SON OF REBELLION

About the Author

Born in Surrey in 1934, Sally Harris was of school age the very month that World War II broke out. Therefore in the desperate and patriotic days of the early forties, the story of Boadicea as told in H. E. Marshall's "Our Island Story" made a lasting impression upon her.

She now has a grown up family and a border terrier and teaches at an East Anglian primary school. She has taken groups of children to search among the archives at the record office and to view the mounds of earth and holes in the ground which herald a current archaeological dig, in the hope that some of her pupils will catch from her a lasting enthusiasm for the puzzles and stories of the past.

SON OF REBELLION
A Story of Boudica's Britain
by Sally Harris

Anglia Young Books

First published in 1989
by Anglia Young Books

Anglia Young Books is an imprint of
Mill Publishing
PO Box 120
Bangor
BT19 7BX

Illustrations by Edward Blake

Design and production in association with
Book Production Consultants
25–27 High Street
Chesterton
Cambridge CB4 1ND

British Library Cataloguing in Publication Data
Harris, Sally
Son of rebellion.
I. Title
823'.914 [J]

ISBN 1-871173–05–1

Typeset in 11/15 point Palatino by Witwell Ltd,
Southport
and printed in Great Britain by
Ashford Colour Press Ltd

AUTHOR'S NOTE

I hope that this story, woven around Boudica's rebellion against the Romans, will make the young reader want to find out more about the Romans and the people who lived in Britain nearly two thousand years ago.

Boudica's rebellion happened so long ago that we must rely on Roman and Greek writers, who lived at about that time, for our information. The Britons who lived then did not write down anything, so that some imagination is required to understand their point of view.

Even the spelling of Boudica is in dispute. Until recent years she was known by the Victorian spelling Boadicea, which then reverted to Boudicca as Tacitus, the Roman writer spelt her name. Now the most likely Celtic form is thought to be Boudica with only one 'c'. Nor is it entirely clear if the revolt took place in A.D. 60 or A.D. 61, or if Prasutagus had been king of the Iceni before the first disarming and minor revolt in A.D. 48–49, nor is there any evidence to enlighten us about Boudica's death. One classical writer says that she fell ill and died and another that she poisoned herself. It is agreed that the Romans did not capture her, for nowhere is there evidence or mention of her body being found.

It is not known for sure if the Iceni king had a palace or, if so, where it was situated. Recent excavations near Thetford in Norfolk have revealed a large building which has the traits of both Celtic and Roman building patterns. For the purpose of the story I have visualised this as the palace of Boudica and Prasutagus.

Nowhere are the daughters of Boudica named and the story of Andractus, Allocine and Tamantine is pure fiction, yet the background is as authentic as our knowledge allows and the story line permits. For instance, conversations between Romans and Britons would have posed language problems, which is not made clear in the story. But the bronze head from a statue of Claudius *was* found in the River Alde this century, and archaeological evidence shows that the three towns mentioned were burnt and the foundations of the hated temple of Claudius may be seen beneath the Norman castle in Colchester.

Finally I should like to thank Mr John Fairclough of Ipswich Museum for lending me books and archaeological papers and for talking to me about the subject.

Map showing likely routes taken by Boudica and the Roman Legions

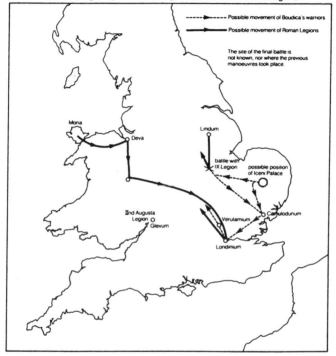

CHAPTER ONE

Andractin was ploughing the cross furrows. Today the pair of oxen who were pulling the ploughshares did not answer to his signals easily and he was trying so hard to keep the lines straight that, at first, he did not hear the rhythmic thumping. Then, as he became conscious of it he shuddered, for it reminded him of the sound that had accompanied a mystic rite performed by the druids.

It grew steadily louder – thump, thump, thump, thump – and there was a gentle clanking of metal too. It was definitely approaching, coming towards his family's farmstead. It was even and relentless. He knew that it was not the druids, yet he was still frightened. He let go of the ploughshare handle and rushed over the criss-crossed fields, up the track, through the gateway and into the fenced farmyard.
'Father!' he shouted, 'what is it!'
His father got out of the clay-lined store-pit which he was examining for cracks. Immediately he heard the steady thumping.
'Roman soldiers – it must be.'
Andractin's father, Brunicon, had been to Camulod-unum (Colchester) and he had seen and heard Roman soldiers before. Brunicon ran towards the farm

1

entrance, Andractin beside him, and suddenly there were the soldiers, coming round the corner of the forest!

Their armour was glinting in the spring sunlight. One of them was on horseback and his metal helmet was crowned with waving red plumes. Andractin thought that warriors from his own tribe, the Iceni, were finer and more ferocious, but these men were relentless in their approach, geometrical in their order and marched as one man.

He was aware that his grandmother, Allocine, his sister and some of the others had come out of the roundhouse and were just behind him. He was unable to move, fascinated by the silent determination of these soldiers. As one man they stopped at the end of the farm track and the horseman trotted up to the boundary fence. Andractin felt the women withdraw a little, but his father stood firm. The horseman halted at the entrance.

'In the name of the Emperor Claudius allow us entry! We have come to take your arms and weapons so that everyone is this province may live in peace under the protection of Imperial Rome!'

Andractin's father stepped forward, holding himself as straight and fearless as the Roman in front of him. 'Why do you come here? We are people of the Iceni tribe. We welcomed your arrival in Britain and were pleased that you conquered our neighbours, the Catevellauni. We offered friendship to Rome and it was accepted by your gracious Emperor. We have never used our weapons against Imperial Rome.'

'Our orders are clear. Fetch your weapons!' ordered the Roman.

'We need some for hunting, at least,' said Brunicon.

The Roman gave an order and immediately the troop came up the track. Brunicon, upright and proud, was trembling with rage. Andractin's sister was clinging to her grandmother who stood as straight as her son. She turned to Andractin and Brunicon.

'This had to come,' she said quietly.

'They can't do this to us!' exclaimed Brunicon, and started forward.

'Stay still,' said Allocine. 'You can do nothing against so many.'

Brunicon stopped, but his eyes were burning.

Once inside the fence the troop spread out, looking in the empty corn pits and thrusting lances into the two that had been left full to see the winter out.

Eight men entered the roundhouse and emerged with Brunicon's spear, sword and shield and even the knives used for hunting and household tasks. These were loaded onto a wagon. Then three of the soldiers kindled fire brands which they put to the animals' hay stores. The hay had kept dry this winter and immediately flames and smoke billowed over the whole scene.

Brunican shouted 'Stop!' but Allocine laid her hand on his arm and quietly said 'No.'

The horseman who had stayed at the entrance, watching everything, looked down. Andractin noticed a pale "V" shaped scar across his cheek. He half smiled and the skin stretched more tightly distorting the "V". He nodded agreement with Allocine and his eyes were kind.

Andractin stared in horror as two soldiers approached the roundhouse with fire brands. Not only were their few precious posessions in there but their extra clothes, the weaving loom with half finished cloth on it, pots, skins and many other things necessary for living, which took many days to make – let alone the house itself. Two of the dogs scurried out to join the others, baying and cowering outside, but the cow, heavy with calf, was inside.

Then the horseman gave a sudden command. Everything stopped. The soldiers grumbled, but put out their fire brands. The whole troop reformed, marched down the track and waited, but the horseman still stood by the entrance. He was staring at Allocine. The beauty of her youth was still apparent. Andractin's father had always said that she was beautiful and now Andractin recognised this

beauty. For the first time he observed her unusually pale skin, her rich dark hair touched with silver and her fine bones. For a moment his eyes met those of the horseman who then turned abruptly and galloped down the track to rejoin the troop that he commanded.

The family stood silent, watching them march away, but before they had disappeared, Brunicon spoke.

'Come on,' he commanded, 'this is mainly a job for the blacksmith but let's clear up and stamp out those smouldering fires.'

They had hardly done so when two men strode up to the roundhouse, breathless and dishevelled.

'You still have your house, Brunicon. Ours have been burnt to the ground. We'll not stand for this. We've got to get rid of these Roman beasts.'
'They did not upset our pots nor put out our fire,' said Allocine. 'Come in and have some broth. Others will soon be here.'

Sure enough, before sunset, the roundhouse was crowded with fifteen men and some wives and childen from surrounding farms and villages. Many were drinking the ale which Allocine made each autumn from the barley crop. They shared those clay pots which had not been broken. There was a lot of angry talk in the roundhouse. Andractin heard his father talking to the blacksmith.

'Can you supply each man with one good metal sword within four days?'

'There is enough metal in my hoard,' replied the blacksmith, 'and with help in the beating and polishing it should be possible.'

'Good,' said Brunicon, 'there will be plenty of willing hands! We'll meet here at daybreak, five days from now, and make for our king's village.'

An old farmer spoke. 'Together we will show these Romans that we cannot be treated like cattle.'

'Our children and womenfolk can take care of those and sow the seed if need be, eh Andractin?' said his father.

'I should like to go with you,' said Andractin.

'When you have more weight and height lad,' smiled the blacksmith.

'At the moment you are better fitted to help here,' said his father grimly.

News of the plan spread fast and five days later thirty men gathered at Brunicon's farm. Some of them did not have swords and some men had smeared dye on their faces so that they looked fierce and ready for war. Brunicon was wearing his helmet which he always kept hidden in a hole dug in the floor of the roundhouse for it was not only practical but precious, with its decorative bronze trimmings. All the men carried shields of some sort hurriedly made from wood. Most were not yet covered in skin nor as hard as they should be for battle, but every man looked fierce and determined.

'The Romans will run away as soon as they see you,' said Andractin to his father.

'No son, I'm afraid not. Remember we do not know if we shall fight yet, nor how many men will gather.'

Andractin and some other children ran with them through the forest to the open land where the river gleamed silver in the morning light. Here the men waded across at the shallowest part and the children waved and shouted until they could see them no more.

• • • • •

Barely a month later Brunicon and a few of the men returned. They carried Brunicon in a litter. One of his legs and one of his arms were cut, crushed and useless.

Allocine said, 'Thanks be to our gods that he lives.'

It was at that moment that Andractin silently swore to have his revenge on the Romans.

CHAPTER TWO

Brunicon's brother and his family who had had their roundhouse destroyed, moved in, bringing their cattle and sheep and extending the outbuildings and fields. Brunicon learnt to move around haltingly on his injured leg and could use his good arm to do many jobs around the farm, but Andractin knew that he could never fight again.

After some weeks news reached the family that the king had died of his wounds and a new king, Prasutagus, had taken his place with the approval of the Romans. Midsummer Eve, which was always a feast day when the people of the tribe could gather at the palace, was to be a double celebration this year when the new king would declare himself to his people and accept their declaration of loyalty.

'The Romans imagine that Prasutagus will do whatever they want,' said Brunicon. 'I have seen and heard things about him, and they may be right, but his wife, Boudica, stands above ordinary women in stature and in determination too, I believe. Andractin, you must go to the feast with your uncle and aunt, and Allocine must go as well. In her way Allocine is no ordinary woman either and she may be able to find out what is really happening at the palace.'

So when the time came the party set out with carts laden with warm skins and other essentials for living in the open air. Andractin felt more cheerful than he had for weeks. He was wearing a light woollen check cloak, newly made by Allocine for this occasion. She wore her best checked tunic which was nearly hidden by a light green mantle. But it was her brooch that fascinated Andractin. It was gold set with red stones, of much finer craft than those which the blacksmith sometimes made from bronze, and nothing like those peddled by the travelling metal smith who visited the farm once or twice a year. His grandmother would never tell him who gave her the brooch; she simply said that she had had it forever.

They followed the river through the forest, being continually joined by parties from other farmsteads, until they came to a crossing place made suitable for carts by pebbles and stones laid on the river bed. At last they reached the gently rolling scrubland that seemed to stretch endlessly ahead and to either side of them. Now they travelled faster and could see other groups making their way to the palace – and suddenly there it was, crowning the higher ground across the river.

'It's huge!' breathed Andractin.

'It is indeed. More huge than it was those few moons ago. It must be the work of the Romans,' said his uncle grimly. 'Still it may benefit us I suppose.'

That night they settled in a sheltered spot near the palace. Earlier arrivals had been inside and said that the new outer wall enclosed the original one, and between these two walls on the northern, southern and eastern sides were seven or eight rows of ferocious looking wooden stakes which would daunt any attackers. Finally in the centre of the palace was a third wall, enclosing three buildings which made up the living quarters.

Despite his excitement, Andractin fell asleep before the talking ceased, or the stars were in full array. But he woke as the grey light of dawn was just touching the sky. He sat up fascinated to see so many people gathered in one place, all silent, still apparently sunk in sleep. He was wide awake now. He got up and trod quietly round the wall, intending to walk to the river for an early morning splash, but instead of passing the palace entrance he found himself walking inside.

In the outer courtyard were the war chariots and horse shelters. Behind them and on each side he could see the stakes. The newly split wood shone white in the grey light and the rows looked as orderly and as fearsome as the Roman columns. At the mere thought of the Romans Andractin felt his anger rising. He began to walk noiselessly through the second entrance and saw the shelters for the king's attendants and warriors. A few more paces took him right to the centre of the palace where he could see the king's roundhouses. Amazed at his daring, he was about to return quickly when a figure in white came out of one of these buildings. It was a druid! Andractin stopped, heart thumping, afraid that if he moved he would attract attention. Behind the druid came a tall female figure. This person turned back to face two more druids who came out of the same buildings, and Andractin saw a long plait of extraordinary thickness which could have belonged to a warrior or the king himself, for it hung down well below the waist. But Andractin knew that this person was a woman by the length of her tunic and the tone of her voice, although it came across to him as a mere whisper. Even at this distance he could feel the presence of this woman.

'The Queen!' he breathed.
'Why have you come in here uninvited?'

Andractin jumped. It was the first druid who had spoken. He hadn't noticed him approach round the edge of the wall. In his fear Andractin blurted out: 'I hate the Romans. They have no feelings and they have maimed my father!' It was hardly an answer but the druid half smiled:
'Perhaps you would be better as a warrior than as a sacrifice then. Go!'
Andractin needed no second bidding. He ran silently and faster than ever before, until he reached the river. He flung off his tunic and cloak and plunged

into the cold early morning water, shocking himself back to normality.

The day passed in a whirl of activity and spectacle. First some hunting parties went out, and then there was weapon practice and a display of throwing and parrying. Andractin watched and played some games with the other children. They had their own trials of strength; they parried and thrust with mock stick weapons, and tested their speed in running too.

As the sun started to turn towards the west the war chariots came out through the palace gates. In the first came the new king. Everyone shouted 'Prasutagus!' and held up swords, spears, sticks or simply a clenched fist – and there, in the second chariot stood the Queen. There was no mistaking her. In the full light of day Andractin saw that her thick plait shone like newly polished bronze. Beside her stood a small girl of about four years and in her arms she held a baby.

'That is an extraordinary woman,' murmured Allocine. 'The king will not be like soft clay, as the Romans imagine, not with Boudica as his wife.'

'The Romans did choose King Prasutagus, then?' asked Andractin.

'Certainly!' replied Allocine. Her brooch was sparkling in the sunshine. 'I spoke with the druids,' she continued, 'while you were at your sport this morning.'

'You spoke with druids!' gasped Andractin. He had not told her that he had spoken to one too. He felt stupid and guilty about his morning escapade.

'Oh yes, age and experience open many gateways,' said Allocine and set her lips firmly so that Andractin knew he should ask no more.

There followed hours of sport and display with the chariots and horses. Andractin gasped at the speed of the tough little horses, at the way that the charioteers handled them and, most of all, at the antics of the warriors who could run back and forth along the shaft, wielding their spears, stretch far out from the chariot without falling, jump out of the chariot and sword fight on the ground with a comrade, and then leap back into the chariot as it returned at speed.

At dusk a line of twelve white-robed druids, oak wreaths round their heads and mistletoe in their hands, walked silently from the palace to a small grove of trees to perform some mystic rite. They were joined by the King and Queen. Then the tribesmen began their feasting, games, dancing and music.

It was dark and everyone was happy beyond caring when the druids and the royal party returned to feast within the palace walls.

Andractin was fast asleep when the druid came

quietly to their camp fire, spoke to his grandmother and pointed at him.

The next day, as the sun turned towards the west, Allocine said to her grandson, 'at sunset you are to go to the middle of the palace. A warrior will await you. He will know you by this brooch.' Allocine removed the brooch from her cloak, exchanging it for the bronze pin which Andractin wore as a cloak fastener.
'But ...' gasped Andractin.
'You are to remain here to be trained as a warrior. You have been watched. A druid believes that you have the will, and one of the king's warriors believes that you have the strength and the skill.'
'But the farm, my father,' began Andractin.
'You know that there are plenty of hands for the farm and your father can wish for nothing better than that his son should become a king's warrior.'
Andractin nodded. His heart beat hard, a little at the shock, a little at the fear of a new life, but mostly with the excitement of what he would become and what he would be able to do.

At sunset he entered the palace and at dawn his family left for the farm.

CHAPTER THREE

The warrior took Andractin to stay in his round-house in the king's village. His son was the same age and when he saw Andractin he smiled broadly.
'I'm glad you've come,' he said. 'I'm Camantus.'

Those words were the start of a close friendship which took them both through the rest of their boyhood as well as through adolescence and into manhood. As the years passed they became expert in all the skills required of an Iceni warrior. The palace was a daytime home to them. They tended the horses and chariots within its walls and learnt the skills of close combat. Roman columns appeared at the palace occasionally and were entertained by the king. But Andractin still hated the Romans and always made excuses to be in the village.

The Romans had made the old capital of the Trinovantes, Camulodunum, (Colchester) into a town like those in their own country. There was a temple where the people went to worship the Emperor, Claudius. There were shops, and houses too, with tiled roofs. Prasutagus and Boudica visited two or three times, with a few warriors. They brought back Roman wines, pottery and glass, beads and women's luxuries. They told of houses that were warmed by hot air which flowed in small tunnels under the floor, and of bath houses whose water was warmed in the same way.

Andractin and Camantus soon became as familiar with Prasutagus as with any other adult but his queen, Boudica, never noticed them. Her eyes always seemed to be directed above their heads. For a woman, her voice was deep and strong. She wore heavy gold chains round her neck and bright robes. Often she took the reins and drove a chariot round the open land.

One day when Andractin was watching her skill with admiration, a voice behind him said, 'I should like to do that.'
'But you're a girl,' replied Andractin as he turned round.
'So is my mother, except that she's big,' retorted Tamantine, the eldest daughter of Boudica.
'Well I expect you'll be able to do it when you're a woman.'
'I soon will be a woman,' she replied.
The chariot had come to a halt beside them and the Queen overheard their conversation:
'Well Andractin, take the reins and give her a ride!' commanded Boudica; then as she alighted:
'Come on boy! What are you waiting for?'
'Oh *yes*!' shouted Tamantine and jumped in.

Andractin needed no further bidding and they set off at a gallop.

'Faster! Faster!' screamed Tamantine.

'Go on boy,' ordered Boudica from the sidelines. 'Do as she says.'

Still Tamantine screamed 'faster, faster,' until they were galloping at full tilt round the tract of land.

After three circuits Andractin slowed down and stopped.

'More!' shouted Tamantin.

'No, that's enough,' said Boudica. 'Now to your weaving.' For even royal girls had to be able to perform such an essential craft.

After that Andractin and Tamantine often rode in the chariot. Eventually Tamantine held the reins and controlled the horses while Andractin performed his acrobatic combat skills.

Now he often went into the royal roundhouse in the palace where he played games with Tamantine and talked to Boudica as well as Prasutagus.

One day Prasutagus said, 'I've had word that many of the Trinovantes have been turned out of their homes by the Romans.'

'Why?' asked Andractin.

'The Romans have encouraged old soldiers to live in Camulodunum (Colchester). Many of these are not Roman born, but men of other nations who have fought with the Romans. They are taking the land on the edge of the town for their houses, or villas, as they call them.'

'They take enough goods and money in taxes already,' said Boudica. 'Many farmers have had to leave their land and are starving. I would not allow that to happen to the Iceni.'

'They paid for the reinforcements to the palace and have given us two large sums of money,' said Prasutagus.

'Hmm, they'll probably ask us to give it back,' retorted Boudica. 'I'll not allow *our* people to be treated like those others. We Iceni have a will of iron and the strength to match it.'

Prasutagus sighed: 'Catus Decianus, the new Procurator, has just arrived. Pehaps he'll put a stop to it.'

Boudica snorted again.

That year, at the midsummer feast, Andractin and Camantus were installed as king's warriors and displayed their skills as charioteers and swordsmen before the assembled tribesmen, including his own family.

Andractin always wore Allocine's brooch. It shone on his cloak as he said goodbye to her. Her eyes were bright with tears:

'Well done,' she whispered, 'take care.'

Andractin's father still limped badly but had become

skilled with his one good arm. He said nothing as he embraced his son, but Andractin whispered, 'if it comes to it, we'll trample them underfoot.'

It came to it sooner than any of them could have foreseen. When Catus Decianus arrived he doubled the taxes and, as Boudica had predicted, declared that the gifts of money from the Emperor Claudius and from the new Roman Emperor, Nero, were only loans and had to be repaid with interest – and then Prasutagus fell ill.

Prasutagus knew that his health was failing. He sent messengers to Suetonius Paulinus, who was the Roman general and new governor, and to Catus Decianus in Londinium, declaring that if he died half his kingdom would be given to Rome, whilst Boudica should rule what remained until his daughters were old enough to do so themselves.

'Why?' stormed Boudica. 'This is our land. They have chosen to come to our land and we have been good friends despite thair shabby treatment of us ten years ago.'

'My dear,' whispered Prasutagus, 'the Romans took all the lands of Cogidubnus when he died, yet he had never fought against them and they gave him a palace by the sea, the like of which we have never seen even in Camulodunum.'

'Let them try to take our lands,' breathed Boudica.

'I have made my will. I command you to uphold it,'

replied Prasutagus firmly. Boudica knelt beside his bed. 'I will,' she promised.

That night Prasutagus died. He was buried with his shield and helmet, but Boudica kept his sword.

'Will the Romans come soon?' Tamantine asked Andractin.
'Perhaps they won't come at all,' he replied, but they both knew that this was unlikely.

Boudica gave orders that each man should keep only one weapon and that the rest should be hidden in the forest together with three quarters of the chariots.

Two days later word reached them that the Romans were on their way. It appeared to be a repeat of the disarming eleven years previously, but much worse.

Messengers were sent to the nobles who had estates some distance away and Boudica called the local warriors to the palace; but she had hardly begun to outline a plan for the defence of the palace than a messenger returned.

'They're coming!' he shouted. 'They are on the open land already!'
'Then I shall receive them as if I welcome them,' said Boudica. 'They may respect my husband's will. Go and receive them at the entrance,' she ordered Andractin and Camantus. 'The rest of you await them here with me.'

Again Andractin heard the rhythmic thumping, but this time when the Romans arrived there were more men and more horses. The officer rode up to the entrance. Andractin spoke first:

'The Queen awaits you and welcomes you,' he said.

Boudica stood in the centre of the middle palace yard, regal, graceful, yet overpowering and determined.

'Welcome to my lands,' she started. 'If I had known that you were coming we could have prepared both a feast and an entertainment, but we should be happy to share our normal fare with you.'

'Woman,' replied the officer 'now that your husband is dead, these lands belong to our noble Emperor Nero. We have come to claim them and to ask that you should repay the loan to our Emperor.'

'This land here was not given to Rome in my husband's will. Only half our lands are yours and those repay any loan a hundredfold.'

'A mere wife and daughters cannot claim any land. All the Iceni lands belong to Rome now. Hand over your arms, jewels, chariots and horses!'

Whilst he was still speaking the Romans moved like lightning. Two troopers grabbed each warrior. Boudica raised her sword to strike the officer.

Andractin wished that he could forget what followed. He was disarmed and struck harshly round the face so that he reeled. Boudica's jewels were ripped from

her and she and her daughters were cruelly attacked, while the few warriors within the palace were held down, helpless.

When at last the Romans left, the silence seemed interminable. Then Boudica rose up and took her daughters, one beneath each arm and hissed, 'we'll get them. We'll exterminate them and throw their remains into the sea.'

CHAPTER FOUR

'Andractin! Andractin!' Tamantine shook his shoulder.

Andractin was still lying on the ground.

'I'll bathe your face,' said Tamantine.

'No! I'm fine. It's you, your sister and mother ...'

But as he struggled to sit up he felt dizzy and found that his face was covered in blood.

'Stay still!' said Tamantine. She bathed his face deftly with water and then smeared a paste of herbs on the wound.

'But you?' asked Andractin.

'We have tended each other. A few people have been killed or badly hurt. I was afraid for you.'

'Oh Tamantine!' whispered Andractin.

They clung to each other and for the first time Andractin realised that Tamantine was indeed a woman.

For a few days Boudica hardly spoke. She told the messengers to stay at the palace until she could send them with more definite news.

Then one evening Boudica called Andractin and Camantus to her.

'At sunrise take the best horses and ride in the

direction of Andractin's family farmstead. You should meet a party of Trinovantes and a druid. Escort them here.'

'Trinovantes?' Camantus looked surprised.

'Yes Trinovantes. They have suffered too. We must unite.'

They met them at last by the river near Andractin's home. Brunicon and his uncle were with them. Andractin heard that, although the family had lost all their possessions, no one had been injured.

'We must not delay you. Go safely and fast. There's much to be done,' said Brunicon.

Andractin rode beside the druid. He knew that they were familiar with the furthest lands and peoples of Britain. The druid spoke to Andractin:

'You are the boy who told me one feast day ten years ago how much you hated the Romans.'

'I remember,' replied Andractin, 'but I didn't know that I spoke to you. I hate them even more now. Can we really find enough men to fight them?'

'More than enough. I bring messages to Boudica from the Catuvellauni, the Dobunni and the Durotriges, and word can be sent to the tribes of the north. We must strike soon, while their general is busy in the west.'

'In the west?' said Andractin.

'Yes, Suetonius Paulinus is in control of the tribes of the high mountains of the west and is now in the land of the Deceangli at Deva (Chester). I fear for our holy island of Mona (Anglesey). Most of my learned brothers are there now but I believe that our power is better exerted through the tribes.'

A council of war was held in the palace. Andractin, Camantus, the other warriors, messengers, nobles, the druid, the Trinovantes and Boudica's daughters attended the Queen.

The full moon, just three moon cycles away, was the date when it was decided that men and warriors from all the tribes of Britain should meet at the Iceni earth ramparts. These had been built at the time of the revolt more than ten years before. Speed was essential so that Suetonius Paulinus would still be in Wales when the British army assembled.

'Go!' ordered Boudica, 'and bring all the people to me.'

During the next month swarthy messengers from northern and western tribes arrived and departed again. Iceni tribesmen sowed their fields, and then left their farms and brought those sheep and cattle that the Romans had not taken, to the royal village. Andractin's uncle was there. He had come alone but most came with their families.

Then Boudica announced that they should all move and wait round the earthen ramparts, and that she and her household would join them just before the set date. Andractin and Camantus acted as messengers.

They were able to tell Boudica of the arrival of groups, not only from the southern tribes but from the more northerly Coritani, Cornovii and Brigantes. Once, just before the chosen day, Andractin was allowed to take Tamantine with him.

'I shall demand to drive your chariot when we go into battle,' she said.

'Your mother will want you at her side,' replied Andractin.

'We work well together; she may agree,' said Tamantine.

'But I couldn't bear to see you hurt,' said Andractin.

'Those words aren't worthy of an Iceni warrior and his woman. We must live or die together.'

Andractin held her closely for a moment and, when they separated, he said huskily:

'Tamantine, I want you to have this brooch which I have worn ever since my grandmother gave it to me, when I first stayed here.'

'That brooch,' whispered Tamantine. 'Your very special brooch.'

She stroked it gently with one finger. 'If I wear *your* brooch, please wear mine, then we shall always have a little of each other.'

Andractin took her hand and kissed it. Then he pinned Allocine's brooch upon Tamantine's cloak. Her copper hair seemd to be reflected in the red stones so that they shone more brightly. Her own cleverly fashioned solid gold brooch which she fastened upon

Andractin's cloak was a dainty replica of one which her mother wore.

On their return to the palace, Andractin was able to report to Boudica that a huge array of warriors was assembled.
'Good. Tomorrow I shall speak to the tribes of Britain,' declared Boudica.

The warriors and charioteers who escorted Boudica made an impressive bodyguard. Boudica was wearing her brightest blue cloak and a brightly coloured robe beneath it. She wore a large and heavy gold brooch and her thick bronze hair hung loose to her hips because, she said, 'it is free as we are soon to be.'

As she stood alone upon the highest of the ramparts, the tribesmen fell silent. She grasped a spear in one hand and at that moment was not only the queen of the people before her, but also their goddess. Her voice resounded so that everyone could hear.
'The Romans promised us both wealth and freedom if we agreed to receive them into our land. But we have been made slaves and we are living in poverty. It would be better if we were free and poor. We should have joined together as soon as they landed and pushed them into the sea, just as our forefathers pushed Julius Caesar back into the sea. We have our own huge island and we should be masters of it and leave it to our children as a free land in which to live.

You are here because you hate the Romans and you fear the future – but do not fear the Romans. There are more of us and we are braver. They need to protect themselves with armour, palisades and walls. We believe that our tents give as much protection as their walls and our shields suffice for all their armour. We have an advantage too, in that we know the country better than them. We swim rivers naked – they need boats. We, being less cluttered, can both attack and retreat faster than them.'

Then Boudica raised her spear in the air, loosening the folds of her dress. As she did so a hare ran out from the loosened folds. It ran from west to east, the direction in which the Romans would return to their homeland. Everyone cheered and shouted with excitement and happiness. Then Boudica held up the spear again.

'Thank you Andraste, goddess of all womankind!' she thundered. 'Thank you that I rule over these Britons, who are real men and not like those soft Romans who bathe in warm water and use scented oils, whose Emperor Nero is a man in name only, and who is more fitted to play the lyre than to lead his men in battle. Andraste, lead us to victory!'

Everyone cheered and embraced those nearest to them. Tamantine and her sister stood silent and triumphant, one on each side of their mother. When all was quiet again Boudica declared that their plans

were laid and that they would leave for Camulodunum at dawn.

What a sight it was! It could have been eighty or ninety thousand or even more who wound their way across the scrubland and thence into the forest where they spread out into the woodland pathways.

Progress was slow with so large and varied a band. The horsemen and chariots were towards the front and the women and baggage struggled to keep up with the main body of warriors. Boudica was always in the front.

She detached a substantial group to cover the road south from Lindum (Lincoln). A few bands of the Coritani tribe had joined the rebels and had warned them that the Roman ninth legion was there and likely to attack the rebels from the rear.

'That is the only sizeable Roman force left in the east and the only one which can stop us. Petilius Cerealis is the young Roman in command,' said a Coritani chieftan.

'Then if they are put out of action it will be a greater military victory than to take Camulodunum,' observed the druid. 'I shall accompany you.'

'Cerealis will have several thousand men,' put in the Coritani chief.

'Ha, that is nothing! We can match that or double it!' declared Boudica.

'Yes, but we must not underestimate them,' warned the druid. 'We will try and take them by surprise in a narrow defile. No chariots, just horsemen and foot soldiers.'

Soon after they had left, a scout arrived bringing good news.

'Our friends in Camulodunum are spreading it around that only a small rebel force is approaching. They sent to Londinium for reinforcements, and Catus Decianus only sent two hundred men!'

'It won't really be a fight then,' said Andractin.

'There'll be plenty of booty – and heads!' laughed the scout.

But Andractin felt that he would like to use his martial skills as his forefathers had done against Julius Caesar.

The scout continued: 'The night before we arrive our friends will scare them stiff. They have plans to push over the statue of Victory, lay on queer howlings in the theatre, and women will pretend that they have had dreams of death and disaster. And I have heard that they are scaring the inhabitants of Londinium too, with news of blood red tides and the shadow of the province sinking beneath the water of the Thames.'

'Why do that?' asked Tamantine.

'It'll put them in a panic,' answered Boudica. 'Start

your scare stories on the third night from now. We'll be there before midday the following morning,' she told the scout.

Before dawn on that third morning, excitement among the rebels grew to fever pitch. Boudica came out of the forest with the first chariots, turned hers and waited to address her rebel army.
She looked magnificent again.
'Remember, have no fear but take up your order, keep it and go at a steady pace. The town first and then to the temple!'
Tamantine went and took up her position in the chariot beside her mother and sister.

Then the whole rebel army moved forward. The horses sensed the excitement and the pace became faster as they drew nearer and nearer. Now Andractin could see the hated temple of Claudius, huge and glistening white upon the high ground above the town. Now they could see people scurrying round the houses. At this first sight of the enemy the British battle cries rose. But there were no columns, no Romans to fight at the edge of the town.

Then they *were* there and Andractin found himself hacking with his sword at anything that moved. 'Hateful Romans! Hateful Romans!' kept drumming through his head. There were flames and smoke as they hurled lighted torches into the houses and shops.

He heard someone shout 'Claudius!' It was Camantus, vainly trying to push over a statue of that emperor. Andractin jumped from his chariot again. They both pushed at the bronze and it crashed to the ground. Camantus stamped on the neck and the head came apart from the body. Andractin picked it up and threw it into the chariot. As a trophy, he preferred a metal head to a real one.

The whole town was alight now and the rebels were the only living creatures among the smoke, flames and ruins. They charged on over the open ground and up to the temple. The few old soldiers and auxiliaries posted outside put up a fight worthy of men trained by the greatest military machine of the ancient world, but eventually the sheer force of numbers saw their complete extermination.

The temple was already packed with women and children, old men and a few old soldiers. The rebels settled for the night round this most hated building. Andractin could not settle. He got up and walked away from the smell of battle. The night was dark. He tripped and fell into a ditch and landed upon a body. From the armour he knew that it was a Roman body. As he jumped up the body moved. Andractin gasped and drew his sword ready to strike. At that moment the clouds cleared and the moon shone brightly. The elderly soldier had no weapons, and as the moonlight shone on his face, Andractin saw the

scar distort as the Roman smiled wryly and said firmly, 'go on, get it over!'

'No' replied Andractin, 'there's been enough killing. Many years ago you stopped your men from burning my family roundhouse. Go now! Escape if you can. I haven't seen you.' He jumped out of the ditch and returned quickly to his sleeping patch.

The temple held out for two days until, eventually, torches flung on the roof started to blaze. Again, screams, blood and smoke pervaded the atmosphere.

'They are hated Romans, hated Romans!' Then as a breeze made a clearing in the smoke, Andractin saw the druid.

'The ninth legion is finished,' said the druid. Andractin had almost forgotten this greatest danger to the rebels. He wished that chariots had been necessary and that he had been involved.

CHAPTER SIX

The Roman Governor General, Suetonius Paulinus, had North Wales under control and, moreover, had trapped the druids in their lair. His cavalry had swum the straits to Mona and the infantry had crossed the divide in flat bottomed boats. The Britons, wild, fierce and wailing, awaited him on the shore.

His men pressed on and slaughtered all the druids and their followers. No sooner had this success been achieved in the west than news of the rebellion in the east reached Paulinus. He had with him two thirds of the military force and was two hundred and fifty miles from London. He could not hope to arrive there before Boudica if he crossed the country with both his infantry and cavalry. The second legion, Augusta, was stationed at Glevum (Gloucester). He could dash through the mountain passes with his cavalry and rendezvous near Londinium with this legion. They could at least hold Londinium until his infantry arrived. He sent a messenger to the second Augusta at Glevum (Gloucester) and set off with his cavalry through the mountains.

• • • • •

'That is our greatest victory,' said Boudica to those

warriors and chieftans who had naturally become a select council of war. The druid was there and her daughters. 'To have all but destroyed a whole legion with less than a thousand warriors is victory indeed.'
'Now,' said Andractin, 'shouldn't we hunt out the rest of the legions and crush them before they can combine?'
'Of course that's what we should do – but do you think that even I could persuade my followers to veer away from Londinium, the den of the despicable Catus Decianus?' replied Boudica.
'We might be able to reach Londinium before Suetonius Paulinus,' said the druid.

But no rebel troop was so unsuited for speed as the hordes under Boudica's command.

• • • • •

Suetonius Paulinus and his troop made one short overnight stop and arrived at the place where the second legion from Glevum (Gloucester) should have been awaiting them. They were not there, nor was there a message to explain their absence.

He had two choices. He could wait until he was joined by his infantry from Wales, who should be marching already, but if he did this Londinium would certainly be lost to the rebels, or he could press on with his cavalry and see what defence Catus Decianus had prepared. He decided on the second choice. If

Londinium was in Roman hands, reinforcements from the continent could be landed easily and quickly.

• • • • •

'I believe that Suetonius will be waiting for us at Londinium,' said Boudica.
'I fear that you're right,' said the druid.
'But we are ready for battle, surely?' said Andractin.
'Always!' declared Boudica.

• • • • •

When Suetonius Paulinus arrived in Londinium he was horrified to find that Catus Decianus had fled to Gaul and had left the town without any defence.

Suetonius knew that there was not time to evacuate the townspeople and that he could not defend it successfully with only his cavalry. He was forced to leave it to its fate and go west to rejoin his infantry.

That night when the rebels made camp, Londinium was only an hour's march away. A band of scouts arrived at Boudica's camp fire. Their hair and faces shone red in the firelight. 'There's no-one there! Londinium and Britian are ours!' they cheered.
'Listen fools,' bellowed Boudica, 'Londinium may be ours, but not Britain – not until we have conquered the legions.'

At sunrise, Andractin once again felt the thrill of the chariot beneath his feet as they flew towards the fine new buildings of Londinium. This time he stood beside Tamantine, the bronze head of Claudius raised aloft on his sword point.

'Those eyes are like the jewels in your grandmother's brooch!' shouted Tamantine.
'Then I shall gouge them out and put them in a gold neck ring for you!' laughed Andractin.

Now they were upon the first houses. Andractin urged Tamantine on. 'To the basilica! To the lair of Catus Decianus!' he yelled.

The streets of the busy trading town were deserted but, from the screams and yells, Andractin knew that the houses were not. He searched the basilica for Catus Decianus and found it deserted. He and Tamantine joined Boudica on the open ground beyond the town and reported this to her.
'So as well as being a bully he is a coward,' she said.
'By dark there will be no town,' whispered Tamantine.
'That's true,' replied Boudica, 'but after this we must face the General.'
After a pause she continued. 'There are some sacred groves of the goddess Andraste near here. Tonight we shall perform the victory ceremony in those groves.'
'If we do that,' nodded the druid, 'no-one can expect a pardon from the Romans. When we meet the legions everyone will need to fight to the death.'

Andractin tried to forget that evening when the live bodies of Roman and pro-Roman British women were offered as thanksgivings to Andraste, the terrible goddess of victory.

• • • • •

'We've only got to conquer one more town and we shall be there!'
'Britain is ours!'
'We're free!'
Those were the words and beliefs of the Britons.
'No!' stormed Boudica. 'We pass Verulamium (St. Albans) so we will destroy it. But hear me! After that we must find and defeat the Roman legions.'
'Easy!'
'There are hardly any of them!'
'If we can take two towns with barely a man hurt, we can crush a few soldiers.'

So the horde descended upon Verulamium (St. Albans). Once more the basilica, the theatre, the shops and houses became hardly more than a pile of ashes.

But Boudica was anxious only for news of Suetonius Paulinus.

'We must go further north to find him,' said the druid.
'Why? What is his purpose in going so far?' asked Boudica.

'He hopes that many of the tribesmen will be satisfied with their success and return to their farms.'

'So he hopes that there will only be a handful of us to crush. He doesn't know my iron will nor how loyal we Britons can be when we fight for our freedom.'

'Yes,' agreed the druid uncertainly, 'but there are so many of us to feed.'

CHAPTER SEVEN

The following day Boudica addressed her followers. 'We are not free until we destroy the men who make the yokes for our necks. We have flung off those yokes but now we must find and kill the slave drivers before they remake tighter yokes. You must be orderly and listen to your tribal chiefs, kings and warriors. We will go north tomorrow. Now prepare for departure at dawn. Take up your positions tonight so that we may leave in good order.'

• • • • •

Suetonius Paulinus had to have enough troops stationed round the province to keep the other tribes in check and so was able to muster only ten thousand men to face Boudica's force of one hundred thousand. But he chose his battleground carefully and waited for Boudica.

• • • • •

Boudica sent scouts half a day's journey ahead and it was many days before they brought definite news of the whereabouts of the Romans. The druid and Andractin were in Boudica's tent and heard the scout's report.

'I fear,' said the druid, 'that Suetonius has chosen the battlefield with skill.'

'His force is but a tenth of ours. No chosen position can help him,' said Boudica. Then she turned to Andractin. 'Tamantine will be in my chariot when we fight, but when we have won she can be at your side always.'

Andractin dropped on one knee. 'Thank you,' he whispered.

'Go now!' ordered Boudica, 'and tell her how it will be.'

So Andractin and Tamantine passed the night before the battle in bliss and peace.

• • • • •

There they were! At last Andractin saw them drawn up in battle order. In the centre was a solid block of legionaries and on either side were two smaller blocks of auxiliaries. Each man had two javelins which reached above his head. On either wing was a smaller group of cavalry. The whole force was stretched across the mouth of a narrow valley and, behind them and on either side, was thick woodland which made it impossible for the British to surround the Roman force.

'But we should not need to do that,' thought Andractin. He realised too, that the Britons would have to charge up a slope towards the Romans. Suetonius had certainly chosen his ground with care!

On the British side the Iceni tribe were in the centre. Andractin was in the front with his own driver, and Camantus was next to him. The Iceni were the only tribe who had saved or remade enough chariots to call them a force. On either side the other tribes were assembled. The fortunate ones were armed with a sword, a shield, a helmet and some light armour, but many displayed bare, painted chests and carried only an axe or a knife. They were not carefully grouped like the Romans and Andractin thought they must seem a disorderly mass to those hard and silent men. Not a sound came from their side, whilst on the British side all was noise and jollity, for the wives and families had drawn up the baggage wagons behind their warriors to get a better view of the entertainment.

Then Boudica rode in front of the tribes like a vengeful goddess, standing in her chariot, a daughter on either side. She commanded immediate attention. 'Do not fear the Romans! We have killed thousands already. We outnumber them by ten men to one. Our battle cries alone will freeze them with fear. You are fighting for your country and for freedom. Remember that, and you will win!'

Then the whole horde moved forward and round her with chilling screams and cries. The Romans barely moved forward or uttered a sound. Then, as one man, they lifted and flung their javelins. The Britons wavered an instant. More than one thousand Britons fell at that first throw. Then came the second and the slaughter was increased threefold.

The Roman legionaries did not give way and allow the chariots to penetrate their ranks, so Andractin jumped from his chariot and felt his sword clash and reverberate against those of the hated enemy. Suddenly the whole scene was a nightmare. The Roman infantry blocks had held firm and now the cavalry came in, cutting down the Britons on the flanks. The Britons were turning! They were retreating! But the wagons and wives were hampering their retreat. Britons were lying killed and dying all over the battlefield. So in those few terrible seconds of realisation Andractin's concentration strayed and he, too, slipped into darkness as a Roman legionary struck him upon the head with his shield boss.

CHAPTER EIGHT

He could see a dim light and Andractin knew that he had to reach it. The light was round. It must show the way out of the pit or cave where some force was holding him down. He gave a tremendous shove and sat up. Immediately he felt sick and dizzy and the light disappeared. He had been looking at the full moon and the force which had been holding him down was the spreadeagled body of a dead Roman soldier.

Even before he fully regained his senses he remembered that disaster had befallen them. He looked round carefully. The silver moonlight showed upturned wagons and chariots and bodies of horses and people everywhere.

'Tamantine!' he thought. Was she free and far away with Boudica? He knew in his heart that this could not be so but he had to be sure that she was dead. He had to find her.

The field was almost silent. The Romans had done their job well, for nothing seemed to be alive. They must have withdrawn for the night to make camp by the fort that was situated nearby.

He pushed the dead Roman aside and staggered back down the slope up which he had charged those few hours ago. He tripped a few times over bodies or bits of chariot and then he fell headlong. As he lay there he knew that he must go more carefully; he must pull himself together. As he stood up he shuddered to see that he had fallen over a head. A head whose eyes glittered red! It was the bronze head of Claudius. He remembered that he had promised Tamantine that she should have the eyes. He picked it up and went on.

He saw the bright robe first and then a horribly burnt body. He knew that it must be Boudica. Then he saw the white robe. The druid lay dead too. Andractin realised that the druid had set fire to Boudica's body so that the Romans could not abuse it. Then, at last he saw the other body, the one he knew and loved, lying still beside Boudica. One of her hands was clenched tight and Andractin knew what it was clasping before he looked.

'Oh my darling,' he whispered, 'let them kill me too!' He released the brooch from her grasp and it lay on the ground unheeded as he squeezed her hands, gently closed her eyes and kissed her lips. Then he lay and wept.

'I would have killed you but I saw the brooch of Claudius.'

Andractin was suddenly aware that an elderly Roman soldier was standing over him.

'Kill me! I don't want to live!'

The old soldier knelt down beside Andractin:

'Young man, you spared my life and I shall spare yours. You have got to help build your land again. Every brave and clear thinking Briton will be needed. Your grandmother may still be alive, so go home with her brooch. You will be needed there more than ever before.'

Then Andractin saw his scar.

'You said the brooch of Claudius!' he muttered, confused.

'Yes,' replied the Roman. 'I was in Camulodunum with the first legions to arrive here. Your grandmother was in Camulodunum too and met the Emperor Claudius. He was spellbound by her beauty and charm and wanted her to return to Rome with him. She refused and he gave her that brooch as a token until he should return to Britain – but of course he never did. Your grandmother knows that Romans can be wise and just. I hope that Rome has learnt a lesson from what has happened here and in future will send wise and just governors who will rebuild this province happily. Take the brooch – for Allocine!' urged the Roman.

So he actually knew her name! In spite of himself Andractin took the brooch. He remembered his father, his sister and Allocine waiting. Every day must be a waiting day for them. He sat up.

'Go now, go quickly!' said the old Roman. 'There's one unhurt horse beyond the line of wagons.'

Hours later Andractin realised that he had been riding with his fingers through the eye sockets of Claudius. His fingertips had gouged out the jewel eyes. He looked at it in disgust. He wanted to forget the smell of blood and death.

Days later as he approached the muddy banks of a wide, fast flowing river to the south of his home he angrily flung the empty bronze head far into the water. Then he set his face and his purpose towards home.

1900 years later the head was found.

PLACES TO VISIT

Colchester Castle Museum, Colchester

Cockley Cley Iceni Village,
near Swaffham, Norfolk

The British Museum, London
(Among many other Roman artefacts,
this museum has the bronze head of Claudius)

The Museum of London

British
Librarianship
Today

A Library Association Centenary Volume

British Librarianship Today

Edited by W. L. Saunders

The Library Association/London

First published by
The Library Association
7 Ridgmount Street
London WC1E 7AE. 1976

ISBN 0 85365 498 0

© The editor and contributors, 1976

British Library Cataloguing-in-
publication data:
British librarianship today
    ISBN 0-85365-498-0
    1. Saunders, Wilfred Leonard
    2. Library Association
    020'.941   z682.2.G/
    Library science as a profession

Design: Graham Bishop
Index: Elisabeth Ingham
Set in 11 on 12pt Garamond
on Fyneprint paper

Made and printed in Great Britain by
Unwin Brothers Limited
The Gresham Press
Old Woking, Surrey

Contents

Contributors

Contents

Contributors

G. W. Adamson, BSC, PHD, AIINFSCI
*Lecturer, University of Sheffield Postgraduate School of Librarianship
and Information Science*

Professor W. Ashworth, BSC, FLA, FIINFSCI, ARPS, DIPLIB
Chief Librarian, Polytechnic of Central London

D. E. Bagley, FLA
County Technical Librarian, Hatfield Polytechnic

N. Beswick, MA, FLA
*Lecturer, Department of Librarianship, Loughborough University of
Technology*

R. E. Coward, FLA
Director-General, British Library Bibliographic Services Division

R. J. Fulford, MA
Keeper of Printed Books in the British Library Reference Division

J. C. Gray, MA
Director, British Library Research & Development Department

K. C. Harrison, MBE, FLA
City Librarian, City of Westminster

N. Higham, MA, ALA
Librarian, University of Bristol

M. W. Hill, MA, BSC, MRIC
*Director of the Science Reference Library of the British Library
Reference Division*

H. T. Hookway, PHD, HONLLD, FRIC
Deputy Chairman and Chief Executive, British Library Board

A. C. Jones, DMA, FLA
Library Adviser, Department of Education & Science

F. Liebesny, BSC, FIISC, FIL, ALA

M. B. Line, MA, FLA, AIINFSCI
Director-General, British Library Lending Division

Professor M. F. Lynch, BSC, PHD, ARIC
*Professor of Information Science, University of Sheffield Postgraduate
School of Librarianship and Information Science*

Contributors

G. E. Marrison, BA, PHD, FRAS
*Keeper of Oriental Manuscripts and Printed Books, British Library
Reference Division*

D. T. Richnell, CBE, BA, FLA
Director-General, British Library Reference Division

N. Roberts, BA, FLA
*Senior Lecturer, University of Sheffield Postgraduate School of
Librarianship and Information Science*

Professor W. L. Saunders, MA, FLA
*Director, University of Sheffield Postgraduate School of Librarianship
and Information Science*

P. H. Sewell, OBE, FLA
Senior Library Adviser, Department of Education and Science

G. Thompson, FLA
Librarian and Director of Art Gallery, City of London Libraries

D. P. Waley, MA, PHD
Keeper of Manuscripts in the British Library Reference Division

A. Wilson, FLA
Director of Libraries and Museums, Cheshire County Council

L. Wilson, MA, JP
Director of Aslib

Introduction/Wilfred L. Saunders

A hundred years, as Godfrey Thompson implies in the opening chapter of this volume, is not a very long period of time. The link with the librarians and librarianship of a hundred years ago is often at only one stage removed: there are many elder statesmen of our profession today who in their early years listened to papers by, sometimes indeed met, librarians who in their own youth had known the profession as it was practised in 1877. But even allowing for the inevitable human tendency to magnify the events, the changes of one's own times, it is surely not unreasonable to suggest that short as a century may be, the one which the Library Association completes in 1977 is without precedent in the sweep, the magnitude, the sheer drama of the changes which it has witnessed. Not just the technological and scientific change with which all of us are familiar – often too familiar – but social change, political change, changes in values, beliefs, attitudes, expectations; changes in fact in areas of human activity, experience and knowledge which must have the most profound effects on a profession such as librarianship – a profession which at once reflects and influences the life and times of those it serves. Still, I trust, without being over-susceptible to the significance of what is new, or recent, it is not over-dramatising the recent rate of change to suggest that just as 90% of the scientists (or librarians?) who ever lived are said to be alive and practising today, so has by far the greatest proportion of this century's spectacular changes in our profession taken place within the last fifteen or twenty years. This is not to say, of course, that the seeds and early signs of change were not there before that time. Of course they were; but it is a remarkable fact that if this volume had been published only a dozen years ago there would have been no British Library, no local government reorganisation, no Polytechnic libraries, practically no DES Libraries Division, relatively little international activity, virtually no computer applications, no research and development to speak of – or write about – and a pattern of professional education that seems almost prehistoric compared with that of today.

In saying this I by no means imply that all change is necessarily good – few librarians could do other than grieve at reorganisation which destroyed our finest county library system, that of the West Riding; just as, in a different sector, few of us can feel comfortable about the present health of industrial libraries. But it is only rarely that change has failed to prove at least stimulating and challenging, and this writer has found the last ten or fifteen years the most professionally exciting period in a career that began some forty years ago. Whether in fact the picture of librarianship presented in this volume is to be preferred to that which went before it is of course a matter for personal judgment; from my position of editorial privilege I would assert that on balance it undoubtedly is.

If our predecessors of 1877 were to revisit the world of British librarianship in the Association's centenary year, what features of the present professional scene, one wonders, would have the greatest impact, cause the greatest surprise? Not, I suggest, the technology, the gadgetry, which now so powerfully supports our professional practice; for the Victorians themselves were no strangers to scientific and technological development, and like ourselves were probably conditioned to believing that in the realms of science and technology very little is impossible. What would probably impress and surprise them more than anything, I suggest, is the fact that we can now think, talk, and act, in terms of a national library *system*. The hub of this system is the British Library – and a hint for my successor as editor of the bicentenary volume of 2077 is that the use of this word 'hub' by the British Library instead of the original 'apex' is itself full of nuances of quite fascinating professional and historical significance. The background, the objectives, the role of the British Library emerge with great force and clarity from the chapters by the chief officers of that institution. The logic of its creation seems at this point to have been inevitable. Those who witnessed its evolution and emergence – spearheaded by the NLL under the leadership of the redoubtable Donald Urquhart – know only too well, however, what a tough and difficult route its protagonists travelled, what formidable resistance had to be overcome, what administrative and political barriers had to be surmounted; and with what incredible speed its creation was brought about, having regard to the legal, administrative and attitudinal changes that had first to be achieved.

In these early years of the British Library's existence the signs are almost wholly good. At leadership level we can see a dynamism which is already making this formidable conglomerate the power in the library world that it should be. In a very real sense one is now aware of great resources at national level – systematically complementing and supplementing what is available locally; providing a formidable array of national bibliographical services and carrying out for itself that bibliographical research and development which can only be done effectively at national level; identifying deficiencies and research needs at regional and local level; and what is more, providing the funds and the organisation required to meet them. For the first time one can feel that a powerful and knowledgeable group of librarians is thinking in national terms, with the will and resources to bring about change that will affect the whole national library system.

The story is of course not entirely one of 'blue skies'. With such great power as that possessed by BL must go the possibility, the danger, of over-domination by the centre. At the head of BL's affairs – as one would hope and expect – are men of strong personality and acknowledged professional expertise. They or their representatives are on most of the really significant professional committees; they are directly involved in most of our profession's important decision-taking; and what is more their decisions, their commitments can be backed by the resources and power of an organisation with a budget of £22,000,000 a year. It is fortunate for the profession that those who wield this power have so far shown a full awareness of the dangers adumbrated above. Perhaps, in fact, it is not too fanciful to suggest that the BL itself would welcome a counterbalancing influence of some sort. Its representatives must be only too well aware of the dangers of too easily getting their own way, of over-influencing the profession and the practice of librarianship in this country. If some other major source of power and influence could emerge, occupying perhaps a 'second chamber' type of position, then the long-term benefits for the profession could be great indeed. Is it unrealistic to suggest in this centenary year that a suitably augmented Library Association would seem to have many of the qualifications for this role?

To describe the BL as the 'hub' of our national library system has been quite a useful way of illustrating its role. To extend the metaphor to the rest of the British library system is not quite so rewarding except, perhaps, in the sense that the essential interdependence of the individual spokes in a wheel is not unlike the relationship between the main elements in our national library system – the public, academic and special libraries. It is still legitimate and certainly convenient to treat these elements separately in a volume such as this, but it is a fact that the boundaries are becoming increasingly blurred, that professional thinking is increasingly in terms of a region's *total* library resources, that the 'local library cooperation' recommended in so many reports and 'official' pronouncements is beginning to be a reality. This, one feels, is wholly for the good, particularly at a time when economic stringency makes the optimum use of library resources of *all* sorts a political necessity. It is imperative in such times that librarians should not only be thinking and acting cooperatively, but that they should be seen to be so doing.

It is appropriate at this point to pay tribute to the quiet but pervasive influence on the whole British library scene of the Libraries Division of the DES. As Arthur Jones and Philip Sewell make clear in their chapter, the Division has certainly not limited itself to the public libraries sector, which on a narrow view of its role might seem to be its principal concern. In the field of local library cooperation, for example, it instigated and financed a very comprehensive research project on behalf of the Library Advisory Council for England; while the modest reference to research on automatic data processing for the British Library conceals one of the biggest automation feasibility projects ever undertaken. The Division's small staff of professional Library Advisers have provided the library profession with a more effective link with the Civil Service than could possibly have been imagined by those librarians who for generations resisted the slightest hint of central government involvement with library affairs. All in all, the Division in its comparatively short life has exerted an influence on professional activity and development out of all proportion to the very modest resources which have been placed at its disposal.

If we now turn to consider individual sectors – having made the point that in practice none can be or should be considered in total isolation from the rest – it is not inappropriate to reflect first of all on the position in which our public libraries find themselves in this centenary year. The 1964 Act pointed the way

to advances that promised a new era in public librarianship, but
the expectation of local government reorganisation and then the
planning for its implementation have filled the years since 1964
with activity of a very different type from the extension and
improvement of services. Certainly much has been achieved, but
many man-years of senior staff-time have been diverted from
more immediately creative developments in public library
service to the minutiae of planning for reorganisation. Even so,
this would have been justified – or so it could be argued – once
the larger, more powerful, more streamlined units were created
and began to operate: energies that had been devoted to the
complexities of reorganisation would be released for vital,
creative thought about the real issues of public librarianship. It is
a sad and ironical fact that scarcely had reorganisation been
achieved before economic recession and financial stringency of a
degree unknown since the 1930s changed an environment of
optimism and expectation into one of gloom and pessimism. Far
from expanding and developing their new and enlarged services,
many public librarians are finding it increasingly difficult to
maintain the *status quo*; the real power and potential of the great
machines which they now control must remain for an
unforeseeable time untested. Nevertheless, the *status quo* is one
which looks different indeed from that of a few decades ago, let
alone a century. The role of the public library as described in
Alex Wilson's perceptive and challenging chapter is one which
makes it an indispensable educational and social force in the
complex society of the 1970s.

If the centenary year sees the end of a period of unprecedented
change in local government affairs it also comes at a time when
education at tertiary level is still adapting itself to a sudden
expansion which now shows every sign of having raced ahead of
the resources with which the community is able – or prepared –
to support it. From the time of the Robbins Report in 1963
until the early years of the 1970s, post-secondary education was a
'growth industry'. Universities increased in number and
multiplied in size; and with the advent of the Polytechnics there
was created a new and powerful educational force, side by side
with the universities and intended to complement them. Colleges
of Education prospered and grew and even the Cinderella which
was the Further Education sector came by at least a few new

garments. It is an encouraging sign of the present-day standing of our profession and of the general awareness of the central importance of libraries in the higher educational process that in most cases growth and expansion of library resources have at least paralleled the growth and development of the institutions which they serve.

Again, as in considering the public libraries, it is difficult not to be over-influenced by the financial gloom which currently hangs over the whole of higher education. This is heightened, of course, by the contrast with the gloriously palmy days of the quite recent past, when university concern was not so much with how to avoid bankruptcy as with whether or not universities were getting their fair share of a rich national cake, which had suddenly to be shared with the new Polytechnics; and when the plans of the Polytechnics themselves looked to a future of apparently unlimited growth, new buildings, new plant, and wide-ranging educational opportunities. That higher education is now on a plateau – if not actually going downhill – is undeniable; but equally certain is the fact that it is a plateau at a far higher level than would have seemed conceivable not so many years ago. In university libraries, for example, expenditure on acquisitions has multiplied far beyond what was needed to keep up with inflation; levels and types of service to users have been achieved – often influenced by the former CATS and the new Polytechnics – that are breathing new life into university librarianship; and even more importantly, attitudes have undergone quite dramatic changes in the direction of recognising a more dynamic, outgoing role for the library. A period of consolidation, it might be argued, is no bad thing. A slimming-down, a readjustment to a new situation might be beneficial for institutions (and their libraries) which have developed at such break-neck speed in recent years. But financial stringency is unfortunately not the only cloud on the higher educational horizon. For reasons which are many and complex, the attitudes of the community at large towards higher education have become in recent years not merely less favourable but at times downright hostile. From the perspective of a century from now it may seem that this is just a tiny kink in a curve of favourability which moves ever upwards; but at the time when it is actually being lived through and experienced it is distinctly worrying and uncomfortable for those concerned with higher education and the libraries which serve it.

On a happier note, the reader cannot fail to be impressed by the innovatory vigour which is being applied to the creation of an individuality for the new polytechnic libraries; the willingness to accommodate the resource centre concept, to be outward-looking in the provision of services, to experiment in many directions. David Bagley makes the point, indeed, that the ethos of a polytechnic library owes more to the special library than to the traditional academic library. But, as Norman Higham makes clear, the traditional academic library itself – the university library, that is – brings to its task today very different values and objectives from those of the pre-Robbins era. It is, as has been said, far more service- and reader-orientated than would until recently have seemed conceivable; and what is more, this has not been at the expense of building and developing its collection – which must still remain a central – probably *the* central – university library service to its readers. It must be said, however, that at the time of writing there is ominous questioning in quite high places of the traditional and hitherto virtually unquestioned view that the larger a university library's stock the greater its value to the research community which it serves. No one will deny that there is, in many university libraries, dead wood of little or no value to scholarship, and in need of removal. No one would seriously deny that for each university library to see itself as a potential BM or Bodleian is both ridiculous and unrealistic. But equally, anyone in close contact with working scholars in the humanities and social sciences quickly develops a deep sense of the close relationship between high quality scholarship and the strength of the parent library. That this relationship is not easy to quantify does not necessarily disprove or discredit it, and it is greatly to be hoped that irremediable damage will not be done, in the name of rationalisation, to the numerous good university library collections which in recent years have been moving steadily towards becoming great collections.

At the other end of the academic library scale Norman Roberts has had the difficult and somewhat gloomy task of writing about a group of libraries – those of the Colleges of Education – on which the sun appears to be setting. Dangerously vulnerable, too, are the Institute of Education libraries which have been in such effective partnership with the college libraries since soon after the Second World War. It will be a national tragedy if this network of Institute libraries, systematically covering the information and library needs of the whole country, prolific and vigorous in its cooperative bibliographic ability, is allowed to disintegrate. If this should happen, then before long these libraries will have to be re-invented. Struggling, too, is Roberts's second group – the College of Further Education libraries. His statistics are revealing and make it plain that there are patches at least in the academic library garden that are very far from flourishing.

The Special Libraries chapter of this volume is appropriately written by Wilfred Ashworth, the first special librarian to become President of the Library Association. There can be few people so well equipped to assess the present situation in this sector and the note of doubt and uncertainty which he sounds about certain aspects of the future of industrial libraries cannot be disregarded. The vulnerability of even our biggest and best industrial libraries in times of economic recession has been only too grimly demonstrated in recent years and if industry's loss – in redundancies of senior library and information staff – has sometimes been the gain of other sectors of the library world, particularly perhaps the library schools, this is small consolation for the effect of such changes on the morale of those who remain. It will be a long time before industrial libraries regain the position they had consolidated for themselves in the post-war years; a long time before heads of library schools producing high-class information-trained science graduates will be able with unqualified enthusiasm to point their best graduates in the direction of the industrial sector. This is wholly bad: the freshness of approach, the innovatory activities of industrial librarians over the years, have had a major influence on other sectors. How greatly indebted, for example, are our university libraries to the special librarians who gave them a vision of special library standards of service in a large, general library environment, and thus assisted the extremely important trend towards subject specialisation. How very much have the academic and public librarians who support Aslib gained from the fresh and different approaches to library and information service of their industrial librarian fellow-members. And to what a very great extent is the fact that numeracy is now widely accepted as being an essential part of the equipment of the librarian due to the influence of the cost-effective and number-conscious approach of special librarians, referred to by Ashworth?

What is perhaps particularly depressing in Ashworth's chapter, because it is of such a fundamental character, is his reference to the change in background of those who control industry – the supplanting of the research and literature-conscious scientists on the boards of big companies by accountants whose sole and short-sighted test is likely to be that of the balance sheet. This cannot but affect the attitudes of top management towards their need for information and, though innovation, as Ashworth has indicated, can just as easily be stifled by too much information as by too little, if it has to be a choice the long-term dangers of the former are surely less than those of the latter.

If the chapter on special librarianship carries suggestions of retreat by some libraries from previously strongly held positions, the school libraries chapter is concerned with a sector which has never had a strong position to retreat from, and for which the only way, surely, is forward. In recent years the present writer on visits overseas has from time to time been called upon to talk about the British library scene. In doing so he has been able to present with some pride a picture of vigorous and deeply impressive progress, in which this country stands second to no other – except in one sector, the schools. Of school libraries he has been moved to say on more than one occasion that the present position is a national scandal, and it is reassuring to have this possibly intemperate view corrected to some extent at least by the cautious optimism of Norman Beswick, a leading authority on school library resource centres. What Beswick has to say about the increased acceptance of chartered librarians in the schools is particularly encouraging, for it is in staffing above all that the school library's weakness currently lies. Nevertheless, there must still be a very long way to go when little more than 10% of our 5000 or more secondary schools are staffed full-time by a properly qualified librarian.

It has already been stressed that the structure of this volume – a sector by sector survey of the library scene – has been adopted only for convenience of exposition. The interdependence, the overlap, the interconnection between sectors emerges throughout the volume. When we turn to the professional associations it is quite clear that these provide the cement which holds together the individual bricks: the only cause for regret, as made clear by Godfrey Thompson's powerful plea for unity, is that we should have to be considering associations – in the plural – rather than a single all-embracing organisation. In his chapter on the Library Association, Thompson refers to a substantial article on the Association by Haslam and to a companion volume to this present one, in which Dr Munford considers the history of the Association in the detail appropriate to a centenary occasion. In the circumstances it is unnecessary and inappropriate to dwell at length on the Association in this introductory chapter save to express the confidence than an organisation which has proved itself so resilient in not only retaining but expanding membership during a time when many feared that loss of its educational monopoly must necessarily seriously threaten its position, has little to fear for the future. The great challenge, at this time, is for the Association to think out and establish the new role which a rapidly changing profession will require of it.

It is pleasing and appropriate that the account of Aslib should be written by the man who for the last quarter of a century and more has guided it to its present position of power and influence. Leslie Wilson in this chapter places his primary emphasis on information management, and one of his most telling points has, in these times, implications beyond the relatively narrow field with which he is primarily concerned. He says 'It is to be expected, therefore, that information management will gradually come to be recognised more widely as an integral part of the management structure alongside, for example, personnel management, financial management, materials management and other parts of the management function. When this has ceased to be the exception and become the rule, the horizons for those who work in the information and library field will indeed have been significantly expanded'. The parallel with the public librarian, who now has not merely a Chief Librarian's but a recreational or leisure 'overlord's' baton in his knapsack, is very clear. At a different level there is surely a similar message, too,

for the school librarian with ambitions to move on in due course
to a headship.

The Institute of Information Scientists, like Aslib, is fortunate
in having as its recorder one who had been very closely
associated with its growth and development. The late Felix
Liebesny was in fact one of the Institute's founding fathers and
must have taken a great deal of pleasure in the survival into
sturdy childhood of an infant for which imminent mortality was
not infrequently forecast in its early days. The Institute, it is
clear, is full of vigour, but small, and the present writer feels as
strongly as he did when writing on the subject nearly a decade
ago, that the brightest future lies with some sort of unification of
all the library and information professional associations – that a
whole which includes the Library Association, Aslib, the
Institute of Information Scientists – and perhaps others – would
be much more powerful than the sum of the individual parts.

A word of explanation is perhaps needed to justify a separate
chapter on the computer and its impact on library and
information work. Certainly it is clear from Michael Lynch's and
George Adamson's contributions that in a few years' time the
computer will be so fully accepted a part of the equipment of the
library and information specialist that – like technical processes
such as classification and cataloguing – it would scarcely seem to
call for special treatment in a volume of this character and
structure. At the present time, however, its power and potential
are sufficiently novel and of such obvious significance to
contemporary professional activity that the true flavour of
librarianship and information studies in our centenary year
would be misrepresented if it were not given prominent
treatment.

If in the matter of computer applications it would seem that
we in Britain have scarcely led the field, but have rather done a
very sound and solid job of development and consolidation in
the light of the experience (and mistakes) of others, particularly
the North Americans, it is a different story when we turn to the
field of education and training. Here we can legitimately claim
to have made quite remarkable advances in the last ten or fifteen
years – advances of a truly innovatory and pioneering character.
The chapter on education and training reveals, it is true, a
proliferation of qualifications which it is not easy to justify or

commend, but it also reveals a vigour and a scale of achievement – both in material and qualitative terms – that have made British library schools in recent years a focus for library educators from all parts of the world. Similar remarkable advances have been made in research and development – often in close association with the professional education sector. In looking back over the period since 1965 one is struck, not just by the happy convergence of circumstances favourable to R & D, and referred to in the chapter in question, but above all perhaps by the capacity that was shown by government research administrators – the senior staff of OSTI – for seeing national R & D needs whole at a time when only isolated fragments were perceptible to most of the professionals, and when R & D workers themselves were few and far between and not capable of generating very much in the way of well-formulated research proposals. OSTI (and its successor, BLR & D Department), as mentioned in the relevant chapter, has been unlike the normal research councils in taking a very positive and, in some respects, participative role in the projects which it funds. This could well have certain disadvantages, but on balance, in these early years of R & D, it has amply proved itself to be the effective mechanism which the situation required. OSTI, like the British Library, has been an element in our professional activity which has excited admiration and not a little envy in all parts of the world.

With librarianship and information work in such a healthy position it has not been surprising that recent years have witnessed a very great growth in our professional influence and activity overseas. Ken Harrison's chapter chronicles a formidable range of international activities with which the profession and, particularly, the LA are associated. It is perhaps invidious to single out any particular incident or activity, but it is hard to resist a reference to the 1971 IFLA conference at Liverpool, with the UK as the host country, presenting a superbly organised occasion which evoked tributes and compliments on a scale very rare indeed for a gathering of this type. It is worth making clear, of course, that in addition to the largely librarianship-orientated activity described by Harrison, there is vigorous British involvement in the sphere of international scientific information – Gray describes, for instance, the BLR & D Department's UNISIST and European

Community activities, and there is extensive British involvement in the activities of FID, via Aslib.

The century with which this volume is concerned has seen, it is clear, changes and developments which have produced something as near to a complete 'national library system' as can be found in any part of the world. That this is so has, however, more than a merely national significance. The library and information world into which we are moving in this centenary year is one in which thinking will increasingly be in international, or at least regional, terms. It is no accident, for example, that at the top of UNISIST's list of priorities is systems interconnection; equally, it is no accident that at the same time – and also from within UNESCO – the concept of NATIS (National Information Systems) should have emerged with considerable power and vigour. For the effective systems inter-connection at *international* level to which UNISIST aspires, a basic prerequisite is effective library and information infrastructure at *national* level – which is the objective of NATIS. It is a matter for some satisfaction that British librarianship has made contributions of great significance to UNISIST, to NATIS and to UBC (Universal Bibliographical Control) and that British libraries, as a 'system', are as ready as any in the world to contribute to and benefit from the 'international' librarianship that surely lies ahead. The part to be played by the Library Association itself is far from clear at a time when it is so earnestly searching its soul, but the evidence of its first hundred years suggests a resilience and a responsiveness that should carry it with some confidence into the second century of its existence.

Chapter One

The voice of the profession: The Library Association

Godfrey Thompson

In a volume issued to celebrate the centenary of the Library Association, only one chapter is to deal with the Association itself. This is rather like including as an afterthought on the guest list the one for whom the birthday party is given. It seems typical of the profession's attitude to its Association: venerable, worthy enough of course, but not exciting.

The Centenary itself hardly stirs the general imagination. The picture it presents is at once old and yet not old enough. If it were a celebration of the anniversary of some event in the colourful past, with costumes, swords and general swashbuckling, then we could more easily work up enthusiasm; but not for late Victorians with mutton-chop whiskers, fighting for such dreary things as the removal of the penny rate, the introduction of open access, the opening up of the libraries of the 'new' (now ageing) universities. The Edwardians and Georgians with their little struggles, how very dated it all is, and how far removed from our exciting world of computers and data-banks and management techniques.

If this image is dull, how much duller is the detailed portrait of a century of committee meetings, working parties, agenda and discussions, of men and women growing old in the unpaid service of their colleagues. The battles which they fought have been long forgotten but the conditions under which we work, the services which we provide to the community, our standing in the community, all owe much to a band of people who have, for a century, believed in and worked for the Library Association.

This chapter does not purport to be a history of the Association. The definitive work by Munford[1] is now available while for those who require a succinct and authoritative summary Haslam[2] has published an account both in the *Journal of Librarianship* and (in a somewhat expanded form) in the *International Encyclopaedia of Librarianship and Information Science*.

The title of the Library Association, like the British postage stamp, gives no indication of nationality: to explain why would perhaps involve an examination of the national sub-conscious. Nevertheless the Association is, proportionate to national population, incomparably the largest and most influential in the world.

There is no yardstick on which to judge the success of a professional association; Bingley has pertinently questioned whether librarianship is a profession at all. Nevertheless the Association, with more than 24,000 members, has for a century affected for good or ill the course of library development in Britain (and to a certain extent overseas) and has had an influence far greater than that of any other body. Does it, in the words of its Royal Charter, 'unite all persons engaged or interested in library work'? Certainly not; several attempts have been made to achieve that aim but so far without success. It would be asking too much of human nature and would not allow for the basically fragmentary nature of information-related activities, the human tendency to sectionalise and specialise.

Why is a professional association formed? Why do librarians join one? It must be because people who spend their lives in a particular discipline and on a certain service come to feel that they can achieve more by coordination of efforts, by cooperation and by consultation together. If they work not only for a wage but in the trust that they have, in their expertise, something to give to the life of the community, they come to believe that, with others similarly motivated, they can together sharpen their techniques, find solutions to common problems, assess their aims and have an influence far greater than they could ever hope to achieve individually.

Like most such bodies the LA has grown steadily in membership over the years. At the end of its first fifty years it had about 800 members; twenty years later the number was 6500 and by 1960 had risen to 13,000. Naturally this reflects the growth of libraries but it also mirrors a growing acceptance of the Association's importance in the life of the country, and an appreciation of the work it does. In 1961 the Association deliberately deprived itself of a section of its membership by removing institutions from full membership in order that it could become a true professional association. Despite this loss, the number of members rose, between 1960 and 1976, from 13,000 to over 24,000. Any cynic who attempts to write off membership figures as showing only the need for the professional diploma would be hard put to explain away this phenomenal growth.

Although the overall picture of the last twenty years has been one of exponential growth, the Association has at times deliberately restricted its activities when it has clearly seen that to do so would be in the best interests of the profession. One example was by restricting voting membership to professional librarians, as mentioned above; a second and much more striking example is the phased withdrawal from library education. By the outbreak of the Second World War almost all library education was controlled and indeed provided by the Association: the exception was a single small library school. When the war ended the LA decided as a matter of long-term policy that full-time education should be the norm and that the work of providing and fostering part-time and self-help learning and qualification should be run down and gradually phased out. This was not an easy, nor a popular decision to take; there were very many, and there are still some, who believe that it was wrong, but none can deny that it was both a courageous and an unselfish decision.

Although the phasing-out of part-time education is now far advanced, the LA still controls jealously the professional standards implicit in the granting of its qualifications. To obtain admission to the Association's Register of Chartered Librarians – now widely accepted as a degree equivalent – the student has not only to graduate from a school of librarianship but also to

3

meet standards of approved library service and experience laid
down by the Association. Moreover, the library schools
themselves, whether part of universities, polytechnics or other
colleges, cooperate by having their syllabi and general
standards approved by the LA before their diplomas are accepted
as leading to entry on the Professional Register. As a part of this
cooperation, representatives of the LA serve on the various
boards of teaching establishments – fifteen of them; there is also
an LA representative on the CNAA board. The Association still
does carry out its own examining, although now on a much
reduced scale, and also operates a Mature Registration Scheme
for candidates, often distinguished in their own fields who may
have come into librarianship late.

When attempting to describe the work of the Association to
others, one is frequently baffled by the very simplicity of the
question 'But what does the LA actually *do*?' Whatever it does
necessitates over seventy staff and creates a turnover of more
than £700,000 per annum, so it must be something on a large
scale. A quick glance at the Annual Report shows that it
published thirteen new titles last year and that over a hundred of
its publications are in print. Another glance shows that these
publications made a fairly considerable profit, despite including
a number which are professionally worthy but which no
commercial publisher would touch; this profit helps to shield
members' subscriptions from the full effects of inflation. These
however are 'normal' publications: there are an enormous
number of others: reports, standards, guide-lines, research
papers and other less glamorous publications were produced for
the simple reason that they were necessary. If they are little
known to the average member it is because his interests are on
the whole confined to his own field; when he does venture on
unfamiliar ground he may be very glad indeed that documents
such as these have been produced to assist him.

The serial publication best known (and best loved? – this is no
place for controversy) is of course the *Record*. Begun in the
nineteenth century it still thumps on to each member's doormat,
receiving a predictably mixed reception: who can keep 24,000
librarians happy? But in addition to this, and in response to a

known need, the LA has steadily added to its list: *Journal of Librarianship, British Humanities Index, British Technology Index, Library and Information Science Abstracts* (with Aslib) and now *Radials Bulletin*. To these can be added the Research Papers and the *Year Book, Students' Handbook* and Examination Papers. Some of these are 'commercial' in that they make a profit but others are a *service* to the membership and their production means a *contra* against the profits of the general publications.

One mentions the 'publishing' of standards as though it were purely a matter of arranging text for the printer. In fact to recommend standards which ought to be applied in certain fields is an exercise which must occupy for a very long period not only the Secretariat but also a number of senior librarians. The resultant publication has to be absolutely accurate, up-to-the-minute and meticulously phrased because those in office who do not wish to see an acceptance of a particular level of excellence will certainly take the opportunity to discredit it if the recommendations are slipshod. One can imagine therefore the time and effort which has been expended by the LA – and by many of its members – in the production in recent years of published standards for 'Libraries in the fields of Higher Education during reorganisation', 'School Library Resource Centres', 'Colleges of Further Education', 'The New Polytechnics', 'Hospital Libraries: recommended standards' and so on – this is far from a complete list but it indicates something of the range. Again this work and its results are unknown to the average member until he happens to need the help.

Professional standards are not *decreed* by the Library Association: those bodies (and office-holders) who bear this responsibility have to be guided, led, persuaded, coaxed, shamed into doing what we librarians believe to be the right thing. This is not only done by publication but also by encouragement, by publicly presenting such honours and rewards as can be devised to those who, we believe, have served the profession, or literature, well. The Association's McColvin, Besterman, Robinson, Kate Greenaway, Carnegie and Wheatley Medals try to do this and, given the active help of members, can often make a real impact.

A third way of improving standards is by the provision of research grants; this is obviously only possible on a limited scale with LA funds but every opportunity is taken of making representations to other, better financed bodies. 'Representation on other bodies' is not an inspiring description of something which occupies a great deal of time-consuming work; more than thirty bodies invite and receive LA representation, members giving of their time for this kind of work; this number does not take into account the various British Standards Committees who are glad of the Association's help.

Perhaps the way of 'keeping up standards' which makes the most immediate appeal to the membership is that relating to the salaries and conditions of service of librarians of all kinds and at all levels. The LA is not a trade union but the activities of the various trade unions in all branches of librarianship would be far less effective without the specialist advice, guidance and prodding which is always necessary to make the needs of the librarian known to organisations which may represent a wide range of professions and trades. This is hard work, and highly skilled work, requiring an encyclopaedic knowledge of awards, recommendations and government rulings, not only current but often going back a number of years. Moreover. its work has to be carried out not with a single union representing all librarians but with a great number: NALGO on NJC matters, the Institute of Professional Civil Servants, the Association of University Teachers and many more – among whom some are not trade unions but professional bodies similar to our own. Parallel with this work is that of collecting and publishing information on salaries and conditions of service, for example the annual 'Grading of public library posts' list and 'Conditions of service of librarians in universities', to assist members who may be negotiating locally.

To the serving librarian this work is of the first importance; it is inevitable perhaps that the LA should be blamed when salaries awarded turn out to be less than some members would wish. Perhaps it is a backhanded compliment to the LA's standing that so many letters arrive asking 'Why doesn't the LA get the

Minister to . . . ?' or 'When is the LA going to give us better salary scales . . . ?'

Some of the most important and least known tasks ever carried out by the Association take the form of 'making representations' to a Minister or Government official. The most formal way is to submit evidence to a Royal Commission or other official *ad hoc* body. In the last decade alone the LA has supplied specialist comment on behalf of the profession to more than twenty such bodies; names such as Roberts, Bourdillon, Robbins, Dainton, Parry, Haint, Briggs, Bullock, Layfield, Whitford may be a form of shorthand to many, but they represent important occasions where our professional lives, and in a small way the life of the country, would have been affected differently if the views of librarians had not been presented authoritatively.

The most immediate examples of such work occur when legislation appears to be planned which might affect libraries and librarians: here the need is for the presentation and pressing of views to Ministers and often to MPs who may be susceptible to our influence. Often this action has to be taken as a matter of absolute urgency, and the real democratic control of the Council has to be suspended by the Executive Committee so that the moment may be seized. If members as a whole are not fully aware of what is going on, this is a built-in condition of such activities. The Council can hardly announce that 'Mr So-and-so, MP, was lobbied' or that 'the Minister assured us, off the record, that . . .'. Often the answer to the question 'why doesn't the LA . . . ?' is 'We do, but we can't publish a report'. The current example is the action affecting the book expenditure of Buckinghamshire County Library which has been subjected to cuts out of all proportion to those inflicted in other areas of that Council's activities. Here the LA has spent many, many hours on behalf of that library, but also on behalf of any other libraries which might suffer if this step were to become a precedent. How successful will our efforts be? We cannot guarantee or predict; only make sure that all is done which ought to be done; and hope.

This record of 'what the LA does' could go on and on. Suffice it here to say that it also runs an information service, feeds the press, compiles statistics, carries out research, organises hundreds of meetings, conferences and seminars – performs in fact a million or more small actions which do not matter except that they need to be done and that no one else would do them.

The field in which the association operates was quite clearly set out in the Royal Charter, granted in 1898, to be 'libraries' 'library work', 'librarians' and 'bibliographical study and research'. In the context of the times this was the inevitable description. The librarians who founded the Association twenty years earlier were the heads of scholarly libraries – the British Museum, the Bodleian Library, Cambridge University Library, the Advocates Library, Edinburgh, the Athenaeum, the London Library and so on: ironically the very group which is least strong in its association with the LA today.

That these librarians should have taken the lead in founding the Association was praiseworthy: that librarians of public libraries and present-day libraries in the field of education should not have been prominent in 1877 was inevitable. The passing of the Public Library Act of 1892, plus the benevolent activities of Andrew Carnegie, stimulated such an explosion of public library creation that thirty years after the founding of the Association, the number of towns which had started public libraries had multiplied by eight; the inevitable consequence of this was that public librarians came into the Association in ever-increasing numbers and that more and more of its time and energy was devoted to public library affairs. This in itself was counter-productive in that learned, university and college librarians were less likely to join, or even to remain as members as they became more and more outnumbered and their direct interests less central to the discussions.

From this trend flowed a number of actions, particularly the founding of rival bodies, which now appear to many librarians to have been unfortunate, but it is not easy to fault those who ran the Association's affairs at that time. As a democratic body with open elections its Council quite naturally acquired a majority of public librarians and they, equally naturally, were concerned primarily with the service in which they, and the great majority of the membership, were engaged. Today we order things differently, recognising that the needs of all branches of the profession must be served and that any library, however small, can make its contribution to the needs of some section of the community. To do this it has been necessary to tamper drastically with the workings of pure democracy: councillors for particular kinds of libraries are elected only by those working in those particular fields who thus have *extra* votes in the running of the Association's affairs. There are also councillors representing the eleven 'branches', ie geographical divisions, thus tending to offset the preponderance of member-numbers in the larger built-up areas.

In 1924, mainly because of dissatisfaction with the LA as it was at that time, the Association of Special Libraries and Information Bureaux (now Aslib) came into being. It too has gone from strength to strength; has attracted considerable support from government by its development of research facilities in the fields of science and technology. It represents mainly institutions and has become a major publishing and guiding authority in its field. Paradoxically, at the same time, the Library Association itself was developing into a different kind of organisation: one specifically planned to be hospitable to special interests. In the 1920s the University and Research Section and the County Libraries Section were formed. The Medical Section was founded in 1948 and the Reference and Special Libraries Section in 1950. These were followed in the 1960s by Colleges and Institutes of Education, Cataloguing and Indexing, Colleges of Technology and Further Education, Hospital Libraries (now Health and Welfare Libraries) and so on to the present total of sixteen Sections, now called 'Groups'. Each one of these was founded because a number of people working professionally in a particular field of resource use felt that they had sufficient in common, and were sufficiently different from others, to warrant the forming of their own group. Of course they were right: the librarian working with a mobile public library has very different problems and technical difficulties from the indexer, the librarian in charge of the audio-visual resources in a college, the librarian working in a school or the curator of a rare books library. In order to promote technical discussion, to hold conferences and to publish the result of study in the special field, a concentrated, specific membership is inevitable. But the great success of the growth of groups within the LA is that this difference can be recognised and catered for without ignoring the similarity of the aim, the commonalty of the profession, without fragmenting the whole and shattering its influence for progress.

The motives of those who founded bodies outside the LA were genuine and represented real needs. At the time the reasons were strong but some of them have little relevance today. The best example of this is Aslib which had excellent grounds for coming into existence – the complete inadequacy of the LA as it was in the 1920s for information workers in the field of technology. That does not apply today. The tragedy is that such an organisation, once founded, attracts loyal and devoted workers who would indignantly reject any suggestion that their body no longer has grounds for a separate existence. These feelings are very human: they must be respected, but they are not a valid argument for the continuation of pointless fragmentation. This is not to say that there is often conflict between the two bodies in the services or the advice that they give, or that there is no communication or cooperation between them. This can hardly be the case when the members of the respective Councils, to say nothing of chairmen of the leading committees of the two bodies, are so often the same people. Further fragmentation took place in 1958 with the formation of the Institute of Information Scientists which now issues its own professional qualification; again a number of professionals working in a field which was at the best on the fringe of, and, as they thought, outside the 'main' field of librarianship, formed a separate association. The Institute has said that 'information science is primarily concerned with the organisation of *information* and not of the sources of information; information scientists *use* libraries (and other sources of information) but do not organise them'. There are many thousands who, while believing that their life's work is covered by this definition, still feel aware that their contribution is a part of the whole – the provision, organisation and use of information in all its various forms. In a similar way, although in a completely different part of the forest, those professionals who are concerned with the care, conservation and exploitation of manuscript, and above all archival, sources, formed their own body in 1948 as the Society of Archivists. Again the reason was that the LA was too much concerned with certain major fields of printed-book librarianship and that the special concerns of a group of people working in a certain area needed a separate body.

If we admit that these younger bodies were formed because of the then inadequacy of the LA, why have steps not been taken to heal the breach now that the Association has remedied the faults of its structure?

The gains under such a proposal seem high; the problems probably capable of solution; it seems odd therefore that nothing should have been heard of the idea. In fact there is in existence a Joint Committee consisting of the LA and Aslib (joined later by the Society of Archivists, the Institute of Information Scientists and SCONUL). Since 1967 it has worked towards a closer linking of interests but hopeful ideas came to nothing and the Joint Committee has never made any practical recommendations to the various parent bodies. In 1970 it published the following statement 'We agree there would be many advantages in a greater degree of cohesion or even unification among the organisations active in the library and information field. There are, however, many practical difficulties which preclude any all-embracing solution. Nevertheless we are satisfied that, as far as Aslib and the Library Association are concerned there is enough common ground and mutual confidence between the two Associations to justify further joint measures in pursuit of the common interest'.

This may sound statesmanlike: in fact it was a confession of despair and failure. Today, five years later, could not goodwill overcome the combination of personal ambition and petty restrictions which lead to that depressing statement? In recent years the Committee has met very infrequently, contenting itself with recommending that its officers should 'keep in touch'. Nevertheless the Joint Committee does exist and could become the basis for a wider assembly.

Why was no progress made? The reason lies in the varied
nature of the organisations and in the imperfectibility of human
nature. Pride and perhaps vanity (on all sides, including the LA,
let it be hastily added) seem to have been more important a
factor than the serious assessment of advantages and
disadvantages. Oddly enough – if one doesn't accept human
nature as odd – one of the greatest difficulties is the title of any
possible federation. It could not be called the Library
Association because that would imply surrender to an existing
body. Other suitable words have peculiar connotations of their
own: information, media, resources, bibliographical,
communications – all have flavours which cannot be instantly
replaced in the generic mind.

The elements which make up the service of the professional to
the people of this country in the general field of book,
manuscript, data bases, audio-visual resources and so on are
almost all paid for in their various ways from public funds and
thus out of the pockets of the people served. Those which are
truly 'private' – libraries and information services in firms and
research associations – institutions, trade unions and so on,
although mainly financed from private funds, are nevertheless
planned to serve the common weal and their servants are
educated and trained in common institutions. Of course, they
are all 'different'. The jobs we do differ greatly in method, in
intent and in the materials we use, but under the leadership of the
British Library they exist to serve the nation, and the more
effective they are, the richer our lives become.

What, then, has the profession itself to gain from such an
amalgamation or federation? Firstly, there would be the
enormous advantage of coordination; conflicting voices would
no longer be heard, conflicting advice no longer be given,
differences being ironed out among a family, not before
outsiders. Secondly, there would be an enormous accession of
that energy and ability within the profession which is at present
split between several bodies. There is a limit to the time and
energy which librarians of goodwill can give to national
professional affairs and much of it is at present wasted on mere
organisational details of so many separate bodies. Paperwork,

office routines and publication could be pooled with immense savings and gains in effectiveness.

Among its other assets the LA owns the freehold of its own headquarters, part of which is at present let to outside bodies. This represents a natural base for a larger federation and the financial advantages accruing to a hospitable headquarters for all elements are too obvious to need stressing.

At international level, too, such an amalgam would have immeasureable advantages. The Library Association is, of course, the present and obvious British national member of the International Federation of Library Associations but the position is complicated in that IFLA is aware that other organisations claim to speak for sections of the world of British librarianship. If we were amalgamated and had one voice, our position would be much stronger.

Perhaps even more important than all these would be the grouping of the very real and tangible assets which the other bodies, to their very great credit, have built up over so many years. The power, reputation and resources of Aslib, with its important library and information service, is complementary to that of the LA; so are the expertise and special skills of the archivists. Joined together in practical work, although entirely free in policy judgments, all parts of the whole would have much to gain; but what would they have to lose?

If we discount entirely the natural reluctance of officers of each body to give up their independence, and the immediate 'real-estate and personnel' difficulties (which, given goodwill, could easily be overcome), we are left only with the problem of allowing each section its independence of decision in its own field within a federation. To produce such a constitution would not be easy; it would be very difficult indeed, but I suggest that the end-product would be so great an asset, not only to the profession, and to the nation, but as an example to those countries who are at the moment in the process of establishing professional associations and look for a lead to those on whose presumed maturity they have the right to rely.

None of the existing organisations could possibly come into a joint body without considerable safeguards which would have to be worked out in detail between all concerned; it is likely that a much looser structure would be necessary but this could be achieved. The Association has changed greatly over the last century, evolving to meet changing needs. If it had not done so, if it had not in general stayed as one body of professional interest, then the library and information field not only in this country but in many overseas countries, would be much the poorer.

The Centenary which this book is published to celebrate would be the ideal time to see what could be done. That there would be some opposition is obvious but if we do not take such steps we shall all be the weaker. It is absolutely certain that new organisations will arise to cover marginal fields, dispersing the general standing of librarianship as a whole, watering our resources and wasting not only money but that limited stock of professional energy which is our greatest asset.

The next step requires trust and goodwill, not surly reaction. The result could be a giant step forward for the profession. Those who write the history of the next hundred years will judge us harshly if we continue to swim apart in our little ponds and say that it is impossible.

References

1. Munford, W. A. *A History of the Library Association 1877–1977* London, Library Association, 1976. (A Library Association Centenary Volume.)

2. Haslam, D. D. A short history of the Library Association. *J of Librarianship* 6 (3), July 1974, 137–164.

Chapter Two

Aslib and the development of information management

Leslie Wilson

As the Library Association prepares to enter its second century, there can be little doubt as to the far-reaching nature of the changes that still lie ahead in concepts and practices over the whole field of information transfer including the librarianship sector. It is in assisting those developments and monitoring their effects that the major part of Aslib's activity is likely to be extended, as it has been increasingly during the past decade. There is a need, of course, in most fields of human endeavour for some mechanism charged specifically with the task of promoting the healthy development of the field or, to put it another way, of acting as the interface between advanced thought and experimental development on the one hand and the broadly based operational sector on the other. That Aslib should have evolved into such a role – at a pace quickening rapidly in the decade since the Government first formally recognised a distinctive function for information in society by the creation of the Office for Scientific and Technical Information (OSTI) – can be seen as a natural stage of development in its fifty years as a focus for special libraries and information services in a wide variety of environments, and as a development enhanced by the special relationship which it has enjoyed with Government since 1944.

Three phases of growth

The formative influences which have helped to shape the Aslib of today are not too difficult to discern in the three fairly distinct phases in the association's life. From its inception in 1924, through the Second World War and until the late 1940s, it was a classical example of the voluntary association. Its purpose was to provide a framework within which librarians and others beginning to call themselves information officers and working in highly specialised fields could cooperate and support each other through an annual conference and occasional meetings, as well as by direct mutual help in the loan of publications which itself owed much to the personal contacts made at the meetings. Nevertheless, even at this early stage, the association's potential for what it has since become popular to call a leadership role was already evident in the initiatives which it took to gather together the scientific and technical journals trickling into the United Kingdom during the war from enemy-occupied countries. The Aslib Microfilm Service, for which these journals were the raw material, became one of the principal means whereby published scientific and technical information from those countries was made available to the British, American and Chinese Nationalist Governments, and this activity – with the prospect which it offered of helping to harness scientific knowledge to postwar rehabilitation – was instrumental in attracting to Aslib Government interest and, from 1944 onwards, a series of grants on an increasing scale. The fifteen years from 1950 to 1965 were a period of steady growth in both membership and services, with industry and business as the principal targets. This growth, assisted by Government grants related to the amount of subscription income from UK sources and administered by the Department of Scientific and Industrial Research, reflected the general expansion of industry at that time. Membership grew steadily from 1000 to 2800, with industrial organisations forming the largest single category, and the range of services offered – all of a strictly practical nature and responding to the needs of small or medium-sized firms with limited information resources of their own – increased substantially. Literature searches for scientific and technical information were undertaken in addition to the basic function of referring inquirers to an appropriate source of information; a bibliographical checking and interlending service was introduced; the Commonwealth index of unpublished scientific and technical translations was established and membership of the panel of specialist translators was greatly enlarged so as to increase subject and language coverage; a panel of subject indexers was set up as a complement to the panel of translators; the first of the short training courses for newcomers to special library work was introduced at a frequency of one or two a year; the formation of membership subject groups was encouraged, starting with an Aeronautics Group and an Economics Group; and Aslib's publishing activity was extended by the issue of such major volumes as the *Aslib Handbook of special librarianship and information work* and a new version of the *Aslib Directory to sources of specialised information,* as well as the first annual volume of the *Index to theses for higher degrees in the universities of the United Kingdom.* Less successful at that time were attempts to establish a consultancy service, which later experience suggests was in advance of its time, and embryonic efforts to develop a research programme which few then regarded as capable of realisation in the information field, and none was prepared to finance.

This brief retrospect is important since it provides the background essential to understanding of the third and current phase of Aslib's evolution which finally determined the firm orientation of Aslib in the direction of a development organisation on behalf of information services generally. Whatever the earlier pointers towards it – such as the attempts to establish a research function and a consultancy service – this third phase dates clearly from the Government's decision in 1964 to establish the Office for Scientific and Technical Information as a separate unit within the Department of Education and Science. The new unit, with responsibility for grant-aid to Aslib among its formal terms of reference, was to take over and develop the scientific and technical information interests of the disbanded DSIR. One of its first steps was to join with Aslib in a working party to spell out Aslib's future role as an authoritative source of information and advice on information and library science and services, a role which the working party saw rising from a three-fold base of research, consultancy and training. Theoretically, the concept was right; logistically, it was inadequate. So far as research was concerned, there were as yet no ready-made information research workers to be recruited into a formal research unit and time was needed to recruit promising people and to train them in research methods. Moreover, there was no clear means of judging how wide was the gap between the research itself and the membership's interest in it or, indeed, its capacity to apply it. True, a special fund of £40,000 contributed by a small number of member companies provided a launching pad with matching grants from OSTI, but a single pump-priming exercise by a few is no guarantee of a long-term commitment by the many. Then, with regard to consultancy, there was still little evidence of a substantial demand for such guidance, still less of a willingness to pay the relatively high cost of providing it. A lead time of from three to eight years might be needed to create a viable consultancy operation; in the event, it required very nearly the maximum period then envisaged. In the training area, it was thought that Aslib's function would be to transfer the results of its own research to operational units by means of a variety of short courses at a very advanced level. Together, these three elements constituted too narrow a base to support an institution capable of maintaining a financially viable independent existence and it soon became clear that a much broader base, maintaining and developing still further the services element of Aslib's previous activities on at least a cost-recovery basis, would be required.

The three major formative influences

In all this story of evolution, three factors can now be clearly seen as the influences which have had most effect in shaping the Aslib that has emerged. First, a membership of great variety looking for many different forms of support, and encouraged to recognise its stake in the association's future. Second, a healthy working relationship with Government, regularly renewed on the basis of review of past performance and the provision of further funds for work undertaken in the wider national interest. Third, and by no means the least important, a recognition within Aslib that much long-term activity, however intrinsically worthwhile, could only be undertaken from a broad, financially sound, base of operations responding to the daily preoccupations of the organisations within the membership. Such influences could only produce an organisation of some complexity, one which must seek to satisfy both a national interest and a multiplicity of private and public interests, ranging from those of private and nationalised industry to those of local authorities and academic institutions of many levels; and one which must, however, strive to reconcile the promotion of an ideal with the economics of the market place. It is in the confluence of all three of those influences that an explanation must be sought of Aslib's present stance and, conceivably, of its future hopes and aspirations.

A diverse membership united in common purpose

The first of these influences, the membership, is clearly the *sine qua non* of Aslib's existence. It is distinguished above all by two dominant characteristics: the loyalty of its attachment to the association, and the complexity of its composition and, hence, of its varied needs for support. Few memberships can, indeed, be quite so diverse. First, it is primarily corporate in nature and adherence to Aslib must, in consequence, periodically run the gauntlet of both a management and a professional critique; the maintenance of a membership not infrequently depends, therefore, upon a management, rather than a professional, information view of priorities, and upon a subtle interplay between the degree of a management's commitment to information policies and the effectiveness of its information staff in projecting its own role in relation to company performance. The orientation of higher management towards unified information policies and cohesive information systems as part of the management structure itself, which figures strongly in Aslib's current aims, is in the interests, therefore, not only of information staffs but, indirectly, of Aslib itself.

Secondly, there is little homogeneity in a membership which includes large and small industry, financial and commercial firms, central and local government establishments, public libraries, universities and colleges of various kinds and a range of technical and professional societies and institutions. Many are highly sophisticated in their approach to the gathering and use of information. Others are engaged in its dissemination, and others still in the development of services, equipment and systems for its management. Whilst libraries of many different kinds form the largest single category of member, therefore, the membership's boundaries have expanded well beyond the

original concept of an association of special libraries to the
point where Aslib provides a much-needed forum wherein a
whole range of interests concerned with the information process
may meet.

A third characteristic is that, even within a single membership
category, Aslib's relationship can be with numerous different
functional types including librarians, information scientists,
editors, systems analysts, chief executives, marketing managers
and many others. Such a microcosm of the information industry
and its clientele unites in one community the full range of
attitudes and experience which these varied categories represent
and, it must be hoped, enables their interaction to make a
positive contribution to the effective development of
information and library services generally.

Finally, the distribution of 30% of Aslib's membership over
some seventy-five countries outside the United Kingdom,
including most of the industrially advanced countries and many
just beginning the process of economic and social development,
makes Aslib probably the most widely international
non-governmental organisation concerned with information
and library matters anywhere in the world. This situation is no
doubt both a tribute to the unique role of the English language
in world affairs and an endorsement of Britain's approach to
information management. Nevertheless, it poses questions, in a
constantly shrinking world, about the relative status of at least
five main membership groups: those in the United Kingdom
itself, those within the area of the European Economic
Commission, those with a British Commonwealth connection
and an English language tradition, those of North America
sharing with Britain a common cultural and linguistic heritage,
and those in the remaining countries of the world. It is
interesting to speculate whether one day they may all have equal
membership status with some form of representation on the
central governing body and local branches to provide a focal
point for cooperative effort.

That such a diverse membership should display so great a
measure of attachment to the association is almost as much a

matter for surprise as for satisfaction; customers who are also
shareholders are rarely the easiest of people to satisfy.
Nevertheless, it would seem that the great majority of members
in the United Kingdom and Western Europe at least are
conscious of holding a stake in the association and of both
contributing and receiving benefit through it. This sense of
personal involvement doubtless stems from an accumulation of
small ways in which the staffs of member organisations
participate in Aslib's affairs: as both lecturers and students at
Aslib courses, as speakers and audience at conferences, as
members of the three branches and twelve groups formed by the
members themselves, as recipients of service given with a sense
of personal concern by the headquarters staff, and, to a more
limited extent, as members of the Council and its advisory
committees. It is to be hoped that, whatever the extent of the
growth of Aslib in future years, ways will be found of keeping
this vital sense of personal involvement alive.

Importance of the Government connection

The second major factor in Aslib's development is without
doubt its special relationship with Government and the
Government grants and contracts for which it has qualified,
under exacting conditions, continuously since 1944. For those
who too readily assume that a grant of public funds may dilute
the discipline essential to effective management, it should be
recalled that the trend in recent years has been away from
grants-in-aid to support recipients' own chosen programmes of
work, and towards specific projects conceived in the wider
national interest and written to Government's own
specification. This is a healthy trend which leaves each party
free to accept or decline a proposal and subjects each contract to
not one, but two, sets of financial and intellectual discipline. And
since the interests of Aslib members are broadly consonant with
the national interest in securing the most effective use of
information, it can be assumed that the risk of conflict between
membership and Government requirements is remote.

As the nature of Government changes so, of course, does the
nature of its relationships with others and, not unnaturally, the

point of contact between Aslib and Government has some effect upon the balance of emphasis in Aslib's activities. The DSIR connection between 1944 and 1964, for example, tended to emphasise the provision of day-to-day services for industry in the scientific and technical fields – and, in doing so, fairly reflected the membership's own concern at that time. The creation of the Office for Scientific and Technical Information within the Department of Education and Science, with terms of reference virtually restricted to research, tilted the balance towards the academic world and placed a priority on support for development of the research capability for which Aslib had long foreseen a need but could not itself finance. It is self-evident that the wholly novel creation of a major research unit in the information and library field, especially if it is to strive towards financial self-sufficiency through group-sponsored research and consultancy, requires a substantial period of time to recruit promising personnel, train them in research method, work out a set of short-term and long-term objectives, and gain practical experience in the conduct of research. It is indeed doubtful whether Aslib could have achieved this so quickly, if at all, without the priming of public funds to build up a viable research staff and to finance a solid core of research projects over the establishment period. It is, equally, not unreasonable to assume that this special relationship with OSTI was a significant factor in the success which Aslib has met in marketing its consultancy services both to home Government departments like the Foreign Office, the Ministry of Defence, the Civil Service Department and the Department of the Environment, as well as to such international governmental organisations as UNESCO, the Food and Agriculture Organisation and the Economic Commission for Europe.

It is to be expected that the nature of the Aslib–Government relationship will again be changed in some respects by the incorporation of OSTI in the British Library as the latter's research and development department, and by the increasingly common adoption by Government of the so-called Rothschild principles in relation to the funding of research and services by non-Governmental organisations. Already, the broad outline of the relationship under this policy can be seen in the terms offered and accepted for the three years to the end of 1978. First, with regard to research, the terms recognise a mutual commitment, in spite of the present economic climate, to maintain the research effort of Aslib at its present strength which requires expenditure in 1976 of approximately £112,000; of this total £40,000 represents a solid core of special projects – in effect, contracts – commissioned by the British Library and conceived in the wider public interest. In parallel is a general research programme generated by Aslib with a view to the more direct support of its members' work. That this general programme is financed by Aslib and the British Library equally, and that it is monitored by a research committee to which each appoints an equal number of representatives, indicates a full sharing of responsibility for the programme and an equal commitment to ensuring its success. A partnership of this kind with Government, whilst not restricting Aslib's freedom to develop its research function in any way, not only fosters a body of widely supported research in the nation's and the membership's interests, but also serves to maintain a substantial research facility ready with the skills and standards necessary to undertake individual or group-sponsored projects from the membership or any other source if the occasion arises. The Rothschild principle now applies for the first time even more fully to Government support for Aslib's non-research activities and any development project can be considered for support on its own merits without, as previously, the artificial ceiling on total Government funding for Aslib created by linking the public contribution to the amount of subscription income contributed by members in the United Kingdom. Precisely how well this arrangement will work in the non-research area remains to be seen but at least it presents a welcome challenge to develop new activities with potential appeal to a widening audience, and bids fair to help concentrate the limited effort that is available where it is likely to be most effective.

Two further important changes in the relationship are provided for in the current agreement. From the time of the very first Government grants in 1944, it was a condition of grant that full membership facilities – including the journals issued as part of a normal member's entitlement – should be extended without charge to any Government department that required them. Whilst the condition was not initially onerous, the expansion of Government activity in the last two decades led to a very substantial number of what could legitimately be regarded as non-subscribing members. Many of them, in common with other members, contributed handsomely to Aslib's cooperative endeavours in non-pecuniary ways, but this form of relationship created anomalies – for example, with regard to a Government official's right to vote or stand for election to the Council – quite apart from any financial considerations. Under the new arrangement, Government departments or establishments can be recruited into the membership and be required to subscribe in the same way as any other organisation. This can only place Aslib's relationship with them on a more rational basis, and also remove anomalies that had regularly consumed time and effort to disguise. The second change has come about more gradually. Under a grants-in-aid system, it was axiomatic that, for obvious reasons, an organisation in receipt of Government grants should receive them through a single governmental channel. With the greater emphasis on contracted work on the Rothschild principle, any Government department must clearly be free to buy the specialist expertise that it requires in direct negotiation with potential suppliers – and, conversely, the supplier to market his wares directly to potential consumers. Thus Aslib is doubly fortunate in enjoying a close working relationship with one Government agency, the British Library, and at the same time in disposing of skills and experience for which other Government departments – on all fours with potential clients in industry, the institutions, local government and elsewhere – may from time to time have need. Whilst this new arrangement is in some respects looser than its predecessors, it is clearly more in keeping with the free market philosophies of the present time, and the fact that Aslib's skills in research, consultancy, training and the organisation of specialist conferences have already been successfully marketed in the public sector suggests that the arrangement should accord well with its operating methods.

The Marketing Approach

It is in this marketing approach to its work, in fact, that the third major factor in shaping the modern Aslib is to be sought. Our association was perhaps among the earliest of professional bodies to recognise that, in an economic climate of increasingly fierce competition for limited resources, they could no longer take the blanket support of their adherents for granted, but must attempt to define the limits of their market and then provide, at a mutually acceptable price, the products or services that that market was willing to buy. This notion has, of course, a by no means universal appeal. Aslib has not infrequently been criticised for adopting a quasi-commercial approach to its task and for deserting, as some would have it, a traditional educational role based on the provision of a library, the publication of a learned journal, the organisation of meetings for the discussion of current theory and practice – and very little else. In fact, of course, these features remain a significant part of Aslib's activity and have, indeed, been embellished by current-awareness and other information services relevant to the library's intake, by the publication of a variety of other journals and occasional publications, and by annual programmes of meetings and specialist conferences organised by both the headquarters staff, three branches and a dozen industrial or special interest groups. What is much more significant is that a very wide range of specialist services, objectively costed and marketed so that each can be developed to the extent that its market will bear, has been added to the traditional core and that, in the process, the nature of the organisation has undergone a fundamental, if gradual, change. Just as diversification within a coherent framework has imposed itself, during the second half of this century, on both large and small businesses as the mainstay of operational viability in an unstable market situation, so has Aslib endeavoured to widen its product range in order to appeal to a wider spectrum of organisations than conventional libraries.

Such a process necessarily emphasises the degree of dependence upon the concept of market research and of positive marketing which dictates that the business cycle should start with the ultimate user of an organisation's products or services rather than with that organisation's productive capacity – in other words, that the organisation should make what it can sell, not merely attempt to sell what it can make. The application of that principle can only start effectively with analysis and understanding of the community to be served. Thus, in the case of the information community, it is necessary to identify the groups that originate information, the categories of information that are generated, the methods and mechanisms whereby they are communicated and the user groups that have an actual or a potential need for information. Only then is it possible to try to ensure that needs and provision are progressively matched and, also, to determine the nature and the limits of the contribution that a central organisation such as Aslib can make to the development of the whole. Even so, an approach of this nature is unlikely to succeed unless at the same time attitudes can be progressively changed in three important respects. First, there must be a high degree of flexibility as to what is, or is not, appropriate for Aslib to do in meeting a recognised or an emergent need and, with that flexibility, a mechanism for decision-making that can respond quickly and unequivocally to each situation as it arises; if this need does not wholly reverse the traditional relationship between members' representatives and operational staff through committee structures, it does inevitably transfer responsibility for the main initiatives to the staff and imposes an even greater need for disciplined communication to the membership at large, as well as to their elected representatives, on whose behalf all central action is undertaken. Secondly, there must be a willingness, as well as a capacity, to accept the economic uncertainties that accompany the selective purchasing of services; on a strict interpretation of the terms of the British Library grant, as much as 71% of Aslib's income in 1976 could be subject to these uncertainties, and it would not be surprising if the proportion were to increase over the years as new markets for Aslib's services are developed. Thirdly, a marketing strategy requires that every member of the staff should work consciously within its terms of reference and that annual targets of performance, whether of individuals or of departments, should be described in relation to the overall strategy, for only thus can everyone recognise the extent of his commitment and eventually gauge the measure of his success.

It goes without saying that, had Aslib already successfully resolved the problems associated with this approach, it would be unnecessary to describe them here; no living organism is static and, with these matters resolved, Aslib would doubtless now be faced with a wholly different set of difficulties to overcome. It has, nevertheless, done rather more than merely to take their measure and its concentration upon them should carry it forward, purposefully, into the 1980s and beyond.

The Next Objectives

To have concentrated on just three aspects of Aslib, however central to its character and its aims, may suggest an over-simplification of a complex organisation. It is, however, important to distinguish between complexity of operational environment which can be exhilarating, and complexity of purpose which can prove a barrier to achievement. Aslib is fortunate that, however varied its potential clientele and however wide the range of service they may need, the purpose of its existence can be simply stated: to promote the effective use of information as a resource of economic and social progress. In that short phrase may be discerned a whole philosophy of information management in the development of which Aslib has indeed fulfilled a leadership role. Promotion implies the encouragement of others, in this instance to put facts and experience to work; a concept which places the user of information firmly at the heart of things. But the existence of a consumer postulates, in industrial terms, a manufacturer, a product and a distributor also. Thus it is profitable to see the individual elements of the information industry and its clientele not as distinct, and possibly conflicting, groups but as inter-dependent parts of a common process sustained by an over-riding unity of interest; the malaise of one is likely to foretell the malaise of all and it is not by accident that Aslib offers a forum in which generators of information, its distributors, those who chart and control its flow, and finally its users can meet and cooperate in the pursuit of their common aims. Again, concern with the effectiveness of the use made of information implies a view of it as a useable commodity, and an attitude of mind towards the regularity of its acquisition, evaluation and exploitation in relation to its cost. Whilst many organisations, including international governmental bodies, are still prone to establish systems and committees ostensibly concerned with information in science and technology, such restrictive terminology places information services under penalty in the relentless competition for support from managements more urgently preoccupied with investment, corporate planning, human relations and the marketing of goods and services. The need for information in these fields is no less than the need for information in science and technology; and it is matched in hospital and welfare services, finance and taxation, the administration of justice and education and numerous other spheres besides. Indeed, few sectors of the nation's life lie wholly without this area of specialised need. At the heart of information policies, therefore, exists a basic need for a total concept of information, as powerful a resource of progress in society as materials, energy, machines or money. Nobody would question that the deployment of these resources in ways calculated to secure the most effective results for the minimum cost is a central function of management. Precisely the same requirement exists with regard to information in the face of the constantly increasing cost of its acquisition and of the growing complexity of the means available for its communication. It is to be expected, therefore, that information management will gradually come to be recognised more widely as an integral part of the management structure alongside, for example, personnel management, financial management, materials management and other parts of the management function. When that has ceased to be the exception and becomes the rule, the horizons for those who work in the information and library field will indeed have been significantly expanded.

Progress towards this objective must clearly depend upon many factors: the impact made by operating information units on the fortunes of their parent organisations, the range of capabilities that can be attracted into the information field, the readiness of managements and other users of information to understand the role of information in decision-making, and many others. The prospect is, of course, for a long period of almost imperceptible change rather than for dramatic developments. Nevertheless, if Aslib is to sustain its role of a development organisation, it must attempt to see the field as a totality and establish a framework within which initiatives can be taken deliberately and constructively towards the desired objectives. The requirements are indeed extensive and complex: it is necessary, for example, to identify and predict the information needs of all user and potential user communities by continuous monitoring and analysis; to foster recognition and understanding of those needs by a sustained programme of education of potential users and managements in a wide range of social environments; to stimulate the provision of information services by initiatives to bring identified need groups and actual or potential suppliers together; to provide authoritative information and advice for the design and operation of information services and systems through Aslib's advisory and consultancy services, and to monitor their effectiveness; to support information services and systems in their operational role by means of research, specialised training, publication, information and advice, and by providing facilities for the exchange of opinion and experience; and to monitor external developments affecting information services and to ensure that the latter's interests do not go by default. Such programmes, of course, go more easily into prose than into practice. Nevertheless, it is to be hoped and, indeed, expected that they will play a central part in Aslib's next development phase.

Readings

1. *The Work of Aslib* (Annual Reports of the Association), London, Aslib.
2. Aslib. *Report of the Committee on Aslib's Long-Term Objectives and Development, August, 1973* London, Aslib. Unpublished.
3. Wilson, Leslie. Aslib *in British librarianship and information science, 1966–70* Section X: 7. H. A. Whatley, ed London: Library Association, 1972, 670–672.
4. Wilson, Leslie. Aslib. *in Encyclopedia of library and information science,* vol 1. Allen Kent and Harold Lancour, ed New York: Marcel Dekker, 1968, 666–669.

5. Armstrong, Alan. Industrial library news. (Interview with Leslie Wilson to mark Aslib's 50th anniversary) *New Libr Wld* 75 (892), October 1974, 223–5.
6. Wilson, Leslie. The Aslib–Government Relationship. *State Librarian* 23 (2), July 1975, 16–19 and (3), November 1975, 30–34.

Chapter Three

The Institute of Information Scientists

Felix Liebesny

Introduction

In order to appreciate the development of the Institute it may be useful to review briefly the history of professionalism in the related disciplines of librarianship and documentation. The major field of activity of librarians developed in the middle of the nineteenth century, mainly through the passing of the Public Libraries Act of 1850 by which the United Kingdom became the first major country to establish a comprehensive public library system. This led eventually to the creation of the Library Association whose centenary is being celebrated *inter alia* by the publication of the present volume. The principal function of the Library Association was, and still is, to promote the interests of its members, the largest group of whom are public librarians.

Special librarianship developed intermittently and slowly until the First World War, but the creation of industrial Research Associations towards the end of that period and immediately thereafter, brought about an upswing in the provision of special library and documentation services both in such Research Associations and in private industry. Examples of such new establishments include the British Scientific Instrument Research Association (1918), the British Non-ferrous Metals Research Association (1920), the technical libraries of the then Mond Nickel Company Ltd (now International Nickel Limited), and of the British Aluminium Company Ltd.

The interests of such special librarians were felt not to be adequately taken care of within the Library Association and therefore eventually a separate organisation was created in 1924, the Association of Special Libraries and Information Bureaux, now Aslib. The Memorandum and Articles of Association of Aslib stated that in order to attain and maintain high standards in the field of documentation Aslib would be empowered among other things to hold examinations and award qualifications. The early years of Aslib and the economic depression of the thirties did not permit a sufficiently rapid growth in Aslib's activities to implement these provisions. Similarly, the after-effects of the Second World War did not allow any discussions on this topic in public until the middle of the fifties. Then several people began to agitate for a professional qualification in the field of special librarianship and documentation and tabled a motion for discussion at the Aslib annual conference at Scarborough in 1957. This motion was, however, defeated and therefore the above-mentioned action group decided to set up a separate organisation.

The action group consisted principally of A. B. Agard-Evans – in whose office at the Ministry of Works many of the preparatory meetings took place – J. E. L. Farradane, A. Gordon-Foster, C. W. Hanson and F. Liebesny. During these meetings the objectives of the Institute were defined, the Memorandum and Articles of Association worked out and a syllabus was drawn up for a professional examination in 'Information Science'. This name for the discipline together with that for its practitioners, *viz* information scientists, were arrived at after much soul searching and discussion. Although in the subsequent two decades much criticism was levelled at these two terms, it must be conceded that no better term has yet been devised and furthermore these names have now become fairly well established.

In the Articles of the Institute, information work is defined as 'the collection, collation, evaluation and organized dissemination of scientific and technical information'. The interpretation of the words 'scientific and technical' has varied from time to time and recent practice within the Institute tends to give them a much wider meaning than may have been intended originally. However, some further definitions of the

component parts of information work are also included in the
Articles where it is stated that it comprises such practices as:

i   preparation of abstracts and progress reviews
ii   translation of scientific and technical writings
iii   editing of such texts as emerge from (i) and (ii) above
iv   indexing, subject classification and information storage and
        retrieval
v   undertaking searches, preparing bibliographies, reports,
        etc
vi   providing information and tendering advice thereon
vii   dissemination of information and liaison and field work for
        that purpose
viii   research in information work

Again, this definition has been modified somewhat in that it is
nowadays generally recognised by the membership committee
of the Institute that a practitioner in information work should
show competence in at least two of the above-mentioned
activities to merit admission to the Institute.

The professional nature of the Institute and its members has
always been characterised by a combination of academic
qualifications and practical experience. This insistence on
practical experience which is carefully checked prior to
admission by the membership committee, has led *inter alia* to a
decision by the members not to consider teaching of Information
Science as a 'recognised' practice. It is the extent of practical
experience which largely determines the grade of membership
which an applicant may be awarded. It is of course very difficult
to establish overnight any profession or to inculcate
professionalism in a new discipline, but within a few years of the
foundation of the Institute the first advertisements appeared in
'situations vacant' columns asking for applications for posts in
information work in which the candidate was stipulated to be
'preferably a member of the Institute of Information Scientists'.
Constant preaching and propaganda over the years have
obviously helped to make this profession better known, greatly
assisted by the publication *A career in information science*, very

wittily illustrated by K. M. Sibley, and by talks to careers officers, careers conventions, etc.

Membership

The membership of the Institute is a personal one, ie only individuals are admitted – in contrast to Aslib, where corporate membership by companies, universities, libraries, etc is possible. The grades of membership are Fellows, Members, Associates, Student Members, and Affiliates. The last grade is a recent introduction and intended for those whose interests lie in Information Science but whose qualifications are not of a sufficient standard for any other grade of membership. These grades of membership of course reflect the professional attainment of its members in that the higher grades require a longer period of professional activity than the lower grades.

When the Institute was set up in 1958, some eighty-five members enrolled. This figure grew rapidly and on 31 March 1974 comprised 1135 members in the five grades as shown in Table 3.1., showing an increase of 8·4% over the preceding year.

Table 3.1

Fellows	50	4.4%
Members	451	39.8%
Associates	542	47.7%
Student Members	85	7.5%
Affiliates	7	0.6%
	1135	100.0%

Education

The Institute was set up in order to establish and maintain professional standards in the discipline. If such standards are to be established, they must be safeguarded by qualifications. This can only be done effectively if there are examinations leading to such qualifications. Satisfactory examinations for that purpose can only be conducted if there are adequate training courses preparing candidates for such examinations. Therefore one of the primary tasks of the Institute was to arrange for such training courses which were started within three years from the foundation of the Institute.

The first course for the Institute's Certificate started in January 1961 at the then Northampton College of Advanced Technology (now The City University) as a two-year evening course with two-hour lectures twice a week. The first intake consisted of four students.

Over the years the course grew until a full-time MSC course was established by the University in 1967. The head and guiding spirit of that Department was Mr J. E. L. Farradane, who on his retirement in 1973 was followed by Dr R. T. Bottle. At present the Centre for Information Science at The City University runs a full-time MSC course (one year) with over thirty students, and two one-day per week Diploma courses for two years with twelve and thirty students respectively. The full-time teaching staff comprises three lecturers assisted by several outside specialist lecturers.

The early courses at Northampton were followed soon after by information courses elsewhere, notably at the University of Sheffield Postgraduate School of Librarianship and Information Science with a Diploma, which in 1968 was replaced by an MSC, and at the Leeds Polytechnic with a BSC in Information Science. More recently, University College London School of Library, Archive and Information Studies initiated an MSC in Information Science, and an MSC in Information Studies has just been set up at the Loughborough University of Technology.

Meetings and conferences

Another early activity of the Institute was the publication of a duplicated newsletter. In 1967 this changed its name to *The Information Scientist* and became a printed journal with professionally designed layout. Its contents range from papers presented at the Institute's meetings to news of new admissions to the membership, correspondence, and the splendid – and still anonymous – Icarus file.

The Institute believed from the very start in catering for the needs of its members and therefore organised meetings and conferences at frequent intervals. The first two conferences were held at Oxford in 1964 and 1966, followed by Sheffield (1968), Reading (1970), Manchester (1972), Guildford (1974) and St Andrews (1976). From then on it is planned to have these conferences annually, in York in 1977 and Loughborough in 1978.

Presidents

The Institute has had the good fortune of having a series of outstanding personalities as Presidents: Dr G. M. Dyson (1959–1961), Professor Sir Lindor Brown (1962–1964), Dr T. E. Allibone (1965–1967), Professor Sir Harold Thompson (1968–1970), Sir James Tait (1971–1973) and Dr H. T. Hookway (1974–1976). The President is expected to give at least one address during his term of office and these make interesting reading in the pages of *The Information Scientist* about the development of the Institute and the discipline as such.

Council, committees and branches

The activities of the Institute are supervised by an elected Council, which is assisted and advised by several sub-committees such as management committee, membership committee, education committee, meetings committee, development committee, and research committee. Each committee reports regularly to Council, usually through its chairman who is a member of Council.

The growth in membership has led eventually to the establishment of regional branches, of which the Northern Branch is the most successful. This was established in 1965 and is very active in holding conferences, meetings and educational courses. A branch for the Midlands was established soon afterwards, but owing to transport problems in that region it has languished for several years. The development of courses in information science at Loughborough University has, however, created a nucleus there from which strenuous attempts to revitalise the Midlands Branch have sprung. A Scottish branch was formed in 1970 and an Irish branch in 1975. An Indian branch was also formed but owing to the strict regulations relating to foreign exchange transactions this branch became an independent body in India in the early 1960s.

The future

Like so many other professional organisations the role of the Institute has changed since its foundation nearly two decades ago. While it maintains its major function of controlling the admission to its ranks, it is no longer the sole controlling body in the educational field where it has tended to become more a supervisory body, ensuring that adequate standards are being maintained. This development is not unlike that of the Library Association, which has almost completely abandoned its role as a direct examining body. Therefore the principal role of the Institute may well be that of ensuring that standards of all types – including those of professional ethics, which are at present being drawn up – are being maintained and raised.

Since there are obviously several areas of overlap with the interests and activities of other organisations such as the Library Association and Aslib, it would be foolish and indeed wasteful to expand into areas which are already adequately covered by other organisations. Thus, for example, the Institute has not attempted to set up its own library or information department, to conduct research or to hold meetings on topics which could be better covered by others. But in those fields where the Institute has a predominant and important role to play it intends to make every possible contribution. This sphere of activity also extends to the international scene since at least at present the Institute seems to be the only qualifying and examining body in information science in the world.

Readings

C. W. Hanson. The first ten years of the Institute. *The Information Scientist* 2 (1), 1968, 1–2.

J. E. L. Farradane. The Institute: the first twelve years. *The Information Scientist* 4 (4), 1970, 143–151.

The British Library: introduction

Harry Hookway

The past hundred years have been marked by many important events in the library world. Of these one of the most recent and certainly the most exciting has been the creation of the British Library as the culmination of years of effort by librarians, scholars, and many others to provide the United Kingdom with a great new national library having comprehensive facilities. The speed with which the necessary legislation was passed, the good wishes expressed at its birth, and the degree of interest in its subsequent development have demonstrated convincingly that the new library met a hitherto unsatisfied need.

The first steps

No doubt future library historians will wish to trace in detail the events that led up to the formation of the British Library, but I propose to start the clock in January 1971, when the Government of the day issued a White Paper (Cmnd 4572, London, HMSO, 1971) announcing their intention to set up the British Library as an independent corporate body under the control of a board of management to be known as the British Library Board. The White Paper also proposed the establishment of an Organising Committee under Ministerial chairmanship to ensure that the new organisation came into being as a going concern at the earliest practicable date. The White Paper acknowledged the need to make more effective arrangements for the provision of central reference, lending and bibliographic services to all users, whether institutions or individuals, whether domestic or foreign. Before the library was created these services were spread between five institutions

37

operating largely independently of one another: The British
Museum Library; The National Reference Library of Science
and Invention (administratively part of the British Museum);
the National Central Library, which provided lending services
for the humanities and social sciences; the National Lending
Library for Science and Technology; and the British National
Bibliography. It was apparent that effective articulation of the
activities of these institutions would have a profound effect on
the efficiency of the country's library system as a whole. There
was a clear need for central planning and management, so that
unnecessary duplication could be eliminated, new techniques
and systems more effectively used, resources better allocated and
the full benefits obtained of working on a national and
international scale. The Government concluded that this could
only be achieved if the institutions concerned were brought
together in one body, centrally financed and directed. This
conclusion was supported by the main recommendation of the
National Libraries Committee, set up under the chairmanship of
Sir Frederick Dainton (Cmnd 4028, London, HMSO, 1969). The
Trustees of the British Museum and the National Central Library
and the Council of the British National Bibliography were
consulted and agreed in principle with the decision to form the
new organisation. The White Paper was approved by
Parliament, and the way was clear for detailed planning of the
new library to commence.

The organising committee

The creation of the Organising Committee was undoubtedly a
major factor in maintaining an unprecedented pace of
development for such a complex undertaking. The Committee
started its work in 1971; by July 1972 the British Library Act
had become law, the Bill receiving a welcome in both Houses of
Parliament; and then in April 1973 the British Library Board
was set up, followed by the progressive transfer of staff,
functions and collections to form the British Library from 1 July
onwards, the process being completed in August 1974.

It is worth spending a short time describing the Organising
Committee and its activities because it provides a good example

of the way in which a complex organisation such as the British Library can be planned. The Committee included representatives of the organisations to be combined, together with other members who could reflect the needs of the major library, academic, industrial and regional interests. It dealt with buildings, staff, finance, management structure and new library techniques such as automatic data processing. It was assisted by a full-time planning secretariat of librarians, administration and finance specialists, systems designers and operational research workers. This secretariat was in turn closely linked with a network of planning officers located in all the major departments of the institutions which were to form the new library. Special studies by outside consultants were also commissioned, and many useful suggestions came from the library community and other users of central library facilities. The whole planning operation was therefore closely integrated and the main features both of the organisation and the preliminary operations of the new library, as well as the design brief for the new building to be erected in London to house the reference collections, had been largely completed between January 1971 and July 1973.

The British Library Act

The British Library Act of 1972, which was based on the work of the Organising Committee, is designed to provide great flexibility so that future, and as yet unforeseen, developments which may cause radical changes in the methods of operation of the new library can be accommodated. The objectives and constitution of the library are therefore described in wide ranging terms. For example, the Act specifies that the British Library shall consist of a comprehensive collection of books, manuscripts, periodicals, films and other recorded matter whether printed or otherwise. The Act also specified that the library is to be under the control and management of a public authority, known as The British Library Board, whose duty is to manage the library as a national centre for reference, study and bibliographical and other information services, in relation both to scientific and technological matters and to the humanities. The Board is required by the Act to make the services of the British Library available in particular to institutions of education and learning, other libraries and industry. It is empowered to carry out and sponsor research and to contribute to the expenses of those providing library facilities, whether for members of the public or otherwise.

The Act provides for the British Library Board, whose members are appointed by the Secretary of State for Education and Science, to consist of a Chairman and not less than eight, nor more than thirteen other members, and at least one of the members must serve full-time. There is, therefore, a great degree of flexibility both in the total number of Board members and in the choice as between the full-time and part-time membership.

The British Library Board

How, then, has the Board been constituted, and within what sort of framework does the British Library now operate? It was clear that for some ten years the Board would be heavily preoccupied with the problems of building up a new organisation of great range and complexity; with maintaining and improving existing services and developing new ones; and with the development of a major building programme. In such circumstances it is particularly important that the British Library Board should exercise powerful, consistent and effective control of policy. Accordingly it was decided that the Board should have a Chairman serving part-time, and with him a full-time Chief Executive who would also be Deputy Chairman. These two members of the Board share overall responsibility for all the Board has to do in the initial stages of the library's development. Three other full-time members have charge, as executives responsible to the Chief Executive, for the three main operational areas – reference, lending and bibliographic services: these members therefore have a dual accountability; a collective one for policy in their capacity as members of the Board, and an individual one as responsible for services under the Chief Executive. In addition, there are nine part-time members chosen for their breadth of experience and ability to evaluate the policies and performance of the Board. One of these part-time members is appointed by Her Majesty the Queen; three are appointed after consultation respectively with the Secretaries of State for Trade and Industry, for Scotland and for Wales; and one on the nomination of the Trustees of the British Museum. The Board is not part of the Civil Service, nor are its employees, and it bears the same sort of relationship to the Government as the British Broadcasting Corporation and other public corporations; it is accountable to Parliament, but has a very large measure of autonomy as may be judged from paragraph 11 (1) of the schedule to the British Library Act which reads as follows: 'It shall be within the capacity of the Board as a statutory corporation to do all such things, and enter into all such transactions, as are incidental or conducive to the discharge of its functions'. The only qualification is that the Board does not have power to borrow money.

The structure of the Library

The main operational areas of the library are grouped into three divisions – Reference, Lending, and Bibliographic Services. Of these, the Reference Division is formed from the former library departments of the British Museum; the Lending Division combines the functions of the National Central Library and the National Lending Library for Science and Technology; and the Bibliographic Services Division is based essentially on the functions of the former British National Bibliography together with the Copyright Receipt Office. Fig. 4.1 shows the organisational structure of the British Library, and it will be noted that in addition to the main operational divisions there is also a Central Administration and a Research and Development Department. The Central Administration, as its name implies, provides the overall financial, personnel and common management services required by any complex organisation. The Research and Development Department is based on the functions of the former Office for Scientific and Technical Information, transferred to the library in April 1974, and suitably expanded to cover the promotion and sponsorship of research and development related to library and information operations in all subject fields.

It will be seen, therefore, that the British Library has started

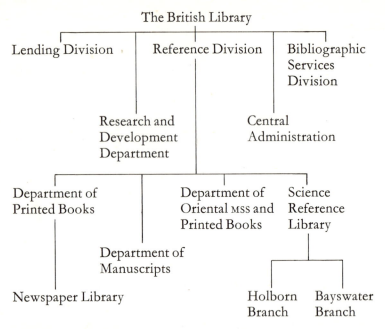

Structure of the British Library

Figure 4.1

with five great advantages. First, it inherited from the British Museum one of the finest and most comprehensive collections of books and manuscripts in the world. Secondly, the library benefits from the statutory right transferred to it from the British Museum by which a copy of every book, journal, newspaper, map and piece of music published in the United Kingdom must be deposited in the Copyright Receipt Office. Thirdly, the interlibrary loan service provided by the Lending Division is without equal in the world. Fourthly, the computer-based bibliographic services operated by the Bibliographic Services Division offer the possibility of providing internal, external and international information services of great value. And, fifth, the Research and Development Department has the power to award grants and contracts to outside bodies so that work may be directed to the benefit of library and information services as a whole.

Given this concentration of central functions and the necessary resources of money, highly skilled staff and printed and manuscript material of all kinds, the British Library is being planned to be at the centre – the hub, as it were – of the country's library services. It has been customary to think of a national library as standing at the apex of the library system, but the apex of such a hierarchically structured system is often remote, difficult of access and somewhat apart from the operational and policy problems of those lower in the hierarchy. By contrast, the hub should be more sensitive and quickly responsive to problems and needs elsewhere.

Of course, local libraries are best fitted to provide many services and the British Library will not attempt to do what these libraries can do for themselves. However, the central services offered to university, technical college, local authority, industrial and other libraries are designed to enable these libraries to make better use of their own resources in satisfying the needs of their users.

Advisory and consultative machinery

To try to be wise all on one's own is sheer folly, and since the central reference, lending, bibliographic and research support services to be provided can have a profound effect on the development of the country's library system, the Board has created advisory machinery to ensure that these services are developed in full consultation with the principal user and institutional interests. An Advisory Council has been set up under Section 2 (3) of the British Library Act to advise on the British Library's relations with other libraries and information services, both national and international, as well as the nature of the central services to be offered to users. Council members are drawn from nominees of the bodies listed in Table 4.2. In addition, Advisory Committees whose members serve in a personal capacity, have been set up to provide the expert advice needed for the successful operation of the library. Five such Committees are at present in existence to advise the management of the Bibliographic Services Division, the Lending Division, the Reference Division (Bloomsbury), the Reference Division (Science Reference Library) and the Research and Development

Department. In all, over one hundred individuals have kindly agreed to take part in this extensive consultative machinery.

The future

Library and information services are under increasing pressure to satisfy from limited resources a wide range of educational, recreational, scholarly, industrial, commercial and other needs. Individual libraries and information services are never likely to meet all the demands of modern society, and yet as much information as is needed should, if possible, be made available throughout the United Kingdom as rapidly as necessary and in the most useful and economic form. Future developments in the British Library will therefore be designed to ensure they make an effective contribution to the further development of the country's library and information services.

Table 4.2.

The British Library Advisory Council

The membership comprises Chairman, nominees of the following bodies, and three independent members:

Library Advisory Council, *Wales* / Library Advisory Council, *England* / The National Library of Wales / National Library of Scotland / The Royal Society / The Standing Conference of National and University Libraries, SCONUL / Aslib / Confederation of British Industry / Council of Engineering Institutions / The British Academy / Council of Polytechnic Libraries / Association of Metropolitan Authorities / Library Association / Association of County Councils / Trades Union Congress / The Royal Society of Edinburgh

This introduction is intended to do no more than set the scene for the contributions which follow. Taken together, these accounts provide the most detailed description of the British Library yet to appear in print. The opinions expressed are those of the authors, and are not necessarily those of the British Library Board.

Chapter Five

The British Library Reference Division

The Division as a whole / Donovan Richnell

The Division and the Library Association

It is perhaps no bad thing to start a chapter on the British Library Reference Division in the Library Association centenary review with a reminder that the connection of the Division in its days as the 'British Museum Library' and since with the Library Association has been, at least intermittently, very close. This is most simply exemplified by the fact that the British Museum Library provided the first President of the Association and that five out of about twenty-three members of the 1877 Conference Committee were members of the staff, and three out of nineteen were on the first Council.

At the International Conference of 1877[1] (titled simply 'Conference of Librarians held in London October 1877') John Winter Jones, the Principal Librarian, presided and among the papers was one by Richard Garnett, Superintendent of the Reading Room 'On the system of classifying books on the shelves followed at the British Museum'. In the discussion after this Melvil Dewey made a short statement about his scheme, and later George Bullen, Keeper of Printed Books, came to Garnett's support after an attack by Dr E Magnusson on the impracticality of classification. In the course of the 100 years since then, one wheel has come full circle – the present writer stating in a preface to the Report of a British Library Working Party on Classification and Indexing[2] chaired by Peter Lewis: 'The Reference Division accepts the recommendations of the Report in general ... It accepts the view that the Dewey Decimal

45

Classification should be accepted as the favoured classification scheme, insofar as a single scheme proves to be necessary'.

What is of greater significance is that during the 100 years of the Library Association's history, the British Museum Library provided the President in fifteen years – and if one adds to that the names of two Directors General of the British Library who have served, it can be said that the British Library has supplied about a fifth of all the librarian Presidents.[3] These facts are stated in part to counteract the widespread feeling of librarians in the recent past that the British Museum Library and the British Library Reference Division has kept aloof from the mainstream of library development. That there is some truth in this impression is indisputable, but it is equally indisputable that the development of British librarianship has owed much in the past to members of staff and to the activities of what is now the Reference Division – and that the integration of the British Museum Library into the British Library opens up scope for an immense increase in the influence of the greatest library in the country on the future of library development.

The creation of the Reference Division

The British Library began to operate on 1 July 1973. But the Reference Division, comprising four Departments – Printed Books, Manuscripts, Oriental Manuscripts and Printed Books, and the Science Reference Library, all of which had previously operated as parts of the British Museum – have by far the longest history of any part of the British Library. This is at once the source of its great strength and of its very considerable difficulties. Its great strength lies in the fact that it constitutes one of the world's greatest reference libraries and 'book museums', and has a world-wide reputation not confined to specialist scholars and actual users, but extending from its relations with Government bodies – eg the role of its staff as advisers on the export of rare books and manuscripts and as custodians of the greatest patents collection – to its complex interrelationships with many learned societies, both national and international.

On the other hand, its very considerable difficulties stem from the fact that it carries with it the immense weight of sheer size, the total inadequacy of its present accommodation and a tradition that stems more from that of the museum world than from the more recently developed library and information systems of the nation in general. True, the Science Reference Library stems in part from a different, but no less historically important tradition – that of the Patent Office Library – but this, too, is strongly influenced by its long and specialised service to the world of technology.

No attempt will be made here to give a history of the past development of the Reference Division over a period of 220 years to its establishment as part of the British Library. This has been most recently and comprehensively done in *That noble cabinet* by Edward Miller,[4] who has also supplied an extensive bibliography on the subject.

Functions and objectives

The functions of the British Library Reference Division were set out in the First Annual Report of the British Library 1973–4[5] (p 4), as follows:

i   to collect, by purchase, gift and exchange, not only all British books and such British manuscripts and papers as are appropriate, but as much as possible of the world's important printed material in all subject fields, and manuscripts of foreign origin in certain specialist fields
ii   to make them available in the reading rooms to users who come to consult them
iii to extend facilities to others by means of catalogues, photocopies, loans (to exhibitions), and information services
iv   to organise exhibitions exploiting the wealth of the collections for the benefit of both specialists and the general public

It will be noted that there is no reference here to a function of collecting material by legal deposit. This is because the Copyright Receipt Office has been transferred to the Bibliographic Services Division, whose function it is to collect all British printed material for inclusion in the British National Bibliography, but, of course, the material then passes to the Department of Printed Books and the Science Reference Library for inclusion in their reference collections of archival copies of British printed material.

In the Second Annual Report, 1974–5,[6] another function was stated explicitly and this I would now extend somewhat:

v   to conserve the materials collected by the best available means, to develop new means of conservation, and to reconcile the needs of conservation with active use of the materials

The objectives of the Division over the next decade may be summarised as follows:

i   to maintain and improve the means of giving effect to these functions by reorganisation, where necessary, by minimising the constraints imposed by inadequate accommodation and facilities, and by introducing new services and techniques
ii   to plan and secure the building of new accommodation which will provide optimal conditions for the performance of these functions and unified identity for the British Library in London
iii   to cooperate with the other Divisions, the Research and Development Department, and the Central Administration in integrating, where desirable, the operations of the British Library as a whole

Development of Divisional activities

Now although the Reference Division came into existence in July 1973, for the remaining nine months of 1973–74 it was little more than a notional concept. It must be remembered that as Departments of the British Museum, Printed Books, Manuscripts and Oriental Manuscripts and Printed Books had stood in the same relationship to the Museum Trustees as all other Departments of the British Museum (the Science Reference Library, as the National Reference Library of Science

and Invention being a part, albeit a very distinctive part, of
Printed Books at that time). The relations of these Departments
to the Trustees was very different from that envisaged both for
relations of the Divisions to the Board of the British Library and
for relations of the Departments to the Reference Division as a
whole. Lacking a Director General and a Director General's
office, however, it was necessary for the four Departments
created in July 1973 to operate independently in relation to the
Board and the Central Administration. This had some
undesirable consequences that have been gradually eliminated.
Only with the appointment of a Director General in May 1974
was it possible to set about the organisation of a unified Division
by the federation of the Departments into a single whole. At the
start the Divisional staff consisted of the Director General and
his personal secretary. It is envisaged that the present provisional
arrangement of having a senior staff member in charge of
Divisional activities will become part of a more permanent
pattern as activities at Divisional level develop.

To create the Division as an organic whole, two lines of action
were possible. The first would have been to reform entirely the
management structure with functions cutting across the existing
Departments. This certainly might have made it easier to create
an adequate Divisional office, but it was rejected as the preferred
mode of action, not only because it would have caused a further
period of dislocation and reorientation and been (rightly)
resisted by the staff, but because the very individual and
specialised work carried out within the four Departments would
have required the re-creation of Departments and Branches on
very similar lines to those already in being. It must be
remembered that the span of responsibility of the Division
ranges from the acquisition and maintaining of Oriental (and, of
course, Western) manuscripts, through the whole gamut of
printed material – books, official publications, maps, music,
philatelic and security printing collections – to the provision of
services to the patent community and on-line computer and
information services to science and industry. The staff of the
Division numbers at present 1125, and its work is carried on in
14 buildings in the greater London area, of which the British
Museum building and the Patent Office are the largest, but

perhaps the least well able to provide working facilities or any
expansion. The only viable method of development, therefore,
was to proceed by stages to federate the Departments through
the identification of various areas of work that were common to
all, or most, of them, and to create Divisional bodies to control
this development by inter-Departmental agreements or by
unification.

The first Divisional body to be established was a Senior
Management Committee drawn from all Departments (all
Keepers and Deputy Keepers from Bloomsbury, and the
Director and Deputy Director from the Science Reference
Library), which holds regular monthly meetings. This should
act as a means of communication downwards of developments in
the Board and Central Administration, as a means of reaching
decisions on certain matters arising therefrom, and as a forum
for the initiation and discussion of policies. The main
achievement in the early stages of the Senior Management
Committee, apart from helping to create a sense of Divisional
identity, has been to decide upon areas of common interest, and
to nominate members of Departmental staff to serve on
committees, working-parties and *ad hoc* groups to develop
Divisional activity in those areas of common interest. These
committees are concerned with major areas of the Division's
work that cut across Departmental activities. Since their work is
also concerned with many of the major issues facing the
Division, it is appropriate to deal with each in turn. The main
ends for which a national library exists, however – collecting,
cataloguing and reader and information services – are dealt with
later under the separate Departments, since, although they are in
many ways interdependent, the activity of each Department
requires a separate approach.

Accommodation

Many of the present difficulties of the Division can only be
solved by the provision of a single new building. On the most
optimistic forecast, over a decade from 1976 must elapse before
this solution is achieved – even in part. Since the new building is
intended to serve not only for the Reference Division, but for all

parts of the British Library except the Lending Division, this is primarily a matter for the Board and Central Administration. But since also by far the greater part of the new building will be occupied by the Reference Division, the Director General and other senior members of staff are engaged at all stages in the planning of the building. This is not the place to describe in detail the long saga of plans, proposals, counter-proposals, postponements and new plans that have occupied decades. Very briefly, until 1974 the Board had planned on the basis that the new building would be on the seven acre site immediately opposite the British Museum known as the 'Bloomsbury Site'. It was only on 19 December 1974 that another Government statement was made:[7]

The Government has been considering, together with the Board of the British Library, how further progress can best be made towards a solution of the Library's longstanding and increasingly pressing needs for a headquarters with sufficient accommodation for its readers, staff, collections and services, while recognising that the intention expressed by past Governments of both parties to use the land adjoining the British Museum in Bloomsbury would involve the kind of large scale redevelopment and disturbance towards which public attitudes have much changed.

A site on former railway land fronting on Euston Road and immediately to the west of St Pancras Station has recently become available. It is less than a mile from the Bloomsbury site and well provided with communications. The London Borough of Camden has indicated that use of the Euston site for the Library would be in accord with their policies for the development of this area.

This site is now being urgently examined in detail by the Government and the Library. Provided that the outcome of this examination is that the site can effectively accommodate the Library, notwithstanding that the preference of the Library remains for the Bloomsbury site, the Government will authorise detailed design work so that construction of new buildings, limited initially to a first phase, can be begun on the Euston Road site in 1979/80 subject to determination of an actual starting date in the light of the economic conditions prevailing nearer the time.

The Board, the Division and the Architect responded promptly, if reluctantly, to this call for a feasibility study. As a result, another Government statement was made on 5 August 1975:[8]

The Government and the British Library Board are satisfied that the site in Euston Road can suitably provide for the Library's building needs. Negotiations have therefore been opened with the owners of the site, the National Freight Corporation and the British Rail Board, so that it can be bought for this purpose. Work on the detailed design of new buildings at Euston will now go forward with a view to a start on the construction of a substantial first phase in 1979–80 if economic conditions at that time permit. The precise nature of the first phase will be determined in conjunction with the Library Board.

At the time of writing discussions are still proceeding on the necessary size of a first phase. From the Division's point of view anything that provides less than enough accommodation to house all the existing basic activities of the four Departments would be unsatisfactory. Ideally, of course, there should be provision for expansion, and a first phase of limited scope only makes sense if it is immediately followed by other phases.

The Divisional Accommodation Committee is more concerned with the problems of the next decade. These are indeed formidable. The Science Reference Library is one of the worst placed Departments, being split between four buildings. Since it is the intention to have a large part of the stock on open access, the stock has to be divided on a subject and form basis, and not merely on the basis of obsolescence. Heroic interim measures to improve the situation are required, but no solution has yet been found. Both here and in the case of the Department of Printed Books, reader accommodation and reader services of an adequate standard can only be maintained by out-housing to closed access depositories. Since the great bulk of the stock of the Department of Printed Books is on closed access already, this would not be quite so serious, but the main depository is thirteen miles away at Woolwich, and over the next decade as much material will have to be out-housed as is taken in. This must inevitably increase the delays in providing books for readers, and other remedies are, therefore, being sought. Reading Room accommodation for all Departments cannot be increased, and this imposes strict limits on new developments. There is a clamant need, also, for better staff accommodation, for lecture and seminar rooms, and for the development of conservation services. No less important are the considerations of the environment in which books are stored. Temporary measures are urgently needed to prevent the deterioration of books and manuscripts. The Newspaper Library at Colindale (which, under present plans, will remain and will not be taken into the new building) is also nearing a crisis of space, and a special study is in progress on the future plans for this part of the Department of Printed Books.

Binding and conservation

Before the creation of the British Library, the binding and book conservation work was carried out by HMSO on behalf of the Museum Departments. The Reference Division has inherited a responsibility to continue to supply binding and conservation work to the four binderies established and run to meet this need – one of which is within the Bloomsbury complex, a second at Colindale, and the other two in London and Manchester. A joint committee of the Reference Division and HMSO has been established to ensure the maintenance of, and improvement to, the output of these binderies. Not all conservation work, however, is appropriate to binderies, and the Departments of Manuscripts and Oriental Manuscripts and Printed Books have small conservation laboratories for their special requirements. But the general problem of conservation is a very grave one, calling for large-scale action. A special consultant was commissioned to prepare a report on immediate and future requirements, and this report was submitted at the end of November 1975.[9] This report paints a grim picture of the state of the collections, and makes massive recommendations for remedying the situation, many of which can be implemented in a relatively short space of time. It calls for an administrative reorganisation, which involves the establishment of a Head of Conservation at Divisional level, the concentration of all available resources, not only on increasing the volume of work, but also on the development of new techniques for dealing with the deterioration of paper and binding materials, and an improvement in the environmental conditions. Pending the implementation of the recommendations of this report, the Binding Committee and other staff working groups are seeking every means to insure against preventable deterioration and to rationalise the flow of conservation work to the bindery to achieve maximum output at minimum cost.

Photography and reprography

Part of the solution of the conservation problem lies in microfilming and other reprographic processes, and a not inconsiderable part of the work of the Divisional Photographic Committee is concerned with microfilming either to reduce the use of the originals or to ensure the preservation in some form of material that is likely to be beyond conservation. One way in which this can be done is by the Library itself offering for sale copies of microfilms etc., produced for internal purposes. The list of *Microfilms of newspapers and journals for sale* is one manifestation of this.[10] It is, however, ironic that the photographic and reprographic processes can themselves be damaging to books and manuscripts – a fact which, if realised, was not sufficiently taken into account in libraries for many years. The Photographic Committee has already taken some steps to reduce potential damage by the introduction of new equipment – and there will be further research and development work in this area.

A large part of the work of the photographic units consists in the satisfaction of users' needs, and the Committee has given consideration to the speed of the service that can be provided. By a review of clerical procedures the waiting-time has been effectively reduced, but speed is all too often the enemy of conservation, and the latter must be the overriding consideration for a national archival library. The Committee has, also, to concern itself with the level of charges for photographic work, and a policy has been formulated to ensure an adequate cost recovery without imposing too heavy a burden on readers.

The scale of the photographic activity, now regarded as a Divisional responsibility, is likely to increase even more with the conclusion of agreements with commercial companies for large-scale microform publication. The Committee has assumed the responsibility for negotiation with commercial firms of charges for reproduction rights of material supplied, and for negotiating large-scale contracts involving royalties. This is one of the relatively few revenue-producing activities of the Reference Division.

Publications

The other main area of potential revenue production is publication. A Publications Committee has been established to control the overall policy and development of Divisional publications. The Committee is a joint one with British Museum Publications Limited which acts as agent for the Reference Division publications (though some minor ones are produced in-house). The major works produced hitherto are products of the work of the Departments, ranging from continuations of the major catalogues[11] inherited from the British Museum Library to catalogues of special exhibitions,[12] special guides, postcards, slides and – in process of preparation – multi-media resources. It is not likely that the major catalogues produced firstly for internal use will show a profit, or can even be produced without subsidy, but there is an intention to develop a programme for more popular material, not only postcards and slides, but commissioned works relating to the collections, which can be expected to produce a profit. This is a legitimate activity for a national library, provided that it does not divert the effort of 'main-stream' library staff from the maintenance and improvement of the free service to users.

The Division is also developing an internal publication programme to provide a current awareness service for the British Library as a whole, based on the Library Association Library, which is now an integral part of the Information Branch of the Department of Printed Books. Its two publications at present are ARP – Addresses, Reports, Papers written by members of staff and presented at conferences or for internal use;[13] and CABLIS – Current Awareness for British Library Staff.[14] The latter may prove capable of development as a current awareness serial for the library profession as a whole. The other serial publication of the Reference Division is the *British Library Journal*,[15] which is a scholarly journal intended to provide articles and news on the collections for research workers and libraries all

over the world. It is printed and distributed by the Oxford
University Press in association with British Museum
Publications Limited.

Exhibitions

This is one of the most important activities of the Departments
at present based in the British Museum building. The King's
Library, the Manuscript Saloon and the Grenville Library
provide space for the deployment of exhibitions of great
importance. In developing the plans for the new British Library
building in London, great emphasis is placed on the provision of
adequate accommodation for a large exhibition centre. It must
be remembered that the exhibitions of books and manuscripts
are the only normal access to the immense riches of the
collections that are available to the general public at all times,
and many hundreds of thousands of people – probably millions,
though no precise statistics are kept – come to the galleries every
year. The Exhibitions Committee is concerned not only with the
'permanent' exhibitions and the problems associated with
adequate equipment, lighting, security and conservation, but
with the organisation of special exhibitions. It has developed a
five-year rolling programme, since prestige exhibitions take a
long time to mature. The Exhibitions Committee works in close
association with the British Museum Design Office, and has
members of staff appointed to the Office.

The Exhibitions Committee is also responsible for
recommending to the Board on matters relating to the loan of
material for display in other institutions all over the world. Such
loans are an extremely onerous and time-consuming activity and
have to be on a limited and carefully considered scale.

Education

There are several different activities that can be regarded as
educational, but they are quite separate. The Education
Committee is responsible for developing a service for the
general public, based mainly on the public exhibitions. A first
step has been to appoint guide-lecturers to the exhibitions, the
next to establish liaison with schools (already done by the

Philatelic Section) and other educational institutions and to produce more suitable literature and audio-visual aids. Professional education for librarians (short-courses, etc) does not fall within the province of this Committee, nor does staff education. These are dealt with administratively at present.

Divisional Office

Indeed, the work of all the Committees must increasingly be supported by administrative staff working at Divisional level, and this is a process of gradual change from the Departmentally based activities. It is, however, right that main operational activities of each Department should be under the control of the Departmental Directors. The remainder of this chapter is given up to an account of these, but the work at Divisional level is now well established and is likely to increase in importance with the growth of the links between Departments and between the Divisions of the British Library.

Department of Printed Books / R. J. Fulford

Except that the Science Reference Library is now a separate department of the Reference Division, the administrative boundaries of the Department of Printed Books are similar to those of the former Department of the same name of the British Museum. It is divided into nine branches or sections – Storage and Delivery, Information Services, Rare Book Collections, Music Library, Map Library, Slavonic and East European, Cataloguing, Acquisitions, Philatelic. The public areas, each with its own reference staff, comprise the famous circular Reading Room, built in 1857, the North Library (for the consultation of rare books), the Official Publications Library and the Map Library, with a total number of seats of over 700. Outside Bloomsbury the Newspaper Repository at Colindale has a reading room with sixty-six seats.

The collection of Printed Books can be regarded as composed of three elements, even though it is not organised and administered as such. Firstly, there is the outstandingly important collection of early books, including the Rare Book Collection proper, which, although it comprises only 2% of the collections accounts for 10% of their use. Secondly, there is the archival collection of British publications built up as a result of the operation of the Copyright Act. In maintaining and servicing the collections in both these aspects the Department has important international as well as national responsibilities and it is these elements of the collections which particularly interest the overseas user. In addition, however, the library also houses the national collection of foreign literature, which is maintained more particularly with the library's United Kingdom clientele in mind. Just over 20% of books issued in the Reading Room are in a language other than English, but because English is an international publishing language the total proportion of use of overseas literature is higher.

As well as the main collections of printed books, the Department administers three special collections of outstanding importance. The music scores form one of the largest collections in the world, while the Map Library, in addition to its uniquely complete set of Ordnance Survey materials and an extensive collection of early maps and topographical material (including some of special importance relating to pre-revolutionary America), acquires current maps from all parts of the world. The Philatelic collection is pre-eminent among the world's historical collections of postage stamps and other philatelic material.

The Department's collection of professional library literature is in the Library Association Library, which provides loan, reference and information services to professional librarians in Great Britain, including especially the staff of the British Library itself.

There are some 8,000,000 items in the Department with nearly a million recorded uses every year. The use of the library, as reflected in the number of issues and the number of readers' tickets, grew by 4% to 5% nearly every year from the end of the second World War up to 1973, since when the economic recession has brought about a levelling off. The use of the collections by means of photocopying has increased much faster, and although the two situations are not closely comparable it is nevertheless significant that the photocopying staff now

outnumbers the book delivery staff. About a third of the
library's on-site users are from overseas. Of both British and
overseas users about a third are university staff, about a third
postgraduate students and the remaining third is composed of
miscellaneous groups such as journalists and freelance writers.
Undergraduate students are only rarely admitted to the library.
Among the library's users there is, as one would expect, a
preponderance of people resident either permanently or
temporarily in the south-east of England, with some 35% of all
users being attached to the University of London. The use of the
collections is fairly even over all periods of publication, and the
average age of a book asked for is fifty years. Users are identified
by passes, which are of two kinds – annual (normally
automatically renewable) and temporary. It is rare for anyone
making out a reasonable case for using the library to be turned
away, except sometimes occasionally at peak periods for the
practical reason that no seats are available.

Many of the problems facing the Department are those of the
Division as a whole and have been described in the earlier
section. Although the only solution in many cases is a new
purpose-built building, important developments are nevertheless
likely to take place in the next decade which will fundamentally
change the relationship of the Department to other parts of the
British Library, to the library system of the country as a whole
and to the public.

A major step in the direction of such change was the
inauguration in late 1975 of a new series of catalogues based on
AACR and MARC for the author/title catalogues and on the PRECIS
system for the subject catalogues. These replace the British
Museum General Catalogue[16] and British Museum Subject
Index[17] in respect of material published from 1975. To begin
with, the main use of the products of the new system, which will
generally be in the form of microfilm, will be as a means of
access to the library's collections on site. Later on, however, the
library community and the public will benefit from the new
possibilities of quick and easy distribution of up-to-date
bibliographic information and information about the holdings of
the library. The Bibliographic Services Division is responsible

for the technical aspects of the maintenance of the British
Library data base and for the distribution of machine-readable
records for internal use by other libraries; but the Department of
Printed Books, as part of the Reference Division, will be
involved in both the creation and the exploitation of the data
base in two important ways. Firstly it will influence the shape
and content of the British Library data base because the records
of non-British material (which will incidentally be the only
other records in the data base wholly consistent with those
created for current British material by the Bibliographic
Services Division) will reflect the selection policies of the
Department. Secondly, the Department, as part of the Reference
Division and therefore in direct touch with the public, will be
involved in the maximum exploitation of the data base for the
public benefit generally and for specialised communities. The
new system opens up many possible new uses of the library's
records which would not have been possible with the former
British Museum system. This will particularly be the case if
other large libraries agree to adopt British Library standards for
input to a common data base. If this were to come about, it
would make possible such projects as combined listings of
resources in the major research libraries of Central London.

The standards adopted for the new series of catalogues are
AACR/MARC for author and title access and the PRECIS system for
subject access.[18] AACR/MARC was the obvious choice for the
author/title catalogues because of its wide acceptance both
internationally and nationally, but the choice of the PRECIS
system for the subject catalogues, using the thesaurus[19] built up
by the British National Bibliography from January 1974, was
more difficult. Given that the manually produced British
Museum Subject Index needed replacement, the most economical
solution would have been to adopt Library of Congress Subject
Headings, because for much of the material acquired by the
library the information could have been lifted directly from the
Library of Congress MARC records and from the published
National Union Catalogue. However, it was decided that the
PRECIS system, which was evolved with the special aim of
making possible maximum exploitation of subject information
held in machine-readable form, offered important potential

advantages over LCSH by way of more effective distribution of improved information about the library's resources, and this consideration outweighed the fact that there would be an increased burden on the professional staff. Original subject cataloguing would be needed for all non-British acquisitions and the prospect of general international acceptance of PRECIS – which might relieve the need for original indexing by the British Library – was a distant one. The Department's experience with the PRECIS system over the next few years is bound to be of prime importance in determining its longterm future.

Because of the pattern of use of the library it is considered necessary to maintain an integrated record of the library's earlier collections. Therefore, because of the uncertain prospect for a national or international retrospective data base, or alternatively a conversion operation by the BL itself, records for non-current items still being acquired will be incorporated in the General Catalogue. The General Catalogue, with supplements which will shortly take it to 1975, is used universally in its published form[20] as a bibliographic reference tool and an approximation to a world bibliography, especially for the earlier periods. The other major published catalogues of the Department are the Subject Index (volumes to 1975 are also in preparation) and the Catalogue of the Map Library.[21] The Catalogue of the Newspaper Library was published in 1976.[22] The only remaining major catalogue still unpublished is that of the Music Library, and unfortunately technical and editorial difficulties make it improbable that it can be published in the immediate future.[23] The Department is also active, either on its own or in cooperation with other institutions, in the preparation and publication of special catalogues of early books,[24] the best known being the *Catalogue of books printed in the XVth century*.[25] It also houses the National Union Catalogue of pre-1800 books, administered by the Rare Book Collections.

The Department's holdings are, of course, nearly all held in closed access. Only 0·4% of the collections are on open access, comprising no more than the most used standard reference works, bibliographies and dictionaries. Service of books from closed access to personal users of the library is by a special team of book supply staff. It is well known, and has from time to time been the subject of correspondence in the national press, that the service of books to readers has in recent years been less efficient than it once was. This is partly because the use of the collections has increased by well over half since the Second World War, while the awkward physical characteristics of the building have remained largely unchanged. However, it is also true that the library has suffered on a small scale in the same way as some much larger long-established public services – the postal services and public transport come to mind – which are labour-intensive and have had to face a situation where no major technical advance has taken place or is in prospect to counterbalance the completely changed situation in the labour market and in labour costs. Some parts of the national economy, such as shops and restaurants, have responded by persuading their clientele to adopt self-service, but this solution unfortunately appears to have no general application in the library. Quite apart from security problems, users would need a long induction course in order to be able to find their way around the collections and the rooms housing them, which are distributed around the building in a peculiarly awkward way. There is, however, one long-term measure which the Department believes could improve considerably ease of public access to the collections, and that is an increase from $0 \cdot 4\%$ to 3% in the proportion of books on open access, or on rapidly available closed access. It is a matter of common observation in the Reading Room that each researcher has by him a mixture of general standard works and more specialised material. It seems probable that investigation would identify a comparatively small number of items in the library which are in fairly constant use and which if they were made available would significantly reduce the load on the book supply staff. The key to the success of this move is constant and careful monitoring of the use of the collections. As soon as the plans for the new building are sufficiently advanced, it would obviously be an advantage for the Department to begin to build up this collection as soon as possible before the new building actually comes into use.

The Department's public role ranges much more widely than the supply of books and information. The senior professional staff

constitute a large fund of specialist expertise and the Department
encourages its specialist staff, whose contribution to
bibliographical and other scholarship has already been
outstanding in many fields, to maintain and broaden contacts
with the relevant communities outside the library, especially in
the academic world. Such contacts are mostly through
institutions such as learned societies, and within the library
world through such organisations as the specialist groups of
SCONUL. In this way the Department, which as part of the
Reference Division is an important element in the British
Library's public image, will be well placed to interpret to the
British Library the requirements of user communities and to
promote the British Library's service to those user communities.
The Department itself involves its specialist staff in outside
activities by organising conferences and seminars, and through
publications and exhibitions. In the new building it is proposed
that specialists on the library staff should be available for
consultation by the public at fixed hours.

A considerable part of the Department's energies and financial
resources is devoted to supplementing the collections. The
purchase grant for 1975–76 (April to March) was £507,090, but
the total value of material received from all sources is estimated
to be twice that figure. A quarter of the purchase grant,
corresponding to about 18% of items received, is spent on
non-current material (defined as being more than five years old)
and selectors, who are organised mainly on a 'language and
culture' basis, are active in filling gaps in the collections in
addition to keeping up with current output. Broadly speaking,
the library's rare book collections are supplemented by purchase,
gift and bequest, and current British output is mostly received as
a result of the operation of the Copyright Act, while literature
from overseas is mostly either purchased (through a network of
agents in most countries of the world) or received by
international exchange.

The library's agents abroad have often been small firms which
take a pride in their connection with the library and go to
considerable trouble to acquire out of the way items which
yield little commercial profit. The library encourages selectors to

visit periodically the countries which are their concern and to maintain personal contacts with their agents. Items for purchase are individually selected; the library does not use the blanket order system, which grew up in the United States after the Second World War when libraries there suddenly found themselves with vast funds for book purchase at their disposal. In Bloomsbury there has been continuity in collection building over a much longer period, and the care of successive generations of selectors, hampered it is true at certain times in the past by being too few in numbers or by book grants which were too small, has made the collection, even though no longer the largest in the world, probably of the highest quality among the world's major collections. The selector's job is to reject as much as to acquire, and it has been estimated, though the figure can only be very approximate, that the Department acquires some 5% of the world's published output. While there are still weaknesses in some subjects and in some geographical areas, it seems improbable that a figure higher than 6% to 7% can be justified even for a national collection.

Exceptionally, there is one type of material in which something akin to the blanket order principle has had to be applied, and that is in the area of foreign government publications. The Department has a network of agreements with foreign governments and overseas national libraries, some of them going back to the end of the nineteenth century, which ensures that the library receives comprehensive coverage of the government publications of many countries of the world, in exchange for British Government publications despatched by HMSO. Similar arrangements cover many international organisations and separate provinces, states, etc, within sovereign states, so that the quantity of material received by this means amounts to some 30% of the total intake (calculated by length of shelf occupied). The use made of this material by the public is well below the average for the collection as a whole, partly because it has never been possible to make the resources of the collections of government publications properly known to those who might benefit from them, though the new catalogue system should make some improvement possible. This is a problem area where the gradual evolution of Universal

Bibliographic Control[26] unfortunately shows little sign of having early impact. Even the Library of Congress catalogues only a limited number of the publications of its own Federal Government and fewer still of the publications of the individual States. The present problem, which no large library appears to have solved, is therefore that information on general subjects in government publications is less likely to become known to those potentially interested than if it were contained in trade publications or in the publications of societies and organisations.

In principle the Department is responsible for providing a library service in all subjects not covered by the Science Reference Library. The library's pre-eminent place in humanities research has always been recognised, but in the social sciences the Department is still in some respects in the process of formulating its definitive national role. The Department's holdings in the social sciences are only marginally less comprehensive than in the humanities, but they are not yet presented in the way which would enable the community to derive the greatest benefit from them. Some research in the social sciences is based, like humanities research, almost wholly on consultation of an archival store of literature, but other kinds of social science research involve a high element of field work, with the consultation of literature merely an incidental element, usually with the requirement for rapid access to up-to-date information characteristic of a technical library and information service. The British Library Reference Division needs to evolve a pattern of library service in the social sciences which meets both types of requirement. Because of the importance for researchers in the social sciences of officially published reports and statistics, the role of the Department in providing a library service in the social sciences, both academic and applied, will be developed on the basis of the already existing Official Publications Library (known to many under its former name of State Paper Room).

Finally, though by no means of least importance, decisions will need to be made over the next few years about the relationship between the Department and the Lending Division.

In the relevant subject fields there is very considerable overlap
between the English language holdings at Bloomsbury and
Boston Spa; nearly all of Bloomsbury's foreign language
holdings are, however, unique within the British Library. The
nature and extent of the Department's involvement in
inter-lending will, once determined, affect the administration of
their collections, their location, and the distribution to other
libraries and to the public of information about the library's
holdings. It seems probable that there will be frequent changes
in future in the relationships between the cost of moving people,
the cost of moving books, the cost of supplying photocopies,
and, in the long term, the cost of communicating information in
digital form, but in any case the use of the collections off site will
almost certainly increase more rapidly than the use of the
collections on site, and the Department's long-term planning
will need to take this into account.

The Department of Manuscripts / D. P. Waley

The collection of manuscripts in the Department, which is the
main national collection of western manuscripts, goes back to
the foundation of the British Museum in the middle of the
eighteenth century. It then comprised the collection made by
Sir Robert Cotton and given to the nation by his grandson, the
Harleian collection formed by the first two Earls of Oxford, the
manuscripts in the Royal Library, presented by King George II
and the manuscripts in the collection of Sir Hans Sloane. Since
then it has been augmented by the acquisition of several
considerable collections, but above all by the steady
accumulation (through purchase, gifts and bequests) of the
series of 'Additional Manuscripts' which is likely to attain 60,000
volumes early in 1977. The collections also comprise very large
numbers of charters, rolls, papyri, seals and ostraka.

The Department in the British Library

The foundation of the British Library and the formation of the
Reference Division have facilitated cooperation between the
Department of Manuscripts and the other Departments within
the Division. This is particularly noticeable in the organisation

of joint exhibitions with the Department of Printed Books, while it also simplifies (for example) the acquisition of collections comprising both printed and manuscript material. The role of members of the Department in activities now organised at Divisional level has drawn them into the wider concerns of the Library. The department has provided secretaries for both the Publications and Photographic Committees.

Meanwhile the Department is no less closely linked with various external institutions and activities than it was in its British Museum days. The role of the Keeper as *ex officio* expert adviser to the Department of Trade on the export of manuscripts remains an important and onerous function, as well as an interesting one. The connection with the Reviewing Committee on the Export of Works of Art is particularly close and time-consuming, but cooperation with the Royal Commission on Historical Manuscripts and the world of archives and record offices generally remains an essential feature of the Department's existence.

The organisation of the Department

There is no formal allocation of functions to Branches within the Department, but certain important administrative responsibilities are allotted to each of the three Deputy Keepers, one of whom is concerned with cataloguing and all publications, one with accommodation, conservation and photography and one with exhibitions and loans. The Students' Room is superintended by a senior Assistant Keeper, this administrative duty, in common with most others at both Assistant Keeper and clerical level, being performed in rotation. In the case of all senior posts, administrative functions are combined with academic expertise in a special field and it is hoped to preserve this form of fluidity so that any individual's combination of duties and interests should not be formalised as requirements of a successor. A division between 'administrative' and 'academic' specialists in the senior posts would be an undesirable development. Versatility in both the academic and more general sense is a strong and excellent tradition within the Department and is essential to its efficiency and morale.

The current situation and problems

Of the problems facing the Department the most difficult are perhaps those concerned with the output of printed catalogues. The innovation of publishing the 'Rough Register' of acquisitions (undertaken by the List and Index Society)[27] is a notable gain, but it is particularly true of a collection of manuscripts that it can only be used adequately if its contents are divulged to potential users – and at the time of writing the most recent full catalogue of *Additions* covers the years 1936–45.[28] This leaves a thirty-year period whose acquisitions can only be known through the 'Rough Register' and the selective lists published by the Historical Manuscripts Commission and the Institute of Historical Research.[29] The most serious threat to progress with the catalogues is the vast and continuous growth of routine administrative tasks, such as those concerned with photographic orders and with enquiries by post. Meanwhile the policy of emphasising the cataloguing of more recent acquisitions is itself a controversial one. We hope to close the thirty-year gap by providing Catalogues of Additions in which, on first publication, the most 'difficult' and voluminous material will receive a summary description only. Yet it could be argued that the task of providing adequate catalogues for the earlier collection, such as the Cotton manuscripts, should be given priority over cataloguing the acquisitions of 1946–75. A balance should be maintained between cataloguing and recataloguing, as well as between cataloguing and exhibiting, lending and other preoccupations. But it would be wrong to end this paragraph on an entirely pessimistic note. Work is well advanced on catalogues of the Ashley manuscripts (the very important collection of mainly nineteenth-century literary material purchased from the widow of T. J. Wise), the Yates Thompson illuminated manuscripts and on an *Amalgamated index* to all the published catalogues as well as on catalogues of the acquisitions of the years 1946 to 1960.

Anxiety about the burden of cataloguing new acquisitions may be misplaced in a time of economic difficulties and heavy taxation. It seems highly probable that gifts and bequests – the source of most of the Department's rich store of historical

papers, as well as of many of its literary and artistic holdings –
will bulk less large in the future. If fiscal developments cause
owners to offer for sale the country's greatest collections of
private family papers, the Department's purchase grant, storage
space and cataloguing efforts will be earmarked for decades to
come. Lack of storage room has already caused the Department
to postpone acceptance of the last collection of plays submitted
for censorship to the Lord Chamberlain (1900–1968) but work in
progress in our present premises should make it possible to
house these before the end of 1976.

The problems mentioned in the preceding paragraphs are, of
course, no more than a selection and may be typical of those
facing other institutions. We have also to decide how much of
our funds should be devoted to conservation and whether we
can maintain the perfectionist but expensive standards which
have prevailed in the past. No accession to our collections
remains unbound, but such a policy is, of course, an extremely
costly one. What proportion of our purchase grant should be
spent on acquiring microfilm of manuscripts? Can we make the
move towards machine-readable indexes which has been made
by the Public Record Office, but which would surely be far more
difficult for us on account of the nature of our accessions?

Whatever the problems of policy and priority, our most pressing
tasks remain those defined in paragraphs (i) and (iii) quoted
above (p. 47) which refer to acquisition and cataloguing. Our
preoccupations thus involve us closely also in the sales-room
and at times with outside institutions which give generous
financial assistance in purchases, as well as with the publishers of
our catalogues.

The Department of Oriental Manuscripts and Printed Books / G. E. Marrison

The foundation collections of the British Museum (1753)
contained some oriental manuscripts and printed books. The
Department of Oriental Manuscripts was formed in 1867 and
this was enlarged to become the Department of Oriental Printed
Books and Manuscripts in 1892. On the inauguration of the

British Library in 1973, it was renamed the Department of
Oriental Manuscripts and Printed Books. In 1975 the Oriental
Exchange Unit, which acquires Government Publications was
transferred from the Department of Printed Books to OMPB.

The Department has 40,000 manuscripts and 400,000 books in
the languages of Asia and North Africa and currently subscribes
to about 4000 journals. The Oriental Exchange Unit at the
present time is dealing with 26,000 titles. Catalogues of
manuscripts and of printed books are published for separate
languages or language groups.[30]. The staff includes language
specialists who, in addition to the care of manuscripts and books,
are consultants on the literature they handle, and its
background of religion, history, sociology, art, politics and
economics. The Department has a Conservation Workshop
which specialises in the care of documents and oriental materials
such as papyrus, parchment, palm leaves, silk, bone and paper.

The Collections

All the languages of Asia and the literary ones of North and
North-East Africa are represented in the collections. The
manuscript materials represent one of the world's great
collections, comprising Hebrew religious texts from the Middle
East and Mediaeval Europe, some splendidly illuminated; major
collections from the Christian Orient: Syriac, Coptic, Ethiopic,
Armenian and Georgian; Islamic materials in Arabic, Persian
and Turkish, including beautifully illuminated Qur'ans, and a
great range of Persian illustrated manuscripts; South Asian,
covering Sanskrit and the modern languages, with important
Buddhist collections from Sri Lanka, Burma, Nepal and Tibet;
unique Javanese material; while the Far East is represented not
only by manuscripts but some of the world's earliest printed
texts in Chinese, Japanese and Korean.

The printed book collections have been developed to provide a
comprehensive representation of the literature of the countries
concerned, not only in their classical aspects (where in particular
the books support the manuscript collections), but equally in
modern themes, not only literary, but also official documentary

publications and like materials required for the current study of
Asia and North Africa. Some of the strongest collections are
from Commonwealth countries, and were in part acquired
through former Copyright provision. Other growing
collections such as the Vietnamese and Indonesian have been
built up more recently. The Department also has monographs
and journals in western languages relating to its regions, but the
bulk of materials of this character is located in the Department of
Printed Books.

Public services

The Department has a Reading Room with a reference collection
on open shelves. Enquiries from scholars and the general public
are dealt with both personally and by correspondence all over
the world. With its collections of calligraphic and finely
illuminated manuscripts, representing the major world religions,
many styles of oriental art, and the history of the book, the
Department makes a significant contribution to the British
Library's programme of exhibitions.

Acquisitions, cataloguing and publication

The aim of the Department is to acquire all significant materials
in the realms of the Humanities and Social Sciences in the
languages of Asia and North and North-East Africa. The bulk of
the monographs and academic journals are obtained by direct
purchase from booksellers in the country concerned, whereas
the acquisition of Government publications through the
Oriental Exchange Unit is maintained almost wholly through
official exchange agreements, in most cases at Government level.
Though these aims have been realised reasonably well from most
regions, there is a special problem relating to Japanese
publications because of the large publishing programme of that
country and the high cost.

Because of the linguistic problems, the language specialists are
involved both in the selection and cataloguing of the materials
from their areas. Separate catalogues for individual languages or
language groups are printed and published from time to time.
Many of the volumes in this series have provided the first, and

remain the leading, bibliographical authorities in the world for the literatures they cover. Current cataloguing is by cards, which are accessible to users in the Oriental Reading Room.

Among publications which will be ready shortly are a *Guide to the Department,* a *Catalogue and subject index to Persian illustrated manuscripts,* a *Supplementary catalogue of Ethiopian manuscripts,* a *Catalogue of South-East Asian manuscripts,* a *Union catalogue of Manchu books and manuscripts* and a third *Supplementary catalogue of Arabic printed books.*

Conservation

The main problems in the conservation of oriental documents are: the many materials specially used in Asia and North Africa, such as papyrus, palm-leaf, silk, wood and bone; the illuminations and miniatures included in many of the manuscripts; and the poor quality, including high acidity, of much recent printing from certain countries. The Department's conservation workshop has developed new techniques for dealing with these problems, which benefit not only the British Library, but also a wider international clientele.

External relations

The Department has close links with other parts of the British Library where collections of oriental interest, but mostly not in oriental languages, are maintained. It also keeps in touch with other Orientalist libraries in this country through a series of Library Groups: the Middle East Libraries Committee, the South Asia Library Group, the South East Asia Library Group and the Japan Library Group; as well as the British Academy Oriental Documents Committee which is concerned with the recording, cataloguing and publishing of archival materials in oriental languages from British collections. Many of these activities are coordinated by the SCONUL Group of Orientalist Libraries, which holds an annual conference in London or elsewhere.

The Department participates in the International Congress of Orientalists, and its successor, the International Congress of

Human Sciences in Asia and North Africa, and in an organisation closely associated with it, the International Association of Orientalist Librarians, which arranges Seminars at these Congresses. Besides these formal links, world-wide contacts with institutions and individual scholars are maintained and these are made more fruitful by periodic visits of members of the Departmental staff to the countries with which they are specially concerned.

The Science Reference Library / M. W. Hill

The last of the four main departments of the Reference Division, the Science Reference Library, is the only one whose functions are delineated in terms of subject matter. The presence in the Division of a component like the SRL, so different in character from the other three Departments and with responsibilities that cut across two of the others, illustrates that the BL is, despite its size, flexible enough to admit or evolve solutions to particular requirements which are not simply subsets of the more standard components of a national library. The ability to maintain a genuine unity in Reference Division and yet allow effective idiosyncrasy to continue is the strength of the federal system of management described earlier.

The character of the Science Reference Library is very largely an inheritance from its predecessors the Patent Office Library and the National Reference Library of Science and Invention, although significant developments have already occurred since it became part of the British Library in 1973. Despite its importance and, during the period up to 1920, influence on the library scene, no full account of the history of the Patent Office Library seems to have been compiled, though one is currently in course of preparation. Gravell[31] and Hutton[32], however, give some indication of its nature.

The Patent Office Library was originally required to have 'mechanical and scientific works of every age and people for use of the Public' and to contain material 'indispensable to the right direction and advance of British Industry'. Add to these the fact that this library, though open to the public, had its stock arranged on open access, forty years before the first public library introduced this feature, and the advanced thinking of the library's founders becomes obvious.

Partly as a result of financial stringency, partly as a result of the growth in patenting activity, and partly as a result of the introduction of scientifically qualified patent examiners, the activities of the library became more and more narrowly patent orientated and the coverage of 'the works of every people' was reduced to those either entirely in a western European language or at least containing a summary in such a language. Periodicals took precedence over books even in the inter-war period.

The development of the Patent Office Library into the National Reference Library of Science and Invention[33] widened the subject spread of the library to cover all sciences and technologies, with a few clearly defined exceptions, and reintroduced the coverage of literature from all countries irrespective of language, but eliminated the 'works of every age'. Holdings, with certain exceptions, were to be limited to fifty years. Though it contains some errors of fact, an account of the NRLSI can be found in the *Report of the National Library Committee*, Cmnd 4028, 1969.[34] An account is also given by Hill.[35]

Today, the objectives of the Science Reference Library are to provide 'a national centre for reference, study and other information services in relation to both scientific and technological matters'.[36] These terms of reference are very wide indeed and would admit again of the historical sector and also of student and lay interests, both expressly excluded by the NRLSI, but because of physical constraints and the importance of maintaining services to industry, to the patents and trade marks community and to the world of scientific research, both pure and applied, the SRL's current targets are much more limited and must remain so until proper accommodation is provided.

Accommodation

Because its accommodation difficulties are the major constraint preventing the fulfilment of its proper role, it is worth spelling them out at this stage, particularly as some knowledge of them is essential to understanding the peculiar arrangement of stock and services. Currently the library contains about three quarters of a million bound volumes, a very large number of unbound issues of journals, leaflets, etc and something of the order of half a million items in microform. This is arranged between five buildings:

i   Sir John Taylor's beautiful library in the Patent Office in Southampton Buildings
ii A converted basement of nearby Chancery House, also in Southampton Buildings
iii A converted warehouse in Kean Street, near Aldwych, about ten minutes' walk away
iv Two floors of Whiteley's department store in Queensway, Bayswater, about three miles distant from the last three buildings
v   A section of the Woolwich Arsenal

The first three of these house what is designated the Holborn Branch of the SRL and are still for most practical purposes the continuation of the former Patent Office Library. The fourth building houses what is designated the Bayswater Branch and which still largely consists of the stock and staff which were amassed as the Patent Office Library was expanded into the NRLSI. The fifth location, at Woolwich, is simply a storehouse for overflow material, particularly from the Holborn Branch, which can no longer be centrally housed.

Because of the way the library was built up, keeping the Holborn Branch running with only minimal extension to coverage but adding all the new literature – both new subjects and material in subjects covered at Holborn but in other languages – to the Bayswater Branch, there is no clear division between them in terms of subject coverage. This situation is currently being rectified so that by the end of 1977 the situation should be as follows. Holborn Branch: physics, chemistry, engineering, and associated technologies; industrial property (patents, trade marks, registered designs) and related law; technological trade literature. Bayswater Branch: mathematics, geology, mineralogy, astronomy; life sciences and associated technologies (eg public health, medicine, food science, agriculture).

However, there will remain an anomaly in that most scientific material written in non-Roman scripts, mainly Russian and Japanese material, will be housed in the Bayswater Branch irrespective of subject content except, of course, for industrial property material. Nevertheless, the outcome will be relatively easier to understand, even if the collocation of subjects proves particularly frustrating to those who are conducting multi-disciplinary searches and find travel from building to building inescapable. Since so much of the library's proper role depends on the provision of an integrated multi-disciplinary stock, much on open access, its potential can never be fully realised until it is properly housed in a single building. Indeed, even with a new building in sight by the middle of the next decade, it will require near miracles of organisation to prevent significant deterioration in reader service during the interim period.

Users of the library

Two surveys of the use of the NRLSI (for all practical purposes of the Holborn Branch alone since the Bayswater Branch had scarcely opened and had at that only a closed access reading room) were carried out in the second half of the last decade[34,37] and provided a useful supplement to a survey of the Patent Office Library made in the early 1960s.[38] The picture revealed was that the majority of readers were, not unexpectedly, concerned with service to industry, either direct to research and development or via the industrial property field. Though a significant number of readers came from universities and other academic institutions, and there was a sizeable number of abstractors technical journalists and other categories, including market researchers, as a proportion of the total use their share was not large. An interesting feature was that, although there was a body of users who spent almost the whole of every day in the library, the average duration of a visit was about two hours. Quick reference is a feature of the use of the library as well as in-depth research.

Use of the Bayswater Branch is growing steadily, despite the closed access nature of the library, but is very small compared with that of the Holborn Branch.

Stock

This is not the place to give statistics about stock levels. The more important feature is the extent to which reliance can be placed on the SRL fulfilling its role as a library of last resort and having a required item or, more usually, group of items. The area of effective coverage of the world's publications is still largely that of the NRLSI: literature of value to modern scientific and technological research and development. In those subjects covered by the Holborn Branch, almost everything still of research value published since 1910 is held.

In the subjects covered by the Bayswater Branch such a claim can be made only in terms of material published since 1960 but there are large holdings of earlier material, particularly UK publications back to 1930 and even earlier for taxonomy. Access can also be arranged to 19th century material held by the other Departments of the Reference Division. Certain subjects excluded by the NRLSI are still excluded by the SRL, notably the philosophy and history of science – but not of technology – and biography. Publications of purely local interest are also still excluded. Clinical medicine, formerly excluded is now being selectively covered particularly to provide on-site back up for the Medline service available in the SRL.

As with medicine the SRL is making every effort to avoid space limitation preventing it from responding to new requirements. Thus resources to enable readers to bridge the gulf between technological and commercial information being currently developed. Science policy has already been added to the subjects covered and now the concern over the effect of technology on the environment and on the quality of life has led to a study of the need for coverage of ethical considerations.

Eventually, microforms may ease the space difficulties, but so far only a small part of the stock is stored on film or fiche. To make it practicable to bring together all the very extensive holdings of spectroscopic data, microforms were accepted but so far extensive use of microform for the huge patents collections has not been practicable or acceptable to readers.

Services provided by the SRL

In its approach to services from the library and the housekeeping operations on which services are based, the SRL takes its precepts from the world of industry. In particular, great emphasis is placed on categorising material according to its potential importance to users, giving priority in handling to the more important categories and, in general, regarding the achievement of speed of action and response as of more importance than perfection at considerable expense and delay. That is not to say that care and thoroughness are ignored, far from it, but it is realised that many clients need the latest publications at the earliest practicable moment and that, in the case of many enquiries, a partial answer given quickly is of more value than a complete answer which takes some time to reach.

To counter any impression this may give of a slipshod approach, the meticulous attention to dating serials is worthy of mention. Although most periodicals parts are shelved on the day the SRL receives them, the remainder first thing the following morning, each one is dated with the date it actually appears on the shelves and the same date goes in the records. Serials librarians will appreciate the problem of identifying, scanning and, in some cases, diverting for special action issues of 30,000 current serials within such a time scale. Not all the three-quarters of a million patent specifications handled each year achieve quite this speed, though many do, but here too each one is individually dated and the date in the records and that on the specification must both agree and be the date on which the item was shelved. Amendment slips have to receive the same treatment too.

Reference service and referral

A wide range of normal reference services is provided not only to readers but in answer to queries received by post, telephone and telex. Although anyone may use the service, discretion is used whether to accept the query or whether the enquirer should be referred to another library. In a significant number of instances the outcome is a mixture of part answer and part referral. It may be that with some suitable guidance he is referred to his local public library or in other cases he may be referred to a specialist source of help such as, when historical studies are involved, the Science Museum Library. Nevertheless, the great majority of queries received are appropriate for handling by SRL staff and are dealt with to the extent that time and resources permit.

Information services

Since reference and referral is a form of information, probably a better title for this section would be research services, with its implication of study in depth. But the point needs to be made that the SRL is a major component of the information world. Its stock is essentially an immense store of information and data and each and every use of the library is to obtain information. Although many of the queries that need some research are couched in the form 'can you tell me what has been published in . . .', which are answered with short select bibliographies usually with some form of commentary, others do ask for 'hard' information.

The SRL plays a very active role in the world of scientific and technical information. A major illustration of this, and of the way the several parts of the British Library can make a coordinated response to a developing situation (see the entries on R & DD and on Lending Division), lies in the provision of mechanised bibliographic facilities. The SRL now provides facilities whereby anyone can be given access to the major on-line computer based bibliographic services, most of them housed on computers in other countries. Services thus available include Medline, the ESA Recon set of data bases and the Lockheed Dialog bases via Tymshare. All major data bases can therefore be accessed in the SRL, probably the only such centre in the UK. Incidentally, just as the Patent Office Library was probably the first library to provide open access for the public at large, so the SRL was probably the first library to

allow the descendants of that same public access in person to
computer terminals to conduct their own searches. This has led
the SRL into the area of commercial services (previously only
photocopies were charged) whose relationship to conventional
'free' library services will take some time to be properly
determined.

Publications

The policy guiding the production of publications by the SRL is
based on four of the library's tasks:

i To inform current and potential users of the library's
   activities and services
ii To assist readers to use the resources effectively
iii To inform librarians and scientists about publications of
   value to them
iv To transmit information of relevance about developments
   in publications practice of information searching

To meet these requirements, four newsletters, each aimed at a
different readership, are published: *Notes to readers, SRL news,
Industrial property news* and *Periodicals news*. Bibliographies of
substance, guides to particular search tools and other
miscellaneous items of some significance are produced in an
Occasional Publications series. Introductory guides to a subject,
intended for those starting to search a topic with which they are
not familiar, are published as *Guideline to . . .*, which are
roughly equivalent to the Library of Congress *Tracerbullets*.

So far accessions lists only of the Holborn Branch are published
but plans are in hand, which may have reached fruition by the
time this appears, to print out on fiche complete new accessions
lists. Handlists of current serials are produced at intervals, the
last one about five years ago.

Looking ahead, one sees continued development in publications
practice, particularly when print-outs from the computer stored
catalogues are available to reduce the time subject qualified staff
have to take over compilation. The role of the SRL will essentially
be the production of highly selective annotated bibliographies;

comprehensive ones will be computer produced probably *via* the
agency of BSD.

Photocopy supply

An immediate service of supplying photocopies of articles from
journals and copies of foreign patent specifications has long been
a major feature of the SRL and its forerunners, probably dating
back to the early years of this century. For regular customers,
accounting is greatly simplified by the use of deposit accounts
but the service also caters for those who only rarely want copies
and have neither deposit account nor BLLD forms to hand. In
1974 over 2,000,000 pages were supplied, mainly by post but
also to readers in person.

Educational activities

Since the late 1960s the library has been developing a significant
educational role. This takes the form of instructional courses on
the effective use of the library, of technological literature
generally or of some special sector of the collections. In
particular it has concentrated on courses in the use of patents
literature for trainee patent agents and other specialists, but
courses for chemists and biologists have also been held.
Another field of activity is the production of tape-slide teaching
aids, some of which are available for use in other organisations.
Several of the staff take part in courses run by other
organisations.

Linguistic help

Complementing the translation service of BLLD, is the SRL's
linguistic aid service.

It is intended to help readers understand either the substance or
some specific part of an item held by the SRL written in a
language the reader does not know. A member of the staff with
sufficient competence in the language, though probably not in
the subject will, with the reader's help, attempt an oral rendering
of selected portions of the item. Frequently it is found that a
short session is quite sufficient to satisfy the reader's interest in
the item: occasionally it is established that a full translation is

worth having – but the reader is satisfied that the cost of the translation is justified.

Patents, trademarks, registered designs

A few words about the SRL's continued special relationship with the world of patents, trademarks and designs is essential. Just as the Reference Division shows its great depth by accommodating a unit as diverse in character from the other components as the SRL, so the SRL shows its ability to provide for singular, non-standard needs by its extensive provisions for those concerned with industrial property. Not only does it house as comprehensive a collection of industrial property literature as is to be found anywhere in the world but also the library compiles a series of registers of patent status and applications indexes, holds judgements of the various courts, catalogues of recent exhibitions, books on heraldry, hall marks, an extensive collection of directories of unregistered trademarks and above all, perhaps, has in its vast collection of scientific and technological journals the outstanding resource for establishing obviousness or prior disclosure.

With the coming changes in the patents world – changing UK practice, the European Patent Convention, the Community Patent Convention and the Patent Cooperation Treaty – and with the advent of computer stored patent data bases, the SRL has a leading role to play in helping the UK to establish an effective network of patent document access and documentation and information services to meet the requirements of the 1980s. In so doing, patterns may be established which, with appropriate adaptations, will serve as models for other sectors of activity.

Conclusion

The previous sections illustrate ways in which the SRL is setting about the various roles it is required to play in its designated subject fields and for its main categories of user. Two roles can be called traditional, that of a research library of last resort, accessible to all, and that of the premier reference library of first resort for in depth, multi-disciplinary studies, for combined science and technology and for industrial property. In the field of STI, however, it is required to be much more than the traditional style of reference library. It is a focal point in the network of information centres and services which cover the UK and a link with corresponding points abroad. Though concerned entirely with published information, it facilitates access by all to its own holdings of STI, provides an entry point to an even wider range of published STI material and provides a switching centre to enable enquiries to be directed to other centres and services.

References

1. *Conference of librarians held in London October 1877: transactions and proceedings* ed Edward B. Nicholson *and* Henry R. Tedder. London: 1878.
2. British Library. *Working party on classification and indexing: final report* BL Research & Development Department, 1975. (BLR & D Report no 5233).
3. Library Association. *Year book 1975* London: LA, 1975. 'Past Presidents of the Library Association', 23–24.
4. Miller, Edward. *That noble cabinet: a history of the British Museum* London: Deutsch, 1973.
5. British Library. *First annual report 1973–4* London: BL, [1974].
6. British Library. *Second annual report 1974–75* London: BL, 1975.
7. *Hansard House of Commons Parliamentary debates* 19 December 1974: written answers 567–568.
8. *Hansard House of Commons Parliamentary debates* 5 August 1975: written answers 143.
9. Seeley, Nigel J. *Conservation in the British Library Reference Division: a survey of the conservation facilities and requirements of the Reference Division* 1975. Unpublished.
10. British Library Reference Division. *Microfilms of newspapers and journals for sale* BL (issued at 3–4 yearly intervals: a list of positive microfilm at 35mm).
11. eg British Library Reference Division. *General catalogue of printed books: five year supplement 1966–1970* London: BMP Ltd, 1971, 26 vols.

12. eg British Library Reference Division. *Petrarch: poet and humanist 1304–74* ed John Barr. London: BMP Ltd, 1974.
13. *Addresses, reports and papers by British Library staff* British Library (Library Association Library), 1–, 1974–, occasional (10–15 per year), not publicly available.
14. *CABLIS: Current Awareness for British Library Staff* British Library (Library Association Library), 1–, 1975–, 10 issues per year, not publicly available.
15. *British Library journal* BMP Ltd, for the British Library, 1–, 1975–, two issues per year.
16. British Museum. *General catalogue of printed books* London: British Museum, 1966, 263 vols.
17. British Museum. *Subject index of modern works.* London, British Museum, 1881–. *1941–1945*, 1953; *1946–1950*, 1961, 4 vols; *1956–1960*, 1966, 6 vols. 1951–55 and 1961–70 are in preparation.
18. *see* Austin, Derek. *PRECIS: a manual of concept analysis and subject indexing* London: Council of the British National Bibliography, 1974.
19. The PRECIS Thesaurus has not been published.
20. British Museum. *General catalogue of printed books op cit.*

21. British Museum. *Catalogue of printed maps, charts and plans* London: British Museum, 1967. 15 vols and vol of corrections and additions.

22. British Library Reference Division. *Catalogue of the newspaper collection* BMP Ltd, for BL, 1976, 8 vols.

23. *but note* British Museum. *Catalogue of music in the Hirsch Library* London: British Museum, 1951.

24. eg British Museum. *Short-title catalogue of books printed in the Netherlands, and Belgium, and of Dutch and Flemish books printed in other countries from 1470 to 1600* London: British Museum, 1965.

25. British Museum. *Catalogue of books printed in the 15th century now in the British Museum* London: British Museum, 1908–. Parts I–X [1971] so far published.

26. Anderson, Dorothy. *Universal bibliographic control: a long-term policy, a plan for action* Munich: Verlag Dokumentation, 1974

27. List and Index Society. *Special series volume 7 of acquisitions by the Department of Manuscripts 1961–1965* The Society, 1974. Available to members.

28. British Museum. *Catalogue of additions to the manuscripts in the British Museum 1936–1945* London: BM, 1970. 2 parts.

29. Royal Commission on Historical Manuscripts. *Accessions to repositories and reports added to the National Register of Archives 1973* London: HMSO, 1975. Annual, latest published.

30. British Museum. *Catalogues of the oriental printed books and manuscripts* by F. C. Francis. London: British Museum, 1959.

31. Gravell, F. W. 'The Patent Office Library', *in* Irwin, R. *and* Staveley, R. (eds). *The libraries of London* 2nd rev ed. London: Library Association, 1961, rpr 1964.

32. Hutton, R. S. 'Contribution to a symposium: the National Reference Library of Science and Invention'. *Docum J* 17 (1), 1961, 3.

33. Nicholson, E. M. 'Contribution to a symposium: The National Reference Library of Science and Invention'. *Docum J* 17 (1), 1961, 15.

34. Great Britain. National Libraries Committee *op cit*.

35. Hill, M. W. 'The National Library of Science and Invention' *Libr Wld* 71 (832), October 1969.

36. Great Britain. Statutes. *British Library Act 1972 op cit*, Para 1 (2).

37. Sandison, A. *and* Preskett, M. *Library effectiveness survey 1970* National Reference Library of Science and Invention, 1972.

38. Kyle, B. R. F. *Patent Office Library: report of a survey* 1963. Unpublished.

Further reading

British Library: *Introducing the British Library: what it is – how it is run – what it does* London: British Library, 1975.
'The British Library'. *Aslib Proc* 26 (5), May 1974, 168–76. Includes a bibliography.
British Library Reference Division. *Guide to the Department of Oriental Manuscripts and Printed Books* London: British Library, 1976.

British Library Reference Division. *Guide to the Science Reference Library* London: British Library, 1974.
British Museum. *Oriental manuscripts* ed J. Losty. London: British Museum Publications, 1973.
British Museum. *Report of the Trustees 1969–1972* London: British Museum Publications, 1972.
British Museum Publications Ltd. *Books in print 1975* London: British Museum Publications, 1975.

The British Library Reference Division

Esdaile, A. *The British Museum library*
London: Allen & Unwin, 1946.
Francis, Sir Frank, ed. *Treasures of the
British Museum* Rev ed. London:
Thames and Hudson, 1975. (1st ed
1971) Ch 6. Manuscripts, by
T. S. Pattie; Ch 9. Oriental Printed
Books and Manuscripts, by A. Gaur;
Ch 12. Printed Books, by H. M. Nixon.
Gardner, K. B. *and others.* 'The
Department of Oriental Printed Books
and Manuscripts of the British
Museum'. *J Asian stud* 18, 1959,
310–318.
Great Britain. Department of
Education and Science. *Principal
documentary evidence submitted to the
National Libraries Committee* London:
HMSO, 1969. 2 vols.
Great Britain. Department of
Education and Science. *The scope for
automatic data processing in the British
Library* London: HMSO, 1972. 2 vols.

Great Britain. National Libraries
Committee. *Report of the National
Libraries Committee* London: HMSO,
1969 (Cmnd 4028). The 'Dainton'
report.
Great Britain. Parliament. *The British
Library* London: HMSO, 1971 (Cmnd
4572). The 'white paper'.
Great Britain. Statutes. *British Library
Act 1972, Eliz II 1972 Ch. 54* London:
HMSO, 1972.
Hosking, R. F. *and* Meredith-Owens,
G. M. *A handbook of Asian scripts*
London: British Museum, 1966.
Woodward, K. R. *The British Library: a
bibliography* Coventry: CADIG Liaison
Centre, 1974.

85

Chapter Six

The British Library Lending Division

Maurice B. Line

Within a month or two of the birth of the British Library in July 1973, the marriage took place of the two national libraries concerned with interlending, the National Central Library moving from London to Boston Spa to merge with the National Lending Library for Science and Technology and become the British Library Lending Division. Thus was created what is probably the most centralised interlibrary lending system in the world, and almost certainly the only national lending library to enjoy equal status with the national reference library.

In essence, the Lending Division is a comprehensive national document supply service, relying mainly on its own resources, but supplementing them by the resources of other libraries. As at March 1976, it has a stock occupying some fifty-six miles of shelving, as well as many microform cabinets, employs 650 staff, and handles nearly 10,000 requests per working day.

The National Central Library was established as long ago as 1916 as the Central Library for Students, and gradually became a national switching centre for interlibrary loan requests, operating by means of union catalogues containing entries of the holdings of many libraries of all kinds. It also built up a very substantial lending collection, by donation and purchase, but in 1951, as the result of a report on interlending, a critical decision was taken that this nucleus should not be built on, but that henceforth union catalogues should form the basis of interlending.

The published literature was already growing fast, and in the next ten years demand continued to grow, especially in science and technology; industrial libraries in particular found that they could neither obtain all they wanted nor could they obtain items as quickly as they needed. Meanwhile, Dr D. J. Urquhart was studying the use made of the Science Museum Library, the chief supplier of scientific serials, and formulating his plans for a national lending library, on the principle of providing a stock that fitted demand as closely as possible. This seemingly obvious principle went counter to all accepted ideas of central loan collections, which, where they existed at all, consisted mostly of material that few or no other libraries had. The NLLST, as it became when it was established at Boston Spa in 1962, not only acquired materials in demand in as many copies as required, but aimed at a comprehensive collection of scientific serials, together with scientific monographs, especially in English and in Russian – the latter because it had begun to be realised how little Russian scientific literature was available to, or used by, British industry.

The story of the NLLST is now a matter of history.[1] Between 1963, the first full year of operation at Boston Spa, and 1972–73, its last year of independent existence, demand increased by a factor of nearly six, as is shown in Table 6.1. A latent demand of unsuspected dimensions had been released, and Britain now has a far higher ratio of interlibrary loans to population than all but one or two countries. That it was created at all is due to a combination of several factors: the inadequacy of other interlending arrangements in 1960; the fact that it came within the province of the Department of Scientific and Industrial Research, of whose total budget expenditure on the library formed a relatively modest proportion; and, perhaps most of all, the fact that Dr D. J. Urquhart was given the responsibility for designing the system, on such a sound basis that the principles on which it was based remain as sound as ever fifteen years later. First reactions varied from cautious optimism to suspicious hostility, but attitudes changed radically as the service proved its value.

When the National Libraries Committee reported in 1969, the

87

Table 6.1.
Growth of interlibrary loan demand, 1962–1974/5

BLLD and precursors. Requests received (000s)		Regional systems Loans made (000s)
NCL	NLLST	
1962/3	92	(1962) 118	226
1963/4	100	(1963) 217	235
1964/5	112	(1964) 290	261
1965/6	120	(1965) 376	257
1966/7	127	(1966) 484	266
1967/8	131	(1967) 592	275
1968/9	149	801	277
1969/70	175	966	292
1970/1	183	1,032	279
1971/2	249	1,280	341
1972/3	277	1,480	337
	BLLD		
1973/4	1,912		369
1974/5	2,164		330
1975/6	2,471		

NCL and NLLST were almost ready for partnership, although the
enthusiasm of the Yorkshire bridegroom was greater than that
of his London bride. The NCL had in the 1960s, in spite of the
1951 decision, begun to build up a good collection of recent
American monographs in the humanities and social sciences, and
the NLLST had acquired social science serials. A study of the
possible use of automation in the British Library, commissioned
by the Department of Education and Science and carried out in
1970–1971,[2] looked at the whole interlending system; it
confirmed the principles on which the NLLST was based, and laid
down some guide-lines for the future. All that was needed to
prepare finally for integration was for the NLLST to start buying
humanities serials and the NCL to buy British monographs in the
humanities and social sciences, and for agreement to be reached
on the procedures to be adopted. After the first few months of
the British Library Lending Division at Boston Spa, integration

was so complete that the two libraries had effectively lost their separate identities. All subjects, and nearly all categories of printed material, are now dealt with, so that with very few exceptions the Lending Division can claim to offer a comprehensive service for the supply of loans and photocopies of the printed word.

The basic principle of the NLLST system was, as explained, an original one so far as interlibrary lending was concerned. It seemed to many at the time, and still seems to some, extravagant to build up specially for interlending a collection that duplicated to a great extent the holdings of other libraries; certainly most of the books in heaviest demand were known to be held in other British libraries, often in several. Doubts as to the wisdom of creating a separate loan collection partly explain why other countries have not followed the example of the UK.

It is true that most books requested from the Lending Division can be obtained from other sources. Of the five serials in heaviest demand, two at least, *Science* and *Nature*, are found in very many libraries. Yet most libraries do in fact prefer to use the Lending Division most of the time, because they have a much higher chance of satisfaction than from other sources, and because the speed of supply is greater, often much greater – in short, the system is faster and more reliable. There are other advantages, such as the simplicity of using one standard system and of sending all requests to one place. If all costs are taken into account, it is rather cheaper to use the Lending Division than either the regional systems or other libraries direct.

There are several reasons why the Lending Division is able to give a faster, cheaper and more reliable service than other libraries. In the first place, an item in a local library may be in use at the time it is requested on interlibrary loan; it may be confined to the library for reference purposes; it may be in process of rebinding or recataloguing, or otherwise unavailable. Many books wanted on loan are very recent publications, and libraries are understandably reluctant to lend items they have only just bought, often at the specific request of one of their members.

Even when a library is able and willing to lend an item, its first responsibility is always to its own members, and its system must be geared to serve them, not other libraries; response may therefore often be delayed. When, as often happened in the past, and indeed still happens sometimes, a request has to pass to two or three libraries before it can be satisfied, delays can be prolonged. A survey carried out in 1974 found that the percentage of items finally supplied as the result of locations of other libraries given by the Lending Division was less than 70%, and the median supply time was fifteen days.

There are other reasons why a central loan stock is justifiable. Comprehensive central acquisition and availability mean, not that each local library need not acquire a substantial collection for its own users, nor that less money need be spent on local libraries, but that selection can take account of the high probability that items not bought locally will be available on loan if required later. Libraries can thus gear their selection policies closely to local demand. The conventional method of trying to ensure comprehensive national availability, by means of cooperative acquisition schemes, is usually expensive to operate, often ineffective in practice, and vulnerable to economic pressures (since libraries are bound first to cease buying new books they do not need themselves). Moreover, it is much harder to ensure that books required under a cooperative scheme are retained, so that one copy at least is always available for use. Finally, without providing an adequate source of supply of British publications, the BLLD could not play a full part in international lending; this is discussed more fully below.

The principles on which the acquisition programme is built are two-fold. In the first place, as already noted, the supply is fitted as closely as possible to the demand. Since most demand is for serials, in various languages and subjects, and for monographs in English, wherever published, these are acquired as comprehensively as possible above a certain level (determined mainly empirically, according to demand), with the exclusion of fiction, for which other loan sources exist. Interlibrary loan demand for 'lower-level' material is so low as to scarcely exist. If demand changed, the acquisition programme would so far as

possible be adjusted to meet it – as has happened in the past,
where the original level of science books had to be lowered
somewhat to meet demand. If the demand for a particular serial
or monograph requires it, additional sets or copies are bought.
In practice, this is relatively easy for serials, since past demand is
a good guide to future demand, which can thus be anticipated;
moreover, photocopies of articles are supplied where possible so
that one or two sets of serials are often sufficient. For
monographs, however, neither of these considerations applies,
and heavy demand may appear without warning for a book,
which may be American, so that extra copies cannot be obtained
quickly, or may, less commonly, be out of print. Indeed, one of
the major deficiencies in the service is the fact that about 25% of
monographs requested are on loan when wanted, but this very
fact emphasises the need for a central loan stock, without which
the supply would be much poorer.

There are other categories of material that are acquired, not
precisely on the principle of satisfying heavy demand, but rather
where the demand is high in relation to the cost of acquisition:
conference proceedings, British official publications, Slavonic
scientific books, translations into English, and music scores.
These also are acquired as comprehensively as possible, except
that orchestral parts and multiple copies of vocal works for
performance are not bought.

The other main principle of acquisition is that items in occasional
demand and not likely to be available from other sources are
bought. This applies to well over three-quarters of the 47,000
serials currently received; 90% of demand falls on fewer than
8000 of the current serials acquired by the Lending Division. It
also applies to report literature, most of which comes in
microform, and to many English language monographs;
another very good reason for buying these is that advance
identification of little-used monographs would be so difficult
that it is simpler to buy all above a certain level. Another type of
material in the same category is dissertations, British and
American. As already noted, comprehensive purchase along
these lines gives libraries an assurance that most of what they do
not buy they can borrow.

Selection of serials is made first on the basis of coverage by indexing and abstracting services, secondly by notification of new serials published, and thirdly from unsatisfied demand. For monographs, blanket orders are placed with suppliers, whose efficiency is monitored by scanning the *British national bibliography* and *Publishers weekly,* and also, more practically, by requests received. Failure to receive significant works does, of course, occur, especially with obscure foreign publishers. As for report literature, most of it is produced in large series, and the rest are picked up as well as possible. The library has perhaps the best collection in the world, although it is still deficient in such categories as local government reports.

The main categories of material not acquired comprehensively are foreign language monographs and foreign official publications. The number of these that is published is huge, and the demand relatively very small and unpredictable. Foreign language monographs that are requested from the Lending Division and are not readily available from elsewhere in the UK are usually bought if in print. The stock built up in this way, and from the comprehensive acquisition of Slavonic scientific books, enables the library to meet as much as 25% of current demand for foreign language monographs.

If the Lending Division had fully comprehensive collections of the main categories of material, retrospectively as well as currently, up to 97% of demand would be satisfied from stock. However, full comprehensiveness is not and never will be possible, because the books are simply not now available. Many back sets of serials have been acquired, and indeed the Lending Division has as many sets of dead as of current serials; also, older monographs tend to come the way of the Lending Division as they are donated by other libraries. Nevertheless, most of the unsatisfied demand is still for serials and English language monographs not held in stock.

A higher proportion of requested items will be available in the course of time, since the comprehensive acquisition programme has been operating fully for less than five years. The present satisfaction rate from stock of nearly 84% should gradually increase. Nevertheless, it will always be necessary to have a supporting system, not only for those items that the Lending Division does not have, but for those that are held but are in use when wanted. The supporting system used by the NCL has been both simplified and extended recently, in particular by the cooperation of the Reference Division and the other legal deposit libraries, as well as of several other large private libraries that played little or no part in the interlending system previously.

Supporting libraries fall into two categories. The first comprises several, some of them very large, such as the other libraries that receive British publications on legal deposit, the London Library, and the Royal Society of Medicine, and some of them small private libraries such as the Linnean Society and the English Folk Dance and Song Society. These libraries are either not supported by public funds, or do not normally lend; they are therefore paid the estimated full cost of fulfilling requests. The other libraries are mainly university libraries, but include also many public libraries and some special libraries; these are paid the value of the BLLD loan/photocopy form, but not the full marginal cost of supplying items. In the case of the special paid back-up libraries, requests are normally passed directly to them by the Lending Division; other libraries are given as locations to requesting libraries, which then pursue the requests themselves.

For serials not held in stock, requests are passed first to the Reference Division if there is a probability that the items are held. This system has been in operation for two years, and now provides access also to the Newspaper Library at Colindale. The next sources of supply tried are the other legal deposit libraries, the Royal Society of Medicine and the Science Museum Library; these are now handling a large number of requests, with high satisfaction rates. Next the *British union catalogue of periodicals* is searched, and locations are given; or other probably sources may be suggested. Finally, requests are sent abroad if necessary.

The procedure for works other than serials is that the union catalogues are first searched, and locations from them are given to the requesting library. The union catalogues now include not only the author/title catalogues brought from the NCL, but the lists maintained by the regional systems of ISBNs of items acquired by member libraries (mainly public libraries); these latter are especially useful as giving additional sources of items held by the Lending Division but already on loan. Next, requests may be sent to the special back-up libraries; these are tried after the union catalogues, since they do not normally lend at all, and when they do it is only for consultation in the requesting library, not for home use. Possible sources other than those given in the union catalogues may also be offered; and finally requests may be sent overseas.

Clearly, each extra stage of searching for items not in stock requires additional work. To avoid spending undue effort on items that are not wanted urgently, or perhaps not wanted very badly, libraries are asked to grade requests according to the level of search they want. Additional charges are not made for extended searches, because the effort of collecting the additional money would probably be out of proportion to the number of requests for which additional searches have actually to be made.

The Lending Division does not handle requests for some types of printed material, some of which have been mentioned. They include fiction, monographs in oriental languages, and orchestral parts. For some of this material, however, the library accepts some responsibility for ensuring availability from other sources. For example, it is giving financial help to the construction of a union catalogue of orchestral parts, and intends to maintain the machine-readable records on a continuing basis. The School of Oriental and African Studies in London has a good stock of oriental monographs, and also maintains the Union Catalogue of Asian Publications; to support this activity, the Lending Division pays SOAS for the loan requests it satisfies, and also pays for the maintenance of UCAP. As for non-book materials, if there proves to be sufficient demand for them on interlibrary loan, provision for these also may be considered, although they raise severe problems of storage and transmission, and would cost more to handle than printed material.

Because the Lending Division aims at the comprehensive acquisition of current English language monographs, it is no longer necessary to require other libraries to submit entries for such items for incorporation in the union catalogues. Entries are still required for foreign language monographs and older English language books, but in fact these are not bought in any significant quantity by more than sixty or seventy libraries, mostly university libraries. Thus, the union lists of the future will be very much smaller and easier to control than those of the past, which had become increasingly difficult to use as very large numbers of libraries submitted entries for all their acquisitions. The new union lists will also be superior, since they include some major libraries that did not contribute previously.

To improve retrospective access, the catalogues of a few libraries have been filmed. Birmingham University Library filmed its catalogue for its own purposes, and a copy of this was bought. Manchester University Library's catalogue was filmed specifically for the purposes of the Lending Division. The other microfilm catalogues are all of small special libraries.

The foreign language union lists are now kept separately from the English language lists (to which most newly added entries are of items acquired for stock). The foreign language union lists may be kept in machine-readable form, with short author/title entries, and produced on COM at frequent intervals for use in the Lending Division (not for publication and distribution).

The ISBN lists maintained by regions have already been mentioned. LASER is converting its catalogue to machine-readable form, using as a base the conversion of BNB back to its beginnings in 1950, and this catalogue will be of considerable use to the Lending Division. It is possible that the same base can be used to convert other regional catalogues, and there could even be, in the course of time, a comprehensive catalogue of regional holdings. As for serial union lists, it is doubtful if the *British union catalogue of periodicals* will need to be maintained in future, since all the titles recorded in it after a certain date should be accessible from the Lending Division or by photocopy from a few other selected libraries, such as the Reference Division and the other legal deposit libraries.

Table 6.2.

Sources of requests received by BLLD.

	%	
Academic	38	
Universities		25
Polytechnics		7
Other		6
Special	43	
Industrial & Commercial		21
Government		13
Other		9
Public	8	
Overseas	9	
Miscellaneous	1	
	100	

Note. Due to rounding-up the percentages shown above do not total 100%.

Table 6.3.

Subjects of requests received by BLLD.

	%
Science and Technology	75
Social Sciences	13
Humanities	9
General and miscellaneous	3
	100

The number of British libraries registered as users with the Lending Division is 5100; this must include all but a very few libraries in the country. As can be seen from Table 6.2, universities account for most requests, followed by industrial and commercial libraries. The small proportion accounted for by public libraries is explained by the fact that interlibrary loans do not play nearly such a large part in public libraries as in libraries used mainly by researchers and students, and that at present

two-thirds of interlibrary loan requests from public libraries are
satisfied through the regional systems. However, the proportion
of public library requests coming to the Lending Division,
directly or indirectly through the regional systems, is increasing
and seems likely to continue to increase. Requests from overseas
are considered later.

Three quarters of the demand (see Table 6.3) is for scientific
material. This is partly a genuine reflection of total interlibrary
loan demand in the UK, but partly due to the fact that in May
1974, when the survey from which the figures are taken was
carried out, libraries had not yet become accustomed to thinking
of the Lending Division as so obvious a source for material in
the humanities and social sciences as in science and technology.
A gradual change in the proportions may well occur. Similar
considerations apply, to a slightly smaller extent, to the
categories of material demanded (see Table 6.4); monographs
will probably gain a little at the expense of serials, which will,
however, probably always account for well over half of all
requests.

The performance of the Lending Division was measured in 1974
by a survey of nearly 13,500 requests. The results of this are
summarised in Table 6.5. Surveys of this kind will be carried out
regularly, since to remain efficient the service must be constantly
monitored. The high percentage of requests referred back to
libraries may seem surprising. Some of these are not traceable, at
least without a great deal of effort; some are quite simply wrong;
and some are for books that have been announced but not yet
received, or even published. Some items, mostly monographs,
are on loan when requested, and libraries are asked to wait if
alternative locations cannot be given.

It will be seen that the satisfaction rate varies considerably
between different categories of material. At the extremes, there is
a 96% total success rate for English language serials, compared
with a 75% success rate for foreign language monographs. The
differences between proportions satisfied from the stock of the
Lending Division are of course much greater: they vary from
93% for English language serials to 26% for foreign language

Table 6.4.
Forms of requests received by BLLD.

	%	
Monographs	23	
English language		21
Foreign language		2
Serials	67	
English language		56
Foreign language		11
Conference proceedings	5	
Reports, Official publications, etc.	4	
Dissertations	1	
	100	

Table 6.5.
Satisfaction rates for different categories of request

	Referred back to requester % of total received	Valid requests satisfied (%)				
		From BLLD stock	From locations supplied*	Sent to back-up libraries	Sent abroad†	Total satisfied
Monographs	14	61	18	5	1	86
English language	14	64	18	4	1	87
Foreign language	12	26	13	17	10	75
Serials	7	91	1	3	0·5	96
English language	7	93	1	2	0·5	96
Foreign language	8	85	1	6	1	93
Conference proceedings	17	81	4	1	0·5	86
Reports, Official publications, etc	14	84	3	1	1	88
Dissertations	22	73	1	0	14	88
All categories	10	84	5	3	1	93

* *Calculated at 70% of items for which locations are supplied.*
† *Satisfaction rate not known at time of survey: counted as 'satisfied'.*

monographs. The 64% satisfaction rate for English language monographs will rise as the stock grows.

As would be expected, the satisfaction rate from stock is higher in science than in other subject fields, but for recent books there are good satisfaction rates for the social sciences and, especially, for the humanities. The level of satisfaction drops with the age of the book, again as expected.

Charges are made for supplying items, the prices being based mainly on the cost of posting loans and making and posting photocopies. At the end of 1975, the average marginal cost of supplying an item – that is, the average cost to the Lending Division of satisfying each additional request – was about 80*p*, and the charge made to libraries in the UK was 46*p*. Thus, rather more than half the marginal costs are recovered. No charge is made for searching for items not held by the Lending Division, the money going instead to the library that supplies the item. To avoid the expensive and complex reclaiming and accounting systems that used to exist in Britain and still exist in many other countries, requests are only accepted on prepaid forms, charged at a standard rate. This system is so simple and effective that BLLD loan/photocopy forms are now used in regional systems and for direct transactions between libraries that do not involve the Lending Division at all.

To supplement local resources effectively, speed is very important. The Lending Division aims to deal with the great majority of requests the same day as they are received. This is not possible with requests that require further checking of one kind or another, or for which locations cannot be quickly found, but about 80% of items that are in stock are sent by first class mail the same day as the requests are received. At the time of writing, an alternative system for sending requested items to libraries, using rail and van services rather than the Post Office, is under consideration. The use of Telex for sending requests saves at least a day over first class mail, and often two or more days over second class mail. A PDP 11 computer has now been linked with the Telex; this transfers Telex requests to BLLD forms, thus facilitating handling at the library, and it also enables much faster response to be made in the case of locations, queries, or non-supply. Requests from the US National Library of Medicine and the Center for Research Libraries in Chicago are now received direct by computer, which may prove an important means of regular requesting in the future.

The systems used at the Lending Division are strictly functional. Since there is no open access in the library apart from a Reading Room containing reference books and a Staff Library for use of the staff, the stock can be arranged for the fastest possible retrieval. All serials are arranged in alphabetical order, although there is one main division by date. This enables the first approach to be made to the shelves, and only when this fails are the records of serials held checked; very often this check shows that the requested item is indeed in stock, and enables it to be tracked down. For monographs, the position is rather more complicated, particularly since the NCL and NLLST stocks were arranged on quite different principles. For the future, all foreign language monographs and older English language monographs will be arranged in a numerical sequence, with access by means of a catalogue consisting of minimal entries made by clerical staff. Current English language monographs acquired during the last few years will be kept in alphabetical order of title, so that, as with serials, the shelves are checked first and the catalogue records afterwards. Each year there will be removed from this sequence the oldest items, which are then shelved in a numerical sequence. The optimum length of the title order sequence will be determined in the light of experience. The numerical sequence, access to which is by means of short entry catalogues, will thus contain all older English language monographs; there is a similar numerical sequence for all foreign language monographs. The reason for limiting the length of the title order sequence is that title sequences over a certain size are very difficult to keep in order, and also use diminishes gradually with age, so that the benefits of direct access are reduced. For many current English language books, no records have to be made, since they are provided by suppliers; it is hoped that it will in future be possible to extract short records either from MARC tapes, or, preferably, from the pre-publication tapes used for the Cataloguing In Publication programme.

For certain categories of material no records at all are made. Most report literature is in numbered series, and the published lists are quite adequate to provide access to it. Similarly, official lists provide access to British official publications. For some categories of material, however, additional records have been created. The chief example is conference proceedings. Conventional catalogue entries for conference proceedings tend to make conferences almost unfindable. Since requests reach the library in a great variety of forms, it is much simpler to enter conferences under key-words in titles. These records are kept in machine-readable form, and since they provide a useful means of access to other libraries than the Lending Division, the key-word indexes are published – as a monthly list, in annual cumulations, and eventually in five-year cumulations.

When requests are received, they are sorted according to the area of the stock in which they are expected to be held, and further sorted when they reach the appropriate area. If they are in stock, the request form is inserted in a transparent folder, which is put in place of the book itself on the shelves. Items on loan and wanted by other libraries are quickly identified when the requests come in, and overdues are traceable by the colour of the folder, which is changed regularly. This system makes it unnecessary to keep any separate record of issues. Photocopying is used as extensively as possible within the terms of the Copyright Act. This leads to increased availability of stock, and well over half of all requests – about 70% of requests for serials – are now satisfied by photocopies. Copying machines are distributed about the stores to speed up copying and re-shelving.

There are various links between the regional systems and the Scottish interlending system, now operated from the National Library of Scotland, and the Lending Division. The British Library has for three or four years supported the production of ISBN lists of regional acquisitions, the regions being responsible for the input and output and the BL for the processing. These ISBN lists are changing the nature of regional interlending, since libraries that acquire these lists in COM form are able to request items direct from other libraries. The proportion of requests that are made in this way will increase in the course of time; at present, requests for older items still have to go through the regional bureaux. Nearly all regional interloan requests come from public libraries, and local government reorganisation has, by reducing the number of public libraries to about a third of their former number, further changed regional interlending. The new library authorities have a much higher degree of self-sufficiency, and requests that are not satisfiable within one of the new library authorities will tend to be for more esoteric items, which have much less chance of being obtainable through the region than from or through the Lending Division. One would therefore expect regional interlending to grow very slowly, if at all, and for an increasing proportion of public library requests to come to the Lending Division. The present indications are that this is happening, with the exception of the London and South East Region, which deals with about as many requests as all the rest of the regions together, and which has the special advantage of enabling loan requests to be satisfied very quickly between libraries in London, a function the NCL was able to perform before it moved to Boston Spa.

As already shown, the demand on the library has increased at a rapid rate, the greatest increase being between 1973–74 and 1974–75. An interlibrary loan costs the requesting library on average over £1·50 (end of 1975), including the cost of the BLLD form. Libraries which, like some universities, borrow more than 10,000 items a year are incurring substantial expenditure, and many libraries are now restricting interlibrary borrowing by one means or another. As a result of this, the growth of interlibrary loan demand from British libraries appears to be slowing down. Nevertheless the increase in demand on the Lending Division was in 1975/6 still high (about 13% per annum), probably because interlibrary lending is becoming concentrated on the Lending Division. Three or four years ago, the NCL and NLLST together were probably dealing with about two-thirds of all interlibrary lending in Great Britain. A year ago, this has probably risen to 75%, and it may well rise to 80% or more. It is unlikely to go much higher than that, because there will always be a place for local interlending, which enables items wanted urgently to be collected the same day as the request arises, often within an hour or two.

Indeed, the future pattern of interlending may well be somewhat different from the present one. Instead of the present regional systems and local schemes (often concerned more with information queries than interlending), it may prove more satisfactory to have a two-stage system, with nothing between the extended locality or conurbation and the Lending Division. Libraries outside the conurbations would not be attached to any system, but use the Lending Division direct, whereas those within conurbations might well have a slightly increased degree of interlending among themselves. One of the great virtues of the ISBN lists is that the same records are used throughout the country, so that the files can be combined or divided in any way desired; this provides great flexibility for the future. Further, if, or rather when, a national serials data bank is set up in machine-readable form, localities can draw records from it and add their own locations to the file, obtaining a local union list of serials at modest cost. However, these are mere speculations. Some regions are now re-examining their scope and functions, and it is important that decisions are made in the framework of a coherent plan for the future, rather than on grounds of temporary expediency or past traditions.

The relationship of the Lending Division with other parts of the British Library has already been touched on at various points: the Lending Division now obtains large numbers of photocopies of serials held in the Reference Division, which also helps in the bibliographical checking of some difficult requests, and it cooperates closely with the Bibliographic Services Division in the mechanisation of the foreign language union finding lists and the ISBN lists. There will be cooperation between all three Divisions in the production of serial records and a national bibliography of report literature. What has still to be discussed in detail is a common acquisition policy; for much material, particularly foreign language monographs, one copy in the country might serve the purposes both of reference and of lending, and a greater number of titles could be acquired by avoiding some of the present duplication between the Lending

Division and the Reference Division. There is no doubt that other forms of cooperation will become apparent, but already the value of bringing together the various activities within one British Library has become clear.

Even faster than the growth of demand from British libraries has been the growth of demand from overseas.[3] (*See* Table 6.6.) In

Table 6.6.

Growth in demand on BLLD from overseas, 1967–1974/5

Requests for photocopies*		Requests for loans†	
1967	9,700	1966/7	8,000
1968	16,300	1967/8	8,200
1969	34,800	1968/9	8,800
1970	54,300	1969/70	9,300
1971	64,300	1970/1	9,500
1972	103,800	1971/2	11,300
		1972/3	12,100
1973/74	159,700	1973/4	13,000
1974/75	208,000	1974/5	10,500
1975/76	286,000	1975/6	15,400

* Figures for NLLST to 1972   † Figures for NCL to 1972/3

1975–76 over 285,000 photocopy requests were received from overseas libraries, constituting perhaps as much as a half of all international transactions. The fast growth of this demand is again due to the comprehensiveness and speed of the service. Foreign libraries can often apply to the Lending Division with a greater expectation of success than they can achieve within their own countries, and with comparable or greater speed; a library in Western Europe sending a request by Telex can expect to receive the item within five days, a library in North America within six, and a library in Australia within eight. The overseas service, unlike the British service, recovers its full marginal costs. The Lending Division can thus give a good, and not expensive, service to other countries without in any way harming the service to British libraries. Half of all overseas demand comes from Western Europe, and it seems doubtful whether another such comprehensive loan collection is needed in Western Europe. Outside Western Europe, the heaviest user is the USA, whose demand is growing faster than that of any other country.

The Lending Division lends books abroad as well as providing photocopies. Unlike photocopies, of which relatively few are obtained from abroad for British libraries, incoming and outgoing loans are roughly in balance. It may lend any book requested, but it accepts an absolute responsibility to lend from its own stock any British book requested from abroad, and to search in other British libraries for books not in stock. It is only if such a principle is accepted by all countries – it was accepted by IFLA in 1973 – *and* if it is put into practice, that the availability of items on interlibrary loan can be improved to more than a limited extent, since the natural and obvious source for a book is its country of publication. The concept and implementation of Universal Availability of Publications will play a major part in IFLA's immediate future programme, parallel in importance to Universal Bibliographical Control, and indeed an essential partner, since bibliographical control is of little use if the books are not available.

The Lending Division's central role in international lending has been recognised by the establishment there in 1975 by IFLA of an Office for International Lending. This aims to facilitate and improve international lending in several ways: by collecting statistics and noting trends, by keeping track of relevant developments in as well as between countries, by devising and encouraging improved requesting, accounting and transmission procedures (eg by the design of a new IFLA request form and by the routine use of air mail for sending requests), by producing regular guides to international lending, by studying barriers to lending such as copyright, and possibly by acting as a switching centre or clearinghouse for very difficult requests.

One of the functions of the Lending Division that is intimately related to its main role is that of a national repository for material of which libraries wish to dispose. Libraries have always offered to the NCL and NLLST material surplus to their requirements, but the increasing size of their stocks, combined with much tighter restrictions on new building, may now lead them to withdraw material in far greater quantities than hitherto. So far as accommodation and staffing permit, the Lending Division accepts such material and adds to its stock all that it does not already hold. Since it already has many of the items offered, especially serials, and since also there is considerable overlap between the items offered by other libraries, a great deal of space is saved nationally. The books themselves, many of which were previously unrecorded in union catalogues, are made more widely available, and the Lending Division's service is improved accordingly. Moreover, libraries can withdraw material and offer it to the Lending Division in the confidence that it can be obtained quickly on loan if subsequently required. Just as the Lending Division's acquisition policy affects the selection policies of libraries, so its repository role affects their retention policies.

In addition to its prime function as a central service for the supply of loans and photocopies, the Lending Division carries out other activities, related to the main service more or less closely. As well as collecting all available translations into English, the library commissions translations on request of articles in most languages – most of the present demand being in Russian and Japanese – and even of a few books. This service aims to recover its full marginal costs; this practice of cost recovery has enabled the service to be extended to a much wider range of languages than hitherto.

Another activity that now recovers its costs is the programme of courses in the use of the literature. These were instituted in the mid-1960s by the NLLST, not so much as a means of training users directly in the use of secondary services and other means of access to the primary literature, but as a way of spreading instruction much more widely by first instructing library staff, mainly in academic libraries. These courses have had a considerable influence on the development of user instruction in British academic libraries. More recently, courses have been given for staff of public libraries, and extended also into the humanities.

The final large activity of the Lending Division is the operation of the MEDLARS centre in the UK. This is at present, apart from the British MARC data base, the only large-scale computer-held data base for which the British Library acts as the main access point in the UK. This service has changed substantially since it was first started, and many searches are now carried out on-line to the data base held in the US National Library of Medicine.

Inevitably, the Lending Division now occupies an important central role within the library system of the country. Most academic, and many special, libraries have become very dependent on its services, and indeed their own acquisitions and services are planned in the light of the Lending Division's services. This central role carries with it obvious responsibilities, primarily that of maintaining the comprehensiveness and speed of the service. It is important also that the library's role is not misunderstood. It was never intended to be, and must never become, an alternative to adequate local provision. Every library must have on its shelves a high percentage of those items wanted by its own readers, partly because it is obviously more economic to acquire for stock items that are wanted more than occasionally, partly because, without access to a reasonable range of material, research, learning and leisure all become increasingly difficult. There is no danger that librarians will ask for less money because the Lending Division exists, but there is perhaps a danger that the authorities come to consider local provision less important. It cannot be overemphasised that the library cannot fulfil its role properly unless it is recognised as what it truly is, a service *in support of* the library system of the country, not a service intended to replace it.

References

1. Houghton, Bernard. *Out of the dinosaurs: the evolution of the National Lending Library for Science and Technology* London: Clive Bingley, 1972.

2. Department of Education and Science. *The scope for automatic data processing in the British Library* 2 vols. London: HMSO, 1972. Annex D: Interlibrary Lending and Copying.

3. Davey, J. S. *and* Smith, E. S. The overseas services of the British Library Lending Division. *Unesco Bull Libr* 19 (5), September–October 1975, 259–267.

Further reading

Line, Maurice B. Access to resources through the British Library Lending Division. *Aslib Proc* 27 (1), January 1975, 8–15.

Line, Maurice B. The British Library and the future of interlibrary lending. *BLL Review* 3 (2), April 1975, 37–43.

Chapter Seven

The British Library Bibliographic Services Division

Richard E. Coward

Introduction

In August 1974 the Bibliographic Services Division was established within the British Library. Its function is to provide centralised cataloguing and other bibliographic services related to the needs of the national library and the library and information community. After many years of planning it exists as a firm base for the future development of centralised bibliographic services in the UK.

The conviction that such services would be necessary was strongly held in the library profession in the immediate post-war era and by 1949 the major institutions of the profession, including the British Museum Department of Printed Books, came together to form the British National Bibliography. After a shaky start the new service took root and by the early 1960s, when the profession began to explore the more comprehensive concept of a national centre for coordinating reference, information and bibliographic services, the BNB was the obvious focus of a new national bibliographic service. A few years later, in 1966, the theme of a national bibliographic service was developed in the influential Parry Report on Libraries and the same year saw the appointment of the National Libraries Committee (Chairman Dr F. S. Dainton) which recommended in its report that a national library be created and that within the national library there should be a National Bibliographic Service which would amalgamate the bibliographic activities of the component institutions of the National Library. This new bibliographic service would

i   produce the national bibliography
ii   compile other national catalogues and union lists
iii undertake research
iv   coordinate national and international networks
v   continue the centralised services developed by BNB
vi   further BNB contributions to international bibliographic
     development

The Dainton Report was published in 1969 at a time when the
library profession was about to experience its major post-war
upheaval. By 1970 the first effects of computers on library
systems could be seen and their ultimate impact could be
imagined. In 1972 the Local Government Act created a new
map of library services. Compared with 1969 the Bibliographic
Services Division had been born into a dramatically changed
world of new large library authorities and new automated
systems. The library community now has technical expertise to
handle advanced computer-based operations and services. It is a
major function of the Bibliographic Services Division to provide
bibliographic input to these systems.

The basic approach of the Division to its bibliographic function
is to integrate the internal processing operations of the British
Library with external services to the library community so that
its cataloguing, classification and indexing activities create
records which can be used for any required purpose. To achieve
this measure of integration the Division is adopting
bibliographic standards which will in future be used throughout
the British Library.

On a wider front the Division is also profoundly concerned to
integrate its own cataloguing activities with those of other
major national centres. To provide comprehensive bibliographic
services to the library community at large implies providing
access to a vast store of bibliographic records. An international
MARC (MAchine Readable Cataloguing) network is being built
up to provide the supply of records. It is in the interests of the
library communities of all countries to develop international
standards for use in this network and thus greatly increase the

utility of the system. A significant part of the Division's activities is directed towards this objective.

Within the Library activity is concentrated on the primary objective of transferring the majority of cataloguing operations to a computer-based system. The first major step towards this objective was taken in 1975 with the transfer of the Science Reference Library cataloguing operations. In 1976 all copyright and English language material will be processed through the computer system. While this programme is being steadily extended it is hoped to start backfile conversion operations beginning with the complete Science Reference Library catalogue and the Reference Division, Department of Printed Books card catalogue holding records for all material acquired after 1970.

Organisation of the Division

The Division is organised into a Central Management Office, a Systems Development Department closely linked to Bibliographic Standards and Subject Systems Offices and an Operations and Services Department. The Central Management Office is responsible for the financial control of the Division's operations and services and acts as a focus for the coordination of systems development and operational services. All projects and operations affecting the Reference and Lending Division of the Library are coordinated through appropriate mechanisms. The Division has a strong formal link with the library community in its Advisory Committee and extensive informal connections through a network of committees and user groups.

Systems development

The Systems Development Branch of the Bibliographic Services Division is responsible for

i   management of computer operations associated with bibliographic services
ii   the extension of the computer system to provide new services
iii   the design, specification and implementation of a new

computer system capable of meeting the current and future
requirements of the British Library and the library
community and in particular offering on-line services to a
national bibliographic database

With the exception of the management of computer operations,
these responsibilities are shared with the specialised offices
within the BSD (the Bibliographic Standards Office and the
Subject Systems Office) and with line management responsible
for maintaining services.

Existing computer operations

All computer processing is handled through bureau services
using mainly IBM 360 and 370 machines. The amount of use has
steadily increased and is currently running at about eight hours
per day, seven days a week. In a typical day rolls of paper tape,
magnetic tapes and boxes of punch cards are received from
installations within the Library, or from outside libraries. These
are processed overnight and by morning new magnetic tapes or
line printer output is delivered ready for the next stage in
technical processing or proofreading. MARC network tapes
carrying a weekly output of new bibliographic records are sent
directly to other libraries where further processing is done on a
wide variety of computers. Most other magnetic tape output is
handled on specialised computers for end product processing.
Computer typesetting machines produce the printed national
bibliography and COM (Computer Output Microfilm) machines
produce microfiche and microfilm catalogues.

The main thrust of systems development activity in the
Bibliographic Services Division is now related to the new
computer system. Nevertheless, the impetus of the British
Library automation programme is such that there is a continuing
transfer of operations and services from existing manual systems
to the IBM-based computer system. To accommodate this the
Systems Development Branch has developed a generalised set of
programmes which can be used as the basis for any new service.
These programmes, which have been given the generic
description of 'Library Software Package', consist of three main
modules:

i   a suite of programmes for the selection of MARC records
        from a file and the selection of a specified set of data fields
        from a record
ii   a suite of programmes for processing the records and for
        adding local records to the file
iii   output programmes for locally specified catalogues in
        microform or line printer output

These programmes are designed to run on IBM 360/370 and ICL
System 4 machines. They are the basis of the MARC full catalogue
service and are available from the British Library for local use.

Future developments

Although the MARC software developed in 1968 by BNB has
proved robust enough to carry a vast range of activities and
services, it was essentially designed to support batch processing
operations and does not form a suitable basis for future British
Library bibliographic service operations. A new system with
advanced authority file and on-line access features is required.
This is being designed and will be operational in 1977. The new
British Library system is called MERLIN (MachinE Readable
Library INformation System). The nub of MERLIN is a central
database and the system and the database will be set up on one of
the new ICL range 2970 computers. To begin with, this will be on
a bureau basis but a dedicated machine will be required to
support the extensive on-line facilities to be introduced in 1978.
The basic design features of MERLIN, ie its database, authority
files and facilities, are outlined in the next few paragraphs.

The MERLIN database will hold catalogue records for all British
and Library of Congress MARC items (including back files to
1950 and 1968 respectively) as well as non-MARC current
acquisitions of the Reference Division, the serials file of the
International Serials Data Centre and the records of any local
library which uses MERLIN services. There will also be smaller
specialised databases such as the British Catalogue of Music and
the ILEA Media Resources Centre Catalogue. The database will
be designed to hold multi-media records and will also allow for
the identification of the ownership of records and fields within

records. The initial capacity of the database will be approximately one million records.

Authority files will be incorporated as part of the database structure. In a machine system an authority file can be both consulted and used in the preparation of a new record. In MERLIN all author headings, subject headings and index terms are held separately with links to the records to which they were applied.

MERLIN facilities will include:

i   Interrogation by record number, subject, names, titles, keywords, forms, etc. Not all of these keys will be available initially. The choice of retrieval keys in MERLIN is basically open-ended; a new field could be chosen as a useful entry point to the database and keys based on that field could be created

ii   A flexible input and editing system using off-line techniques (ie magnetic tape, paper tape) or terminals providing direct access to the database

iii   Output in a flexible and wide ranging set of options covering physical layouts and physical forms. Users will be able to define full or simple records appropriate to each catalogue

iv   The processing of an exceptionally wide range of characters (Roman, Cyrillic, Greek, etc). Output facilities will depend on the capacity of the output hardware available in the form required

MERLIN will be introduced in several phases. Phase 1 will comprise the new system for producing BNB, MARC tapes, the Selective Record Service and the MARC Full Catalogue Services for new users. These will be produced through batch processing techniques as at present but the new system design and new software will provide much greater flexibility, speed and economy. In addition the new system will be capable of handling other valuable databases such as the new International Serials Data System file and will support completely new bibliographic services such as a current serials bibliography.

Phase 2 sees the introduction of on-line operations within the British Library and the establishment of an experimental on-line network to a cross-section of libraries. This phase is dependent on the installation of an in-house computer at the British Library. The priority will be to develop a completely flexible catalogue service using ISBNs, BNB numbers, LC numbers, and so on for access to the file.

There is no sharp distinction between phase 2 and phase 3 and, in practice, the priorities of phase 3 will be determined by demand. The two areas of development are an extension of access to the file by a wide range of keys – author, title, keyword, etc, and an extension of processing facilities to include acquisitions, on-line catalogues, information retrieval, etc. Phase 3 will see the utilisation of the full potential of the computer and the MARC network.

MARC network services

The British Library's MARC Network Services have been developed out of the UK MARC project. The general objective of this project was to develop, in collaboration with the Library of Congress, a system for providing machine-readable catalogue records on magnetic tape for use by the library community. A permanent commitment by BNB to maintain a MARC service was essential and it was decided from the start that magnetic tape records created as part of the UK MARC project should be used as a basis for all BNB services. Subsequently the BNB Card Service was transferred to the computer based system in 1969, the BNB itself in 1970 and all other services by 1976. All services supplied are derived from a database which now contains

i   The retrospective UK MARC file 1950–74
ii   The current UK MARC file 1975–
iii   The retrospective Library of Congress MARC file 1968–74
iv   The current Library of Congress MARC file 1975–

These files now total over a million records. As the international network develops they will steadily be augmented by records received from European bibliographic services.

Three types of service are supplied from these databases: complete tape services, selective record services and local catalogue services. The complete tape service and selective record service are designed for those libraries that have established their own computer based operations and are using the central system as a source of data. For libraries not having or not wishing to use local computer facilities, the local catalogue service provides computer produced catalogues derived from the British Library database. These catalogues are tailored to the requirements of individual libraries. Records selected from the database may be amended and local material may be added. Local records may also be added. The output which is normally on microfiche or microfilm is locally defined. Entries may be full or brief. The sequence may be alphabetical or classified; updating is at the discretion of the user. Flexibility made possible by the use of the computer is the key-note.

The significance of the MARC local catalogue service is that it is a comprehensive attempt to produce customer specific services through a central system. The potential for such services is very considerable. In the future they will probably co-exist with on-line catalogues. The two techniques offer a combination of the economy of microform with the unmatchable up-to-date capability of on-line systems.

International Standards

A major responsibility of the Bibliographic Services Division is to distribute cataloguing information to the UK library community. This responsibility cannot be met in isolation. The Division must necessarily collect catalogue data from other national centres and distribute it. It is a basic policy of the British Library to promote the development of an international system which facilitates this. This is the responsibility of the Bibliographic Standards Office, whose activities are very largely devoted to British participation in the development of a new international bibliographic system now known as Universal Bibliographic Control.

The work of the Bibliographic Standards Office is concentrated on the specification and use of standard systems for bibliographic interchange within the international MARC network focussed on various aspects of the MARC II international exchange format which was adopted by the Library of Congress and the British National Bibliography in 1967. The machine structure of MARC II was accepted as an international standard in 1973. It now forms the foundation on which the international bibliographic exchange system is being built.

The next level of standardisation in the area of international bibliographic exchange is the specification of a new and more complex standard which will define how data elements must be identified in MARC records which are being exchanged between national agencies. This system, known as UNIMARC, will mark a tremendous advance in international bibliographic cooperation. When operational – perhaps in 1977 or 1978 – it will be possible to receive bibliographic records from anywhere in the world and pass them through an automatic translation program which will convert the foreign record into a national format record which could be used in any UK library computer system. By making exchange not only possible but relatively simple, the UNIMARC system provides a powerful incentive to reaching agreement on higher levels of bibliographic standards covering cataloguing codes, transliteration, filing conventions, etc. Work in these areas is the responsibility of the Bibliographic Standards Office.

The main functions of the Bibliographic Standards Office are:

i To assist in the drafting and promotion of international bibliographic standards
ii To promote the use of national bibliographic standards within the British Library and in the UK library community generally
iii To assist with the training of the cataloguing staff within the British Library

In the international field the work of the Office is heavily concentrated on the Anglo-American Catalogue Rules Revision programme. Work on this will continue until 1977. The new edition of the Anglo-American Cataloguing Rules will form the basis of cataloguing standards for most of the English-speaking world. As a new code is adopted by national libraries and national agencies, an increasing proportion of traffic in the international MARC network will match UK library requirements. The economic benefits will be very considerable.

Closely associated with this programme is the work of the Office in the development of International Standard Bibliographic Descriptions. In 1975 a generalised description, ISBD(G), was accepted by the international library community as a basis for a family of bibliographic descriptions for all types of material. The standard for monographs, ISBD(M), is already accepted. Standards for serials, maps, music and audio-visual material are in preparation.

The Office is also responsible for the development of a set of filing rules for the British Library. These are based on a set of filing principles which the Office prepared for consideration within ISO (International Standards Organisation) as a basis for an international standard. The rules themselves will be applied within the British Library and in the bibliographic services produced by the Bibliographic Services Division. They will be presented through BSI (British Standards Institution) as a preliminary draft for a national filing standard. Across the next few years the Bibliographic Standards Office will have a special responsibility for the development of national MARC formats for special types of material. Draft national formats for serials and music were produced in 1975.

Progress in the field of MARC format and cataloguing standards is nowadays so rapid that the once impossible dream of a universal cataloguing system seems within our grasp. Regrettably this optimism cannot be extended to the other component of catalogue services – that is the use of subject systems, be they classification systems, subject headings or indexing terms. In this area no existing system seems to be the right base for a standardisation programme. The one genuinely international

system – the Universal Decimal Classification – is not widely
used in the MARC network, the one widely used system – the
Dewey Decimal Classification – is maintained by a private
foundation. In addition there is no consensus as to the essential
functions of a classification scheme. Shelf collocation or subject
retrieval? Most schemes have ambitions beyond the former,
while falling well short of the requirements of modern retrieval
systems. On the whole the time is not yet right for further
progress in this area. In spite of the problems of language it
seems that subject term systems offer the most chance of
progress. Research and development in this field is the task of
the Subject Systems Office of the Division.

The main functions of the Subject Systems Office are to:

i   Design and test indexing systems for use in the British
    Library and in the bibliographic services produced by the
    Bibliographic Services Division
ii Carry out research related to the general problems of
    indexing and to specific indexing techniques which might
    be developed for use in the multilingual MARC network

Most of the work of the Office is closely related to the
development of PRECIS (PREserved Context Indexing System) as a
universal indexing system. An early version of PRECIS was
adopted for use in BNB in 1971 and an extensively revised version
(PRECIS II) in 1974. During 1975 the system was extended to
cover the requirements of the British Catalogue of Music and
the British Education Index.

PRECIS was planned from the outset with computer production
in mind. The original research in the system had the following
objectives:

i   The computer not the indexer would generate all the index
    entries. The task of the indexer was to prepare an input
    string containing the terms which were the components of
    the index entries plus certain codes which would serve as
    computer instructions during entry generation
ii Each entry should be co-extensive with the subject as
    perceived by the indexer; that is, none of the terms necessary

for a summary subject statement should be dropped from any entry. This should be seen in contrast to the chain index where only the final entry is fully co-extensive and with a system of subject headings where a given heading may express a part but not the whole of the subject

iii   Each entry should be meaningful according to 'normal' frames of reference: that is to say, the order of terms in the entry should correspond sufficiently closely to one of the accepted orders in natural language to allow the user to interpret the entry correctly with a minimum of instruction in how to read the index.

iv   The terms in the index should be supported by an adequate system of reference (*See* and *See also*) from semantically related terms. These too would be generated by the computer from a machine held thesaurus

v   The system should incorporate an open ended vocabulary: that is to say, new terms were to be freely admitted as they occurred in the literature

PRECIS research was concentrated on an examination of the relationship between terms. Firstly the syntactical relationships between terms in index entries and secondly the semantic relationships between terms in a thesaurus which would serve as a source for *See* and *See also* references.

In PRECIS II the objectives of the research and development begun in 1968 have been largely achieved. Development work continues to test the application of the system at the most specific indexing levels in different disciplines but the system is now regarded as stable at least as far as indexing in English is concerned. The next stage of development will be to test the multilingual capacity of the system. Three areas will be investigated:

i   whether the syntactic relationships and mechanisms in PRECIS can support the generation of index entries in a wide range of languages

ii   the use of PRECIS in translingual switching systems from a source to a target language possibly *via* an artificial intermediate language

iii the simultaneous application of PRECIS in more than one
     natural language

These investigations are seen as a basic contribution towards the
long term objective of designing a common indexing system for
use in MARC and UNISIST networks.

Operations and services

Most of the staff and resources of the Division are devoted to the
production of regular internal and external publications and
services. The central operations of cataloguing, classification
and indexing form the core of these activities. At present these
are still closely associated with particular publications but the
general trend is towards specialisation according to process
rather than publication. As the flexibility of the computer
system is more fully exploited, most records will be held in a
common database and will appear in a variety of publications.
Although the Division's processing activities now extend far
beyond handling the national output, it retains and will always
retain a special responsibility for cataloguing UK current
publications. These are received through the Copyright Receipt
Office.

Under the Copyright Act of 1911 (as amended by the British
Library Act 1972) the British Library is entitled to receive,
within one month of publication, a copy of every book,
newspaper or other publication issued in the United Kingdom.
The British Library is one of six Copyright Libraries, the others
being the Bodleian Library, the Cambridge University Library,
the National Library of Scotland, the National Library of Wales,
and the Library of Trinity College, Dublin. The Copyright
Receipt Office now handles over 300,000 items each year. These
include 150,000 newspapers, 100,000 periodical issues, 23,000
books, 12,000 maps and 4,000 items of music.

The British National Bibliography is based on copyright intake
and since the formation of the Division much effort has been
applied to obtaining, as promptly as possible, all material due
under the Copyright Act. A continuous monitoring process has

been set up to check trade announcements and trade bibliographies. This has already significantly increased the amount of material being deposited under the Act. It is anticipated that the introduction of Cataloguing In Publication will result in further improvements in performance. The Copyright Office is one of the main sources of intake into the descriptive cataloguing and subsequent operations within the Division.

The descriptive cataloguing operations in the Bibliographic Services Division at present cover the English language intake of the Reference Division plus the very small percentage of copyright intake in other than English. This is the first stage in the very complex operation of integrating the BNB cataloguing systems with those of the Reference Division.

BSD cataloguing is firmly based on the Anglo-American Cataloguing Rules which were adopted by BNB in 1968. Cataloguing which is at present done elsewhere in the BL is also brought into line with AACR as the system is transferred to the computer. Within BSD the majority of items for cataloguing are still received through the Copyright Office. On receipt, a record is immediately made of the ISBN. This is subsequently transferred to a machine file so that a record of all items in progress is held. An automatic overdue message is printed out by the computer if, after a period of time, the ISBN is not linked with a BNB number which indicates that processing is complete.

At this pre-cataloguing stage all books without ISBNs are identified and a special request form is sent to the ISBN agency for the number. This cooperative arrangement ensures that virtually all books entered in the British National Bibliography ultimately have ISBNs.

Cataloguing is done on MARC record bibliographic forms in what has become almost a traditional technique. The operation differs superficially from cataloguing for manual systems in that a fairly detailed tagging system is applied by the cataloguer to the record but there is a more fundamental difference in that the cataloguer is preparing a book description which does not conform to any particular output situation. This book description is converted into machine readable form and processed through a suite of computer programs which check the accuracy of the ISBN and validate the data fields. Two forms of output are produced by the computer. The main diagnostic conforms closely to the manuscript input form for checking purposes. In addition the entries are manipulated to produce a full set of index entries which are produced in a line printer form. This reveals filing errors and other inconsistencies which are not readily apparent on the full diagnostic.

After editing, a second suite of programmes links the descriptive catalogue entries with their subject data fields and finally magnetic tape output is prepared for computer typesetting machines which produce the page negatives and from which the issues of BNB are printed.

All records prepared in the Descriptive Catalogue Section are permanently held on magnetic tape. Some of these are incomplete when first entered as it is BSD's policy to enter records in the weekly issues of BNB as quickly as possible and not to wait for missing information such as the price of a book. Some records contain errors and sometimes the form of an entry is changed as further information comes to hand. These amendments and additions are applied to machine files as part of the regular input routines so that the cumulations which are automatically prepared by the computer contain the latest and most correct information. Cumulations are produced in both microform and printed form although at present the microform versions are only available as internal files.

Apart from requiring cataloguers to work in terms of a total book entry which can be machine manipulated to form catalogue entries, the introduction of the computer into the BSD has as yet done little to change the traditional work of cataloguing. More significant changes are ahead. The new BSD computer system which will be introduced in 1978 will provide on-line access to a vast store of foreign records which will substantially provide pre-existing records for the non-copyright British Library intake. With this facility non-copyright cataloguing will be a 'search and amend' operation rather than an original cataloguing operation.

Classification and subject indexing

The majority of books processed are classified both by Dewey and Library of Congress systems and are given Library of Congress Subject Headings. All books are PRECIS indexed. Combining these operations into an integrated system is one of the most complex processes within the Division.

The processes of classification and indexing begin with the subject analysis of a document. The indexer examines the document and mentally formulates a title-like phrase which comprehends the concepts and the relationships between them which make up the subject of a work. After some training the indexer automatically formulates the subject in the form of a PRECIS string. This string, or any concept in the string, can be checked against authority files which show whether the concepts have already been indexed and whether the particular combination of concepts has occurred before. Assuming that the particular combination is new to the system, the indexer prepares a PRECIS string which is a sequence of terms with syntactic links. This string, which is a highly formalised subject statement, is passed together with the document through the Dewey classification operation, the Library of Congress classification operation and the Library of Congress subject heading operation. In each system the task is to assign a number or subject heading which matches the subject analysis contained in the PRECIS string. This is not always a straightforward operation due to the peculiarities and special features of Dewey and Library of Congress systems, but in the vast majority of cases the intellectual analysis can be expressed in DC or LC terms. When these 'conversions' are complete the PRECIS string is permanently related in the authority files and in the computer system to its DC and LC equivalents. As and when the same string is applied to another book it is not necessary to go through the special subject system routines. The book is already classified in all systems. The subject packet as it is called now goes to the indexer responsible for building up the thesaurus of

terms. Each term is examined from the special viewpoint of
semantic logic and the necessary array of synonyms and generic
links added. The complete subject packet is finally given a
number which acts as a machine address. This number is the
only item which need be applied to the next book on the same
subject. The computer generates all subject fields and all
references.

The particular significance of the PRECIS system to indexing and
classification theory and practice is the basic notion of a neutral,
formal subject statement which is used as the point of control
for the application of all special systems. PRECIS can be used as an
index system linked to any classification. This characteristic
gives it a very special potential in the development of national
bibliographic services and in the development of concept
switching systems in an international MARC network.

The operations of cataloguing, classification and subject
indexing complete the technical processing activities. They are
repeated in more or less identical sub-systems for each of the
main services produced by the Division.

BSD publications

The most important publication of the Division is the *British
national bibliography* which first appeared in 1950 and has been
published weekly ever since. The objects of the *British national
bibliography* are to list, with certain exceptions, new books
published in Great Britain; to provide an authoritative
catalogue record and Dewey classification number and to index
the precise subject of each item listed.

The items excluded from BNB are maps, certain Government
publications, cheap novelettes and publications without a
British imprint. Only the first issues of periodicals are included.
The number of entries in BNB has grown from about 13,000 in
1950 to 32,000 in 1975, which roughly represents the increase in
British monograph publishing between these dates.

Throughout its quarter of a century of publication the *British
national bibliography* has tended to set rather than to follow

bibliographic fashion. It was born at about the time the theories
of Dr Ranganathan were revitalising the study of classification in
the United Kingdom, and its successful use of facet analysis in
the application of 14th Dewey schedules in a classified national
bibliography was, in those days, a dramatic example of the
practical significance of those theories. Chain indexing as a
technique also made its impact through its use in BNB, becoming
in due course a stable item in the library school curriculum.

While the first objective of the *British national bibliography* is
always to produce a reference tool that satisfies precise
bibliographic and subject enquiries, the period from the early
1960s onwards has been one of increasing concern with
standardisation. Good cataloguing standards were achieved with
the adoption of the new Anglo-American Cataloguing Rules in
1968 and in 1971 the new 18th edition of Dewey was accepted
without modifications. The important and widespread use of
these standards in UK libraries today is in no small measure due
to their early adoption and use in BNB, thus encouraging the
processes of change in library systems.

The most recent pacesetting innovation in BNB was the
introduction of the PRECIS system of indexing in 1971. The
fundamental difference between PRECIS and chain indexing is
that in PRECIS each entry is specific, while in chain indexing only
the entry representing the last link in the chain is co-extensive
with the subject of the book. PRECIS is, *par excellence,* a machine
system although it has been applied in some small manually
produced catalogues.

The future of the *British national bibliography* is not easy to predict
but certain trends seem likely to assert themselves across the next
decade or so. As far as physical form is concerned, printing on
paper is becoming an increasingly expensive and long-drawn-out
exercise. It seems likely that the larger cumulations will, before
long, appear in microfiche form only and that the interim and
annual cumulations will be produced in both printed and
microfiche form. This will enable subscribers to take advantage
of the extremely rapid processes of computer output microfilm
techniques which can produce an Annual Volume in January as
compared with a printed version in April.

While a prediction of no change is almost as hazardous as predicting the direction of change, there does not seem to be any underlying trend which is likely to affect the general organisation of the material in the weekly issues of the *British national bibliography*. A classified arrangement is the most convenient for book selection purposes and the Dewey classification is now more firmly established than ever in the United Kingdom. In the cumulative volumes, however, some change is indicated. There is no doubt that the primary check-point in the Annual Volume is the author or title entry. Presentation of information at this point should be complete. The introduction of computer techniques has made this possible and the logic of the situation is that the Author/Title index entries in BNB should be upgraded. The use of a computer plus PRECIS also makes feasible the production of cumulation sequences arranged under subject headings constructed mechanically from PRECIS strings. The first BNB annual cumulation with citations organised under subject headings has actually been produced, but remains carefully hidden. It may be BNB's next significant bibliographic innovation.

As far as content is concerned the BNB seems likely to change in two respects. As the volume of material increases the present single comprehensive bibliographic service is likely to be replaced by a family of bibliographies covering monographs, report literature, serials, maps, music, etc. In addition the traditional BNB covering UK monograph output will be extended to include Cataloguing In Publication records. With this innovation the BNB will meet, for the first time, the highly desirable requirement of a book selection tool that the entries should be published before the publication of the book itself.

No description of the *British national bibliography* is complete without reference to the inspiring work of A. J. Wells who was appointed Editor in 1949 and who, as Managing Director, saw the BNB incorporated into the British Library in 1974. The impact that BNB has made on British librarianship during that period was very largely a result of his unflagging enthusiasm and leadership across a quarter of a century.

A national catalogue card service was established by the British National Bibliography in 1956. Although much of the operation has since been transferred from manual to computer systems, the essential feature of the card service operation remains the production of a master stencil from which entries are printed on demand. A massive file of half a million of these stencils is now held.

Although British libraries have never depended to the same extent on a centralised card service as US libraries, the BNB card service has been a significant feature of British library systems throughout the 60s and early 70s. During that period approximately 3,000,000 cards were produced and sold each year. The main market was the local authority systems where acquisitions policies closely matched the entries in the *British national bibliography*. Since 1974 the demand for catalogue cards has declined and while this is partly due to the reduced book budgets there is little doubt that the change is now structural. Card catalogues are now steadily being replaced by microform catalogues. While the heyday of the card catalogue is certainly now over, there is still no certainty as to the form of the next generation of catalogues. In the early days of computers, before the development of COM (Computer Output Microfilm) system, there was talk of a revival of the book catalogue. Microform catalogues are now on the way in – but probably also on the way out as reductions in computer storage and terminal costs make on-line systems economically feasible. A period of experimentation lies ahead.

The first issues of the *British education index* were published by the librarians of the institutes and schools of education as a small private circulation journal. Between 1962 and 1969 it was published by the Library Association and from 1970 onwards by the British National Bibliography. In 1960 BEI covered some 50 British journals. In 1975 over 160 journals were indexed. These fall into three main categories:

i   The mainstream educational journals, both general and specialised which are indexed from cover to cover
ii   Journals dealing with various aspects of the curriculum.

Articles from these journals on the techniques of teaching
the subject are indexed

iii Journals, usually of major importance in their own fields
which contain important articles relevant to educationalists,
eg *British Journal of Psychology*, *British Journal of Sociology*, etc

In addition to journals the *British education index* has, since 1972,
indexed papers from the more important conference proceedings
listed in the *British national bibliography*.

The preparation and production of BEI will be transferred to the
BSD computer system in 1976. To achieve this a special 'subject
heading' version of the PRECIS system has been developed so that
citations can be arranged under an alphabetic sequence of
headings derived from PRECIS strings.

The *British catalogue of music* is a record of new music – with the
exception of certain types of popular music – published in
Great Britain. In addition it records foreign music available in
this country through a sole agent. Entries for books about music
which have appeared in the *British national bibliography* are also
listed. BCM has been published since 1957. The catalogue appears
in two interim issues and an annual volume.

The catalogue is presented in three sections: Classified section,
Composer and Title Index section and Subject Index. The
Classified section is arranged by the E. J. Coates Music
Classification, using alphabetic notation and a faceted
construction. This has proved to be eminently suitable as a basis
for the arrangement of a music catalogue but the use of special
schemes is now in conflict with the general policy of the
Bibliographic Services Division which is to adopt standard
systems and codes wherever possible. Special consideration is
therefore being given to the possibility of utilising the music
schedules in the 19th edition of Dewey for future issues.

Books in English is the first of the British Library's major
bibliographic services to appear only in microform. In fact the
number of entries in *Books in English* is so large that the form of

publication is ultramicrofiche which has a packing density of 2380 frames per 6 × 4 transparency. An annual volume in this physical form consists of about half a dozen transparencies containing about 14,000 pages and over 300,000 entries.

The source of *Books in English* is the British Library and Library of Congress MARC files. These files are merged week by week throughout the year, and every two months the complete file, less foreign language material, is processed into a BIE master tape which is subsequently converted first to 35mm microfilm using COM techniques and then to a microfilm of the microfilm.

Apart from the obvious importance of *Books in English* as the largest and most up-to-date current bibliography of new publications in the English language, it also marks a new stage in the development of bibliographic services. By fully utilising computer technology to handle massive files and COM technology to obtain reduction ratios of 150 : 1 it is possible to achieve a currency, coverage and economy that cannot be matched by traditional print services. The microfiche bibliography created directly from databases holding MARC records supplied from many national agencies will be characteristic of the new world of bibliographic services.

The National Serials Data Centre

The National Serials Data Centre was established in 1975. It has four main functions:

i   To register all new serials published in the United Kingdom and to allocate an ISSN (International Standard Serial Number) to each

ii   To liaise with the International Centre of the ISDS (International Serials Data System) in Paris and to organise the transmission of machine readable serials records between the two centres

iii   To respond to demands from UK libraries for ISSNs for existing serials and to initiate a regular programme for the numbering of all existing UK serials

iv   Generally to promote the use of ISSNs within the UK

The British Library Bibliographic Services Division

The Centre is a national node of the International Serials Data System established within the UNISIST programme and consisting of a network of national and regional centres coordinated by an international centre in Paris. The international file which will be available to libraries through the NSDC will carry ISSNs which uniquely identify each journal and which will become increasingly important in serials processing.

British Union Catalogue of Periodicals

The National Serials Data Centre is also responsible for the preparation of the *British union catalogue of periodicals*. BUCOP, which is published by Butterworths, first appeared in 1955. It records the serial holdings of about 500 British libraries. Of these about 150 contribute on a regular basis. The production system is semi-mechanised using IBM punch cards. The publication appears quarterly with annual and multi-annual cumulations.

Since its first appearance BUCOP has been an important part of the interlending apparatus of the country. With its record of the holdings of older material not available through BLLD the existing volumes will retain their value. However, the interlending system in general has dramatically changed since the first appearance of BUCOP and in Annex C of the National Library's ADP Study it was noted that 'if the central collection were extended, BUCOP would cease to be necessary for the majority of interlending of recent material'. The central collection has been subsequently extended to the point where the vast majority of all periodical interlending is met directly from BLLD. A reappraisal of the form and content of the national serials listing service is now necessary.

Cataloguing In Publication Office

The function of the Cataloguing In Publication Office is to organise the provision of advance information professionally compiled on newly published British books. The information appears in the book itself and will be issued on MARC tapes. It is intended that it should appear in the *British national bibliography*. Thus the entire library community will find the information available in a convenient form for selection, acquisitions and cataloguing purposes.

The development of a CIP system has been a special feature of MARC services in the 70s. The original project was launched by the Library of Congress in 1971. Similar systems are now being developed in the UK, Canada, Germany and Australia. Rapid development of CIP into an international operation is now certain. It is one more stage in the progress towards a national centralised cataloguing service for libraries and it will complement the MARC records made available by the British Library.

Cataloguing In Publication requires a very high level of cooperation from publishers who are required to supply front matter (title page, introduction, etc) and, if possible, page proofs at the earliest possible moment to the British Library. The publisher is also required to fill out a cataloguing data sheet giving details about the book. From this information an authoritative catalogue record including tracings, DC and LC class numbers and Library of Congress Subject Headings is prepared and sent back to the publisher who has the information set and printed on the back of the title page as a CIP entry. When the service is fully operational the record itself may appear on MARC tapes and in BNB up to three months in advance of publication.

ISBN/BNB Number Location Service

The organisation of interlending of recently published material in English forms a predominant part of the work of the Regional Library Bureaux. From the 1950s onwards most of the Regional Bureaux have maintained their new 'current English' catalogue in BNB number sequence and have received locations in the form of lists of BNB numbers from their constituent libraries. This system was found to be efficient although there were disadvantages in that the operation was still largely manual and, more seriously, that the reporting library had to identify a BNB number for all books. Both of these disadvantages have now been removed with the transfer of the operation to an ISBN base.

ISBNs are immediately available in the book itself and the task of providing information on locations and deletions is reduced to a minimum. As more and more library systems automate their acquisitions and cataloguing operations the ISBN location data can be provided quite automatically.

In the collaborative system evolved between the BL and the Regional Library Bureaux the British Library receives location information by ISBN from the Regional Library Bureaux. This information is used to update a master location file which already in 1975 held more than half a million records under ISBNs and BNB numbers. Some of these records may have hundreds of locations. Every two months the file is output onto magnetic tape and converted, using computer output microfilm systems, to ISBN Location indexes for each library bureau.

The potential of this system is considerable particularly as the British Library operation is upgraded to an on-line system. This will provide a direct link between an ISBN and the bibliographic record as well as the possibility of direct interrogation of the database to identify holdings of a particular title.

Non-Book cataloguing services

The cataloguing activities of the Bibliographic Services Division are traditionally concentrated almost entirely on the recording of printed material. There has not yet been time to respond to the increasing awareness of the significance of non-book material – film, sound discs, tapes, slides, etc – as information carriers, but it is accepted that there is an urgent need for improved bibliographic control and recording of this type of material. The problems are considerable. There is no general archival collection similar to the printed material collection in the Reference Division; there is no legal deposit requirement; and there is no listing remotely resembling the *British national bibliography*.

However, valuable experience has been gained over the past few years through collaborative programmes with specialised institutions concerned with audio-visual services. The BSD computer system is used to produce the *Audio-visual materials for higher education* and the *Higher education learning programme information service* catalogues, both published by the British Universities Film Council. Materials covered include films, video tapes, sound recordings, tape slide programmes and film loops.

The Division fully recognises its responsibilities to provide a strong lead in this field by fostering the preparation and use of standards and by providing central processing facilities for bibliographic services. As a preliminary step a two-year pilot experiment has been designed with the assistance of the major audio-visual institutions and mounted within the Library to establish the technical feasibility of decentralised cataloguing with central processing of records. This will test the capacity of the new British Library computer system to handle complex non-book media data. The experiment will, it is hoped, provide part of the framework for a national cataloguing service in this area which should attain in time the same quality of service that the Division already offers for printed materials.

Conclusion

The British Library, through the services of the Bibliographic Services Division, has now permanently linked national library processing with national bibliographic services. This complex and difficult operation has been achieved in time for the United Kingdom library system to obtain the maximum benefit from the national on-line database services which are being designed today and will be implemented in the late 70s. As the system is developed the libraries of the United Kingdom, including the British Library, will become more and more the nodes of a single bibliographic system and a single bibliographic resource.

Bibliography

Reports:

Great Britain. University Grants Committee. Committee on Libraries. *Report* London: HMSO, 1967 (Chairman: Thomas Parry).

Report of the National Libraries Committee London: HMSO, 1969 (Cmnd 4028. Chairman: F. S. Dainton).
    The scope for automatic data processing in the British Library: report of a study (directed by Maurice B. Line) *into the*

feasibility of applying ADP to the operations and services of the British Library (edited by Maurice B. Line and Andrew Phillips) London: HMSO, 1972.

Manuals and Guides to Services:
Austin, Derek. *PRECIS: a manual of concept analysis and subject indexing* London: Council of the British National Bibliography, 1974.
  British Library MARC Services: a guide for intending users London: British Library, Bibliographic Services Division, 1975.
  UK MARC Manual. 1st standard ed. London: British Library, Bibliographic Services Division, 1975.

Background Articles and Papers:
Chaplin, A. H. Basic bibliographic

control: plans for a world system. *Aslib Proc* 27 (2) February 1975, 48–56.
  Linford, J. E. Books in English. *Microfilm Rev* 1 (3), July 1972, 207–213.
  Shaw, C. M. The *British education index:* current practice and future possibilities. *Educ Libr Bull* 17 (3), Autumn 1974, 1–10.
  Wells, A. J. New patterns in bibliographic services: the role of the Bibliographic Services Division of the British Library. *In: Proceedings, papers and summaries of discussions at the Public Libraries Conference held at Aberdeen, 16th September to 19th September 1974* London: Library Association, 1974, 53–58.
  Woodward, A. M. The National Serials Data Centre. *Program* 9 (3), July 1975, 158–165.

Chapter Eight

The British Library Research and Development Department

John C. Gray

It is perhaps a little presumptuous to contribute extensively to a centenary volume on an organisation that has lived for only one decade of the century. But the eleven years of OSTI and the British Library Research and Development Department have been so packed with incident and with changes in outlook and interest that I feel sure the contribution can provide in analytical depth what it lacks in historical span.

The origins of OSTI – the Office for Scientific and Technical Information – lie in para 35 of a forgotten annual report of a now defunct Advisory Council on Scientific policy for the year 1959–60. (Cmnd 1167. London: HMSO, 1960):

The second aspect of the [information] problem, towering above and behind the first, is created by the enormous growth of the output of scientific literature in all countries, which exceeds the capacity of the individual, even in his own specialised field, to deal with. Arrangements to "document" this material grow more and more necessary, and more and more elaborate and expensive; and in some cases it has become necessary to digest the digests, in order to keep control of the mounting mass of information. We feel that this problem will continue increasingly to impede progress unless it is recognised as meriting research in its own right, and techniques are devised for the recording and presentation of scientific information in a form in which its significance can be most readily appreciated by those who have to use it. The Council feel that serious research into the whole problem of collation and dissemination of scientific information should be undertaken forthwith, possibly under the auspices of the new National Science Lending and Reference Libraries and in association with international efforts in this sphere.

It fell to the then Department of Scientific and Industrial Research to see what it could do about the Council's recommendation, and a small number of information research projects were financed in the early 1960s out of funds for support of scientific research in universities and colleges. When DSIR was dismantled in April 1965, the information research activity went neither to a research council nor to the (then) Ministry of Technology, but to the Science Branch of the Department of Education and Science, where OSTI was born and, until April 1974, bred. It has never been under the 'auspices of the new National Science Lending and Reference Libraries', but it has always regarded them as brothers (perhaps sisters) in the DES family and these ties of kinship have been much strengthened since the merger of all three bodies in the British Library.

I have stressed the 'science' and the 'information' components of this background in order to show how much the concept and practice of a national research facility has broadened over the last ten years. OSTI quickly learned to make no distinction between natural and social sciences or between academic disciplines and areas of application in its use of the word 'science'. It also defined 'social sciences' as broadly as possible and the Library Association's Advisory Board for Research, at its first meeting, noted that very few areas of knowledge lay outside OSTI's remit. In the R & D Department of the British Library that remit has been extended to fill the gaps, though I should perhaps add that there has been no spontaneous rush of proposals for research in humanities information.

OSTI also quickly extended its interests to libraries and librarianship, avoiding as far as possible the age-old argument as to whether libraries are a subset of information or vice versa. Within two years of its creation it was supporting library-automation projects and by 1968 it had provided support for the setting up of a Library Management Research Unit at Cambridge University and a National Reprographic Centre for documentation at Hatfield Polytechnic, as well as individual projects in academic libraries, library schools, and Aslib. OSTI was not empowered to support research of interest specifically to public libraries; but the British Library is free from such restraints and, following an expression of interest in such research by the Library Advisory Council for England, it has agreed to devote part of its research funds to this purpose. The present list of supported projects is almost certainly more balanced between library and information research than at any previous time.

The present functions of the R & D Department can be arranged under two main headings: those functions that relate to the objectives of the British Library – which, of course, include the objectives of the former OSTI – and those that are delegated by DES in order to assist in the attainment of national and international policy objectives.

British Library objectives

The Board has identified five major objectives for the Library, which can be briefly summarised as follows:

i   To develop the best possible BL library services
ii To promote reference and lending networks
iii To ensure the provision of appropriate bibliographic services
iv To promote the development and use of flexible facilities for information transfer
v   To provide BL information services, where appropriate

Each of these objectives has implications for R & D, but not necessarily for the R & D Department. The first objective is mainly the concern of the Reference and Lending Divisions and most of the associated R & D is likely to be their responsibility. The same is true of the Bibliographic Services Division in relation to the third objective. The second and fourth objectives are the principal concern of the R & D Department. The fifth is one that must be tackled gradually, as need arises, and responsibility for it and for the required R & D and experimental operation is likely to be allocated on an *ad hoc* basis in the initial years. A first project, in which services for users in education will be run experimentally from (mainly) British Library data bases, involves the Bibliographic Services Division as the provider of the services and the R & D Department as coordinator of the project and supplier of funds for the research.

Taking the second and fourth objectives together, the R & D Department has the triple role of identifying priorities for research, stimulating and supporting research, and promoting application of results. It may support any sound project that can influence the effectiveness of:

i   Primary, including preliminary, publications
ii   The informal flow of information
iii The classification, cataloguing, indexing, storage, retrieval and translation of information
iv The operation and use of libraries and formal information services
v   The education and training of librarians and information specialists

In all areas of research the Department, and OSTI before it, have promoted the development and evaluation of potentially useful systems and techniques and the economic assessment of alternative methods of operation. Where necessary for research purposes they have supported the creation and evaluation of experimental services, either completely new or based on existing services, and the Library has been prepared to encourage the establishment of permanent services, for example, MEDLARS, where this appears to be in the national interest. There has also been an attempt to secure a balance between applied studies leading to immediate applications and more basic studies which can advance library and information science.

In identifying priorities for future research, the R & D Department starts from the fact that unsolicited proposals do not always match priorities, as identified by research workers and practitioners. Many unsolicited proposals are well worth supporting, but they need to be supplemented by projects that are first identified as important and then 'sold' to research teams either for developing in their own way on a grant or for conducting to specification on a contract. Methods of identifying priorities have included review studies, committees and seminars (first recommended to osti by its Advisory Committee), an r & d Department task force and an *ad hoc* working group of the Board. In autumn 1975 the Board set up an Advisory Committee for the Department, which is concerned with priorities among other matters.

In disseminating the results of research, osti and the r & d Department have been anxious that the normal channels of professional discussion – Aslib, the Library Association, the Institute of Information Scientists, the Standing Conference of National and University Libraries etc – should be preferred wherever possible. However, small *ad hoc* seminars are often needed at short notice, and then the Department is always ready to run them. Also many advisory committees exist as much to educate potential users of the results as to give expert guidance to the research itself. Finally it is necessary, as a complement to support of research, to ensure that every opportunity it taken to improve the facilities for education and training of librarians and information specialists, both on basic courses and on short courses or seminars; that sound professional information and advice is available to them when trained; and that more effective use is made of the services they offer.

Achievements and problems

It is difficult to assess the achievements of an organisation from within; much easier to assess the problems. However, I would like to say a little about what I believe to be its main achievements of the last eleven years.

First, the research has helped those responsible for the policy and management of library and information services to assess more clearly the scope for use of computer and allied technologies in various kinds of services. This has meant support for a wide variety of projects, since the potential scope for use of these technologies is wide.

Projects concerned with the computer-typesetting of bibliographies, including abstracting journals, demonstrated how to overcome the operational problems of using the techniques concerned. They also provided data on costs and showed how, in preparing the material for typesetting, one could also produce a unit record of each item in a convenient form for retrieval. The experience gained by INSPEC on this work enabled it to draft for the International Council of Scientific Unions and UNESCO a standard manual of bibliographic descriptions. This manual, after revision, is gaining world-wide support; and, at the request of UNESCO, the British Library's R & D Department has created a small UNISIST centre to maintain and promote the manual. At the time of the research computer-typesetting proved to be marginally more costly than traditional methods; but it attracted because it provided a cheap data base for other information services. Recent increases in labour costs have made computer-typesetting marginally cheaper and so have strengthened its practical advantages.

OSTI-supported projects on computer production of printed subject indexes also provided data for policy-makers and managers on the technical, operational and economic aspects of these methods. In addition they helped to develop and test new techniques of indexing, notably the articulated subject-indexing system developed by the library/information science school at Sheffield University. These techniques have had a marked influence on the development of indexing procedures in several UK information centres.

Perhaps the biggest single achievement lies in the use of computers for cataloguing and other library procedures. When OSTI received its first proposal in these fields, there was a rapidly growing interest in the possibilities of automation, but little expertise for exploring them. A serious danger existed that large resources might be wasted on a variety of incompatible local systems which later generations might come to regret. OSTI's small resources were therefore concentrated on a fairly systematic programme aimed at exploring thoroughly each group of library procedures – notably cataloguing, serials handling and monographs handling – and at determining the respective roles of local systems (in individual libraries), cooperative systems and national systems. The main results of the programme, which was mostly completed by 1973, are as follows:

i   Build-up of expertise
ii   Demonstration of a number of operational systems
iii   Stimulation of others to plan and develop their own systems
iv   Development of a cost-conscious approach to library automation
v   Greater awareness of the implications of automation for library management, especially for the need to choose between local, cooperative and national approaches to processing

Part of the success of this programme lies, I believe, in the close attention given by OSTI staff and cooperating librarians to the dissemination and understanding of results. Current and future research is likely to take this function a step further: it can consolidate the progress made on previous work, permit deeper consideration of the practical options before librarians – now that rising labour costs have increased the attractiveness of automation – and introduce the possibility of interactive library networks of the kind pioneered by the Ohio Colleges Library Centre in the USA.

Projects concerned with computerised information retrieval, though only in recent years planned as a systematic programme, have also provided policy makers and managers of services with valuable data which they can interpret and use in relation to their own decisions. The initial projects were concerned either with the development and/or evaluation of techniques or with user-orientated experimental services provided by what are known as batch-processing techniques. Together they contributed significantly to the growing body of knowledge on the strengths and limitations of batch-processing techniques both for current-awareness services and for retrospective retrieval. A similar contribution has been made in recent years by a coordinated series of user-orientated experiments with services based on on-line interactive techniques. The combined results indicate that user response to on-line retrospective search facilities – whether in the USA, in Europe or in this country –

will be positive provided that prices are at the levels envisaged by service suppliers at present and provided that the UK economic situation does not deteriorate further. Use of batch-processing systems for retrospective searches is likely to decrease in importance: but they can cheaply provide 'macroprofiles', ie current-awareness print-outs for multiple sale, and they may well continue to be used for this purpose, alongside manual systems. The prospect for selective dissemination (SDI) to individuals and single teams is more uncertain because such a service is expensive, whether done by computer or by hand and brain.

The achievements of projects not involving computers are less easy to group. Experiments with information analysis centres have provided helpful data for planners and operators of such centres on the objectives one can hope to attain with small resources and on the problems of launching and establishing centres and of securing participation by working scientists. The National Reprographic Centre for documentation has built up a substantial reputation at home and abroad for its information services, its evaluation of equipment and its forward-looking studies on reprographic techniques, especially in relating to computer output on microfilm and the reproduction of literature from remote locations.

The research contribution of Aslib, with regular support from OSTI/BL funds, has been built up to a substantial size and quality; and Aslib courses, seminars, discussion groups, lectures and conferences have become important channels for the dissemination of new ideas resulting from library and information research of all kinds. The combined work of Aslib, the Library Management Research Unit and other institutions on management problems and techniques has been widely used in existing practice and in the schools of librarianship and information science. These schools, of course, have been able to draw on completed research in many ways in order to develop or improve courses. But they have also benefited from research into the use of certain educational techniques – programmed learning, management games and demonstration of on-line systems – which OSTI and the British Library have supported.

The joint efforts of the National Lending Library and OSTI (now together in the British Library) have done much to promote interest in the improvement of user education. The contribution of NLL (Lending Division) has been to demonstrate simple forms of education for use by those responsible for giving formal education on a regular basis. OSTI (R & D Department) has supported a variety of experiments with information and liaison officers designed to identify what functions such intermediaries might perform in academic institutions, especially in relation to user education. One of these experiments was in the social sciences and formed part of a long-term programme of research designed to provide a better understanding of information needs in the social sciences and to indicate ways of encouraging rational growth of social science information services.

Two main problems must be set against these achievements. The first is the failure of information science to develop as a discipline (or a focus of disciplines) through a wide range of basic research. In all countries, even the USA, significant basic research is done by very few individuals or teams, and the UK is no exception. Despite continuous encouragement from OSTI and the British Library, hardly any new teams have come forward with original ideas and the bulk of current work falls under project heads who were already in the field five to ten years ago. This shortage is serious because there are a number of unsolved problems in information science which restrict the effectiveness of systems and services and the satisfaction of users and which can only tackled by rigorous basic research. The British Library is trying to deal with this problem by building up teams or small centres for solving specific problems – for example, one in Sheffield University to promote better methodologies and more compatible results in user studies, and another in University College, London, to develop a sound approach to the modelling of national information 'systems' and from the modelling to discover what research needs to be done in order to fill vital gaps in knowledge.

The second problem is one of maintaining a substantial flow of good unsolicited research projects in all significant fields of research – applied as well as basic. Earlier in this chapter I said that unsolicited proposals do not always match priorities as identified by research workers and practitioners. The British Library has developed (or inherited from osti) fairly satisfactory techniques for determining priorities. And before deciding to commission high-priority research on a contractual basis, it usually tries to find a suitable research worker who is sufficiently interested to work up a proposal in his own way and apply for a grant. But the flow of new research ideas can only remain healthy if a sense of priorities develops spontaneously among research workers in librarianship and information science, and a reasonably high proportion of high-priority work is genuinely unsolicited.

Organisation of research in The British Library

The discussion of British Library objectives on page 138 reveals that some of the research necessary to achieve them must be the responsibility of the operational divisions, namely that which is related mainly or entirely to the development and management of divisional operations or to the allocation of functions and physical resources between divisions. The R & D Department concentrates its effort on work which is of no more concern to the operational divisions than to any other organisation; or which can help to determine the role of the British Library in the broad network of library and information services.

This arrangement clearly calls for good coordination, ie for a forum in which needs for research can be continuously reviewed, new proposals from any part of the library can be assessed, responsibility for new projects allocated, any necessary cooperation started between the divisions and the R & D Department, and the results monitored for their implications for the Library. This forum is provided by a high-level Strategic Planning and Research Coordination Group, which is gradually creating a range of useful functions, including a regular assessment of the role that research can play in the formulation of future policy. Projects that have already germinated within this group include alternative means of transporting literature between libraries and the study of practical options in library automation which is mentioned on page 141–142.

National and international objectives

OSTI's combination of research and non-research functions made it an informal national focus for scientific and technical information. However, as Government departments and agencies enlarged their interest in information science, the need for a more formal national focus grew and such a focus was created in the Science Branch of the Department of Education and Science when OSTI became part of the British Library. DES is helped by an Interdepartmental Coordinating Committee for Scientific and Technical Information, which brings together departments and agencies with a substantial interest in information, notably DES, Department of Industry, Department of the Environment, Department of Health and Social Security, Ministry of Defence, Ministry of Agriculture, Fisheries and Food, British Library, UK Atomic Energy Authority and the Research Councils. Still in its infancy, the Committee is building up a range of functions in relation to both domestic policy and international participation in inter-governmental organisations, especially EEC. Both Chairman and Secretary of the Committee are in DES, but under an arrangement made with the Library when OSTI was transferred to it, DES delegates to the R & D Department a wide range of functions related to the operation of the national focus, including the supply of papers to the Committee, the sponsorship or coordination of research which can inform national decisions, and day-to-day liaison with other departments and agencies. On the library side, the R & D Department keeps in close touch with DES and its library advisers so that the research it supports can be of maximum value in the development of national library policy. It performs formally delegated functions on the handling of postgraduate awards in librarianship and information science. (*See* Chapter Nine, The Libraries Division of DES.)

DES also provides, through the Library, national representation on three inter-governmental committees – the UNISIST Steering

Committee and bureau (rapporteur), the OECD Information
Policy Group and bureau, and the EEC Committee for
Information and Documentation on Science and Technology.
Participation in EEC is of particular importance to the Library's
research effort, since the nine member countries are committed
to the establishment of a European network for scientific and
technical information and the Commission (the permanent
officers) have substantial funds for R & D which they spend
mainly by contracts to national organisations. The Library has
the dual role of helping, along with the Department of Industry,
to ensure that UK expertise is fully mobilised for this purpose and
that European projects, whether done in the UK or elsewhere,
are closely coordinated with the Library's work.

The EEC Committee has created several working groups and at
present the R & D Department provides national representation,
as do the relevant government departments, on groups
concerned with the technical, economic and training aspects of
the European network and with cooperation on information
activities in agriculture. Its representative is chairman of the
training group. It has arranged for the Science Reference
Library to provide representation on the industry and patents
groups and for the Lending Division to cover the groups on
biomedical and environmental information.

In July 1975 the Community decided to entrust to the PTTS (ie the
postal and telecommunications offices) the task of creating a
physical network for the communication of information. Details
are now being worked out by the PTTS which expect the network
to become operational early in 1978. The British Library,
through its R & D Department, and the Department of Industry
are together considering the implications of European
developments for the future supply of information services in
the UK and are feeding their conclusions to the Interdepartmental
Committee.

UK participation in UNESCO information activities (the established
UNISIST programme and the newer NATIS programme)
is assisted by a British National Committee with a wide
range of information, library and archive interests. The

R & D Department provides the chairman and secretary of this committee.

Finally the Library continues OSTI's practice of encouraging bilateral cooperation on research. It has jointly financed projects with its opposite numbers in the Federal Republic of Germany, France and the Netherlands and is stimulating cooperation between selected UK and US research teams, notably those engaged in modelling studies.

Further reading

OSTI – the first five years: the work of the Office for Scientific and Technical Information, 1965–70 London: HMSO, 1971.
List of grants and contracts awarded by the British Library Research and Development Department 1970–1975 (including projects taken over from the former Office for Scientific and Technical Information but excluding a few minor awards) London, British Library, 1975. (Obtainable from the R & D Department.)
OSTI Newsletter, 1966–74; *British Library R & D Newsletter*, 1974–.
Gray, John *and* Perry, Brian. *Scientific information* London: Oxford University Press, 1975. Ch 8.
UNISIST: Study Report on the Feasibility of a World Science Information System Paris: UNESCO, 1971.

UNISIST: Information Policy Objectives (UNISIST proposals) SC/74/WS/3 Paris: UNESCO, 1974.
Bundesministerium für Forschung und Technologie. *Programm der Bundesregierung zur Förderung der Information und Dokumentation (IUD-Programm) 1974–77* Bonn: 1975. (English translation due in 1976.)
Ministère de l'Industrie et de la Recherche. *BNIST Bulletin Trimestrial d'Information*, 1975–.
Commission of the European Communities. *Report on the activities of the Committee for Information and Documentation on Science and Technology (CIDST) of the European Communities for 1972 and 1973.* (EUR 5177.) Luxembourg: 1974.
Second report – 1974 to mid 1975. Luxembourg: 1976.

The Libraries Division, Department of Education and Science

Arthur C. Jones *and* Philip H. Sewell

The Department of Education and Science and public libraries

Until 1920 the central authority for the purpose of the Public
Libraries Acts was the Ministry of Health, which had inherited
its powers and duties in this respect from the former Local
Government Board. The passing of the 1919 Public Libraries
Act led to a change in these arrangements: responsibility for
confirming bye-laws, consenting to certain types of sale and
approving of the application of the proceeds, was transferred to
the Board of Education by the Ministry of Health (Public
Libraries, Museums and Gymnasiums Transfer of Powers)
Order, 1920. Only powers relating to sanction of loans and audit
of accounts were retained by the Ministry of Health. In addition,
the following powers were allocated to the Board by the Public
Libraries Act, 1919:

i   To approve the terms on which the Library Authority in an
    existing library area agrees to relinquish its powers and
    duties to the County Council
ii To make an Order rescinding, as respects a particular
    district, the resolution passed by a County Council for the
    adoption of the Public Libraries Acts
iii To confirm an Order for the compulsory purchase of land
    by a Library Authority which is a Local Education
    Authority for the purpose of Part II of the Education Act,
    1902

In its annual report for 1933 the Board set out the nature of its
responsibility for public libraries, drawing attention to the fact

149

that public library provision was discretionary, not mandatory, and that

the public library service has no essential connexion with any Government Department. The Ministry of Health sanction loans for libraries as for other services; and the Board of Education confirm, allow or disallow byelaws made by Library Authorities with respect to libraries under Section 3 of the Public Libraries Act, 1901. Certain other semi-legal powers are also vested in the Board of Education who have exercised a benevolent interest in the progress of the movement. But neither Department has any power to inspect or regulate the conduct of public libraries.

This situation remained unchanged until, in 1957, the second of three White Papers on the reorganisation of local government mentioned that the Minister of Education proposed to set up a committee to consider the exercise of local government functions in respect of public libraries. The committee, under the chairmanship of Sir Sydney Roberts, was appointed later that year. Its report, published in 1959 and supplemented by the reports of two specialist working parties on library cooperation and standards of public library service in England and Wales, paved the way for the Public Libraries and Museums Act, 1964. This Act designated library authorities covering the whole of England and Wales, allocated to each the duty to provide a comprehensive and efficient library service, and gave to the Secretary of State the duty 'to superintend and promote the improvement of the public library service provided by local authorities in England and Wales, and to secure the proper discharge by local authorities of the functions in relation to libraries conferred on them as public library authorities by or under this Act'. The 1964 Act therefore significantly changed the role of the Secretary of State, and hence of the Department of Education and Science.

The role of Libraries Division

From 1957, when the Roberts Committee was appointed, responsibility for public library matters within the Department had been allocated to a Libraries Section within other branches, ultimately 'Further Education II' Branch, which was concerned with various aspects of informal further education including the youth service, the Sports Council, and adult education undertaken by the 'responsible bodies', namely university extra-mural departments and the Workers Educational Association. In April 1969 Libraries Division and the Office of Scientific and Technical Information (OSTI) were brought together to form a new Libraries and Information Systems Branch. This, however, was shortlived, and a change in the alignment of ministerial responsibilities resulted in July 1970 in the formation of the present Arts and Libraries Branch, while OSTI became for a time a division of Science Branch before being transferred in 1974 to the British Library. The post of Library Adviser, which had been created by temporary secondment in 1961, was permanently established in 1964, a second Library Adviser was appointed in the following year and the team has since built up to four. The present (1976) position of Libraries Division within the Department is represented in Fig. 9.1.

Although Libraries Division came into existence as a result of the Public Libraries and Museums Act 1964, it is concerned with matters affecting libraries of all kinds. Current responsibilities of the Division include:

i   National Libraries policy and all general policy matters relating to libraries
ii   Financing of the British Library
iii Administration of the Public Libraries and Museums Act, 1964, in respect of libraries
iv Postgraduate awards in librarianship
v   Public Lending Right

In addition the Department of Education and Science is concerned to ensure both the effectiveness of a wide range of educational institutions from schools to polytechnics, and liaison with universities, in each of which the library must play an important part. Libraries Division is the part of the Department which provides advice and professional assistance in these areas, complementary to those of Her Majesty's Inspectorate.

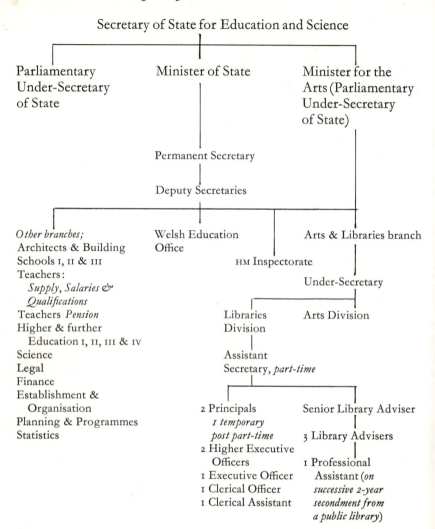

Secretary of State for Education and Science

| Parliamentary Under-Secretary of State | Minister of State | Minister for the Arts (Parliamentary Under-Secretary of State) |

Permanent Secretary

Deputy Secretaries

| *Other branches;* Architects & Building Schools I, II & III Teachers: *Supply, Salaries & Qualifications* Teachers *Pension* Higher & further Education I, II, III & IV Science Legal Finance Establishment & Organisation Planning & Programmes Statistics | Welsh Education Office | Arts & Libraries branch |

HM Inspectorate

Under-Secretary

| Libraries Division | Arts Division |

Assistant Secretary, *part-time*

| 2 Principals *1 temporary post part-time* 2 Higher Executive Officers 1 Executive Officer 1 Clerical Officer 1 Clerical Assistant | Senior Library Adviser 3 Library Advisers 1 Professional Assistant (*on successive 2-year secondment from a public library*) |

Figure 9.1.

The wide range of responsibilities of the Division, with its implicit recognition of the inter-dependence of libraries, is reflected in the 1964 Act. The Act required the appointment of two Library Advisory Councils, one for England and one for

Wales, with a duty 'to advise the Secretary of State upon such matters connected with the provision or use of library facilities whether under this Act or otherwise as they think fit, and upon any question referred to them by him'. Libraries Division provides the Secretariat and professional assessors for the English Council, and one of the Library Advisers also serves as assessor on the Welsh Council, so that the full scope of the Councils' interests is reflected in the work of the Division.

The interests of the Councils and the activities and specific responsibilities of the Division have varied so much from year to year since 1965 that it is necessary briefly to review the period as a whole to convey something of the Division's work. An appreciation of the many changes in pattern and programme during the last ten years may provide some basis for anticipating the likely nature of the work during the next decade.

Studies of public library services

In April 1965 the Department issued Circular 4/65, which explained the new Act and the responsibilities which would henceforth fall upon library authorities, and drew attention to the report of the Working Party on Standards of Public Library Service which contained useful guidance as to what constituted a comprehensive and efficient library service. There was an urgent need at this time to establish criteria by which to determine the extent to which authorities were meeting their obligations. This was especially important because Section 6 of the 1964 Act made provision for the assessment of library services in county district authorities with populations below 40,000 and in those cases where the Secretary of State was satisfied that the result would be beneficial he was empowered to recommend to Parliament the transfer of library powers to the respective county councils. With the cooperation of the authorities concerned, therefore, the Library Advisers undertook trial inspections of library services in two counties (Shropshire and East Suffolk) and two county district library authorities (Widnes and Kidderminster) which would not have been affected by this provision in the Act, and established certain methods of assessment which were developed later. The 1964 Act was, however, soon followed by proposals for the thorough-going reorganisation of local government, and this Section of the Act was never implemented. Eventually the Local Government Act, 1972, removed library powers from all the authorities to whom it might have applied.

Since 1965 the Library Advisers have carried out an extensive programme of inspections, studies and less formal visits to library authorities, and up to 1973 – the year before local government reorganisation – seventy-seven library services had been examined and reports sent to the authorities concerned. During the late 1960s inspections usually came about in one of three ways – by invitation of the authority, as a result of complaints received by the Department, or on the initiative of the Department. At first, library services were usually examined comprehensively, but this was a considerable undertaking, involving the preliminary collection of data, a week or so 'in the field', and the drafting of an exhaustive report which might be spread over many months. Later, therefore, it became more usual to study particular areas of library provision, such as the effect of inadequate bookfunds, the provision of mobile libraries as compared with small static service points, or proposals for resiting a branch library. By 1970 the Division was beginning to devote more of its attention to studies which would be beneficial to libraries as a whole. The most considerable of these was an examination of the implications of local government reorganisation for library services throughout south and west Yorkshire. This occupied the Library Advisers for much of 1971 and provided the basis not only for reports to the authorities involved but also for a publication of more general interest, *The Public Library Service: Re-organisation and After*, which offered guidance on many aspects of public library service which were likely to come under review. The report of a complementary study of Devon and Cornwall, in which some of the problems of rural areas were examined, has been made available by the two authorities concerned.

After a gap of two years while local government underwent reorganisation, the programme of visits was resumed in 1975. The main need now was to establish contact as quickly as possible with librarians in the new authorities, to assess the ways in which library services had been restructured and to acquire some appreciation of outstanding problems. The method adopted has been a series of one-day visits, mostly taken up by discussions with chief librarians and other senior staff, and it has been possible during the first year to make informal visits of this kind to one third of all the library authorities in England and Wales. The lessons learned will help to determine the Division's own future pattern of work, and may well provide the basis for a further publication. In the meantime the Division and the Advisory Councils are drawing on the fruit of these contacts in considering what steps may best be taken to preserve the essential basis of public library service during times of economic stringency.

Legislation

Three areas of legislation, or potential legislation, have occupied the attention of Libraries Division within the last decade – the British Library and Public Lending Right (which are discussed later) and the libraries function as part of the general reorganisation of local government as eventually provided for by the Local Government Act 1972. In respect of public libraries the main decision to be taken by Government was whether responsibility for the library service should be allocated to authorities in the first or second tier. During the period leading up to legislation many interested bodies, including the Library Association, the Society of County Librarians, and the Smaller Public Libraries Group, offered their advice in writing and in interviews with the Minister. The duty of the Department's professional advisers in this situation was to ensure that the arguments being put forward, and their implications, were fully understood both by Ministers and by senior civil servants.

Two other duties fell to the Division as a consequence of the Local Government Act 1972. Section 207 of that Act provided that the new district councils in Wales which met certain criteria could apply to be designated as library authorities – the only category of library authority whose designation was at the discretion of the Secretary of State. Each of the many applications received had to be carefully evaluated, and a factual statement prepared for consideration by the Minister. The Division was also involved in arrangements to receive the series of deputations, from both districts and counties, which sought to supplement their written statements.

Section 101 of the Act allowed designated authorities to enter into arrangements for the delegation of certain functions which became known as agency arrangements, and the Division was concerned in the drafting of Circular 5/73 which contained advice as to those aspects of the library service which might be considered for possible agency arrangements. Local authorities which failed to reach agreement on agency for public libraries could seek a direction from the Secretary of State, and the processing of such applications was a further responsibility of the Division during 1973. It will be apparent therefore that the period of local government reorganisation was a busy one for Libraries Division as well as for library authorities, and the decision to suspend for a time the programme of visits was not taken solely in the interests of the authorities.

The Library Advisory Councils

The two Library Advisory Councils appointed under the 1964 Act provide the principal means by which the Minister and Libraries Division keep in touch with informed opinion concerning libraries. The Branch and the Councils form a partnership which has become increasingly productive in recent years as methods of working together by means of groups and working parties have evolved. From their combined discussions and studies have come a number of reports of considerable practical value, and the Councils have submitted observations to several Government committees, including the Russell Committee on Adult Education and Bullock Committee on Reading and the Use of English. In 1976 the major preoccupation of the English Council is with library services for the disadvantaged, while the Welsh Council has a working party studying library services in rural areas. The English Council recently asked the Department to forward to the British Library a statement of its views as to topics in the public library field which urgently need research, and the Welsh Council has submitted to the Minister proposals for the organisation of industrial and commercial library services in Wales. A small joint working group of the two Councils has been examining, with representatives of the book trade, the scope for bookselling in public libraries. These examples illustrate the range of interests and intensity of activity of the two Councils, to whose work the Division contributes technical papers, supplementary studies and secretarial services. Year in and year out, it is likely that a quarter of the effort of the Division is channelled through the Library Advisory Councils.

A glance at the involvement of Libraries Division in statistics and manpower will serve to illustrate relations between the Division, the Library Advisory Councils, the Library Association, other Branches of the Department and other bodies.

Library statistics

The first *Public libraries circular letter* issued by the Division, in April 1965, explained that instead of collecting its own statistical data annually from public library authorities the Department had arranged to make use of the public library statistics already collected and published annually by the Institute of Municipal Treasurers and Accountants (now the Chartered Institute of Public Finance and Accountancy) and the Society of County Treasurers. These associations agreed to adapt their questionnaire to meet the needs of Libraries Division, and since then the Division has taken the lead in calling one or two meetings each year at which representatives of the bodies concerned, including the Library Association and the Statistics Branch of the Department, monitor progress and consider the need for further modification of either the questionnaire or of the published tables.

In 1967, at the request of the Library Association, a study group was formed to examine the country's requirements for library statistics in view of the likely requirements of UNESCO, and in 1970 representatives of Libraries Division, the Library

Table 9.2

Public Libraries Circular Letters

No	Date	Reference	Subject/heading
1	20 4 65	A 41/12/20	Public Libraries and Museums Act 1964 – Public Library Statistics
2	15 12 65	A 41/12/56	Public Libraries and Museums Act 1964 – Library Model Byelaws
3	1 6 65	PL 1/ 5/04	Public Libraries and Museums Act 1964 – Loan Sanctions, Tenders
4	24 5 68	PL 1/ 5/07	Public Libraries and Museums. Capital Expenditure 1968/69
5	6 2 69	PL 1/ 5/014	Public Libraries and Museums. Capital Expenditure 1969/70
6	22 1 70	LS 11/ 5/023	Public Libraries and Museums. Capital Expenditure 1970/71
7	29 9 70	LS 11/ 5/026	Public Libraries and Museums. Capital Expenditure 1971/72
8	27 11 70	AL 7/ 4/04	Capital Expenditure on Public Libraries and Museums
9	17 3 71	AL 1012/02	Library Services in Hospitals
10	2 4 71	AL 4/ 6/02	Library Advisory Councils for England and Wales – Survey of Serials
11	26 4 71	AL 14/ 6/04	Collection of Library Statistics 1971/72
12	23 5 71	AL 1010/013	Staffing in Public Libraries
13	12 1 72	LS 19/ 8/014	Library Advisory Councils for England and for Wales: Report on Public Library Service Points with Notes on Staffing
14	13 5 72	PL 30/ 4/011	Public Lending Right
15	14 7 72	AL 1044/03	Documentation on Community Law and the Laws of Member States
16	31 10 73	AL 3/ 4/010	Transport for Inter-Library Loans
17	31 12 73	AL 1044/038	European Community Law and the Law of Member States
18	1 7 74	AL 1032/026	Public Lending Right
19		AL 1077/01	Programme of Work with Adult Illiterates
20		AL 1034/025	Local Library Cooperation in Support of Higher Education
21		AL 1032/032A	Public Lending Right
22	10 3 75	AL 6/18/02	Automation Guidelines for Public Libraries
23	25 3 75	AL 1010/070	Public Libraries and Cultural Activities

Note: A number of these circular letters are merely covering letters attached to the appropriate report.

Association and the Standing Conference of National and University Libraries (SCONUL) were included in the committee of experts called together by UNESCO with the object of achieving a greater degree of rationalisation and standardisation of library statistics. Steps have since been taken to bring United Kingdom statistics closer to the form recommended by UNESCO.

For many years statistics relating to university libraries have been collected by the University Grants Committee and published in the Department's Statistics of Education series. In 1974, after having assisted the Library Association's Colleges of Technology and Further Education Group to collect statistics for several years, the Department assumed responsibility for publishing Statistics of Libraries in Major Establishments of Further Education for the United Kingdom for the year 1973–74. This has made possible a much fuller return from colleges of data which is in line with UNESCO's Recommendations on Library Statistics.

The staffing needs of libraries

In 1965 the Library Association drew to the attention of the Department the importance of making a study of the number of qualified librarians likely to be required in the foreseeable future. At the first meeting of the Library Advisory Council for England (LAC(E)) in February 1966, they were asked by the Minister to undertake this study, including the implications for education and training. A joint committee of the English and Welsh Councils submitted a report (which became known as the Jessup Report) in 1968. This made a number of recommendations about the initial and subsequent education and training of librarians and included estimates of likely demand which had been prepared by Libraries Division. These estimates showed a likely level of production of qualified librarians considerably in excess of the anticipated demand, and suggested, therefore, that no further expansion in the output from schools of librarianship was likely to be justified in the immediate future. This view, and the intention of the Secretary of State to hold at its present level the output of qualified librarians, was communicated to authorities in Circular 6/69, and followed up by a Circular Letter in 1974 (from the Branch directly responsible for librarianship education) when output again seemed likely to exceed demand.

It was fully recognised that the estimates contained in this report were based on a number of assumptions, particularly with regard to staffing standards in public libraries, which needed further study, and in their next report, on Public Library Service Points (1971), the Councils urged that investigation should be undertaken as soon as practicable into the utilisation of staff of different types and qualifications in public libraries. The outcome of this recommendation was a research project funded by the Department and undertaken by LAMSAC during 1971–73, which had as its main object the identification of criteria by which to establish staffing standards for all types of public library staff other than manual workers. The report of the project was published in 1976.

Other studies in connection with manpower planning have been undertaken by the Division in association with the Statistics Branch of the Department. At six-monthly intervals, starting in 1970, the output and employment of newly qualified librarians has been monitored with a view to determining whether the capacity of library schools is adequate or excessive. In March 1972 the first census of staff in librarianship and information work in the United Kingdom was carried out and the second will be in 1976. Then, with the cooperation of the Association of British Librarianship and Information Science Schools, more detailed data has been collected since 1973–74 on those entering and leaving full-time courses.

The Jessup Report's concern for the initial and post-experience training of librarians has been followed up both by the Department's Committee on Postgraduate Awards in Librarianship and Information Science and the Committee on Short Courses. Both these bodies are the joint responsibility of the British Library's R & D Department and Libraries Division, the latter being set up under the aegis of OSTI. The Division also keeps in touch with developments in professional and sub-professional librarianship education and training through representation on appropriate committees (currently eight in number, plus their working groups).

Buildings

Until 1971 Libraries Division received information about all proposals for public library building in England and Wales, and was required to select, on grounds of greatest need, those which should be recommended to receive loan sanction from the limited sum available. A most valuable by-product of this exercise was the many consultations which took place between a Library Adviser, one of the Department's architects, and officials of the authority submitting the proposals. From April 1971 public libraries have been within the category of 'locally determined schemes', for which an annual block allocation of capital payments has been made available directly to authorities. Since then, therefore, the recommendation of loan sanction has ceased to occupy the time of the Division, and the amount of information passing through the Division about new library buildings has been greatly reduced.

As early as 1968 the Library Association submitted to the Department proposals for a comprehensive research project to examine and evaluate trends which may influence the future development of the services and buildings of libraries of all kinds. Although it was not possible for the Department to find the funds necessary to support such a comprehensive study, it did sponsor in 1971–72 a more modest piece of research, the supervision of which was undertaken jointly by Libraries Division and Architects and Building Branch. This was a study of public libraries and their use, the main object of which was 'to identify the factors which influence, or should influence, the grouping, location, distribution and inter-action of library services within the community'. The report of this study concluded with the recommendation that the Development Group of Architects and Building Branch should undertake a public library development project, on similar lines to the development projects which it had hitherto undertaken for schools and other educational buildings. This recommendation was accepted, and Libraries Division cooperated in the

identification of a suitable project and in the preliminary studies
of existing libraries. One of the Library Advisers is a member of
the team which is undertaking design work for a projected new
library at Penrith in Cumbria.

Library cooperation and National Libraries

Both the Roberts Committee and the 1964 Act, while concerned
mainly with public libraries, recognised the interdependence of
libraries of all kinds. The former gave rise to the establishment
of a Working Party on Library Cooperation which reported in
1962. The latter included not only Section 2, which gave the
Library Advisory Councils a very wide remit, but Section 3,
requiring the establishment of regional systems for the purpose
of library cooperation. In the event, because of the need to wait
first for local government reform and then to give time to assess
the impact of the British Library on requirements for regional
cooperation, statutory regions have not been set up. However,
the Division has kept closely in touch with developments in
regions. This has involved encouraging the former National
Central Library's policy of central book supply, assisting the
formation of the London and South Eastern Regional Library
System and its experiments with computer applications, and
keeping regular liaison with regional developments via the
National Committee on Regional Library Cooperation.

With the special needs of public libraries in mind, the
Department's library advisers, following the area study referred
to earlier, encouraged the development of the Yorkshire and
Humberside Joint Libraries Committee which added to the
interlending role of the former Yorkshire Region a number of
other services, many based on those provided by the former
West Riding County Library. Certain kinds of cooperation
between libraries can best be carried out in local informal
groups. With the needs of those engaged in higher education in
mind, the Department commissioned a two-year study by the
University of Sheffield Postgraduate School of Librarianship and
Information Science of the needs of such people and the
resources available to them in a locality to explore possibilities
of making the maximum use of local resources.

The Division has, of course, been continuously involved with the evolution of policy on national libraries. The first official minutes on the need for a rationalised national library system originated in Libraries Division in April 1965. The Division was represented on the UGC's Parry Committee and maintained close liaison with the Dainton Committee on National Libraries, particularly through the Library Advisory Council whose recommendations to that Committee clearly carried weight, as may be seen in their published Memorandum of Evidence. Following the Government's acceptance of the main recommendations of the Dainton Report, the Division was involved in the preparation of the White Paper on the British Library and the British Library Act 1972 and in the work of the Library's Planning Committee. The Division now has responsibility for certain aspects of the implementation of the Act, particularly in respect of buildings and finance.

The advent of the British Library has, of course, had an impact on the work of the Library Advisory Council for England which in 1974 invited its Chief Executive, Dr Hookway, to address it. The Council set up a Working Party in 1974 which reported on the allocation of resources of libraries of all kinds. It is now considering the case for further provision for national library planning and coordination.

College and school libraries and resource centres

In addition to the functions mentioned, the presence of the Library Advisers within the Department has led to their being called on to help in the formulation of standards for libraries in colleges of further education, colleges of education and polytechnics. The last decade has seen an unprecedented expansion in college library facilities and the Advisers have been called on, in conjunction with the Department's Architects and Building Branch, to comment on plans for expanding old library premises and building new libraries. Links with the university library sector have been maintained both informally, through SCONUL, and by invitations to serve on relevant UGC Committees or Working Parties. Much informal advice has also been given to college authorities and their librarians, and the

Advisers have contributed to HMI short courses for school and college librarians and to those organised by the Further Education Staff College. This advice and contact with college librarians was especially necessary in view of the lack of up-to-date published guidance.

Attempts have been made to issue a revised version of Circular 322, 'Libraries in Technical Colleges', issued in 1957. An agreed version was drawn up but delay in publication, due first to economic pressures, then to the changed situation following the White Paper 'Education a framework for expansion' (Cmnd 5174), caused the document to become outdated.

Both the Advisory Councils and Libraries Division have been concerned with school libraries. The nature and quality of the support services offered by public libraries have been an obvious point of interest, but this has inevitably had to be extended to the operation and use of school libraries themselves. Hence the Advisers have made many visits to schools with HMIs, and are currently involved, with the Library Association, School Library Association and the former Association of Teachers in Colleges and Departments of Education, in discussion of the training requirements of school librarians.

In recent years the Advisers have played an active role with the Council for Educational Technology, the British Library and with HMI in involving policy and mechanisms for using non-book materials in association with traditional library provision. The LAC(E) has before it a Report on New Media in Libraries, and the Advisers are involved with the British Library in developing bibliographical controls. The development of these media has also, of course, implications for the design of school and college buildings, for public library support services and, indeed, for maximising all publicly provided multi-media resources (as has been demonstrated so well at Newcastle). It has implications also for professional education and for the staffing of school and college libraries and resource centres. All these matters have in various ways called for consideration in Libraries Division.

Special library services

Since April 1974 the areas of public library authorities have, with a few exceptions, been coterminous with those of Area Health Authorities. This makes possible more effective cooperation between public libraries and medical and hospital library services. Possibilities for furthering this cooperation have been studied both in the context of the LAC's Working Party on Library Services to the Disadvantaged and in specific areas such as Wales and Cheshire.

The Division has also cooperated with the Home Office in reviewing standards of provision of libraries in penal establishments. The possible contribution of public libraries to the provision of library services to local government officers and members has also been studied. The Division and the LAC(E) took the initiative in encouraging the establishment of a special library service to immigrant groups by the Birmingham City Libraries.

Research

Reference has already been made to several research projects sponsored by Libraries Division as part of the Department's research programme. Other similarly financed projects whose reports have been published have dealt with the use of automatic data processing in the British Library, automation guidelines for public libraries, and transport for inter-library loans. For each of these the Division has provided not only financial support but also guidance and consultation through the Library Advisers and, often also, a steering committee. The Division can only finance research projects which are considered necessary to enable it to carry out its own responsibilities. Support for projects of more general interest has to be sought elsewhere, notably from the British Library Research and Development Department, with whom the Library Advisers keep closely in touch.

Cooperation with Her Majesty's Inspectorate

Close working relations have been established with HM Inspectorate. The Library Advisers regularly attend meetings of the HMI Libraries Committee and members of the Inspectorate serve as assessors on the two Advisory Councils. Local HM Inspectors are consulted as a matter of course about any major inspection undertaken by Library Advisers, and Library Advisers have been invited to participate with HMI in several studies of the provision and use of books and libraries in schools and colleges. In 1971 inspectors and advisers worked together in an evaluation of dual-purpose libraries which combined service to the public with service to a school or college.

UK and international involvement

The Division is of necessity involved in, and frequently contributes to, a wide range of conferences in the UK and, occasionally, abroad. One of the Library Advisers has acted as Adviser to the Department of Education of Northern Ireland on a secondment basis since 1967, a period which has seen the preparation and implementation of the Northern Ireland Education and Libraries Board Order 1972. (Scotland has, of course, its own administration for libraries, a post of HM Inspector (Librarianship and Library Services) was created in 1975, and the Library Cooperation Committee of the National Library of Scotland has been formally recognised as the official advisory body on library services in Scotland).

The DES Advisers have contributed to the revision of the International Federation of Library Association's Standards for Public Libraries, particularly those for buildings. The Division was represented in the UK delegation to UNESCO's NATIS Conference in 1974 and it is also represented on the British National Committee for UNISIST and NATIS. Its advice is regularly sought by the Ministry of Overseas Development on library matters relating to UNESCO and advice is also given via their Books Coordinating Committee on the detailed work of the British Council's book presentation programme.

Although the main burden of liaison with the EEC's Committee for Information and Documentation on Science and Technology rests with the Department of Industry and the British Library's R & D Department, the Division is represented both on the

Working Group for the Training of Specialists and on the UK's main briefing body for liaison with Europe: the Inter-Departmental Coordinating Committee for Scientific and Technical Information. Overseas visitors who are interested in library policy and development are regularly received.

Public Lending Right

Libraries Division has for many years been involved in considering the case for reimbursing authors for the use of their books in publicly-supported libraries and the mechanism for doing so. Consultations have been held with the Arts Council, the Library Association and the Society of Authors and more recently the Writers' Action Group. There was evidence of support from members of Parliament on both sides of the House for the introduction of a Public Lending Right. A series of technical investigations has been carried out by a Group established to explore the feasibility of a practical scheme, and the results have demonstrated that a scheme can be worked out. The Queen's Speech opening the current session of Parliament reaffirmed the Government's intention, announced in 1974, to present proposals to Parliament. The Minister for the Arts has given assurance that no charges will fall on public libraries in any scheme for making payments to authors.

DES Publications relating specifically to libraries

Circulars:

4/65 *Public Libraries and Museums Act 1964.*
6/69 *The future supply and training of librarians.*
5/73 *Local government reorganization and the public library service.*
6/73 *Constitution of district councils in Wales and public library authorities.*

See also Table 9.2 for a list of Public Libraries Circular Letters.

Library Information Series:

1. *The purchase of books by public libraries* HMSO, 1972, 20*p*.
2. *The public library service: reorganisation and after* HMSO, 1973, 47*p*.
3. *Aspects of public library management* HMSO, 1973, 47*p*.
4. *Public libraries and their use* HMSO, 1973, £1·10.
5. *Public libraries and cultural activities* HMSO, 1975, 65*p*.
6. *Automation guidelines for public libraries* HMSO, 1975, 95*p*.
7. *The staffing of public libraries* 3 vols, HMSO, 1976.

Other Reports:

Library Advisory Councils (England and Wales) *A report on the supply and training of libraries* HMSO, 1968.
Public libraries service points: a report, with some notes on staffing HMSO, 1971.
Royal Institute of Public Administration. *Local Government operational Research Unit. Transport for*

inter-library loans DES, 1973.
Department of Education and Science *Census of staff in librarianship and information work in the United Kingdom, 1972* DES, (1975).
– *Public Lending Right: report of the Working Party appointed by The Paymaster General* HMSO: 1972, 30*p*.
– *Public Lending Right: an account of an investigation of technical and cost aspects* HMSO: 1975, £1·50.
– *Public Lending Right: final report of an investigation of technical and cost aspects* HMSO: 1976, 80*p*.
– Reports on Education. Number 34, February 1967. *Public libraries and education*. Reports on Education. Number 57, July 1969. *The Public library service today*. The scope for automatic data processing in the British Library 2 vols. HMSO, 1972.

Reports of research sponsored by DES but published elsewhere:

W. H. Shercliff *and others. College of Education libraries research project: final report* 2 vols. Manchester: Didsbury College of Education, 1973.
T. D. Wilson *and* W. A. J. Marsterson. *Local library cooperation* University of Sheffield, Postgraduate School of Librarianship and Information Science, 1974. (Occasional Papers no 4.)

Other papers:

E. M. Broome. Library manpower planning. *Aslib Proc* 25 (11), November 1973.

A. C. Jones. Dual use of libraries. *Trends in Education* 31 July 1973.
P. H. Sewell. Government concern for libraries in *British librarianship and information science, 1966-70*, ed H. A. Whatley. Library Association, 1972.

Surveys of students of librarianship and information science completing courses in UK colleges appeared in *Libr Ass Rec* 75 (10), 1973; 76 (8), 1974; 77 (1), 1975 and 77 (12), 1975.

Public libraries

Alexander Wilson

The external environment of the British public library service
has changed rapidly and fundamentally since 1965 and further
change, mostly for the worse, can be anticipated in the period up
to 1980. As a result of structural reorganisation in local
government, the great majority of the population are now served
by a library authority large enough to afford to give the
'comprehensive and efficient library service' which became a
statutory responsibility under the Public Libraries and Museums
Act, 1964. Owing to the relatively low priority given to library
development, by no means all of the new library services have
access to such resources although the minimum standards
recommended by the Bourdillon Working Party in 1962 have
been attained or exceeded by most of the urban authorities, with
the county authorities more or less attaining these levels of
provision.

A considerable number of library systems are now controlling
their acquisition, cataloguing and circulation systems by
computer. The profession has shown an ability to absorb an
unprecedented rate of expansion and structural change. It is a
less healthy sign for the future of the service that professional
objectives, activities and the organisation to provide them have
not changed very much when compared with the best current
practice forty years ago. The number of people using public
libraries has remained fairly steady over the past ten years and in
many places people in authority have an unfairly limited view of
the usefulness of the service and of its social importance. This
may in part be a matter of presentation since the continuous

provision of lending and reference library services on however large a scale does not provide good copy for the mass media and there are rarely policy issues to draw the attention of decision makers.

Central Government

Central Government began to take a renewed interest in the library services of the country with the appointment of the Roberts Committee in 1957 at which time there were about 500 independent public library systems in England and Wales alone, of which seventy-four served populations below 20,000. The Roberts Report[1] paved the way for the Public Libraries and Museums Act, 1964 which conferred statutory responsibility on library authorities in England and Wales to provide a service to standards which would be determined by the Minister responsible for education. There are powers in the Act to allow what is now the Department of Education and Science (DES) to review the efficiency of authorities under 40,000 population but these were never exercised because implementation of a good deal of the Act was inhibited by the onset of local government reorganisation which has restructured library authorities throughout Great Britain and Northern Ireland on a much larger scale than envisaged in the 1964 Act. In 1969 the DES formed an Arts and Libraries Branch which includes a small team of professional Library Advisers. Their indirect influence on the development of public libraries has been out of all proportion to their numbers. Indeed, the combination of economic stringency and local government reorganisation has prevented much direct pressure by central government to improve library services at the local level. Librarians were over-sanguine in expecting that superintendence by the DES would involve the direct control over programmes and finance which is customary in the schools system.

The DES has a wide remit within which public libraries, museums and the arts take their place with adult education and youth and community services as desirable rather than basic provision.

Authoritative advice on local government reorganisation from the DES undoubtedly influenced the placing of libraries on the

same tier of administration as education everywhere except in
Scotland, where the Wheatley Commission classified libraries as
an amenity service suitable for the lower tier and thus effectively
separated public and school library services.

As a result of further advice from the DES, central departments
responsible for the hospitals and prisons have accepted the
public library system as an agent for rechargeable library and
information services. Various DES publications[2] have been of
considerable value to chief librarians in urging better provision.
Even before the Act many smaller library authorities were
persuaded by the Roberts Report to improve services under the
threat of possible loss of library powers. In its turn, the
Bourdillon Report[3] has been most influential in raising
provision to standards which were in 1975 generally
approaching or surpassing the minimum standards
recommended in that document. These were based on best
current practice about 1960. The Library Advisory Councils for
England and for Wales set up under the Act may have
disappointed the profession by an apparent lack of impact which
is explained by the reluctance of central government
departments over recent years to recommend proposals
involving additional expenditure by local authorities.

Nevertheless, the Advisory Councils have themselves been
responsible for several valuable reports guiding library policy on
topics like library management and the provision of cultural
activities.

The LAMSAC Report on the Staffing of Public Libraries is by far
the most important research project to be funded by the DES.
Although this is not officially published at the time of writing, it
is likely that the work study carried out by a mixed team of
management experts and librarians over a period of two years
will prove invaluable to library managers in assessing the
manpower implications of basic and specialised public library
services. It was necessary for the investigation to begin by
establishing norms of activity for a range of services, some of
which had previously been described only in philosopical terms
or as reports of local initiatives.

Library expenditure

The mechanism of central government control of public library expenditure has changed during the period under review. At first the DES had direct control over loan sanctions for new capital expenditure and although the amounts available at £3·6 million to £5·7 million per annum were disappointingly small in relation to need the DES did in a short period establish a system of priorities and cost limits. Value for money was further obtained by the adoption of systems building and standard designs for many of the new county branch libraries. It has been estimated that in 1960 Britain needed from 600–800 new library buildings, including the replacement of many obsolescent central libraries. Large inroads have been made in this programme including the erection of major buildings in some provincial cities. Prime mention must go to the new Birmingham Central Library which is currently the largest public library building in Europe until it is exceeded by the major extension to the Mitchell Library at Glasgow. From 1971 local authorities were allowed to decide their own priorities for building in what were called non-key sectors including libraries. Freed from the DES control which had rationed developments to less than 40% of applications in some years, a number of enterprising local authorities embarked on ambitious programmes only to be halted indirectly by the general government restrictions on the total allocation of funds to these Locally Determined Schemes. This allocation will be reduced considerably over the next few years and it is unlikely that many new libraries will be commissioned before 1980.

Revenue expenditure on library services has been far more buoyant as will be seen from Fig. 10.1. This represents significant growth in real terms although much of the increase has been to compensate for the extremely high rate of inflation.

Urban library authorities, and particularly those in Greater London, had by 1975–76 attained higher standards of provision than the county libraries, but even the counties had in total more or less reached the minimum staffing standards recommended by government. The relative performance of the three groups of new library authorities is shown in Table 10.2.

Figure 10.1

Growth in local authority expenditure on public libraries, museums and art galleries to 1972/3.

From 'Local Government Trends 1974' (CIPFA)

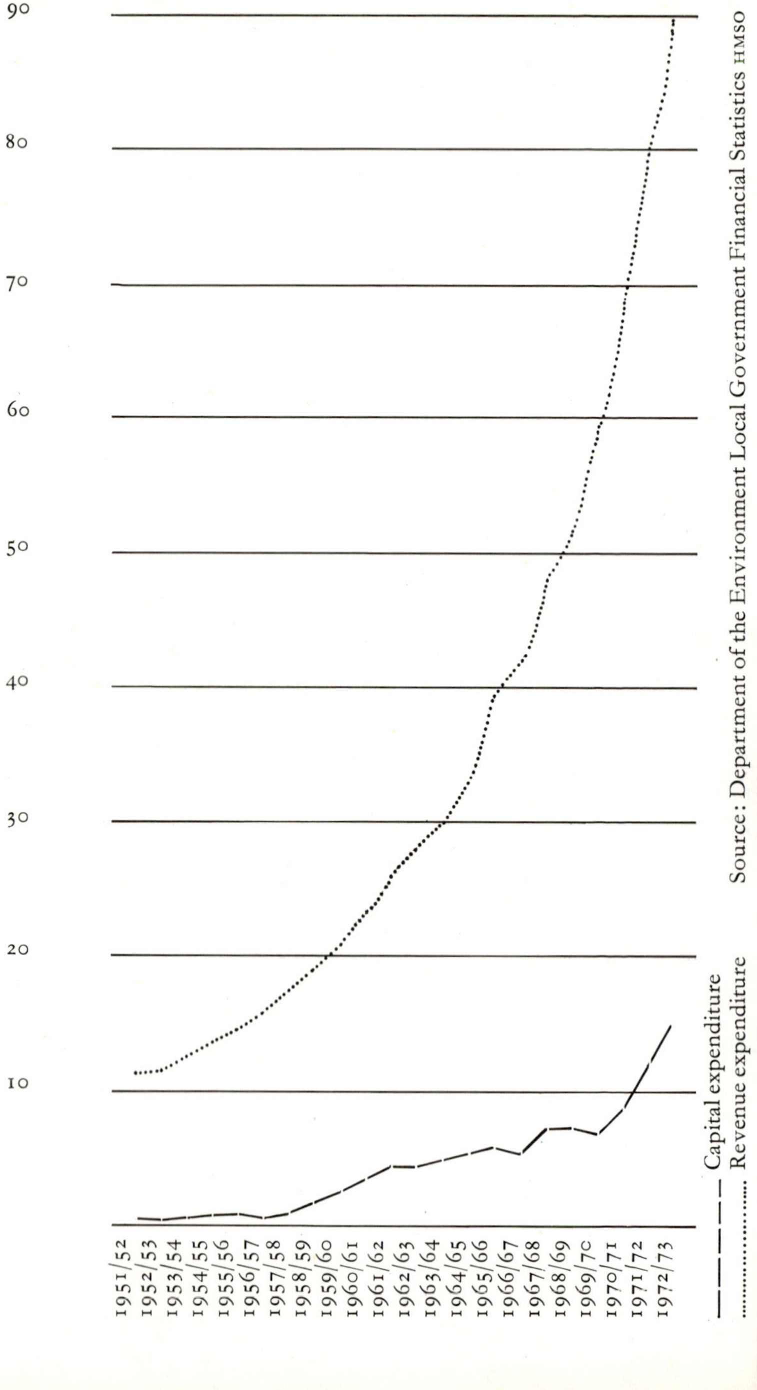

Source: Department of the Environment Local Government Financial Statistics HMSO

——— Capital expenditure

············· Revenue expenditure

Table 10.2

Staffing of the new Public Library Authorities in England and
Wales, 1975/7
(Based on CIPFA Public Library Statistics: estimates 1975/6

	Population 000's	Non-manual staff		Professional staff %age	
		Recommended Standard	Actual	Recommended Standard	Actual
London Boroughs	7,111	2,844	4,952	25/33	39·6
Metropolitan districts	11,671	4,668	5,766	25/33	33·4
Non-Metropolitan County Councils	30,261	12,104	12,668	33/40	32·3

Librarians struggled with reasonable success to keep the book
purchase funds in line with the increase in book prices. In the
1970s cost of living increases and improvements in the
remuneration of local government officers, particularly in the
clerical grades, resulted in the library payroll taking up an
increasing proportion of total expenditure. Shift payments and
extra pay for working on Saturdays began to have an effect on
library opening hours contrary to the efforts to exploit libraries
as cultural and community centres.

Unfortunately, public libraries are amongst a group of local
government services which seems to be used by central
government as something of an economic regulator. For most of
the post-war period, libraries in the academic sector have not
been so much affected by recurrent economic crises. This has
resulted in the loss of many trained librarians to the developing
university and college libraries. Public librarians are well aware
of the support which reference services in particular give to
students and school children and it is perhaps understandable
that they should resent a crude classification as an amenity
service, much as they value their contribution to leisure
provision. The gloomy forecast for local government finance
and in particular that of the library service will be discussed
later.

Local government reorganisation and the new library authorities

Social policy since the war has conferred ever greater
responsibilities upon local government to carry out statutory
powers and duties. To a very large extent local government is an
agent for policies and programmes determined at the centre. A
desire for efficiency led to successive waves of reorganisation
beginning with local government in the Greater London area
(1965), followed by England and Wales (1974) and Scotland
(1975).

The reorganised local government service in Britain is on a two
tier basis of county and district. In the conurbations of Greater
London and the provinces the districts are the 'most-purpose'
authorities including education and libraries; elsewhere the
non-metropolitan county councils control these services, except
for four county districts in Wales. The forty-seven
non-metropolitan county library systems of England and Wales
have an average population above 600,000 and about one-third
of the English counties serve above 900,000 population. The
London Boroughs are for the most part serving less than
250,000 population but ideas of economic size are increasing so
that the later thirty-six provincial metropolitan districts are
much larger on average although few of them exceed 350,000
population.

As to resources of libraries in England and Wales, total book
stocks in 1975–76 were approximately 113 million; there were
2,398 full-time libraries, 963 part-time libraries and 589 mobile
libraries, and it can safely be said that almost everyone among the
total population served of 49,346,500 has regular and convenient
access to a public library service point.

The new county libraries incorporate many formerly
independent urban library systems, some of them serving very
large towns and cities, as for instance Southampton and
Portsmouth (Hampshire), Bristol (Avon) and Stoke on Trent
(Staffordshire). Thus the historical separation of town libraries
from their rural or suburban hinterland has been largely
eliminated and the new counties have the opportunity to create

logical networks of libraries supported by large resources and able to develop the specialised reference services lacking in most former counties. In the words of S. G. Berriman 'In past years we were always arguing about county and municipal libraries, about small systems and big systems'. The Public Libraries and Museums Act 1964 was a compromise on this issue but now there are just public libraries.

Political compromise raised its head in the passing of the Local Government Act 1972 which permitted districts within non-metropolitan counties to continue to exercise library powers on an agency basis. There was a real danger at one time that municipal library authorities would seek to perpetuate their independence in this way and it is once again thanks to the advice of the DES that there was not a good case for administrative devolution but rather for local advisory bodies which ensured that no significant degree of library agency resulted. The individual citizen determines his use of libraries by convenience, disregarding administrative boundaries, and the extra-district charges which unpleasantly reminded him of these in the past have largely disappeared.

Cooperation

There is no limit to the desirable size of network in terms of a truly comprehensive library and information service so that the DES has rightly pressed the need for continued cooperation between the new larger authorities. This is particularly desirable in the conurbations where the large cities such as Birmingham, Manchester and Leeds, which have long provided reference library services of regional importance, find themselves with more or less the same rateable value as before reorganisation, as one of a number of districts of the same metropolitan county. Such reference libraries, providing comprehensive collections of books and serial publications, could be regarded as quasi-national in some respects. At least they regard themselves as an intermediate level between the services of the British Library and local libraries. In committing themselves before local government reorganisation to the building of major new reference libraries, Birmingham and Glasgow amongst others have shown that a city which has the will can well afford to maintain a high standard of library and information services. Public library expenditure is only about 2% of the budget of most local authorities. However, one has to remember the special economic and social problems of metropolitan cities in all western society.

It may well be economic for adjoining metropolitan districts to subscribe to library and information facilities from the major city. Adjoining non-metropolitan county libraries which do not have a major central library within their own area may likewise develop a partnership with a major existing reference library. There is no legal difficulty in such arrangements. Meanwhile the British Library Board is taking the widest view of its responsibilities to integrate the national libraries for the benefit of the whole library community. The DES have commissioned research into the actual infrastructure of library use and the forms of cooperation possible between the different types of library in an urban area. The Board has power to make grants to other libraries. The metropolitan county councils offer yet another possibility of financial support for regional library services: several of them have assumed some responsibility for museums and the arts on a county basis.

Scotland and Northern Ireland

The library profession, and in particular the Scottish Library Association, were very disappointed by the recommendation of the Wheatley Commission that Scottish public libraries should be regarded as an amenity service and relegated to the district tier of responsibility except in certain areas of very sparse population. Whilst there was a welcome improvement in staffing structures and budgets of the new Scottish library authorities in May 1975, the structural weakness will be of more lasting impact. Whereas the Scottish Library Association had advocated a minimum population of 100,000, the thirty-seven library districts vary widely in size, with three of less than 30,000 and 50% less than 100,000 population. Admittedly there are many areas of dispersed population in Scotland and just eighteen of the new library authorities contain 80% of the population of the country. But there are 'cases of the needless truncation of existing county library services and the substitution of district authorities without a large centre of population capable of providing an effective central library'. Considering that the new Scottish authorities have wholeheartedly accepted the concepts of corporate management, it is quite anomalous that the new education authorities are developing separate school library services.

Some public librarians, disillusioned by the low priority given to their service over the years in local government, envy the Northern Ireland solution of autonomous education and library boards reporting direct to the provincial government.

Rationalisation

It is natural for new administrations to seek to level up provision in all areas to the best which they have inherited. This laudable if costly policy resulted in a very great improvement in the standards of the London Borough libraries at reorganisation, giving them a lead over the rest of Britain which they have managed to preserve in relative terms. DES advice ahead of the main reorganisation in England and Wales anticipated the same process of levelling up, or at least advised that the new authorities should ensure that no constituent library system would suffer any reduction in standards. Unfortunately, the economic background to this reorganisation could not have been less propitious and the result has been rationalisation rather than overall improvement. Scottish reorganisation followed soon afterwards and curiously enough this did create a definite upgrading of standards in many authorities. Admittedly these had been below the standards in the rest of Britain.

Rationalisation of inherited book stocks will take effect automatically over time but the immediate challenge to library management was the retraining and redeployment of professional manpower. The new library systems have inherited too high a proportion of qualified staff, many of whom lack the appropriate experience for the reorganised cultural and information services of the future. Former library authorities,

especially the municipal libraries, had made considerable
progress towards the upper level of 40% qualified professionals
recommended in the Bourdillon Working Party Report. In fact,
Bourdillon did mention lower levels of 33% (which accords with
international thinking) or even 25% in major conurbations.
However, the higher figure was inevitably the target of
professional ambitions. Bourdillon was not based on any
systematic work study and subsequent investigation in
individual counties and by LAMSAC is likely to show that at the
junior level many librarians are employed to an undesirable
degree in administrative and clerical duties. Cost differentials
between junior professionals and experienced clerical assistants
have been much eroded by the general trend to improve the
remuneration of lower paid workers but apart from the residual
cost advantages there is a need to improve job satisfaction by
the creation of an intermediate grade, whether regarded as
sub-professional, technician or library supervisor, for people
trained and experienced in general library housekeeping and
elementary bibliographical work. Centralisation of technical
processes, and in particular the use of the computer, have
reduced the need for 'behind the scenes' library technical skills.
Interpretive work at the individual library has been facilitated by
the provision of COM catalogues and improved
telecommunications with larger libraries. In terms of narrowly
conceived public library objectives, therefore, a reduction even
on the 33% professional figure may be envisaged as desirable
provided that a library technician grade emerges in sufficient
numbers. To produce the intermediate grade without enhancing
the role of lower grade professional staff will be self defeating.

Corporate management

At the more senior levels of the profession, new approaches to
local authority organisation and management have adversely
affected the status of many chief librarians and have reduced that
independence of the public library service which has been a goal
of the Library Association for many years. Traditionally a local
authority in Britain regarded itself as a corporate body
responsible for providing specific services under legislation.
Accordingly the council of the authority delegated its powers to

a series of service committees each advised by a professional chief officer, supported by his department. Coordination at the centre was more of a financial constraint on the ambitions of powerful service committees than any kind of corporate policy making.

Virtually all of the new local authorities have adopted the recommendations of the Bains Committee[4] (England and Wales) and the Paterson Committee[5] (Scotland) both advocating a corporate planning approach, whereby '. . . a local authority appraises and plans its activities in relation to the needs and problems of the area and of those who live and work in it'. There are three interrelated themes:

i   a community approach to local government
ii   a planning orientation
iii an organisational focus

An authoritative observer of local government has expressed the opinion that the new authorities have been more active so far in devising corporate organisations and planning processes than they have been in achieving a true community approach. With this caution, it can be claimed that many authorities are now seeking to influence the quality of life in their localities in a systematic and positive way rather than presiding over the administration of a series of independent services.

At the political level a powerful Policy and Resources Committee directs and monitors overall progress, supported by a series of programme committees each responsible for a broad area of public concern; such as planning and transportation, education, social services, public safety, or leisure. One or more service departments will be accountable to a programme committee. In the case of libraries this would usually be the leisure committee (under a variety of titles) or the education committee.

At the officer level a Chief Executive is head of the professional service, supported by a management team of chief officers equivalent in its way to the Policy and Resources Committee in having corporate responsibility under the leadership of the Chief Executive for all the concerns of the Authority. In some authorities administrative logic has created a series of directorates, one to each programme committee, where the head of the libraries department would probably be a second or third tier officer within a directorate. In many authorities, however, the heads of each professional service, perhaps twelve or more in all, are each regarded as a chief officer. In this type of authority it is usual for only a few principal chief officers to be members of the management team, their minor colleagues attending by invitation. There are, however, a minority of authorities in which all chief officers are regular members of the management team.

Public libraries in corporate structures

Where do public libraries fit into the new structures? A survey by the Library Association in late 1975 indicated that in England and Wales sixty-four chief librarians report to a leisure committee, two to the education committee or a sub-committee, eighteen to a cultural committee (ie excluding the recreational element of leisure) and two to a general purposes committee. Seventy-one chief librarians claimed chief officer status but only twenty-seven were members of the management team. An INLOGOV survey of about the same date indicated that of all professionals the librarian was least likely to be on the team.

The idea of leisure management is a new one, no discipline can claim to be especially relevant to direct leisure services; obviously the main qualification is a high degree of managerial ability. A few librarians have become directors of leisure or amenity services and where a mini-directorate of cultural services has been created the chief officer is normally a librarian. The degree of administrative integration within these conglomerates varies greatly. Many chief librarians are still exercising virtual autonomy within an educational or leisure department. It is yet to be proved that corporate management will produce the greater flexibility and greater relevance to community needs that is claimed for it. Certainly the philosophy has generated much energy and commitment amongst senior local government officers, although inevitably there is a degree of administrative empire building in any large service. Realism compels the young librarian with ambition to recognise that progress in the hierarchy of the new local authorities calls increasingly for skills in management at each higher level and that there comes a crossover point when managerial ability outweighs professional skill.

Why have librarians not fared very well from the opportunities of corporate management? There is a variety of reasons, among them the dedication of many librarians to purely professional concerns. This perhaps explains the poor attendance of librarians at management courses for senior local government officers. Only fourteen librarians were among 450 students who have attended the advanced courses organised by the Institute of Local Government Studies, University of Birmingham, since their inception in 1967. Only seventy-two places have been taken up by librarians out of 2600 students attending shorter courses held in various polytechnics since 1969. It may well be that local authorities have not thought of nominating librarians, who do not dispose of a large amount of resources, but it is still disappointing because the profession of librarian, concerned as it is with the control of information, ought to be an excellent discipline for the future senior manager. In spite of this, it is of course a fact that many senior librarians do play a valuable part in the general management of their authorities.

Library management structures

It is possible for the management style and even the management structure of a department to be quite different from that of its organisational environment. For historical reasons large public library systems tend to be bureaucratic, to use the word in its exact sense. The routine administration of a very large volume of repetitive transactions with relatively slow change in resources and demands provides an atmosphere in which bureaucracy may be the most effective management style. However, the rapidity of change which will be revealed in some part by this chapter is compelling the new library authorities to adopt a more flexible and participative style of management exemplified by the flatter hierarchies of some of the new systems.

For too long public librarians ambitious for promotion have had to eschew specialisation because promotion lay in the line of general administration. Some of the new authorities have created promotion ladders for functional specialists equivalent to those in general administration and this process will probably go farther when a true corps of specialists has emerged.

The new cultural departments are providing opportunity for librarians to work not only with specialists of their own kind but with museums curators, archivists and arts administrators. One kind of librarian specialisation is to be deplored and that is the tradition of producing amateur specialists in transport, personnel, exhibition design and other functions. Where there is an accepted professional qualification it is to be hoped that such posts will be filled by appropriate professionals. Yet in 1975 only two library authorities in England and Wales employed a full time professionally qualified personnel officer, although the training and staff development needs of the new library systems are considerable. The tradition for a deputy librarian to be a pure administrator was wasteful of professional and managerial ability. The new library authorities or the directorates within which they are often located, frequently have a specialist administrative branch.

The new authorities often possess a wide range of management services available to departments on a part time or consultancy basis including personnel management, computing, work-study and other management services, and accountancy. Public relations and research and intelligence are two of the more recent specialisations which have arrived. Judicious use of such advisers should strengthen the ability of chief librarians to integrate and develop the considerable book and information resources now at their disposal and to plan for eventual development of services. Since corporate planning is the reason for the existence of the new structures, senior professionals find themselves in turn expected to make a contribution to community planning.

Returning to the library department there is usually a superfluity of two kinds of professional experience: library administration and general professional practice in lending libraries. The soundness of basic public library training proved itself in an unwelcome way during recent years by providing large numbers of librarians for the expanding services of universities, colleges and industry. Now the public library sector itself has need of specialists who must learn by a combination of short courses and practical experience. The library schools have shown themselves anxious to assist in this task as one way of establishing a more meaningful relationship with the practising profession. It will be realised from the foregoing that public libraries are not exempt from the dictum of Donald Schon that all organisations are becoming 'learning systems' but if the practising profession are consciously learning and developing on a scale never before experienced, so must the library schools become work-integrated organisations if their contribution is to remain relevant.

The more obvious librarian skills which are needed lie in the areas of subject bibliography, local studies, information service and the handling of non-book materials. Attempts to be more responsive to the needs of the local community compel the service to develop in addition expertise in meeting the needs of particular groups of people. Children's librarians were being appointed in a few public libraries in the 1920s but only recently has this aspect of librarianship achieved general acceptance as a worthwhile specialisation, although the fault for this does not lie entirely on the side of library managers. Now we need to add skills in identifying and meeting the needs of the disadvantaged persons in society, students, local government members and officers and many other groups.

Participative management

Before a professional person becomes committed to a new kind of work and a new style of working, it is first necessary to persuade him or her that the old way will not do. Some professional librarians do not see the need to change and blame the pressures of society upon the sins of management with its misunderstanding of what librarianship is really all about. Management consultants of wide experience who have researched the public library field are invariably impressed with the dedication of librarians and also with the strongly personal nature of their commitment to the public service. Faced with this situation, the library manager must accept that development of plans and policies by working groups is ultimately the only effective way of working, although it is one which is extremely frustrating at times to all concerned and is demanding upon the latent democratic instinct of senior staff who have behind them the greater part of a professional life-time spent in an atmosphere of more or less benevolent autocracy.

In terms of delegation, the metropolitan library authorities have a fairly free choice between geographical or functional division. Geographical problems of the counties more or less compel delegation to some form of area management with a balancing county-wide group of advisors and specialists. The degree of delegation as between the centre and the districts is more of an option and requires considerable judgement. If the chief officer is determined upon a systematic change in objectives and style of management, centralisation should be stronger in the first phase. Once the new system is well understood, the objectives clear and the programmes defined, one can safely delegate far more responsibility to librarians in the field by giving them freedom along with accountability for achieving agreed results. The strategy in one new library authority was for a high degree of decentralisation at the time of reorganisation, in order to achieve initial rationalisation without too much disturbance to the public or the staff. Once the system had attained reasonable integrity of operation, senior librarians from the field were involved more and more closely with central development. Ultimately perhaps the balance will again move the other way, with groups of libraries as cost centres.

The Library Association and professional education

The Library Association has its own chapter but one should perhaps mention that the welcome growth of professional membership over recent years has been very largely in non-public library employment so that the once predominant library sector now represents very little more than half of the practising membership of the Association. There were signs that the drive to enlarge the representation of other sectors of the profession had led to a certain neglect of the problems of public libraries and indeed the Library Association has not been apparent to them as a major influence in the recent critical years. However, the recent formation of a Public Libraries Group should ensure that it will not be forgotten that librarians in this sector remain by far the largest occupational group in the Association. This is not to call for renewed separation in librarianship; on the contrary, the greatest need of practising professionals in public libraries is for the Library Association to take an ecumenical approach to the other cultural and information professions. Librarians who are trying to work more closely with museums officers, archivists and arts administrators are only too well aware that professional institutions define themselves by exclusion, whereas the corporate approach and the growth of reprography and non-book materials are factors blurring the boundaries between professions which define themselves in terms of information materials or techniques. For various reasons there is a greater fraternity between senior librarians in all sectors of the profession than has ever obtained in the past and it is to be hoped that remuneration and conditions of service at middle management levels may be sufficiently compatible to encourage a degree of movement between types of libraries on the part of specialists and those ambitious of rising to the higher posts.

A DES survey of the broad pattern of employment of newly qualified librarians by types of library and information work, during the period 1969 to 1974, shows that nearly two-thirds of students entered public library work. The public library contingent accounts for three-quarters of the non-graduates, and an increasing proportion of those with first degree status, rising to more than half of them in the last year of the survey. Actual numbers in 1973–74 were 290 non-graduates, seventy-seven with first degrees, 224 with a postgraduate diploma and five with a master's degree in librarianship: a total of 596 compared with 232 to academic libraries and 163 to special libraries.

Mention of graduates recalls the problems of enhancement of the qualifications of those non-graduate public librarians who have proved their merit but feel disadvantaged in the search for promotion by their lack of graduate status. There is a radical answer for those who are able to suspend gainful employment for a year or two to attend a library school but for the majority the answer may be the Open University, which confers recognised degree status upon graduates who have studied by a mixture of correspondence course, television and radio lectures and attendance at Summer Schools. This is no easy answer as it involves three or four years of arduous part-time study. At present few of the chief and deputy librarians of British public library authorities are university graduates and it is likely to be some years before the possession of a degree becomes the universal requirement.

The need has already been expressed for an intermediate category of worker in public libraries. In order to establish a proper identity and status for these library technicians or sub-professionals, an external qualification will be required which is of a higher standing than the existing Library Assistants Certificate awarded by the City and Guilds of London Institute. It was partly due to the opposition of public librarians that the Library Association refused to assume responsibility for the Library Assistants Certificate. The insecurity of professional status which was the reason for opposition to this Certificate has surely disappeared and the Library Association would do well to consider embracing a range of qualifications. Most of the public library authorities have in-service training courses for experienced library assistants which many of them regard as preferable to the City and Guilds Certificate.

Booksellers and authors

The principal theme of this article and possibly of the centenary volume is that of change for integration forced on by the developing scale of technology, the need for better management of limited resources, and increasingly sophisticated and extensive demands on services. A certain degree of systems integration

has taken place between public libraries and the large
booksellers specialising in that market. Prevented by trade
restrictions from competing on price, they compete in service
and much of the processing of new stock for public libraries is
carried out at quite low charges. Computer links between such
suppliers and the new library systems can be expected to
develop, improving on the existing current awareness service of
new books which they already give.

A more controversial development is that of central purchasing
of books by a consortium of large local authorities. Most
librarians are conscious of the need to use the public purchasing
power at their disposal to support reputable local booksellers.
Indeed libraries do much to promote the buying of books as well
as the borrowing of them. Many schools now run a paperback
book sales point, whilst universities and polytechnics often give
some sponsorship to a complete book-shop on the campus. It
would not be appropriate for every central library to house a
book sales point; there may be legal and other difficulties.
Certainly it does not appear that it would be economic to run a
hard back book-shop dedicated to sales to library users.

At the beginning of the chain are the authors and it is unpleasant
to report that relations between the professional associations of
writers and public librarians have not been good over the last
few years due to the bitter campaign to establish a Public
Lending Right which would entitle authors to remuneration in
respect of the borrowing of their books from public libraries.
The report of a working party was published as long ago as
May 1972 but at the time of writing the responsible Minister has
indicated that a long-delayed Bill will be laid before Parliament
in the coming (1976) session. A feasibility study has indicated
that it would be practicable to analyse loans from selected
libraries on a computer-based method and this has been
preferred to the simpler alternative of analysing library
purchases. The fears of the local authorities have been to some
extent assuaged by assurances that no cost will fall upon them
and that the authors' remuneration will come from central
government sources. Librarians are still divided upon the pros
and cons of this issue, but the majority dislike the Public

Lending Right proposals, criticising especially the high cost of administration and the decision that payment will be proportionate to the popularity of an author. There is a discernible side benefit that, if the detailed census of borrowing is published, public librarians will have additional background information on stock control. Provision has been made in the estimates for the Arts in 1977–78 to pay the first annual instalment to authors under Public Lending Right.

Library networks

The contemporaneous rationalisation of national libraries and public libraries should now be succeeded by the creation of a truly national system for the delivery of documents and information to users in all parts of the country. The technology is there in computers, telecommunications, facsimile transmission and reprography and within a few years there should be the capability to employ them in a network. Feasibility studies are already in progress on the best administrative network and particularly the role of a regional or intermediate grouping between the local university or public library system and national resources. Various groupings are operational including a local consortium based on the university and public libraries of Birmingham which offers full cataloguing services to any subscriber, the long established regional library bureaux and the direct lending of books, serials and photocopies from the British Library Lending Division. The future national system may be based on more than one administrative network.

In so far as the local public library is a place of first resort for access to documents and information, each new public library system has its own hierarchy of branches and mobile libraries, district libraries and county special collections which may be based on a county headquarters or main city library or alternatively may be based on a system of subject specialisation by various district libraries. *Public library service points*[6] updated the Bourdillon standards on the provision of a network of library buildings and one should also consult John Taylor's DES project on *Public libraries and their use*. The DES have also sponsored operational research into transport systems for interlending. Most public library administrative headquarters are on telex and a few systems have installed telex in a number of their main libraries.

Management for recession

Library managers in Britain have been accustomed to think in terms of development led by a steady growth in real resources, even though it has sometimes been a struggle even to maintain the budget in real terms. For the next few years librarians will have to learn management for recession. Contingency planning for five or more years ahead may be optimistic or pessimistic according to local prediction, but it is certain that in the near future librarians must seek to reduce costs in ways that will not seriously diminish the number of active users of libraries and which will continue to provide them with at least adequate standards of service. Management service units can often help to improve efficiency by work study and organisation and methods surveys, but it is doubtful whether these measures will suffice to cover the budget deficiencies in many authorities. Undoubtedly reductions will have to be made in staff costs and in the fund for books and materials since these constitute about 80% of the budget.

Cost reduction seeks out under-used or wasted resources. In a regard to stock it is hoped that a systematic programme of stock control may bring about real savings with only marginal loss of reader satisfaction. The pioneer studies by A. W. McClellan[7] have been one of the most valuable contributions to professional thinking in the past generation. If his ideas have been slow of adoption this is because the elaborate checking of supply and demand by manual systems in a large number of interest topics was too expensive. The Public Library Research Unit at Leeds Polytechnic Library School have been working with Bromley Public Libraries for some time on a feasibility study to create a computerised model of the stock situation. There is a simpler alternative of arranging most of the books in small to medium sized libraries according to a manageable number of reader interest categories, say thirty, and then comparing issues with shelf stock on a weekly basis. This would have the effect of making clear to readers as well as staff any glaring mis-match between supply and demand, which might be a valuable discipline upon librarians too concerned with theoretical considerations of what should be available. It would require a user-orientated approach to service. Other methods of improving efficiency would include the planned acquisition of stock for groups of libraries with a bulk exchange system. This should provide for the interests of minorities and for changing the aspect of stock provision at the lowest cost.

Staff cuts are heralded by the reduction of the hours of opening, particularly in the evenings and at week-ends, taking place in many public library systems in late 1975. This action is justifiable in the sense that most readers will continue to use the library at other times and it is more efficient to concentrate demand on a shorter period of opening. But it hinders the development of the library as a cultural and educational centre. Research shows that the great majority of people using lending and reference libraries work on a self service basis and this trend must increase with the shortage of staff. Therefore we must frankly adjust to the supermarket situation by making it easier for people to make proper use of the facilities. The installation of security systems against theft is likely to increase. The economics of automation depend on the policy of individual authorities about recharging central computer costs. It is an artificial situation so far as the chief librarian is concerned.

Public participation and the use of volunteers is another potential source of help, not only for economic reasons. Britain has a great tradition of voluntary service and authorities are seeking to channel help to public services by the establishment of volunteer service bureaux in many towns. Areas particularly suitable for the involvement of volunteers are cultural and promotional work with children, service to housebound people and those in residential establishments, sound and photographic surveys for local studies, indexing of local studies material, promotion of exhibitions, lectures and cultural activities and the provision of service to the general public in small communities. Libraries have suitable openings for certain of the offenders sentenced to a period of community

work under recent legislation. Although all volunteers need to
be selected very carefully on the basis that they are willing to
give regular service over a period and capable of doing the work
to an adequate standard, they are a source of help which no
public service can afford to ignore, least of all the public library
which has prided itself on being widely acceptable to all groups
in the community.

The Free Library principle

British public libraries were known for generations as 'free'
libraries and the principle of free use was continued in the
Public Libraries and Museums Act 1964 with the exception of
small clerical fees and penalties for non-return of books. There is
also a loophole in the Act whereby library authorities are
enabled to make a charge for the loan of material other than
books. Few London libraries have taken advantage of this
provision but many in the provinces have done so and are likely
to do so in the future. The government is awaiting the report of
the Layfield Committee on the financing of local authorities and
at least one of the local authority associations has submitted an
appeal to be allowed to make a direct charge for services,
particularly those which are regarded as desirable rather than
essential. Whether one regards the idea of a free service as a
principle or an historical tradition, it is likely that the
introduction of even a small charge would meet with
considerable consumer resistance to the point of losing many
present borrowers. Evidence for this can be found by comparing
the user of gramophone record libraries which do or do not
make a charge and, in a related field, research into pricing policy
for public swimming pools shows that revenue actually drops
beyond the quite small charge of 10*p* for children and 20*p* for
adults.

Those who take the amenity view of public libraries may argue
that there is no logic in having a free loan of recreational
literature when people have to pay an admission charge for
theatres, concerts, adult education classes and other
recreational facilities. Professional opinion remains solidly
against charging for the use of libraries and it may be thought

unwise even to discuss the matter in print as the issue is not yet a live one. The justification is that it is likely to be so by the time this volume is published.

The public library user

The remarkable correspondence of international thinking shown in Withers' *Standards for library service: an international survey* [8] may be due to a tendency to follow best current practice rather than the coincidence of original research, but it enables one to assume that the average British public library by 1974 had attained standards of provision in staff and stock which would be regarded as very satisfactory in most western countries. An audit of buildings would show a worse result, for as late as 1971 about half of them were in need of extension or replacement.

But do British libraries give value for money to their public? An academic who is a great user of university and public libraries, in an affectionately critical comment on librarians, said that they appeared to have the ideal of a British standard reader, around whose model requirements they were able to erect complicated and elegant systems of cataloguing, shelf arrangement and service.

Certainly the image of British public libraries is very uniform. The typical library serves a small town or a suburb of some larger town. It will either be of post-1960 period, open plan on one floor or with a mezzanine, carpeted wall to wall, with plate glass windows; or it will have been built in the other great period circa 1895–1914, in which case the interior design will be of three rooms around an entrance hall in a building of very solid construction with adequate fenestration. This older building will have been modernised and very well adapted as the former reading room has been used for expansion of lending library facilities. These typical libraries will carry a shelf stock of between 10,000–20,000 volumes and will provide either a separate room or at least an area for children up to ten years of age, there will be some study facilities and a quick reference collection and whatever display space is available will be taken up by notices of local events, book displays including one of specialised material from the central library and there may very well be a colourful show of artwork from some local school. At most times a professional librarian, usually female, will be available in the public rooms and through her computer-produced union catalogue of the system holdings will be able to obtain any book on request. In the more modern type of library there may well be a small meeting room popular with local cultural societies and adult education classes. The staff will usually limit themselves to cultural activities for children, probably a weekly story hour.

The typical central library is less easy to specify in terms of scale but in organisation it will be the branch library writ large with adult lending, reference and children's departments, plus a local history library, meeting rooms and possibly a general purpose hall or even a theatre, which may or may not be managed by the librarian. Very few of even the largest city libraries have adopted the system of subject departments plus a general library and where they have done so the general library will be crowded because something like 65% of the readers are using it as their local 'branch library'.

Uniformity in the scale of provision for similar populations is echoed in the stock, where subject coverage and the range of popular material will be comparable; although quite small libraries, formerly independent, will exhibit strength in certain subject areas and possess a scattering of non-fiction titles not represented in much larger libraries.

These are rather shameless generalisations for the sake of illustration but, if it can be accepted that there is a standard set of British public library images, do these reflect a mere desire for administrative uniformity or is there a strong similarity between the needs of readers in all parts of the country? Although there is no authoritative survey of public library use comparable with Berelson's work in the USA almost thirty years ago, we have been fortunate in the geographical distribution of several sociological surveys[9] of British library use in recent years; Groombridge in London, Luckham, Marsterson and Mann in the North of England. Although it is based on operational rather than sociological methods, John Taylor's study which was based on several areas in England helps to confirm the other results. Marsterson, in comparing some of the results concludes

This paper has drawn attention to similarities between three studies in the age and socio-economic status of library users; in the sources of encouragement for library membership; in the extent of the use of other libraries and of book ownership by library members; in the frequency and purpose of library visits; the number and purpose of books borrowed; in the extent of borrowing for others; and in the extent of 'shelf–failure'. The areas of similarity are extensive, while differences are largely confined to the nature of the population served and the scale of service. If library users display broad similarities in different environments, the implications for library management and for the sociology of library use are worth further study. Survey methods may be standardised; library methods found successful in one environment may be confidently applied elsewhere; organisations serving different types of environment through one service may be as successful as organisations serving one type only; and so on.

In his own work at Maltby, Marsterson identified

a core of intensive library users, associated with extended education and high occupational grade, who not only used Maltby for work or hobbies and ensured best use of available resources by approaching the staff or reserving books in case of failure, but also made use of other libraries and owned personal libraries.

Similarly, it is interesting to quote Luckham on the typical public library user at Chester and Eccles:

Overall, one can see that the typical library member is of higher social status, younger and more active and interested in his community than the non-member . . . but although membership is selective, it is not exclusive. Some people of all types and backgrounds are enrolled.

These conclusions broadly justify the type of provision made by public library authorities in terms of the traditional objective of satisfying the needs of people for hard-back books. When we compare the findings of the Government Social Survey with the percentages of library user to population, it is seen that libraries have been very successful in attracting a large section of the potential market for hard-back books. The Social Survey finds that only 40% of the adult population regularly read such books yet public libraries have just under 30% of the catchment population in regular membership. Only 60% of the population claim to read hard-back books at any time; if we add proxy borrowing, lapsed members and others who claim occasional contact with public libraries, the user rate rises to between 70% and 80% of the catchment population.

On reference provision the public library emerges from the Clements Survey[10] as an extremely useful and widely used multi-purpose information source, and he notes 'the large extent to which public reference libraries are used as a source of technical and commercial information by a wide range of users – especially in local industry, commerce and public service'. The biggest user group (52·5%) were students although this average figure conceals very large variations locally. This probably reflects the physical deficiencies of the library provided by the students' own institution since 'approximately half of all students in the reference libraries required merely a quiet place and a desk'. One may suggest a subjective influence also in that students like to escape from the campus into the wider world.

There may be some over provision in large reference libraries since the information required by people using them for their work was only 10% at post graduate level. Most users had a need for straightforward factual information; they served themselves and mainly used recently published material such as periodicals, text books, general works and directories. Where the staff were consulted, a much wider range of material was drawn upon. 62% of the users reported complete success and only 24% recorded failure which is regarded as a good result for a basically self help situation.

On the level of medium to small town reference library services, a survey in one county has confirmed remarkable correspondence with the results in two American studies by Rothstein and Weech. Provisional results of the Cheshire survey show that existing provision, whilst strictly uneconomic in terms of costs per inquiry, has considerable social value. People used the reference libraries for many purposes and a very high percentage declared themselves satisfied with the service they received. However, it was noted that several studies elsewhere indicate the subjective nature of satisfaction which depends on the level of reader expectation.

Experienced public librarians will be gratified but not surprised by the confirmation that their service is regarded as satisfactory by a large proportion of the serious reading public in the community.

Cultural, community or documentary centre?

Why should the DES and leading professional opinion be urging the need for diversification into cultural activities and social outreach? Single purpose services of good quality are most likely to be successful, so why blur the image? The answer from the local authority would be that the library service is paid for by the whole community and must ally itself with other community services in order to provide for the cultural, educational and information needs of the majority of the population who do not ordinarily read books. Even on grounds of organisational survival, one may discern disturbing signs. Television, radio and domestic sound reproducers and newspapers and magazines absorb the great majority of the time which people in all social classes can devote to indoor leisure pursuits; a massive adult literacy campaign has followed the revelation that at least 4% of the adult population are functionally illiterate and the number of library users has remained static over ten years.

Even in the smallest public library there are elements of service to the Arts and concern for social uplift. The historical origins of the public library were the Mechanics Institutes, which included a library within a wide spectrum of cultural and educational provision. Victorian legislators and philanthropists were motivated by the need to reduce the inequality of educational opportunity. Corporate management will support the many librarians who are now seeking to develop and redesign their services to local needs. It is likely that British libraries may be more heterogeneous in the future, with an image somewhere

along the spectrum between two extremes, cultural centre or
community library and information centre.

The élitist concept of the cultural centre is well accepted and it is
fairly closely matched with the social profile of existing library
users. In prosperous suburbs and commuter towns around
major cities the library based arts centre will be most popular.
Inner city areas of decayed housing often have the oldest and
shabbiest libraries whose stock and services are relevant to only
a small minority of the local population which might consist to
an extraordinary extent of elderly people, poor families and
immigrants. One response to such a situation is to restock the
library with more suitable material, set up a community
information centre, provide space for meetings and a 'market
place' for information exchange. The professional and some of
the clerical staff will be despatched into the community to serve
the housebound and support community education workers.
Recognising that convenience of access is paramount in such a
community, small library deposit centres will be established in
many places of public resort.

Since community librarianship is less common than cultural
activity, it may be worthwhile to cite two examples. In the
London Borough of Lambeth the library service has been drawn
into the large scale community education and leisure campaign
of the Director of Amenities who happens to be a librarian by
profession. The City of Birmingham have designated libraries in
the inner zone as a special area for development and have
completely reorganised the approach to service.

As the objectives of a particular library polarise towards either
extreme as cultural or community centre, so the traditional role
as documentary centre becomes diminished in importance. The
cultural centre requires a team effort involving museums officers
and arts administrators as well as librarians. If the centre is on a
scale such as to justify provision of a museum specialist, theatre
or concert hall, these may be managed separately or, if there is
overall management, there is no particular reason why the
person should be a librarian. At the extreme of the community
library the debate is not only between professions but between

professionals and amateurs. If the populist approach is to be
accepted as sincere then community leaders must be given the
opportunity to share in determining policy and the librarian
could find himself the servant of local pressure groups.

So far we have been looking at development through a change
of objectives but there is another road to development through a
change of style towards a corporate approach to library and
information provision.

The corporate library and information service

At national level the DES is in a strong position to coordinate or
at least influence policy in all publicly supported libraries. At the
local level these will always include hospital and school library
services and often libraries in local government departments and
in the larger towns and cities there may also be a university or
polytechnic library. The Birmingham consortium has shown the
advantages which can come from an integration of certain
services as between the city and university libraries whilst there
is a close coordination of school and public library provision in
many of the county library areas. The need for economic use of
scarce resources requires still greater coordination of school and
public library services to children, as exemplified in the dual-use
type of library of which quite a few now exist. Another positive
development is that of team librarianship whereby a group of
branch librarians are organised into a team of specialists
spending a good deal of their time in the community seeking to
identify and meet the needs of specific groups of people be they
actual or potential library users. This approach has been
pioneered in counties with many small libraries which scarcely
justify the full-time attendance of a professional librarian, but it
is nonetheless valid for the urban situation. Working as a
specialist member of a team out in the community is a novel
experience for the professional librarian: it requires a change of
style from passive to active, from response to initiative. Even
within the library these specialist teams will work to identify
'client groups', that is groups of readers with a common interest.
They will attempt to serve the needs of these groups both
indirectly, by such means as programmed stock control,

displays and publications, and directly by seeking to meet individual readers with these interests, particularly officers of local societies and other key people.

Perhaps we can illustrate the positive approach to the conventional library role by describing the transformation which has taken place in the approach to local studies. British municipal libraries in particular have built up notable collections of material over generations, often overlapping in their collections of historical materials with the more recent record offices (manuscripts) and with local museums (prints and drawings). It is natural that the catchment areas of local collections frequently overlapped with those of other towns and the county as a whole. The new county library authorities will seek to establish a strong central collection adequately staffed by specialists whilst preserving and developing existing local collections. The positive approach to local studies is prompted by the development of reprography and audio-visual materials and the concept of educational resource centres which seek to draw without distinction on the resources of libraries, museums and record offices. In some of the new authorities a cultural department including libraries, museums and archives is providing a resources service to schools parallel to the school library service.

There is no reason why the resource centre approach should not be adopted in meeting the needs of the general public. If we extend local studies to embrace time past, present and future, we can form links with planning departments. Bibliographical control of the very wide range of local photographic records, plans and graphic material held by agencies other than the public library may be obtained by use of computer-based coordinate indexing, subject to agreement on standards. Local photographic societies may carry out photographic surveys on behalf of the collection; local history societies may compile archives of sound recordings including interviews with senior citizens. The general public have a keen interest in history at the local level which may be encouraged by the creation and sale of local publications, of reproductions of old maps and of specially compiled handlists to answer the more repetitive queries which can be widely distributed to schools and information centres.

Public librarians, faced with a whole community to serve, have been dominated for generations by a concept of the individual reader as their customer. If staffing levels permitted one to operate on the American scheme of the reader's advisor, interviewing new members in order to provide them thereafter with a personal current awareness service, this ideal would be workable. We now have to recognise that libraries are in a self-service situation and that much more effort must be put into improving the facilities for readers to help themselves and into work with identifiable groups of any kind.

Conclusions

The public library service in the United Kingdom in the Centenary Year will find itself in a very strong position both as to its resources and as to a public support which, although drawn disproportionately from the middle class, does include an equal number of skilled manual workers and their families. The widespread infrastructure of libraries and mobile vehicles will be unexcelled in its accessibility. The individual public library system will be supported as never before by national and academic library resources. Faced with an indefinite period of economic recession the service will require leadership which is competent in the skills of management and highly market oriented. The existing uniformity of library provision will give way to a more heterogeneous response to local need, polarising upon the concepts of the cultural centre and the community library. Coordination of all publicly supported library services will take place at local level, linked with the service of the British Library to create a truly national library and information service. It will be an anxious time involving a painful rate of change, but a clearer recognition of the social objectives of the public library may permit steady progress towards our goals even in the decade of the 'slimmed down' public library.

References

1. Ministry of Education. *The structure of the public library service in England and Wales* Cmnd 660. HMSO, 1959.
2. Department of Education and Science. Library information series. HMSO. No 1. *The purchase of books by public libraries* 1972. No 2. *The public library service: reorganisation and after* 1973. No 3. *Aspects of public library management* 1973. No 4. *Public libraries and their use* 1973. No 5. *Public libraries and cultural activities* 1975.
3. Ministry of Education. *Standards of public library service in England and Wales* HMSO, 1962.
4. Department of the Environment. *The new local authorities: management and structure* HMSO, 1972.
5. Scottish Development Department. *The new Scottish local authorities: organisation and management structures* HMSO, 1973.
6. Department of Education and Science. *Public library service points* HMSO, 1971.
7. McClellan, A. W. *The reader, the library and the book* Bingley, 1973.
8. Withers, F. N. *Standards for library service: an international survey* Paris UNESCO Press, 1974.
9. Groombridge, Brian. *The Londoner and his library*. Research Institute for Consumer Affairs, 1964. Luckham, Bryan. *The library in society* Library Association, 1971. Mann, P. H. *Books, buyers and borrowers* Deutsch, 1971. Marsterson, W. A. J. Users of libraries: a comparative study. *J of Librarianship* 6 (2), April 1974, 63–79.
10. Clements D. W. G. Use made of public reference libraries. *J Docum* 23 (2), June 1967, 131–145.

Sources and recommended reading

Berriman, S. G. *and* Harrison, S. G. *British public library buildings* Deutsch, 1966.

Chartered Institute of Public Finance and Accountancy. *Local government trends. Annually* 1973–. Invaluable source book on the institutional, social and economic factors impinging on public libraries and other services.

– *Public library statistics: estimates. Annually* 1961–62.

Gans, H. J. *People and plans: essays on urban problems and solutions* Basic Books, 1968.

Greenwood, R. *The organisation of local authorities in England and Wales: 1967–75* University of Birmingham, Institute of Local Government Studies, 1975.

Hill, Janet. *Children are people: the librarian in the community* Hamish Hamiton, 1973. An inspiring account of contemporary professional philosophy in practice in the London Borough of Lambeth.

Library Association. *New library buildings, (1969–1970)*, 1973 and *(1971–1972)*, 1974.

– *British librarianship and information science, 1966–1970* 1972. Quinquennial.

Library Association. County Libraries Group. *The new public libraries: integration and innovation* 1972.

Murison, W. J. *The public library, its origins and significance* 2nd ed, Harrap, 1971.

University libraries

Norman Higham

A considerable expansion of university education began in the 1870s with the creation of a number of colleges, the precursors of the modern provincial universities. The first fifty years of their existence saw a generally slow growth in their libraries, and professors' rooms were often the homes of their choicest collections. Though there were honourable exceptions, the central libraries of these institutions were hobbled by regrettably small book grants. Thus it was that the oft-quoted remark of the University Grants Committee in its report of 1921: 'The character and efficiency of a university may be gauged by its treatment of its central organ – the library', shone like a good deed in a naughty world.

Today, at the end of the second half of this century of development, after the second great expansion in numbers following the publication of the Robbins Report of 1964, the position is very different from a hundred years ago. This is not to say that university libraries are lavishly, or even adequately, endowed, but their role is respected, and their essential position in the educational programme of universities is established. If the situation is brighter, it also presents a very complex picture embracing the great and ancient libraries of Oxford, Cambridge and the Scottish universities and the newest and fast-growing technological universities.

It is not possible, in one chapter, to present a picture which delineates the variety of activities carried out in so many disparate institutions. At Oxford and Cambridge there is a wealth of library provision that is the envy of the world, while many new university libraries are still struggling to provide collections adequate to the needs of their users. Indeed, even the libraries of some of the 'middle-aged' universities are also still struggling.

Neither can the chapter provide an account of modern university librarianship in all its manifold branches. Such accounts can be found in recent books devoted to the subject, for example those by K. W. Neal and James Thompson. All that is attempted here is to pick out areas of development and of special concern among university librarians today, and indicate trends in thinking.

There is one basic function common to all university libraries whatever their size and stage of development, and it may be briefly stated thus: *to acquire and make available all books, periodicals and related material required by all members of the university for teaching, research and study, in accordance with the educational objectives of the university, and within the limits of funds allocated to it.* Every substantive word or phrase in this statement requires expansion to take into account the many activities contained within a library service, eg acquisition implies identification, selection and ordering; making available implies cataloguing, classification, display, storage, guiding, lending, rendering assistance and exploiting resources. But the statement includes all that is fundamental to a basic service. The fact that a university library may be a national or an international centre of excellence in some or all fields of study, rendering a unique service to scholars outside its university precinct, is in all but a few cases an additional role beyond its basic task; it exists to serve its members to its best ability and to the limit of its financial resources.

Finance

Finance obviously is a major element in a library's capacity. A poorly endowed library will be a drag on the educational aims and development of a university. The responsibility for the adequate funding of its library lies squarely within the university itself. The University Grants Committee, which provides almost the entire funds of provincial universities and a major part of those of Oxford and Cambridge, makes block grants which are at the autonomous disposal of the universities, with only occasional directives for their use. It is up to librarians and their library committees to lay claims for funds, and to indicate to their universities where their enlightened self-interest lies. It is superfluous to say that within universities as elsewhere the financial situation at the present time is very grave. But it is particularly the library that has been hardest hit. The rise in costs of books and periodicals is second only to the rise in salary costs and, since approximately half of the library's expenditure must be devoted to salaries, it suffers a double blow.

The expansion that has been required of each university following the Robbins Report, coupled with the enormous increase in the output of literature, not merely in books, but also and especially in periodicals, have placed crippling strains on the ability of libraries to build their collections and maintain them to adequate standards. And this is the activity most basic to the work of the library. There is no adequate alternative to a strong collection, and whatever steps might be taken to provide alternatives are likely to involve serious constraints on the highly important free-ranging personal exploitation of the resources of the library by its users. Where such methods come into their own is as a supplement to a strong collection. While it is true that a library succeeds only if its collections are actively used, a library that is strong on services and weak on collections has an in-built failure factor.

Given that the funds available to the library must serve equally adequately the needs of research, teaching and undergraduate users, the establishment of priorities is a complex activity, and the process of selection becomes ever more difficult, especially since material is required urgently and there is generally little time for the leisurely scrutiny of a reasonable range of book reviews. It is more than ever essential that the fullest cooperation exists between the library and teaching staff so that use may be made of their specialist knowledge of fields of literature.

Subject specialisation

One of the contributions to this cooperation has been the growth of the subject specialist approach within the library. The concept is not new. The library of University College London has employed subject specialists for twenty-five years. Moreover, wherever departmental libraries exist, the librarian in charge has become a specialist by the nature of his duties. A departmentalised – or rather sectionalised, since many branch libraries cover more than one department and in a large number of cases serve a faculty – library system has always carried an in-built subject specialist element. But in such cases the specialisation is a part of a functional structure; the specialist is also a library administrator. An essential feature of the subject specialist approach as such is that certain senior staff are employed specifically to be responsible for a subject or group of subjects, and any administrative or managerial responsibilities are additional to this.

In some libraries they will be entirely responsible, directly to the Librarian, for acquisitions in their field. In others they may be responsible to the Deputy Librarian, or the Sub-Librarian (Acquisitions), or the Head of Technical Services, acting as liaison between these and departments, as well as initiating suggestions themselves. In a well-organised system, whatever the place of the subject specialist, the result for the university will be the same – a collection based on the needs of the users of the library and satisfying the demands of teaching departments subject to the necessary right of the Librarian to exercise discretion on the grounds of balance, of standards and of funds available.

Through his developed knowledge of certain subjects and their bibliography the subject specialist can render effective assistance to readers in his field. Users benefit from the awareness that there is one member of the senior staff from whom they can seek information. The need for help is not confined to undergraduates, unsure of reading lists, but is particularly evident among postgraduate students beginning their assignments and requiring advice on research tools. But it is also noticeable that teaching staff, themselves experts in their fields, are among the most frequent users of the assistance of library specialists; they are likely to know them already through contacts at the book selection stage and they find the subject specialists' bibliographical knowledge useful when their research takes them into related fields.

Of more recent development in university libraries is the concept of the information officer, not necessarily a specialist in any subject sphere, but trained to know his way through information sources. It mainly came in with the establishment of the technological universities, which evolved out of colleges of advanced technology. These institutions were already in close contact with industry, its libraries and information services, and they recruited largely from industry. Although it is an over-simplification, there is some truth in the contrast between the industrial researcher, reluctant or unable to spare the time to search the literature, and the academic researcher for whom use of the literature is a part of the search for knowledge in which he is engaged. However, in the technological areas of universities there has been shown a genuine need for a service of this kind and its value has already been felt. Moreover an information service is of considerable benefit in many other fields such as medicine and the social sciences and indeed every librarian has at some time acted as an information officer, not merely steering the user towards the sources of information, but extracting information from those sources himself and presenting it to the user. This cautious, or it might be said, naïve way of describing such a service is intentional and serves as a reminder that the academic is principally concerned with the personal pursuit of knowledge and its communication to others, and the more he acts as his own information officer, with the help of the library and its staff, the wiser investigator and better communicator he is likely to become. Indeed there is many a scientist who would claim that nobody but himself can carry out a literature search in his field, since only his brain is attuned precisely enough in that field to separate the relevant from the irrelevant, and to identify the relevant within the apparently irrelevant. It is significant that the majority of the products of information science courses in our library schools go elsewhere than university libraries. All this being said, information service in its broadest sense is a developing element of university librarianship which is expressed in the encouragingly healthy beginnings of the recently formed information services group of the Standing Conference of National and University Libraries.

A factor in this service, and the third major element of the subject specialist approach, is the development of instruction in the use of libraries. For many years, the majority of university libraries were able to give no more than token instruction to new students, comprising a talk by the Librarian or a senior staff member and a brief tour of the library. Coming as it often did – and in many cases still does – at the beginning of the student's university career as part of, or at the end of, a bewildering period of registration, induction and union society 'bazaars', its absorption by the students was no more than superficial, and only the enthusiastic student was likely to carry information from such instructions into practice. Improvements in the technique have often produced extremely useful films and tape-slide presentations whose visual impact carries the message deeper and more permanently into the memory of the student. But the subject specialist is able to communicate much more effectively to a small specialist group of students, provided that he is given the time and has it at the right stage. In what are often considered overcrowded courses there is likely to be resistance to giving up subject teaching time to library instruction. It is therefore necessary to put the case, and support it, that library- and literature-knowledge are basic to effective learning. Clearly it is easier to involve postgraduates, not so constrained by timetables, but these require more individual, more specialised and therefore more time-consuming attention from library staff. The same applies to teaching staff, with the proviso that they must first of all be convinced that they *need* to learn more about the use of libraries and the literature. The establishment of priorities among the three main functions is one of the problems of the subject specialist system.

Another problem has given some concern to librarians wishing to give their senior staff managerial experience to take more senior administrative posts. A subject specialist (since he or she often is responsible for more than one subject it is convenient to use the term divisional librarian) is involved in academic activity, scholarship and teaching, and with public relations, rather than with personnel direction and administrative problem-solving. The longer he works at the job, the better qualified he is for it, but he may not gain that breadth of experience which will be of use in a managerial situation. One way of overcoming this is to organise collections into sections separately staffed, as departmental libraries are, so that the specialist has an administrative role. But this requires a level of staffing that may be difficult to achieve.

Provision for undergraduates

The role of the library as instructor in its own use raises particularly the question of provision for undergraduate students. This is an area of university librarianship which has perhaps seen more change in this century than any other of its services. In the past, a different teaching situation made it possible to provide a minimal service. One copy of a book, or at most two, was considered sufficient to meet the needs of students who provided their own basic library of texts, and sought background reading to extend their studies. The growing practice of supplying books in schools rather than leaving pupils to provide their own, coupled with rises in the price of books, led to a reduction in the tendency of students to acquire books for university courses. In addition the range of reading required for courses tended to increase, with tutors reluctant or unable to differentiate between essential texts recommended for purchase, and the rest. Demands on the library grew and dissatisfaction with its service intensified.

The provision of an extra copy of essential works, confined to the library, ceased to be the exception and became a commonplace. Latterly the tendency to increase the number of copies of undergraduate texts has become standard practice, and this has enabled a variety of levels of availability to be introduced. Provision may now range from total confinement, through a three- or four-hour loan, an overnight loan, a two- or three-day loan, to a termly loan. Such flexibility of provision provides a more efficient method of obtaining optimum availability, avoiding on the one hand frustrating delays in obtaining required reading, and on the other hand a wasteful saturation policy of providing multiple holdings in all cases.

Such a variable loan policy requires careful monitoring to ensure that supply is keeping pace with, and not excessively outstripping, demand. In a conventional, manually operated lending system this can represent a very time-consuming operation, if it is not to remain only a crude tool.

Consideration of the problem of provision for undergraduates led in the United States of America to the movement towards separate undergraduate libraries. Arguments for and against these can be found throughout the literature of librarianship but there is scarcely a university library in Britain today that does not have a students' collection of some kind. The principle is clear; there are a limited number of works in heavy demand by large numbers of students and these can be identified with relative ease; to provide quick and easy access to such works it is convenient to group them together and to provide a congenial environment for their study. Thus has grown the concept of the Undergraduate Reading Room, providing reference copies of works in demand, in addition to the loanable copies available either there or in the main collection. As long as the collection is within easy access of the main library (preferably contained within the same building), it can, if sensibly organised, provide ideal conditions for student use. If it is too far from the main collection it either tempts the student to confine his reading to what is available there, or involves wasteful and tedious journeyings between two places of study. Given the right relationship between the two, the undergraduate library or reading room, staffed by those experienced in understanding and catering for students' book needs, is a considerable educative force within the university.

Provision for research

If it is true that eighty per cent of library use is devoted to 20% of its stock, then the question of provision for research, the justification for that remaining eighty per cent bookstock, is seen to be one of frightening proportions. The problem of research provision is as difficult as it was a hundred years ago: how to provide within a reasonable budget for the unforeseeable needs of those carrying out research in many and widely differing fields. Even the largest and oldest university libraries are not self-sufficient in meeting all the needs of their users. Yet it is true that the larger the collection and the more it satisfies its users from its own shelves, the greater the research potential of the institution it serves. The researcher works most effectively within an immense collection close at hand. Any recourse to other sources places constraints on the free-ranging scope of his studies. In library provision, while *large* does not necessarily mean *good*, *good* necessarily involves *large*. The principle must be understood in comparative terms; a large collection, adequate for the needs of scholars in one subject, may be numerically smaller than that sufficient for scholars in another subject. But deep and rich it must be if research activity is to flourish unchecked. So ideally collections must be built up massively and maintained. However, none but the largest libraries can ensure this in traditional subject fields, and the remainder must concentrate on meeting as far as possible the expressed demands of faculty for new material, and either search for the rest on the second-hand market or rely on the interlending system.

Special collections

The second-hand market becomes ever more difficult to shop around, as prices escalate. Reprint programmes have helped, but at present are not free of publishing difficulties, and every library has files of orders for speculative and unlikely-to-appear reprints. Special collections, built up with great care and shrewd opportunism in the early years of the century, are ossifying in many university libraries through lack of funds which nowadays appear as more urgently needed for bread and butter purposes.

The Rare Books Group of the Library Association is performing a valuable service in keeping alive a tradition and encouraging a concentration of the attention of librarians on an activity upon which the spotlight of cost-effectiveness casts a glare which some consider baleful.

But if a library becomes a national and international centre for research in a number of fields on the strength of its collections of scarce materials, or if even one collection in a library is regarded as a unique national source, then it is justifying the use of funds to maintain it as an active collection. Thus in the university library field today the scarce resources available for early books are being devoted to the nurturing of those collections already established as research sources.

But not all special collections are of early books, and it is possible, and desirable, to build and maintain collections in comparatively recent fields. The expansion of studies in politics, in labour history and in transport history require the conservation of printed and manuscript sources of study, which are frequently in such a form that they have been vulnerable to destruction as ephemera. A large number of university libraries, without the funds to compete for early material with wealthy book collectors, have established important modern collections related to research activities in their own universities, which provide invaluable research support, without making excessive demands on the library budget.

Interlending

The other alternative to the purchase of current material, the use of the interlending system, has been one of the major advances in the history of the library service. The first formal service between university libraries was in fact established through the initiative of the Association of University Teachers in 1925, and a central bureau established, which was later to be incorporated into the National Central Library. Now that the NCL is incorporated with the British Library Lending Division, there can be seen the logical culmination of those earlier efforts. The development of interlending systems among public libraries into regional systems gave university libraries another source of supply through their local regional bureaux. It is true that today all but the smaller and newer university libraries lend more books locally than they borrow; this is inevitable since they are often the only libraries in the area catering specifically for academic research and likely to have the unusual material which the public library user may not find on its shelves. Nevertheless a judiciously used regional bureau can be a quick source of material in certain fields. And where a university offers more to the region than it receives, it forms an appropriate service to the local community at comparatively little cost to itself.

A university library, therefore, has three main sources of supply in interlending, namely other university libraries, its regional library system and the British Library. Naturally it uses other sources, the London Library, Lewis's, the Colleges and Institutes of Education library network and the many informal contacts with individual libraries. Inevitably, given the stage of development of the BLLD, most university libraries direct most of their borrowing requests there. It is estimated that about three-quarters of university library borrowings are from the BLLD and its outlier libraries. The establishment in 1962 of its precursor, the National Lending Library, made a revolutionary change in the accessibility of scientific and technical literature. The rate of increase of requests from science-based departments since that date is evidence of the increased satisfaction level in this field.

Of course it must be said that not every loan from the BLLD is necessarily a research problem solved, or even helped. Just as making a photocopy can often be a substitute for reading, so an impressive list of borrowings may hide a reluctance to develop one's own work. This should not be the concern of a university library. If its users request it to obtain from other libraries what it does not hold, it is, in principle at least, its duty to obtain it, on the grounds that it has failed to provide on the spot for its users' needs. However, at the present time the cost of postage is so high, staff are both expensive and, when pressure to freeze vacancies in hard-hit universities is so great, difficult to obtain, that libraries are re-examining very carefully the logistics of interlending.

There are two main methods of reducing the cost of interloans. One is by reducing the number of requests despatched, and the other is by making a charge to users. The former method involves some kind of selective process, limiting the categories of those who may use the service or limiting the number of requests that users may make. An obvious application of the first method would be to limit undergraduate use to those requests countersigned by tutors as being necessary for curricular purposes, and since undergraduate curricular needs should be capable of satisfaction from a library's own holdings, reducing unnecessary interloan requests, and as a result transferring some of them to purchase orders. The second method, of limiting numbers of requests, is more difficult to apply since it is open to abuse without a labour-intensive recording system.

This problem demonstrates the principle that borrowing from BLLD or elsewhere is not necessarily an economic alternative to adequate provision by a library for its users' needs. And as has been stated earlier, it is not a satisfactory alternative academically. Nevertheless, an efficient, fast national interloan system is an essential supplement to a library's in-house provision and a necessary support system for a national library service. The British Library Lending Division contributes uniquely to this system, but its success is placing it under considerable organisational stresses. This is a problem for the British Library, but it is also a matter of concern to university libraries, whose users are generally in a hurry, that there should be no falling off of speed of delivery or request handling. There is at times evidence of delays, and of inadequate checking, especially when outlier libraries are involved, and the question must be posed whether a movement towards entire reliance on a central supplier is a wise one. It is essential to ensure that there is a fail-safe situation nationally, and to avoid ending up with only one basket, however large, for our national eggs. But we have a long way to go before the overwhelming benefits of a national lending library, increasing steadily, especially in the social sciences and the humanities, are in serious danger of being replaced by the frustrations of a clumsy, bureaucratic machine.

Accommodation

Questions of local as opposed to national holdings of library materials raise the problem of accommodation. The University

Grants Committee set up in 1975 a working party to consider capital provision for university libraries.[1] The Committee was naturally concerned, at a time of economic difficulty, at the number of very expensive library buildings that had been erected in recent years and even more concerned at the number of buildings and extensions under submission. It was inevitable that an examination should be made of the possibilities for the use of cheaper storage facilities at a local and national level. However, the concept of external storage is not new to university librarians. They have long been familiar with the problems of accommodation, and have used some or all of the methods under current discussion. Closed storage was once the normal method of housing the greater part of the university library's stock, and today large proportions of the stock of some libraries are either completely closed or available only to certain categories of users. External stores of various kinds have been used for as long a period as internal closed storage and are now used perhaps more than ever before. Cooperative storage is not so common, involving as it does difficulties of administration and funding, but the London University Repository at Egham provides an example of the cooperative approach, and also illustrates the problems that attend such a venture, even among the constituent colleges of one university. The transferring of stock considered surplus into the BLLD is a comparatively recent possibility, and one whose growth would have to be controlled with care if it were not to produce an inaccessible heap awaiting processing.

The discarding of any stock other than duplicates has never been a major activity among university librarians. They have always erred on the side of conservation, and erred is probably the right word. But any analysis of the loans from a university library and any sample of the consultation of books in library stacks show evidence that any attempt to select items for discard is risky. Despite the danger, it is true that there is a limit to the number of second and third rate out-of-date works that a library need hold, and a limit to the number of libraries that need hold them, and some rationalisation of national holdings would be desirable. But the concentration of all such material in one repository or even arbitrarily in a small number of repositories could prevent the sort of free access which such material requires. A student of the history of thought, say, in the nineteenth century in whatever field, science, politics, theology, medicine, the arts, etc, needs to have access not merely to the works of the leaders of thought, but to the mediocre, the third rate, the laity. And he needs, since there is so much of it, to be able to scan quickly through it and extract the current thinking that underlies it. For this purpose he does not want to send lists of requests to a repository and wait for delivery, but to browse among such material, using his trained eye and brain to make appropriate selection. If such cooperative storage is practical, perhaps it should be considered on a subject basis; perhaps there should be established repositories which could be centres, not of excellence, but of mediocrity.

In the process of slimming down, a library must not, however, leave itself weakened. Having regard to the time-scale we are considering, a library requires the stamina of a long-distance runner, but it must have in addition the build of a weight-lifter – it must be massive enough for the weight of scholarship which it is called upon to support.

Library buildings

The considerable increase in library buildings which has come about over the last fifteen years or so, and increasingly in the last eight, has been the result primarily of the creation of the new universities, from 1960 onwards, and secondarily of the need to replace outgrown and out-of-date pre-war buildings in the older universities. Even buildings of the late fifties, after nearly twenty years' use are in need of considerable expansion if not replacement. It is not extravagance on the part of universities, or empire-building on the part of their librarians, which has produced the demands for new accommodation. And in the scale of financial values, these claims are not excessive; it is unfortunate that many of these demands are still waiting to be met when the economic climate is so bleak. When inadequate and out-dated or ill-planned old libraries are pressed into the attempt to produce an adequate and up-to-date service, the educational function of the library and of the university suffers.

A well-designed building is a fundamental element in the success of the library as a university service. The library is a place of study for many hours a day for a very large number of students as well as staff, as well as being a place where certain services are provided, so that environment is as critical a feature as administrative efficiency.

Before the Second World War, a number of fine university libraries were built as a result of munificent gifts or bequests. But no main university library since then has been built with private money, and so modern libraries have tended to be built to standards controlled by an official body, the University Grants Committee. Since that body provides the funds for the building, the standards which it lays down are binding on librarian and architect. This situation can be seen as an exciting challenge to the ingenuity of the architect, or as a dead weight on his imagination and aesthetic capability. It certainly sets limits on the soaring imagination of the librarian, and forces upon him a preoccupation with efficient use of space if he is not to find himself administering a failed library.

Fortunately there is today a wealth of experience in library design available to university librarians. The far larger numbers of libraries in the United States have provided very many examples of library buildings to study in detail. SCONUL has an active sub-committee on buildings which promulgates information and organises very useful critical visits to recent library buildings, and by this time there are a reasonable number of buildings in this country which the prospective library designer can inspect at length. It must be said, and it should be evident, that the UGC itself has acquired a good deal of expertise in library planning and has a very informed staff with whom a librarian will find himself dealing. There is moreover a useful and growing body of literature on the subject, paramount among which is the remarkable work by the best-known and respected library consultant in the United States, Keyes Metcalf. This book, *Planning academic libraries,* is a masterpiece of book production in its field and a mine of information, and every librarian has profited from its study. Architects have ignored it at their peril and the wisest of them have copies on their shelves.

Ralph Ellsworth, too, has greatly influenced for good the design of libraries both in the United States and in this country, and there is now no excuse for a badly planned university library.

Given the present circumstances it is inevitable that there will be a certain sameness about modern library buildings. Those earlier privately financed buildings were able to contain features which would nowadays be considered extravagant, sometimes splendid architectural treatments, sometimes splendidly disastrous design elements; but they were often idiosyncratic. But the modern building is constrained by financial considerations, and by current design principles which the majority obey in the reasonable belief that they serve present needs and will meet future and possibly changing demands. Since the main disadvantage of the previous generations of buildings has been their resistance to adaptation for modern needs, one of the main requirements now written into the library building is flexibility.

The word is often abused. Total flexibility is a librarian's dream and an architectural impossibility. The flexibility must be built into a library within certain limits both structural and financial, and the problem for librarian and architect is to achieve the correct balance. The success of the building for the future will hang on whether that balance was achieved. The building must be capable of internal rearrangement (though librarians must not contemplate annual major redesigning sessions) and must be capable of expansion without major reconstruction of the first stage.

What, then, is the concept of a library building which will be acceptable to librarians in general and will satisfy the UGC in particular? The most efficient shape within which to achieve easiest and shortest lines of communication is the cube. Though vertical communication can be achieved quickly with the aid of lifts and paternosters, there are two main arguments against these: they are expensive and they break down. Moreover, for lifts to be useful as public conveyances, there must be so many of them to carry the numbers of readers using the building as to create very serious cost problems. Ideally, in order to use staircases as the main vertical communicators there should be no more than four floors, but the larger libraries may find that floor areas become unrealistically large for horizontal communication. There is, therefore, a complex problem in the three-dimensional geometry of library design to adhere to the principle that internal distances should be reasonably short and communication routes relatively simple.

For maximum flexibility the cube should be a series of empty floors permitting complete rearrangement in the future. But as has been mentioned, this is an impossible dream; there must in the first place be fixed elements like plant rooms, service cores, structure supports and staircases. The skill of the designer lies in the confinement of these elements so that as large an area as possible on every floor is uncluttered. Into these areas will be fitted the bookshelves, reading spaces and administrative and library service areas.

Such requirements will produce a very deep building. To avoid this, some library buildings have incorporated a central light well so that natural light and natural ventilation may be utilised as much as possible. These attempts have avoided too drastic a rejection of the traditional concept of libraries with views of the outside world from all points, and are certainly less costly in terms of environmental control. But they are relatively inflexible and they do not cater as efficiently for maximum capacity for books and readers. The advantage of the deep, square, or near square, building is that it can house its bookstock efficiently in blocks near the centre of the building and place its reading areas round the outside with communication among these elements remaining as nearly as possible the shortest distance. The main disadvantages that the designers of such a building have to overcome as far as possible is the absence of natural light and external views over large areas of the building, and the problems of costly environmental control. The former must be overcome by an attractive interior design and a layout which ensures views of the outside world incorporated into the traffic routes most likely to be followed. The latter problem is one that must be taken into account when initial costings are being prepared. Environmental control is necessarily a major element in the capital and maintenance costs of a library building and must have a high priority in overall budgeting. The UGC, aware of these problems, has laid down that windows should occupy no more than 25% of the total wall area, in order to avoid excessive heat loss, and reduce the amount of mechanical cooling required to offset solar gain. The problem of cooling raises the question of air-conditioning. The majority of libraries built recently have been able to incorporate this within the cost limits laid down by the UGC. There is a large measure of agreement among librarians and ventilating engineers that air-conditioning is desirable, but the argument is not entirely accepted by the UGC, and even some architects, suffering from faulty or badly designed systems, remain unconvinced that mechanical ventilation without cooling provision is insufficient to provide acceptable conditions for books and readers. There is of course a problem in any building of providing conditions which are satisfactory for the permanent conservation of books, and the personal comfort of anything between six hundred and a thousand readers at any one time.

Since a university library does have to provide for these large numbers of readers, particular care is taken over the design of reading areas and the furniture for those areas. The trend is away from open tables with views of hundreds of other readers and the resultant visual distraction, towards a variety of seating patterns, with a predominance of individual screened tables, allowing an element of visual privacy, some open tables, study rooms and easy chairs. The very large seating areas again are visually broken up by fitments which avoid an agoraphobic environment without interfering with the adequate circulation of air. There are two main reasons for the concentration of books in the centre and readers in the perimeter. Books benefit from an avoidance of daylight, and readers enjoy a visual relationship with the outside world. It is additionally possible to accommodate some readers safely outside the structural frame, and thereby to gain accommodation, but it is an essential element of flexibility that within the main framework the floors should be capable of housing both bookstocks and readers, thus ensuring that these are interchangeable in the future, if functional requirements make it desirable.

A university library is a quick service unit and a study at the same time. Students or staff in a hurry may wish to return or borrow a book before a lecture, scan recent additions to the library, check current periodicals in their field, refer to the catalogue to check a holding, or lodge an interloan request. It is important therefore that such services should be available near the entrance both for the convenience of such users and to avoid disturbance to readers. It is important that the issue counter should be closely related to the entrance and exit control and that the catalogue should be strategically placed not only for library users but also for the cataloguing and book order staff who are individually its most frequent users. It is a fact that seconds saved in the library staff's catalogue use are cumulatively a significant feature of the efficiency of the administration of those sections. Thus a relationship complex emerges between the many elements of the library building and it is the role of the designer to see that the optimum satisfaction level is achieved in all these. The bookshelves must be convenient for, but not obtrusive to, the readers. The latter must not be distracted by browsing users, but should enjoy a 'bookish environment'. Service staff should be available for readers, but consultation should not disturb those studying; the process of borrowing should be simple to follow but should not involve loopholes in security, since stolen books represent a failure in availability, and their replacement a drain on scarce resources needed for current literature.

The modern design of university libraries has been criticised on the grounds that the scholar's study has been replaced by a machine for reading. But as long as that machine has been designed to take into account the aesthetics of library use then it will in its own way ensure an environment in which the pursuit of knowledge through books is a pleasure as well as an efficient process.

By the intelligent application of past experience, and the acceptance and utilisation of the constraints surrounding it, the modern university library has become a very efficient building, flexible and amenable to expansion. Its efficiency would become progressively limited if its inbuilt expansibility were not to be utilised, but large parts of its stock relegated to remote stores. Too little is known of 'user behaviour' for us to be happy to alter radically the habits of use which are established, and which modern libraries appropriately serve.

Computerisation

The contemporary library building, systematically based on certain principles, is a product of study over fifteen years or so. That period has also seen the development of computer applications in university libraries which may be said to be still in its infancy, though the last five years have seen a considerable maturation. It was inevitable that once the computer, developed originally for scientific purposes, was seen to be applicable to data handling of many kinds, thereby finding a major application in commerce and industry, its relevance to library procedures should be recognised. The circulation system of a university library is a case in point. Its distinctive features are that it creates one or more large files of book issue records which require daily or more frequent updating; the file must be searched hundreds of times daily when books are returned; it must be further searched for reservations and to issue overdue notices; and it must be capable of providing immediate information concerning items on loan. This last feature is particularly important; university library users require material urgently for course work, and need to know whether a book is on loan and if so whether it can be obtained quickly. It will not do to say that if a book is not on the shelves it will be on loan, since the reference use of a university library is high. Action must be taken at once on the required book which is not on the shelves. A significant amount of reading room staff time is devoted to the creation and maintenance of files which will provide that information.

Another distinctive feature of a university library circulation system is that a high turnover of stock must be maintained. Since a large number of students require for a short time and at certain times of the session a limited number of titles, it is essential that they are returned as soon as possible after use and made available for others. It has been found necessary to operate a reminder procedure to ensure this turnover, and this also is a very labour-intensive operation.

A third feature is that since constant reference is being made to the issue files for reservation and recall purposes, a certain minimum of information, author, title, class number, borrower, etc, must be recorded for each book. In a manual system this involves the completion of a two-part slip by the reader, what has been described as 'cataloguing a book in order to borrow it'.

All this file creation, maintenance and handling can be carried out by a computer more quickly, more accurately and using less staff and reader time. Similarly the computer may be used for book-ordering, in which large files are maintained and a regular reminder service required; and in the cataloguing sector, where the same books are catalogued and classified in scores of libraries all over the country, a central computer-based cataloguing service has obvious advantages. For over ten years projects have been developed in university libraries using computers to assist these housekeeping operations and at the present time a large number of systems, especially handling circulation, are in operation. The British Library Research and Development Department, and the Office for Scientific and Technical Information from which it developed, have given considerable support to experimental projects in the field. But university libraries have laboured under a disadvantage over this period, as their use of their universities' computers has tended to be by grace and favour, since the Computer Board, which controls all university main computers, has ruled that the use of such computers should be restricted to research and teaching purposes, and only an insignificant proportion of their time may be spared for administrative use. Libraries could not afford to purchase for themselves machines adequate to their needs, and so any service would be vulnerable to the constraints of use of a large scientific computer serving research needs. A daily updating of files is a minimum need for a university library circulation system but a university computer unit is not always in a position to guarantee this. However, a number of circulation systems are providing a service even under these conditions.

The development of the mini-computer especially over the last five or six years has placed more potential in the hands of libraries and emphasised the limitations of many existing computer-based circulation systems. One of the problems of these systems is that no more than a daily up-date is likely and even that may not be guaranteed; and yet the old manual system, clumsy as it is, can generally do better than that. If it is required to improve on it, some form of on-line, or interactive, system is required. A mini-computer in the library may be coupled to a university central computer to provide on-line access to at least part of the circulation file. Clearly a further development would be a large enough main computer in the library itself. But as has been said, this is beyond the purse of most libraries. One way of overcoming this problem is for a group of libraries to share a computer and link on-line to it via mini-computers in each cooperating library.

Variations of these alternatives are under development in the country and may indicate appropriate patterns of use. This is to be hoped, because it seems clear that the most successful applications of the computer will require guaranteed privileged access, and will demand the use of machines to their full capacity and therefore at their most economical.

The question of computer economics is a complex but important one. One may cite three main reasons for the use of computers: firstly to improve the service, secondly to effect staff savings (and therefore economies), and thirdly to provide management information. It is in the circulation sub-system that the most apparent possibilities for improvement exist. But it is a fact that a computer application could achieve improvements at some points of the service only at the expense of down-grading the service at other points. If every reader making a book enquiry or reservation is compelled to consult the catalogue to read and transcribe a six-digit number before he can be given information, this is a worse situation than under the old manual system where author/title enquiries were permitted. Similarly if the latest information the reader can be given at 5 pm on one day is that the book he needs was not borrowed before 5 pm the previous day – it may have been borrowed since, but we shall

not know until some time the following morning, by which time
it may have been returned, and we shall not know *that* until the
following morning – then we are providing the reader with a
worse book-enquiry service than is possible, albeit in a
cumbersome way, under a manual system. If there must be
constraints placed upon our use of the computer for circulation
purposes, and for financial reasons this must be the case, then it
is essential to examine these and the corresponding benefits most
carefully to ensure that we are not giving a bad deal to our
users. It may unfortunately be the case that even where overall
improvements can be demonstrated, a university may be forced
so say that it cannot afford an improved service, if the manual
system has not broken down, and if the use of the computer
involves extra expenditure. What, it may be asked, will users do
with the seconds we are saving them in the time they take to
borrow each book? This may not be an enlightened question,
but it is inevitably a part of the thinking of hard-pressed
university purse-holders. An improved service may not in itself
be a sufficient argument for the use of computers.

The second argument must be brought into play. An automated
issue system occupies considerably less staff time at the issue
counter and either staff numbers may be run down by natural
wastage, or staff may be diverted to more productive library
tasks. The use of national or regional computer-based catalogue
production will require less cataloguing time in each library, and
the cataloguing staff may be reduced or set to retrospective
catalogue revision. These are sound arguments if they can be
sustained. But the cost of computer staff or computer bureau
charges must be offset against library staff savings. Those wise in
the experience of computer applications in university libraries
are inclined to say that no savings can be effected, by which they
mean that none have been effected in their experience. Whether
various cooperative applications can improve on this is a
question which only time can answer. What a consideration of
staff costs may do at the least is to establish that considerable
service improvements may be obtained for only marginal
increases in costs. And that would be something.

It is the third argument, the provision of management

information, that is at once the most intangible at this stage and potentially the most powerful. University librarianship provides an interesting example of the economist's concept of decision-making in an uncertain environment. We know far too little about the use of our resources to know whether we are carrying out a cost-effective operation. Whether we are providing the right books in the right number of copies and making them available for the right periods of time are questions we can only answer by rule of thumb. We do not know how much waste is involved in our library service, and what would be the results of improving it in one direction or another. The statistical information which could be extracted from computer-aided operations would give us some quantifiable basis for examination. Since there is no acceptable way at present of quantifying the end-product of a university library system, or indeed of a university education, we shall not have the basis for planning enjoyed by commercial organisations which can relate programmes to profits. But we should be in a better position to steward our resources more accurately and more wisely than we can at present.

If we are to use the computer's potential efficiently, we must learn from the experience of others and proceed with care. The arch-enemy of library computers, and what he calls 'computerators', (those who brandish them), Ellsworth Mason, found an easy target in the United States after a decade of what could be termed the 'colossal blunder' approach. If he generalised too easily from the disasters he encountered, his lesson for those who are prepared to heed his warnings without accepting his conclusions is that the university librarian should proceed step-by-step with caution and consultation. The more cooperation there can be between libraries in this field, the more economically can the benefits of computerisation be achieved. There are a number of cooperative projects in Britain at the present time and much is to be learnt from them. The greatest potential for cooperation lies within the British Library itself whose developments are described in another chapter. Every university library stands to gain from such developments, and there is still time to allow them to mature. The likelihood of its possessing the greatest computer potential of any library in the country will enable it to develop beyond MARC, forms of information service of great benefit. At the moment the use of such computer-based information services as exist is on a comparatively small scale, largely through shortage of funds for what is still an expensive field, but also through an unsureness as to the benefits to be gained from them and their inherent value-for-money. Much work remains to be done on assessment and revision among these services.

'I am sure that the computer can benefit the university library, if it is used with taste', is the remark made a few years ago by a Vice-Chancellor, a scientist of repute, expert in the scientific use of computers. It expresses succinctly, not merely that intelligence and commonsense should be brought to bear, but, because of the nature of university libraries, we need to apply a sense of the fitness of things.

Non-book media

Taste is a quality equally useful to the consideration of new media, audio-visual aids, or non-book materials. Librarians often feel that they have struggled to introduce microforms into their libraries over a large number of years against the assembled resistance of faculty. Who, it is said, would sit before a screen peering at smudgy marks when he could relax with a good book? It is not merely the advocacy or doggedness of librarians but also improvements in photographic techniques and reading devices, that have brought about a grudging acceptance of the medium. And microforms are *quasi* books, whereas the new media are often anything but readable. There is clearly a problem in acceptability. But there is also a problem in establishing what, if any, new media are appropriate to university teaching and learning.

The use of film for teaching and indeed for research purposes is well-established in some medical, technological and scientific fields as, over a shorter period, is closed-circuit television. Their usefulness in these areas has been based on their ability to demonstrate techniques and operations either too large or too discrete or too expensive to present in a lecture-theatre or laboratory. For this reason they have seemed less appropriate in the teaching of the humanities. But in any field the use of audio-visual media to replace teaching at any point has not been popular, and can meet active resistance. Yet the language laboratory has found acceptance for admittedly limited purposes. It is perhaps that the use of pictures, either instead of or additional to the spoken word, appears too juvenile a way of communicating at a university level. Some audio-visual presentations, commercial and home-produced, make such an argument all too tenable, but patience and hard work, especially by audio-visual aid units, but also by libraries, have succeeded in demonstrating that some subjects are responsive to teaching in a rewarding manner by new methods involving AV techniques. More significantly for university libraries, it is being shown that valuable self-instructional presentations can be produced. Controlled experiments on the value of self-instructional tape-slide presentations are being carried out at the Institute for Educational Technology of the University of Surrey. The implications for university libraries are clear; the use by individual students of such devices is analogous to their use of books, in a library which is open for longer hours than teaching departments, and which provides a congenial environment for study. Such a situation is already regarded as commonplace in a few university libraries, and is likely to spread as teaching staffs exchange views in their conferences, and more especially as generations of students enter universities with experience of new media in schools.

Already, through the initiative of the SCONUL Tape/Slide Working Group, with the support of the SCONUL New Media Sub-Committee, a number of tape-slide guides to the literature of various subject fields have been produced, and are in use in libraries. The fact that the series is subject to a reviewing procedure by the working group is an indication that it is not easy to create an effective presentation. But as libraries gain more experience of producing (hopefully in conjunction with their AV unit whose professional expertise can make such a difference) tape-slide guides to the use of their own library, their awareness of the medium's potential, and their ability to select as carefully as they select books, will grow.

With enthusiasm running high, and with costs comparatively low, the temptation to overreach oneself is at the moment strong. The reference to selection in the previous paragraph serves as a reminder that book selection is best carried out in consultation with departments. Similarly with non-book media, it is important to work in collaboration with teaching staffs. Audio-visual aids units are finding that they cannot run too far ahead of their teaching colleagues, however reactionary they may find them. Librarians who are concerned to supply the needs of staff and students must move at their pace, in a field where a few successes already show a considerable potential for the future, but where a number of blunders already indicate the opportunity for failure and a consequent hardening of the opposition. It is well to remember that it was as far back as 1955, that Sir Arthur Elton, a pioneer documentary film maker with John Grierson, presented a paper to Aslib, which was, or should have been, of seminal influence on the use of film in the teaching of history; and to consider how little development there has been since then.

Cooperation

A university library must serve its university, and a university librarian's loyalty is to his or her university. A university's contribution to the community is to carry out its teaching role and its pursuit of knowledge to the best of its ability and in the service of the community. The University Grants Committee allocates funds to universities specifically for those tasks and for no others. Any allocation of resources by a university to functions which impede those tasks is a misuse of funds.

This is why, to take a specific example, a university library cannot throw open its doors and make its resources widely available to other institutions and individuals, if such use reduces its ability to serve its university members adequately. What is sometimes criticised as exclusiveness should be commended as single mindedness. Nevertheless, there are limited areas in which it can cooperate with libraries of other institutions with mutual benefits, and while there is a long tradition of cooperation in some of these fields (interlending has been mentioned), there has been a noticeable development in recent years of closer cooperation among libraries. Effective use of computers will depend to some extent on such cooperation, and if scarce national resources are to be used efficiently, national aid to centres of excellence to enable them to make their own resources more available to other institutions makes economic sense. Schemes of local cooperation are likely to receive encouragement (if of a somewhat sober kind) from the survey carried out among libraries in the Sheffield area. The establishment of the British Library has been an influence for good in this field. University libraries have been able to build in many cases strong research collections which it would be false economy not to share with others. At the same time the creation of working collections adequate for its users is the duty of every library of every institution, and it is its right to expect to be given the funds to create and maintain those collections. No librarian wants to be dependent on another librarian for providing a basic service for his users; pride in one's work is rightly too strong for that; and no library should be denied the funds that will make it the active resource centre of its institution.

SCONUL

Cooperation between university and national libraries is long-established and the links between them were formalised in the creation in 1951 of the Standing Conference of National and University Libraries. From small beginnings it has grown into a powerful organisation with a full-time Secretariat, consulted nationally on a large number of topics, and represented on many national bodies. A conference is held every six months at which business meetings are held and papers on matters of common interest read and discussed. While it is natural that the librarians of autonomous and widely varied universities should differ in their views on many points, and show a healthy dislike of conformism, the strength of SCONUL lies in the breadth of this cross-section, and in its ability, on matters which vitally concern research and advanced educational needs, to speak with a common voice.

Conclusion

This chapter has not attempted a full-scale treatment of the administration of university libraries. In discussing their basic role and considering a few matters of current interest and concern, the intention has been to give an indication of a stage of development over a number of areas, and the questions and problems that will remain or will appear. The future does not look an easy one for universities as a whole and librarians cannot expect it to be easier for them. What they hope for is the financial support to serve the information needs of their users, pre-eminently by collection building of the highest order, and by the exploitation of these collections, and the national resources of which they are a part.

Note

1. This chapter was written before the appearance in 1976 of the Report of the working party.

Further reading

Brook, G. L. *The modern university* Deutsch, 1965. (Especially the chapter on libraries.)
Ellsworth, Ralph E. *Academic library buildings* Colorado Associated University Press, 1973.
Higham, Norman. *Computer needs for university library operations: a report* SCONUL, 1973.

Metcalf, Keyes D. *Planning academic and research library buildings* McGraw Hill, 1965.
Neal, K. W. *British university libraries* Published by the author, 1970.
Thompson, James. *An introduction to university library administration* Bingley, 1970.
University Grants Committee. *Report of the Committee on Libraries* 1967.

Chapter Twelve

Polytechnic libraries

David Bagley

In 1966 a White Paper was presented to Parliament by the
Secretary of State for Education and Science. *A plan for
polytechnics and other colleges: higher education in the further education
system*, Cmnd 3006) was a product of Labour Government
thinking, possibly influenced by its policy of developing
comprehensive education in the secondary sector. Anthony
Crosland introduced the new thinking in a speech at Woolwich
in which he supported the concept of a binary system of
education. This involved the creation of a system based on the
autonomous sector represented by the universities, and the
public sector as represented by the leading local authority
controlled technical colleges. Under the binary system each
sector could make a distinctive contribution to the expansion of
student numbers which had been forecast by Robbins and was
itself generated by the post-war birth rate bulge which was
approaching the secondary and higher education sectors. A
further problem had been posed by the cost of creating more
university places and it was believed that higher education might
possibly be provided more locally at less cost. A further
implication was that teacher training, in colleges of education,
should also be part of the public sector and should therefore
involve a closer integration with technical colleges. In the light
of all this, the White Paper on Polytechnics contains some
significant phrases which should be kept in mind when
considering their library developments. 'The Polytechnics are a
distinctive sector of higher education, complementing the
universities and colleges of education'. They were also intended
to be comprehensive in the range of studies and in the pattern of

courses, from diploma to postgraduate courses and with provision for study by full-time, sandwich or part-time means.

The need to provide vocationally oriented courses was stressed by including the importance of developing direct links with industry, business and the professions. Research would be encouraged, but only where it was directly in response to industrial need and hence preferably sponsored by outside funds. Thirty establishments were proposed as Polytechnics, with the majority being created by an amalgamation of existing local authority colleges of technology, commerce, art and other specialised colleges. In some cases, the amalgamation proposed involved links between colleges up to twenty miles apart or mergers between up to six separate colleges, each with its own satellite annexes. Of the thirty, in fact, only four were created from a single institution and even some of these inherited scattered annexe buildings. Thus although the new Polytechnics were to engage in work of university level and comparability, they were at a sad disadvantage in respect of buildings and were deficient in physical resources and support services. Although the name 'polytechnic' was used deliberately because it emphasised their wide-ranging ideals, it is perhaps unfortunate that there were Polytechnics already in existence and with a very honourable record in the provision of part-time and full-time education, particularly providing courses for professional qualifications in technology and commerce. The pre-1966 Polytechnics were mainly in London: two became full universities, five more became four new style polytechnics whilst two others retained their old name but are no longer technically Polytechnics. This kind of confusion is only gradually clearing as the student output increases and the value of the new-style Polytechnic education becomes more apparent.

The Polytechnics White Paper marked yet another stage in post-war thinking about education after the age of eighteen. Traditionally British policy in higher education had been based on three institutions, the university, the teacher training college (later known as Colleges of Education), and the further education college. Much of the emphasis of development in the nineteen fifties and sixties was concerned with expansion of the university sector, but the mid-fifties saw a realisation of our shortcomings in technological education. Technological development, particularly in the USSR and in USA, had led to a White Paper on Technological Education in 1956 which provided for a major initiative in higher education but in establishments then under local authority control. Eight of the leading regional technical colleges were designated Colleges of Advanced Technology with a brief to develop university level work but outside the hitherto traditional university sector. There are many similarities in the development of these CATs and the later Polytechnics, the major difference being that the Polytechnics were deliberately given a much wider brief to provide a comprehensive range of course.

A vital element of the policy outlined in the 1956 White Paper was the creation of an outside body, the National Council for Technological Awards which provided a mechanism for setting standards for courses which would be designed by the individual colleges, but leading to a NCTA award of degree level, the Diploma in Technology. The NCTA was a licensing body which quickly established very high standards which had to be satisfied to ensure that the Dip Tech award would be of honours degree level. In this way, the Colleges of Advanced Technology can be seen as a pilot for the later creation of Polytechnics which provide courses approved by the Council for National Academic Awards. The Robbins Committee report of 1963, which was primarily concerned with recommendations about full-time higher education, recognised the achievements of these colleges and included a proposal that they should be translated into the traditional university sector, albeit retaining their technological bias. Thus they moved out of the control of local authorities to come under the wing of the University Grants Committee. Polytechnics were deliberately left with the local authorities and expected to reflect locally expressed needs and to exploit the benefits of their existing links with industry and the professions.

The situation with regard to libraries in 1966 was generally grim for the new Polytechnics, but also illustrated a tremendous variety in levels of provision. It must be remembered that in most technical colleges under local authority control library development had never had a high priority in resource allocation, or indeed been considered significant in the teaching role. A major book on technical college work published in 1955 contained no reference whatever to libraries. Development of a university would have been unthinkable without a library being created at a very early stage, and the Colleges of Advanced Technology had to develop their library resources rapidly to cope with their new role. Local authority colleges generally, however, had been built upon a tradition of teaching on a part-time basis, with an emphasis on note-taking and little spare time or encouragement to seek information in libraries. Pressure of time had overtaken the earliest ideals, when Mechanics Institutes were first created by groups of people prepared to share their books for the purpose of self-education. At the time of creation of Polytechnics there were at least a few pointers from the Department of Education and Science. The first hint had come from the issue of DES Building Bulletin 5 in 1955, which recognised the need for a properly planned library in a College of Further Education, and yet was only recommending 2000 square feet of space for a student population of 3000. An administrative note had also been circulated, Circular 322, which emphasised the role of the library in a college, but this also related more to the work of a College of Further Education.

Librarians were becoming more vocal in drawing attention to their potential, especially through the Colleges of Technology and Further Education Section of the Library Association. In July 1968 the Library Association Council accepted a very far-sighted document on Guidelines for Polytechnic Library Development, published in the *Library Association Record* for September 1968 under the title 'Libraries in the new polytechnics'. Earlier standards had been published by CTFE quoting minimal figures for bookfunds and staffing level but the Polytechnic Guidelines used a different approach. Because of the need to think on a totally new scale, and the very wide disparity of existing provision, the Guidelines set out a number of factors to be considered in new library planning and offered examples based on current good practice. For instance, instead of suggesting a global bookfund, it demonstrated how the necessary bookfund total should be calculated by considering the types of courses to be run in different subjects, and the level of support needed allied to the numbers and types of student. The resulting totals produced figures so far in advance of what many of the institutions had previously considered good enough that the Guidelines met with an incredulous response from many librarians.

In October 1969 the Registrar of CNAA circulated to colleges a private paper indicating the standards of library provision which its visiting Subject Boards would consider an acceptable minimum. The paper had been prepared by the Subject Board for Librarianship, an internal committee constituted to examine provision for education in librarianship. The document was an attempt to be realistic in its requirements 'at a time when library provision in Colleges is probably at its most varied and against a background of unusual financial stringency'. Even now these words have a familiar ring! The covering letter to the document stressed its purely advisory nature, but recommendations of CNAA Visiting Panels carry considerable weight in Polytechnics, and the content of the paper caused considerable anxiety amongst Polytechnic librarians.

First impressions were that the whole paper gave a picture of Polytechnic libraries at the opposite end of the spectrum to that contained in the Library Association Guidelines published only the previous year. Minimum figures were quoted which could prove disastrously low if used as acceptable targets, and published figures are often widely misquoted. It is only fair, however, to balance against this the widespread scepticism of colleagues who regarded the 1968 LA statement as being an unrealistic ideal. The CNAA paper quoted a minimum total bookstock of at least 30,000 volumes and 750 current periodical subscriptions for a college with 2000 students. The LA guidelines stated confidently that a basic stock of 150,000 volumes with subscriptions to 3000 periodicals would be a reasonable estimate for 2000 full-time students studying a wide range of degree level disciplines. A similar gulf appeared in the guidance on expenditure. CNAA indicated that although annual expenditure would vary according to the stage of development reached, they would be satisfied to find an average allowance of

£10 per full-time student (1968 prices). Assuming the average of 2000 students, this would yield £20,000 per year for books and journals. The LA Guidelines suggested that it is doubtful whether any Polytechnic could develop adequate resources without an annual budget of £60,000 on books and periodicals, and probably an additional £10,000 for non-book materials. At the time that the CNAA paper was circulated, more than half of the Polytechnic libraries were in receipt of bookfunds exceeding £20,000 per year. However, CNAA were rightly concerned about those below the line and it must be admitted that because of CNAA's powerful position as a body approving course submissions, any statement from them could be used as a strong argument in requesting financial support from local authorities.

The facts about bookfund levels were known to the librarians of Polytechnics, but due to the lack of official statistics it is possible that the CNAA Librarianship Board did not have the full picture. However, since there appeared to be a need for collated information, a standing conference was formed, the Council of Polytechnic Librarians (COPOL). This was seen to be essentially a self-help organisation, a group of librarians facing common problems and in need of material support and assistance. With each Polytechnic in a state of rapid development there had been frequent questionnaires circulating in attempts to establish inter-Polytechnic comparisons. A first priority for COPOL was therefore seen to be the central collection and maintenance of the necessary statistics, and possibly the establishment of agreed standards. Rapid improvements in library services have been taking place since then, due partly to careful handling by librarians of figures demonstrating one's place in the league table as compared to other Polytechnics, and also due to the continuing insistence by CNAA Subject Panels of high standards in support services for all schemes of study put forward for approval. The National Union of Students decided that improving library services in Polytechnics should have a priority in their programme and held demonstrations locally, devoted a full day to a conference in November 1970 and finally called a national day of action to draw attention to their dissatisfaction over the standard of Polytechnic libraries.

Relations between Students' Unions and librarians were usually friendly since everyone agreed on the desirable objectives, differing only on the means of achievement. Finally the CNAA was able to withdraw its document since the essential point had been made and both academics and local authority education departments had generally been made aware of the new scale of thinking necessary for Polytechnic libraries.

Although the White Paper was first published in 1966, individual Polytechnics were not created overnight. Because of the problems of amalgamating separate establishments, the majority of Polytechnics did not receive their formal designation until 1968–1970. In each case the first task was to draw up development plans indicating their academic philosophy and the necessary physical development. Since most occupied city centre properties, physical development posed considerable problems solvable in some cases only by seeking totally new sites. Over half of the thirty have now submitted planning proposals involving new or greatly enlarged main libraries and 1975–76 will see the completion of a number of totally new library buildings. Some Polytechnics planned to move out of city centres and Bristol Polytechnic represented the first of the 'green field' pattern when its new library opened at the Coldharbour Lane site in 1975. In Sheffield, a city centre car park gave way to a new library building opened in November 1975. The present freeze on building projects is making forward planning very difficult, and new libraries will inevitably have to be designed to a lower standard than the post-war universities have enjoyed.

In order to provide guidance on cost limits the DES Architects Branch undertook a major design study at Leicester Polytechnic and this led to a recommendation on space formulae for the allocation of space to teaching, communal and library areas in a Polytechnic building. The earlier Building Bulletin 5 had indicated specific area allocations for bookstock, staff workroom and readers' study space. The Polytechnic guidance, however, adopted a 'broad brush' approach using a formula allowance of 0·8 square metres per Full-time Equivalent student (FTE). This space can be increased to 1·29 square metres/FTE if equivalent space can be reallocated from general teaching areas. Such flexibility allows for decisions to be made locally which could reflect, for instance, the degree to which self-study by students is encouraged. Within the total space the librarian and architect are given design freedom in allocating space to books, readers and staff, thus encouraging open planning. Although a 40% balance is allowed in teaching areas for corridors, toilets, stairwells etc, only 25% balance is given in the library area which again emphasises the need to reduce 'dead' space resulting from internal corridors or rooms. Most academic libraries are now planned as learning resource centres allowing for the use of all kinds of media and the favoured solution in utilising open planning seems to be to allow adequate electric power points in reading areas, rather than to hive off special media rooms or to provide carrels fully wired for all services. Experience gained in the study of use of seats in academic libraries carried out by the Cambridge Library Management Research Unit also points to the value of optimising use through individual or paired study tables in preference to multi-seat open tables. The study also cast some doubt on the previously accepted ratio of at least one seat to four FTE students, but the seating ratio needs to reflect the total academic mix and the teaching methods in use.

The student population of a Polytechnic can be a vital planning figure but a number of calculations can be used in determining the FTE total. For accommodation purposes the DES Architects Branch used a points system where full-time and sandwich students equalled one point each, part-time day students two-ninths, and block release students one-third each. Evening students do not count at all on the grounds that they reoccupy space used earlier in the day by full-time students. Since Polytechnics have a greater variety of attendance patterns for students than universities, these formulae can have considerable effect on library planning. In terms of bookstock utilisation and turnover, a different population count should be used because an evening class can pose greater demands. Students will be more dependent upon reading between classes, and there will be little opportunity for sharing material. Thus the demand on funds for additional copies may be greater although the space FTE formula would take no account of these students. Polytechnics accept as part of their philosophy the need to develop a range of opportunity for part-time study, and this particularly applies to postgraduate courses as these offer facilities for intellectual refreshment, updating and retraining. Bookfund requirements are closely related to the range of disciplines studied and another major problem facing Polytechnic libraries is the policy of offering a wide spectrum of subjects at first degree and diploma level.

The challenge of the two cultures outlined by C. P. Snow was met by the creation of Polytechnics from a wide base of colleges of technology, commerce and art. Library development has therefore required the recruitment of a range of staff, preferably with subject qualifications to match the range of schemes of study offered. The traditions of the constituent colleges indicated a bias towards courses leading to vocational qualifications and hence an emphasis on the practical applications of all knowledge acquired. Polytechnic librarians have reflected this by using subject specialists to develop an active policy of reader education and of the use of information services. The ethos of a Polytechnic library owes more to the special library than the traditional academic library, and thus undergraduate subject knowledge linked to professional library qualifications have been exploited as far as possible. Many development plans have reflected the idea of the library being a major teaching instrument in the Polytechnic and ways of providing reader education have provided a main topic of discussion. Because few librarians have acquired the additional skills provided by teacher training, there has been a good deal of interest in a packaged approach such as is offered by tape-slide programmes. It is slowly being appreciated, however, that neither students nor academics readily accept that there is a need to be taught how to use a library or sources of information. The need is best demonstrated through a project oriented approach since the lesson is often best learned by experience! Students appreciate being taught how to use sources of information if the relevance to their immediate needs can be shown, and the hazards and difficulties of information searching can be demonstrated effectively through a team teaching approach involving subject lecturers. Suitable library education can also be a continuing process. A first year student may be content with simple guidance on the use of local libraries but his final year thesis could well start with a literature search efficiently performed and involving all aspects of inter-library cooperation.

It may be difficult to distinguish between what counts as readers' advisory services and formal teaching. The question of the extent to which librarians should teach in the lecture-room situation is also clouded by the controversy surrounding salary scales. Traditionally, librarians in colleges have been regarded as administrators, and therefore paid on local government scales rather than teaching scales. Broad acceptance of a new role for the library as a fundamental extension of lecture room and laboratory has led some Polytechnics to adopt teaching scales for all professional librarian posts. Other Polytechnics use either all local government grades, or a mixture with perhaps senior posts and 'tutor-librarian' posts on the teaching scales. In cash terms the two types of scales have swung backwards and forwards over recent years in providing more advantageous terms. However, there has always been a more basic difference in conditions of service, with teaching scales offering ostensibly a shorter working week based on class-contact hours and apparently longer holidays. Librarians agree on the need to provide library services for as long as possible during term-time with weekend and late-night opening according to demand. In vacation the library normally expects to continue to provide a full service at least between 0900 and 1700. Use of different scales can therefore cause staffing problems although it is generally accepted that senior staff should be graded as academic staff and the Polytechnic Librarians are paid as Heads of Departments, equivalent to the professorial grades applied in universities. That demarcation disputes do not occur more often is a credit to the commonsense of librarians who are more concerned to develop reader services than to argue about who is paid for what. The line between teaching and advising readers is, however, particularly fine when library tuition is developed through project centred learning.

A full awareness of the value of libraries is achieved by good liaison between library staff and academics, both in formal committee work and through informal discussion in common room and refectory. The appointment of graduate librarians as subject specialists with encouragement to develop their areas in collaboration with users has helped to develop this approach. The Polytechnic Librarian is normally an *ex-officio* member of the overall Academic Board, and it is now usual for the subject specialist to act on his behalf on departmental boards of studies and similar bodies. This provides the Librarian with early warning of new academic developments whilst enabling matters affecting library use to be discussed at a grass roots level. A post as subject specialist in a Polytechnic library thus provides an opportunity for early management development but emphasises the need for careful staff selection. Personality and the ability to communicate are as significant as professional qualifications.

Communication between staff can be a particular problem in Polytechnics because many are in a multi-site situation. The North East London Polytechnic, for instance, has to operate twelve site libraries. The constituent colleges of Lanchester and North Staffordshire Polytechnics are up to twenty miles apart. Split-site working inevitably means expensive duplication for the librarian and a management problem in effective staff deployment. Subject specialists may have to carry a line management function as perhaps a site or precinct librarian, in addition to a polytechnic wide subject responsibility. Ideally, technical services such as book ordering and cataloguing should be centralised but there may be physical complications such as lack of adequate space on any one campus. In the case of the Polytechnic of Central London, for instance, it is also impossible to provide adequate transport between sites.

Computerisation of some routines might seem to be an obvious solution but few Polytechnics can yet offer sufficient dedicated time on their own machines, and insufficient funding can be guaranteed for the use of computer bureau services. The ability of the Birmingham mechanised project to provide a full cataloguing service has persuaded at least three Polytechnics to accept, whilst three others are developing with the British Library service. Mechanisation does, however, imply the acceptance of a degree of standardisation and some multi-site

Polytechnics still have to operate with inherited differences in classification and cataloguing, often due to lack of staff to alter practices in large collections. Whilst a good deal of cash has been injected into the libraries to increase bookfunds, there has been a much slower increase in staffing to support the development adequately. Issue systems demand a high intensity of staff effort because of the complexity of the requirements, but capital to instal computer charging systems may only be forthcoming as part of equipping a totally new building. Currently available computer charging systems such as ALS or Plessey can operate independently to process book and borrower numbers but need fuller computer facilities later to interface with a stock file to identify books, and a borrower file to find names and addresses. A decision to adopt any degree of computerisation thereby implies that the whole system has been considered and a development plan costed to allow for fuller operation within a predictable time scale – not always a feasible proposition where budgets are calculated on an annual basis. It is interesting to note that several Polytechnics, in creating their new senior management structures, have advertised for planning or systems librarians.

There has been much interest in academic circles in the significance of educational technology and at Plymouth and Brighton Polytechnics the library rapidly became designated a learning resource centre. In one case it remained under the direction of a librarian, in the other the senior appointment went to a media specialist. At the City of London Polytechnic, direction of all learning resource development, media production and libraries, was vested in a new post at the senior management level of Assistant Director, and a librarian appointed to that post. Many words have been spoken and written about the relation between libraries, audio-visual media production units and the development of new teaching methods. Essentially, however, the full exploitation involves a team effort harnessing various professional skills. At least one Polytechnic advertised an Assistant Director post to be responsible for Learning Resources, and their interpretation included the full teaching staff and allied staff development, efficient utilisation of lecture rooms, planning for the growth of computer facilities . . . and incidentally, libraries. Others have deliberately created posts for media librarians, perhaps emphasising a belief that the form in which information is contained is of more concern than the subject.

Whilst the management of library services is a major task, the Polytechnic Librarian must be prepared to play his part in planning curriculum developments within the institution. Whilst he will always be alert for the opportunity to stress the advantages of training students (and staff) in the efficient use of sources of information, it is equally important to appreciate the problems of assessing the learning capacity of students and to be able to debate the merits of modular courses. As a professional in the media of communication, membership of a working party on prospectus design and production, or on course publicity may well be part of the day's work. The rest of the day might be spent in committee debates on course planning or resource allocation, and it is quite possible that inadequacy of library provision could lead to the failure of a new scheme proposal.

The Council for National Academic Awards rightly demands high standards before allowing a Polytechnic to offer a scheme of study leading to a CNAA award, a degree or diploma. Not only must their subject panels be satisfied about the quality of the proposal, they must also be satisfied about the quantity of total resources available. These resources will include academic staff expertise, laboratory or lecture room equipment and accommodation, and library support, both in bookstock and space for its use. The Parry Report on University Libraries was content to offer broad guidelines such as the desirability of 150 volumes per student, or an expenditure of £75 per head. These broad figures can be meaningless in the context of CNAA requirements in respect of a single scheme. The Polytechnic may have a long history of academic excellence and adequacy of resources in engineering, for instance, but have only developed in the social sciences over two years and be proposing a new degree in sociology. This would be well within the polytechnic philosophy, and may be a stage of development from earlier lower level work in a constituent College of Commerce. The new scheme will be examined on its merits and the library assessed in relation to its provision of material on the booklists submitted, and its ability to provide further general support for the subject area. Since academics are normally unused to thinking about booklist details, this aspect of course development is in danger of being left to a late stage and the librarian may have to resort to very crude mathematics in endeavouring to assess the financial backing needed to support a new scheme. A gamble also has to be taken on how much material must be purchased prior to scheme approval in order to convince the CNAA panel that further development can be guaranteed. Scheme development can take two to three years before students are enrolled, by which time some staff turnover will have been involved and in the interim changes in the detail of booklists are inevitable. Comparative data from other institutions with similar types of course is very helpful, although each institution endeavours to prepare its own unique aspects of a scheme. In collecting such information the existence of COPOL, the Council of Polytechnic Librarians, has been invaluable since this body has provided the means for library staffs to meet each other and it has collected comparative statistics.

The first five years of Polytechnic library development have seen dramatic improvements, especially in bookfund expenditures. Table 12.1, based on figures collected by COPOL, illustrates the growth:

Table 12.1.

Academic Year	Average expenditure (*books and periodicals*)	Average expenditure per FTE student
1966/67	£ 13,000	£ 6·50
1969/70	32,000	10·50
1970/71	40,700	14·00
1971/72	48,000	16·00
1972/73	68,000	21·00
1973/74	74,000	24·00
1974/75	114,000	33·50

These figures indicate that very considerable development was needed, growth indeed of an order of magnitude for the majority of the constituent colleges and even in 1975 these figures still included a good deal of capital injection. In the last two years inflation has made considerable inroads into the value of those bookfunds although it has demonstrated one advantage of preparing annual rather than quinquennial budgets. At least the effect can be modified earlier but considerable attention now has to be paid to studies of the use of stock, particularly periodicals, and assessing cost-benefits.

Current development is hampered for some by lack of space although, as stated earlier, at least half of the Polytechnics have new library buildings in various stages of design or construction. Bookstocks have reached an average level of 100,000 and these are considered to be collections of 'live' stock for undergraduate study since the Polytechnics consider teaching to be their priority and not research. Many university libraries are nearing the capacity of their buildings and this factor, taken together with the economic climate, is leading to thought of steady-state rather than developing libraries and the potential benefits of cooperation with other academic and city libraries.

Many of the Polytechnics are in centres of population where there are already universities in the vicinity. In the case of Birmingham and Manchester, there is in fact more than one local university. Considerations such as these provoked the Department of Education and Science to sponsor research into possible areas of library cooperation carried out by the Sheffield University Postgraduate School of Librarianship and Information Science. The report, published in 1975, was concerned with an investigation specifically of the needs of students in higher education within the City of Sheffield and may well prove of great significance in future. The question must be asked whether, within a few miles of a city centre, there could not be more collaboration in providing for the library needs of students. One must accept the fact that a student in search of information will not travel far in search of it. Other studies of information-seeking habits have shown how quickly people discard their need for information, or readily accept an inefficient substitute if data cannot be easily found. The rising costs of major services, such as Chemical Abstracts for instance, do cause one to consider the value of shared assets. So far there has been little evidence of a move towards cooperation, with such honourable exceptions as are evidenced in Newcastle. The Sheffield report indicated how political and administrative barriers can act as positive disincentives but there are many services which could be developed cooperatively.

As Polytechnic libraries have developed, the increasing appointment of subject specialists has led to the provision of internally published information services. The use of selective dissemination of information is more familiar in industrial libraries but broader based academic groups can still have their attention drawn to current awareness services. These should not seek to duplicate commercially produced services, but can effectively complement them. The Hatfield Polytechnic filled a gap in the coverage of education literature by producing a fortnightly Review of Further and Higher Education as a service to its local college principals, its own Directorate and for the County Education Department staff. After proving the production schedule over a year and receiving satisfactory user feedback, it was offered to other academic institutions and met with an enthusiastic response. Similarly, Leeds Polytechnic prepare current awareness bulletins based on scanning professional literature in their School of Librarianship. Many other Polytechnics now use this for their own staff development. Plymouth Polytechnic similarly have a specialism in marine engineering and publish an information bulletin. Provided staff do not get too enthusiastic and begin to duplicate fuller abstracting services, these publications could well be exchanged to mutual benefit.

Collaboration on book and periodical purchasing policies may be more difficult to coordinate, but as polytechnics and universities achieve a greater parity of provision so the scope for cooperation increases. The gradual adoption of computer-produced catalogues also offers the prospect of increased awareness of each other's accessions. Computer updated union catalogues again have an increased local value, particularly as postage rates increase and dependence on the National Lending Library becomes more expensive. Eventually, on-line shared cataloguing will provide an instant picture of local availability of material and effective sharing of resources may become much more viable. That computer-based information retrieval can be economic has been proved during the British Library sponsored research project. The Hatfield Polytechnic participated in this research, and although the early stages where only a limited INSPEC data base was available did not prove much, the later link with Lockheed attracted widespread interest. Because Hatfield was able to attract many industrial users through its HERTIS information service to industry, the usefulness of the computer link to the variety of data bases available at the Lockheed centre in California was tested to the full. Comparisons between manual and computer searches provided interesting data on retrieval efficiency and created sufficient interest to warrant maintaining the link as an ongoing service.

This survey of Polytechnic libraries should perhaps conclude with a summary. It cannot yet be said that there is such a thing as a typical Polytechnic library because of the variety in the colleges which amalgamated in their formation, and the different stages of development which they have reached. On average, they spend £33 per student for a population of 3100 students and 480 academic staff. There are an average of twelve academics and eighty-six students to each library staff member and a ratio of 0·87 professional to non-professionals. Multi-campus operation is the norm, involving 5½ sites per Polytechnic and probably multiple service points within the site. The ethos of Polytechnics is 'many arts, many skills for many people' and a recent estimate is that there are about 160,000 students in the thirty Polytechnics, half on full-time or sandwich courses and half on part-time courses. Slightly less than half are on courses leading to degrees or higher degrees, the majority of the remainder on courses leading to higher technician diplomas or certificates. A third of the students are in science and technology, a third in business and administrative studies and a third in creative arts and in teacher training. Thus the community is a total mix of students with a vocational bias. Library services closely reflect this by accepting the primary importance of equipping the student for later life through tuition about sources of information as an aid to self-learning. Many of the techniques adopted by Polytechnic librarians are those of the special library and there is a deliberate attempt to create an awareness of the library as an active information centre rather than a passive collection designed for the research worker.

Further reading

Francis, S. *Polytechnics: a bibliography* 2nd ed. Polytechnic of North London School of Librarianship. 1972.
Cowley, J. ed. *Libraries in higher education* Bingley, 1975.
Whatley, H. A. ed. *British librarianship and information science 1966–70* Sect VIII, Ch 5. Library Association, 1972.
A Plan for polytechnics and other colleges Cmnd 3006 HMSO, 1966.

Robinson, E. *The new polytechnics* Cornmarket Press, 1968.
Department of Education and Science, Architects and Buildings Branch. *Polytechnics: planning for development* (Design Note 8) DES, 1973.

College libraries

Norman Roberts

The editorial directive that 'the main emphasis should be on
present roles and activities with some brief indication of future
possibilities' is peculiarly difficult to follow in this instance.
There are over 650 colleges, or institutions, of further education
in the United Kingdom – excluding the polytechnics from the
category of further education for the purposes of this review. In
this group are to be found colleges of technology, colleges of
art and design, colleges of music, colleges of agriculture and
other specialised institutions, even, a college of librarianship.[1]
Many of these institutions and their libraries have little in
common other than the designation 'college'; even within
ostensibly similar institutions wide diversities of standards and
activities are not uncommon. To make comment on present
roles and the future even more difficult the, libraries of the
colleges of education, which for our purposes have been
grouped with those of further education, are suffering a
somewhat uncertain present with the prospect of a radically
altered future. Since the aim of this chapter is to reflect the main
outlines of the current situation of college libraries and
librarianship, the decision has been taken to treat developments
in the college of education and further education sectors
separately and in rather different fashions. In justification it may
be pointed out that colleges of education have not shared the
traditions of the further education institutions and that, in
addition, much of what is said of college of education libraries,
following the recent reorganisation of teacher education, must
be of an obitual nature, while for the college libraries in further
education a future, however problematic, does exist.

Colleges of education and their libraries: the past

An understanding of the roles, functions and contributions of libraries must be sought in the histories of the institutions and communities which they were established to serve. This commonplace is of general application but it has especial relevance when considering college of education libraries for, without a knowledge of the history of the colleges and their aims, both the achievements and failings of their librarians lack their essential meaning-giving contexts.

College of education librarianship grew to maturity during the 1960s. The long previous history of 'libraries', consisting of small, ill-organised, poorly exploited, collections managed (where such specialised staff existed at all) by professionally unqualified 'librarians', directly reflected the situation of the colleges as educational institutions. Training colleges for teachers rarely exceeded 200 students in number but all followed 'crammed and cramming two-year courses' of what now seems a strangely unbookish nature. In both educational philosophy and in the value attached to library provision the colleges of education were far removed from other institutions in the higher education sector, notably the universities. The developments in college of education libraries during the 1960s were modified transformations of the remarkable changes which overtook the colleges. The force motivating change was the need for more teachers; a need that was rather belatedly perceived and which had to be satisfied rapidly. To meet the situation additional teacher training colleges were established and, more importantly for librarianship, colleges grew in size. Between 1954 and 1971 the student population in colleges of education grew from 24,742 to 118,000 and colleges of over 1000 students emerged. Associated with the growth in scale were other developments of significance to the practice of librarianship in colleges of education. The long-established two-year training course was superseded by a three-year course, the professional degree, the BED, was introduced, curriculum innovation was encouraged to an extent that one observer was forced to conclude – 'gone are the certainties of the past: gone is the rigidity with which so many syllabi were bound',[2] and

greater stress was placed upon forms of student self-education.
All these developments implied more extensive and much more
intensive use of libraries and their resources.

College librarianship developed as librarians and their libraries
responded quantitatively and qualitatively to these new
circumstances. Collections grew bigger, larger libraries were
built to cope with storage and use demands, staff became more
numerous and better qualified, libraries absorbed an increasing
proportion of college budgets. There were a number of
qualitative adaptations and innovations, most of which were
applications of, for want of a better description, positive forms
of librarianship. The shift in emphasis to the active exploitation
of resources which was implied in changing attitudes brought
librarians into closer working relations with their academic
colleagues and invested them with a clearer educational role.
The emergence of the librarian as teacher (in effect) culminated
in the tutor-librarian as a distinctive feature of college of
education librarianship. The tutor-librarians personified, in
telling fashion, the movement towards a more vigorous form of
librarianship and the growing acceptance of the library as an
educational tool. The drive to relate libraries as closely as
possible to the processes of education also carried college
librarians, earlier than most, towards an acceptance of the
implications and challenges of media resource centres. If
educational potential could be increased through the intensive
and integrated use of complementary forms of media then, many
college librarians were willing to argue, the business of
organising the use of such diverse materials was within both the
province and competence of college librarians.

Change and the need to adapt to change obviously had a
profound effect upon college librarianship. However, in one
respect college librarians remained impervious to change.
Despite remarkable institutional transformations they retained
one of their most distinctive characteristics unimpaired: their
close and friendly relationship with their users. This relationship
has often been commented upon; it should not be dismissed
lightly for it was an achievement of significance. It was both
cause and effect in the creation of satisfying and stimulating

working situations for librarians and the basis of high standards of personal service for students and academic staff.

All these developments had collective professional repercussions. There were now sufficiently numerous active, progressive, college librarians to maintain a lively interest group which eventually metamorphosed into the Colleges, Institutes and Schools of Education Sub-Section of the Library Association (CISE). Both within, and outside, their professional groups college librarians were displaying a self-confidence and an enthusiasm which motivated their constant struggle to secure higher standards for their libraries and their users. Perhaps, as a group, they were not as successful as they needed to be to match the developments in their parent institutions but a substantial measure of success was recorded. Much of what the college of education libraries achieved and stood for is to be found in *Libraries in colleges of education*[3] which accurately reflected the state of librarianship in colleges of education following a decade or so of unprecedentedly hectic development. Coincidentally this marking of the high-point of college librarianship appeared in 1972 just as the colleges of education were being prepared for yet another transformation fully as remarkable as that undergone during the sixties. It is one of the sadder ironies of librarianship that changes were to be enforced on colleges of education and their libraries as they were outgrowing the limiting traditions of their past. As a result the history of colleges of education as a major, monotechnic, sector in post-secondary education comes to an end and with it that of their libraries.

Colleges of education and their libraries: the present

The colleges of education were the unwitting victims (if this is the right word) of demographic forces and educational developments. Population forecasts revealed a falling school population and, consequently, a diminishing future demand for teachers. A recent estimate[4] suggests that by the early 1980s the number of teacher training places in colleges and polytechnics will have declined from 114,000 in 1972 to 61,025. In addition, persistent criticism of the long-established monotechnic forms of teacher education, among other issues, persuaded the central government to initiate reviews of the education and training of teachers. Once initiated the movement which ended with the reorganisation of teacher education proceeded rapidly. The James Committee[5] reported in January, 1972, the subsequent White Paper, disarmingly entitled *Education: a framework for expansion*[6] appeared in December, 1972 and the DES *Circular 7/73*[7], which gave effect to the accepted ideas on reorganisation, was circulated in March, 1973. The proposed reorganisation not only advocated a change in the education of teachers by, basically, making their education less specialised but also set out to provide an organisational structure appropriate to the new aims.

A certain number of colleges of education were required to close down because their capacity was no longer needed. The remaining colleges were required to merge, or associate, with larger educational institutions, the polytechnics in the main but, in some instances, with universities or to develop, either independently or in combination as colleges, or institutes of higher education. A small number of colleges of education were expected to retain their monotechnic nature. By January 1976, it was possible to define these latter institutions in terms of their commitment to teacher training. Colleges of higher education were defined as having less than 75% teacher training students; there were to be fifty-three such colleges in all with the prospect of 'the lion's share of training the country's all-graduate teaching profession in the 1980s'.[4] Colleges of education, nineteen institutions, were defined in terms of having more than 75% of places given to teacher training students. As a consequence of these changes it is estimated that the size of teacher training departments in colleges of education will range from 300 to 750, at an average size of 490; colleges of higher education departments will range from 300 to 1500 with an average size of 637. With the colleges themselves in some disarray and much preoccupied with problems of institutional integration and development, there can be no authoritative discussion whether of the present, or likely future, of their libraries but the situation does allow of the discussion of a number of general issues raised by the demise of college of education libraries.

Libraries and education

For nearly thirty years the librarians of Institutes of Education and colleges of education cooperated formally, and informally, to produce, in effect, a loose, but effective, 'system' of libraries specialising in education or aspects of education. This cooperation operated to rationalise the acquisition and storage of educational materials and did much to make accessible books and other material on a national, regional and local scale. One consequence of reorganisation has been the destruction of links which facilitated and encouraged cooperative activities. Not only have colleges of education been merged with, or transformed into, different, more general, kinds of institutions but the links established between educationists by the Area Training Organisations have been severed by the abolition of the ATOS themselves. The significance of this decision for the colleges of education is indicated in the following assessment:

The college of education 'system' was coherent only in terms of its monotechnic focus on teacher training as linked with the Area Training Organisation network. The system cannot survive diversification and the White Paper's expressed intention to replace the existing university based ATOS with new regional committees to coordinate the education and training of teachers.[8]

Reorganisation has left the Institutes of Education with a diminished responsibility for teacher education, a change in circumstances which has brought their important specialist libraries into a new relationship with the libraries of the parent universities. The possibility exists that the Institute libraries will be drawn closer to the main university libraries, in some ways parallelling the coming together of libraries in polytechnics. In both cases the result could be a dilution of specialised and specialising staff, a lesser emphasis upon the development of intensively specialised collections, and fewer opportunities for staff to develop as expert education documentalists. In essence, the trend against the separateness of teacher training as an educational activity which has brought the colleges of education firmly into the general system of higher education, with a consequent loss of clearly defined educational focal points, has also drawn the previously separate, and distinctive, libraries of education into libraries of a general, or more diversified, nature. In addition to this loss of focus it seems probable that the size of the remaining monotechnic, teacher training, institutions – the rump of the colleges of education – will be smaller than previously[4] with, it must be assumed, correspondingly diminished resources for most purposes including libraries. It is too early even to speculate usefully about the consequences of these changes but a guess may be hazarded that since material disadvantages may be mitigated in a number of ways, not least by recourse to the British Library Lending Division, the more serious repercussions are likely to be in the area of human resources and the attitudes shown towards the continuance of the bibliographical separateness of education.

Organisation and staff

The headlong pace of institutional reorganisation has resulted, inevitably, in the exacerbation of problems and difficulties normally attending the merging of institutions with vastly different histories and educational aims. In common with other members of colleges, library staffs have had to suffer the uncertainties, insecurity and anxieties inherent to situations of rapid change. There is little to be said about problems at this individual, personal, level. One would like to believe that every effort was made, and is still being made, to acquaint library staffs with the institutional problems encountered and their probable effect upon library and personal issues, but experience suggests that effective communication was not always established either between, or within, what sometimes came to be seen as contending institutions. In fairness, however, it should be said that few educational institutions have had to cope with such a degree of change in such a short time. In the circumstances, measured, consultative approaches to problems were not always possible even when thought desirable.

As has been seen many college libraries have become part of larger educational institutions, whether with polytechnics, universities or as Institutes of Higher Education 'concentrating on advanced level work in the arts, science and technology, while retaining a teacher training section'. The organisational,

structural and human implications of change on this scale are
many. For example, the 'distance' of the service points from the
policy-making centre will have been increased; the formalities
and necessary bureaucracy of large organisations will be
interposed between staff, functions and users with the result,
unless actively and consistently countered, that user services
become less personal and less personalised. Given the service
and informal traditions of college librarians such changes will
not always be welcomed; there is always the concern that the
imperatives of larger organisations may reduce levels of personal
work satisfaction. Faced with such apprehensiveness and with
other delicate and awkward staff issues such as the establishment
of an acceptable staff structure, differentials, redundancies,
seniority, etc, calling for rapid resolution, it is evident that
library managers have had to spend much of their time engaged
in establishing sound human bases upon which to erect their new
systems.[9] It is fortunate that, as a group, the polytechnic
librarians have moved further than other academic libraries
along the paths of innovatory and participative management.
The advantages of such progressiveness and flexibility cannot be
overestimated during the current period of transitional
difficulties. The creation of a single institution out of many
tends to intensify the human aspects of management problems
and a consideration of these strengthens the conviction that
librarians increasingly will need adaptability as one of their more
important personal characteristics. Even in this paragraph the
staffing aspects of reorganisation have been seen as 'problems';
given sufficient adaptability, however, reorganisation may
offer an environment of opportunity. Membership of a larger
library system can confer substantial benefits upon individual
librarians in terms of enhanced career prospects at higher
salaries and opportunities for greater degrees of specialisation.

The drive by polytechnics to integrate their diverse activities
within a distinctive, institutional, whole has been hampered, in
many cases, by the geographical dispersion of teaching
departments and various other institutional fractions. The
multi-sited nature of many polytechnics has resulted in libraries
of a like nature as librarians attempted to provide services at
scattered points of widely dispersed campuses. The addition of

substantial college libraries, usually at some distance from the
polytechnic complex, cannot make the task of creating a unified,
coherent, library service, working towards common institutional
aims and objectives, any easier. It may be tempting to think that
this problem is best solved by doing as little as possible to
disturb the *status quo*, by allowing college libraries to continue
very much as before except for a nominal subordination to a
conveniently remote chief librarian. College librarians
apprehensive of some of the consequences of reorganisation
have expressed, and found comfort in, such views. Any such
opinions, however, represent a misreading of the situation. The
high costs of reorganisation were not assumed by the
community at large to allow either the colleges of education, or
their libraries, to stay as they were – even under the umbrella of
the polytechnics. Reorganisation is intended as a prelude to
significant educational change; this means that libraries serving
education must also change whatever the extent of the break
with past traditions. One certain implication of this change must
be the acceptance of the concept of a unified library service,
centrally and positively directed, committed to the sharing of
resources and an increasing centralisation of many
administrative and technical tasks both for the sake of economy
and for the realisation of the educational aims of the new
institutions.

Colleges of higher education

The immediate future of the 'merged' colleges is certain to be
much concerned with organisational matters and in attempting
to find ways of imposing unitary ideas of library service upon
physically dispersed units. To the extent that colleges of higher
education are formed through mergers so will they meet
similar problems and difficulties. Merging, however, implies the
loss of identity to that of a senior partner; there are traditions
and guidelines to follow. The colleges of higher education, on
the other hand, are novel institutions in the higher education
sector with reputations to make, roles to be decided, students to
attract. That the change from college of education to college of
higher education is fundamental is evidenced by the great
amount of time devoted by the academic staff to discussion and

investigation of new courses, curriculum design, and so on. Their libraries, too, are concerned with the search for, and establishment of, identity. The transformation of the college implies a transformation of the library, an act that requires as much discussion and investigation as academic matters. There is hardly a facet of the library service that does not need reappraisal – acquisition policies, budget allocations, deployment of staff, breadth and depth of provision in reference materials, necessity for an information service, relationship with academic staff – all these, and more, are likely to come under scrutiny. A number of college of education libraries, preparing for their transformation, have used the occasion to initiate a critical examination of their library services and to develop plans to meet the needs of a less specialised community. Librarians derive professional benefit from such exercises; they also benefit from the greater awareness of library problems that the discussions of such plans within the colleges generate and the establishment of the idea, not always grasped, that the problems of the college are those of the library, as well as vice versa.

Requiem

The college of education library of the past fifteen years or so is dead. For some librarians and their libraries there are stimulating professional challenges to be met in new environments in the higher education sector. In colleges where the main emphasis is to remain on teacher education and where the politics of reorganisation has ensured the continued survival of institutions with less than 500 students a more restricted future may be predicted. In a sense this is where the story of colleges of education libraries began; such small institutions could not develop adequate libraries on such small bases in the past, and it is unlikely that they could do so today. But, however restricted, there is some comfort, in these difficult times, in being librarian of even the weakest of libraries; there is little comfort to offer those made redundant by change. In many ways during this century change has had a positive, benign, influence upon librarianship and librarians; it may be as well to remember that change may have its harsher side even for previously favoured classes such as librarians.

Libraries in the further education sector

The variety of institutions and libraries in this category has been commented upon already but the point deserves stressing. Further education institutions differ widely in size, types, degrees of specialisation and levels of courses offered. The educational range spanned by these institutions collectively with their full and part-time courses is enormous. They are engaged in General Certificate of Education preparation at Ordinary and Advanced levels and prepare large numbers for the Ordinary and Higher National Certificates; courses are offered for the qualifications of numerous professional and other varieties of vocational associations, there is a strong emphasis upon forms of general and adult education and a wide variety of degree and degree-level courses are offered. Work for the higher qualifications tends to be concentrated in the colleges of technology and other specialist institutions with the colleges of further education in the main, concentrating upon lower level qualifications, general and adult education. One reason for this diversity is to be found in the distinctively local character of further education, institutions. They tend, more than other institutions in the post-secondary stage, to reflect local circumstances and the progressiveness, or otherwise, of the local authorities responsible for their existence. In these circumstances generalisations, intended to apply to 'libraries of further education', have to be framed and treated most cautiously. Nonetheless since, in the space available, it is not possible to treat libraries either individually, or as more or less separate, homogeneous, groups, some attempt at generalisation must be made. Any such statements, however, will have a collective, rather than an individual, significance and will tend, in this case, to produce a gloomier, overall, picture than progressive librarians 'in the field' might find acceptable. Of course, there will be exceptions to the general statements and, for those wishing further to qualify the views expressed here, recourse may be had to the few texts treating of the further education sector.[10]

Apart from the striking degree of diversity the most distinctive characteristic of this sector of librarianship is the small size of the units involved. Since this fact has a direct bearing upon the practice of librarianship, it is illustrated in some detail by reference to the two measures of stock and staff.

Libraries of further education: stock

Table 13.1.
FE libraries of England and Wales grouped by stock size, 1973/4.[11]

Number of volumes	Number of libraries
60,000–80,000	5
40,000–59,999	10
20,000–39,999	95
0–19,999	362

Table 13.1 shows a clustering of libraries in the lower quartiles. 98% of FE libraries operate with less than 40,000 volumes, 76% with less than 20,000. The statistics reveal that the majority of FE libraries are much smaller than those of colleges of education but further analysis is needed to illustrate fully the paucity of resources available to FE librarians and the communities which they serve.

The figures in Table 13.2 show that 7% of FE libraries in England and Wales contain less than 1000 volumes, and 21% have fewer than 5000. Compared to the collections in the libraries of universities, polytechnics and colleges of education those of most FE libraries are laughably small, but the real significance of the figures is not to be found in such cross-sector comparisons but rather in the relationship between size and types of communities served and the established professional idea of what practitioners in the FE sector of librarianship think these should be. Such ideas are to be found in *College libraries: recommended standards . . .*[12] published in 1971. The authors make it clear that a

poorly stocked library is as useless as a laboratory or workshop so lacking in equipment that the teaching programme is handicapped [and express the view that] basic stock for a college without degree

Table 13.2.
FE libraries of England and Wales with less than 20,000 volumes, 1973/4.

Number of volumes (000)	Number of libraries
19	13
18	10
17	13
16	19
15	19
14	22
13	12
12	15
11	20
10	23
9	21
8	19
7	16
6	20
5	20
4	15
3	17
2	17
1	14
Less than 1,000	37

work should not be less than 10,000 book titles, and for a larger college with some degree work and specialised advanced courses not less than 25,000 titles. In a college with several degree courses this figure should be considerably exceeded.

The statement lacks rigour but it does have the merit of insisting upon a minimum level of stock provision below which, presumably, modern ideas of library service could not be satisfied. On the basis of this professional estimate, arrived at by librarians experienced in the realities of FE work, 40% of FE libraries in 1973–74 were operating with inadequate stocks. The extent of the inadequacies is spread unevenly among the main categories of FE libraries. On the 10,000 titles standard, 28% of technology libraries are inadequate, 50% of college of art libraries fall into this category as do 55% of the libraries of colleges of further education; numerous specialised colleges also fail to reach the standard.

Unfortunately these standards, although insistent on a minimum, say nothing about the relationship between the size of population served and the size of the library; the relationship employed is that of types of courses and size. Approaching the problem from the point of view of the number of volumes available per head of population served reveals, again, both wide variation and low levels of provision and suggests, in this variety and comparative poverty of resources, at least one reason why the relationship between population served and size of library has not been reduced to a formula.

On average the libraries of the colleges of technology provide 4 volumes per head of population served,[13] the colleges of art roughly the same, the libraries of the colleges of further education 2·75 volumes per head. The distributions are tabled below (Table 13.3); as a yardstick it should be remembered that college of education libraries averaged around forty volumes per head of population served.

The volume per head figure is probably a superior index of the service potential of a library than a gross stock number. While there may be some uncertainty regarding the precise level at which a collection attains adequacy there seems little doubt, making the most generous of allowances, that the majority of FE libraries exist below the 'poverty line' and do not have the capacity to sustain library services conforming to ideas of modern librarianship. Almost 80% of FE libraries make available for their potential users less than six books per person. 88% of college of further education libraries are to be found in this group, 86% of college of technology libraries, 70% of the unclassified college libraries, 50% of college of agriculture libraries and 40% of the colleges of art. These figures conceal great variations and give rise to many questions. Why should one technical institution deem it necessary to provide 55,000 volumes to serve a population of 2728 at a rate of 20·1 volumes

Table 13.3.

FE libraries – distribution according to number of volumes per head of population served, 1973/4.

Vols. per head	Colleges of Technology	Colleges of Further Education	Colleges of Agriculture	Colleges of Art	Other	Total
0	1	12	5	2	11	31 (6·5%)
0·1–0·9	3	10	1	1	0	15 (3·1%)
1 –1·9	13	19	2	3	0	37 (7·8%)
2 –2·9	44	48	2	5	3	102 (21·6%)
3 –	38	39	4	3	3	87 (18·4%)
4 –	29	30	3	2	8	62 (13·1%)
5 –	14	14	1	2	4	35 (7·4%)
6 –	9	10	2	3	0	24 (5·0%)
7 –	3	4	1	1	0	9 (1·9%)
8 –	2	3	0	0	1	6 (1·2%)
9 –	2	2	0	1	1	6 (1·2%)
10 –	3	0	0	0	4	7 (1·4%)
11 –	2	2	0	3	1	8 (1·6%)
12 –	1	0	0	1	0	2 (0·4%)
13 –	0	0	2	2	1	5 (1·0%)
14 –	0	0	1	1	0	2 (0·4%)
15 – 20	1	1	7	5	0	14 (2·96%)
21 – 26	0	1	0	1	0	2 (0·4%)
27 – 32	0	0	0	2	1	3 (0·6%)
33 & over	0	0	5	7	3	15 (3·1%)

per head while another provides 9000 volumes for a population of 6792 persons, a ratio of 1·3 per head? How does one institution of further education manage to meet the needs of its students at a level of 0·9 volumes per head while another needs 6·9? Are the differences a function of kinds and levels of subjects taught? If so, should not standards be based, more precisely, upon such differences? Is it possible to argue that the contribution to educational experience provided by the availability of twenty books per head is ten times greater than two books per head? If not, what may be inferred? What is the educational significance of such differences? Are the differences a product of political and local factors? Are library services in colleges inferior because students are expected to rely mainly upon public library provision? The questions proliferate but convincing answers are not so easy to come by – yet another indication of our professional ignorance of both the causes and effects of our work.

The noticeable lack of correlation between the size of population served and size of library suggests (as with other libraries) that the forces which operate upon libraries do not do so as in simple demand and supply models. Clearly potential demand is transformed into provision of books in a variable fashion. All manner of local circumstances and accidents influence this transformation but, probably, the most powerful influence in producing libraries with generous stock ratios is the combination of ambitious (in the best sense) principals and librarians. The importance of the human factor cannot be ignored or forgotten in any branch of librarianship; it is of particular importance in FE libraries where circumstances are not always encouraging to professional attitudes and where heavy demands are made upon the personal qualities of librarians.

Further education libraries: staff

As might be expected the cottage industry characteristics of a substantial proportion of FE libraries is reflected in staffing figures, as shown in Table 13·4. Not far off a fifth of FE libraries are staffed by less than one person. The magnitude of this figure, which includes institutions without librarians, reflects, perhaps, the status both of libraries and librarianship in a disturbingly high proportion of educational institutions. Could it be an indication of professional failure in this sector? Or academic ignorance? Or both? Given the present state of FE libraries the questions must be asked – repeatedly, and answers sought with the same assiduity. Apart from directing thought towards professional fundamentals this strange figure 'less than 1' serves as a reminder of the heavy reliance upon part-time staff in college libraries. In 1971–72 35% of FE library staffs were part-timers. The proportion appears to have declined very slightly since but is still close to a third. The high proportion of part-time staff is combined with small staff establishments. 54% of libraries employ less than the equivalent of three full-time persons, 81% less than the equivalent of five full-time persons.

Table 13.4.
FE Libraries – Distribution of staff in FE libraries – 1973/4

Number of staff *full-time equivalent*	Number of libraries
24–24·9	1
23–23·9	0
22–22·9	1
21–21·9	0
20–20·9	1
-----------------------	---------------------
16–16·9	1
15–15·9	1
14–14·9	2
13–13·9	0
12–12·9	0
11–11·9	1
10–10·9	4
9– 9·9	5 (1%)
8– 8·9	7 (1%)
7– 7·9	14 (3%)
6– 6·9	20 (4%)
5– 5·9	26 (6%)
4– 4·9	51 (11%)
3– 3·9	82 (17%)
2– 2·9	116 (25%)
1– 1·9	49 (10%)
Less than 1	90 (19%)
1,475	472

Only twelve FE libraries in England and Wales have staff
establishments running into double figures.

For England and Wales these figures represent a total of 1475
persons engaged in further education library activities. Of this
number 728 (49%) are designated as posts requiring professional
qualifications or experience. 609 (83%) of these latter posts are
filled by professionally qualified librarians. Within this sector, as
elsewhere, graduates are making themselves felt; 285 (39%) of

the librarians occupying professional posts are graduates. The ratio of professional to non-professional staff is interesting in its unity, almost 1 : 1. This ratio, as far as can be judged from incomplete data, probably represents an improvement in the provision of support, or non-professional, staff over 1971–72 when it stood at one professional to 0·7 non-professional. There is still some way to go before the recommended standard of 40 : 60 professional : non-professional is attained.

From the available statistics it seems not unreasonable to conclude that, in many libraries, the time of librarians is fully taken up in 'manning' libraries during normal opening hours and in coping with the routines necessary to maintain the libraries in being. In addition, the combination of small staff establishments and a relatively high proportion of professional posts (49%) indicates that task demarcation is a luxury which FE libraries generally cannot afford; librarians, in short, must be jacks (and jills) of all trades. Out of this professionally unpromising situation two schools of thought, or rather action, seem to have emerged. The first accepts that the prime responsibilities of librarians lie within the four walls of their libraries – what might be termed the intra-mural school of thought. In contrast, members of the second group have reacted to the difficulties of their situation by stressing the active, exploitative, aspects of a librarian's role and seeing their libraries as tools to be wielded, to be used for specific, desired, ends. Interestingly the 'philosophy' informing the former view is rarely formally expounded in the literature although the correspondence columns of the professional press, conference gossip and the results of rare surveys attest to a strength of feeling on the issue. Despite their straitened circumstances most of what is written about FE libraries preaches the cause of positive librarianship. In many ways the advocates of the 'library as an instrument of education' were fortunate in the appearance, as early as 1966, of an outstanding exposition of their view by G. H. Wright.[14] In many ways his work *The library in colleges of commerce and technology: a guide to the use of a library as an instrument of education* has yet to be bettered.

Whitworth[15] has seen in these divergencies a clash between traditional, conserving, librarianship and the modern, outgoing, positive forms, between restricted-role and extended-role librarians personified, in many cases, by tutor-librarians. The roots of the differences may lie in personality as much as in professional philosophies but, however derived, Whitworth suggests that institutional assessments of librarians and their contribution to general college goals tend to be favourably biased towards those librarians acting out the implications of the role of the librarian as educator. The issue has been debated many times in less analytical and detached fashion and, as is the way in such matters, positions tend to become unnecessarily polarised. The issue is not whether librarians should be conservationists or exploiters. They should be both or, rather, resources should be available so that libraries and librarians may perform both tasks adequately. The problem is one of resources not contradictory philosophies, for such is the situation of the majority of FE libraries that neither the restricted nor the extended role librarians are achieving their goals.

The future?

A general improvement in the circumstances of FE libraries and in the quality of librarianship would require:

i   a substantial additional allocation of resources to the further education sector
ii   the expenditure of a greater proportion of such sums than hitherto on libraries
iii the establishment of a greater measure of institutional acceptance

The key to the situation is the state and status of the further education sector as a whole and the degree of priority attached to its needs and development by the central government. The development of libraries must wait upon the development of the institutions they are to serve. Currently there seems little likelihood of significant changes in the attitudes of educational planners towards the further education sector. The present economic situation, in addition, does not encourage the introduction of educational improvements requiring substantial increases in resources. In short, the basic condition necessary to the betterment of library services is unlikely to be satisfied in the forseeable future. Given this conclusion the likelihood that libraries will succeed in obtaining a higher proportion of the further education budget is remote indeed. It might be argued that the main concern of further education libraries is not so much that of gaining a bigger proportion of future budgets but of retaining, in real terms, existing proportions of current budgets. Like all libraries in recent years those of further education have been struggling unsuccessfully to cope with the resource-eroding effects of inflation. The point may be illustrated by reference to the years 1973–74 and 1974–75. During 1973–74 total expenditure on FE libraries was £4,866,000 in the ratio 57% salaries 43% on books and other materials. For 1974–75 this allocation was increased to £5,353,000 a rise of roughly 10%. Assuming a constancy of proportion between expenditures on salaries and materials (and this seems a most favourable assumption), rises in material costs, currently increasing at a rate of 47% per annum,[16] were offset only to the extent of 10%. Only one conclusion is possible. A sharp decline in real term resources occurred over the year. Library services based on the availability of materials locally must have been affected adversely. The position is serious enough on the postulate of a constant salary ratio but the effect of a lower turnover of staff due to economic restrictions and of higher salaries in the education sector generally has probably increased the proportion of library budgets devoted to salaries and so diminished further the amounts available for library materials.

Stock inadequacy obviously limits the institutional effectiveness of librarians. Less obviously, but just as certainly, professional effectiveness is also a function of the degree of institutional acceptance of the library as an 'instrument of education' and all that this entails. Only a library so accepted can be put to full and proper use. Despite Lebovitch's[17] optimism this struggle for acceptance has still to be won in many FE institutions. Whitworth, a sympathetic outsider, considers that efforts to improve what he terms the 'centrality' of the college librarian will never completely succeed 'in present conditions'. Conditions in this instance imply the whole range of personal and institutional disadvantages which beset college librarians from status, through academic attitudes to personal characteristics. In short, the future of further education librarianship is constrained by lack of resources and the unsympathetic nature of the organisations they serve.

References

1. Colleges of further education have been taken to mean those listed in the *Statistics of libraries in major establishments of further education for the United Kingdom, 1973/74* published by the Department of Education and Science. The polytechnics are normally included in this sector but, for reasons of emphasis, they have been excluded from this review.

2. R. Fothergill. *Resource centres in colleges of education* National Council for Educational Technology, 1973.

3. P. Platt, ed *Libraries in colleges of education, 2nd ed* Library Association, 1972.

4. *The Times Higher Education Supplement* no 220, 9 January 1976, p 1.

5. DES *Teacher education and training* (James Report) HMSO, 1972.

6. DES *Education: a framework for expansion* HMSO, 1972.

7. DES *Development of higher education in the non-university sector* HMSO, 1973. (DES Circular 7/73.)

8. J. Porter. Teacher education and training implications for the librarian. *Educ Libr Bull* 16 (2), Summer 1973.

9. These concerns find expression in 'Some implications for libraries in higher education during the period of reorganisation.' *Libr Ass Rec* 77 (3), March 1975.

10. D. L. Smith *and* E. G. Baxter *College library administration in colleges of technology, art, commerce and further education* OUP, 1965. Dated but still useful. K. W. Neal. *British academic libraries* Neal, 1973. An unpretentious but interesting collection of essays.

11. All the figures in this, and subsequent, tables are drawn from item no 1.

12. Library Association. *College libraries: recommended standards of library provision in colleges of technology and other establishments of further education* 2nd ed Library Association, 1971.

13. For this calculation and that of Table 13.3 full and part-time populations have been added and used as divisors.

14. G. H. Wright, ed *The library in colleges of commerce and technology: a guide to the use of a library as an instrument of education* Deutsch, 1966.

15. T. A. Whitworth. *The college librarian: a study in orientation and role incongruence* A thesis submitted for the degree of Master of Arts in the Postgraduate School of Librarianship and Information Science, Sheffield University, 1974, *and The role of the technical college librarian,* M SC dissertation, Bradford University, 1969.

16. L. A. Information. *Weekly Newsheet* no 53, 23 January 1976.

17. J. Lebovitch. *College libraries and tutor librarianship: an annotated select bibliography* Hatfield Polytechnic, 1971. Comment on p 23.

Special libraries

Wilfred Ashworth

When I was a young librarian and looked up with great respect and awe to the Grand Old Men of Librarianship I remember being presented to one of them, the forthright H. M. Cashmore. I was introduced as a special librarian and with the preliminary throat-clearing reserved for his more pontifical utterances he tartly enquired, 'What's special about him?' We later became great friends and laughed together about this incident but I have never forgotten it. Indeed it has caused me often to wonder what *is* special about special librarians and their work. This was no easy question to answer then, when special librarianship was new, and I am not at all sure that it has been answered entirely satisfactorily since. Does special librarianship truly exist as a separately-definable and sufficiently-different aspect of librarianship to merit consideration in its own right?

Is it not surprising that librarians, presumed experts in classification, have come to accept a term which is so imprecise in its connotation and which so obviously exhibits the faults of cross-classification? Clearly all types of librarianship have their special facets and both public and academic librarians frequently do work of a specialist nature which is indistinguishable from some of that carried out by special librarians. Nevertheless, the term has become firmly established and everyone imagines he knows what is meant by it but shirks the difficult task of defining it.

The Mechanics Institutes, a unique British phenomenon dating from about 1824, can fairly be said to have been as much part of

special library as of public library history. They undoubtedly
gave to a few socially-minded industrialists of the early 1850s
the idea of setting up private libraries for the moral, spiritual
and educational benefit of their workpeople. Some at least of the
books provided would almost certainly have dealt with the
techniques of the particular industry and these collections could
well have shown the way to establishment of industrial libraries.
If such events can be accepted as the first steps in British special
library history then we were in the field before the Americans
although some of their purely technical industrial libraries came
before ours.

If, on the other hand, the genesis of special librarianship is seen
in government departmental libraries, and there is some
justification for this, history can be carried back many years to a
Library and Librarian at the Foreign Office in the 1780s and a
librarian at the Board of Trade in 1843, though its library was in
existence from 1801. Burkett, however, while referring to
occasional attempts at reaching high bibliographical standards
by a few enthusiastic devotees, expresses the view that the age of
professionalism in these libraries did not start until after the
Second World War and that library services such as we know
today have mostly been developed since 1945. Government
libraries usually showed a tendency to appoint staff with
conventional training in librarianship but people who accepted
posts in these libraries, then regarded as unconventional, tended
to be more open-minded about systems which they felt free to
modify extensively to fit the material to be handled.

Libraries of a specialist nature were first established in America
and the UK at more or less the same time, but the recognition
that they represented a new type of librarianship came some
years later. In a paper I gave at the 1971 Aslib Conference in
Darmstadt on the information scene in Britain I indicated that
the main causative factor in the development of such libraries
was the need to solve problems arising from the rapid growth of
scientific, technical, statistical and commercial knowledge, and
especially from the form in which that knowledge was
communicated as unit papers and reports rather than sizeable
monographs. This is no place to delve into the formation of the

learned and professional societies and the births of their scientific periodicals and abstracts, except to recognise that these were an entirely new kind of literature which by its character and quantity presented hitherto unknown dimensions of handling and exploitation. The industrial revolution, and the social, statistical and commercial problems associated with a rapid advance into a new technological age, brought a sense of urgency to innovation and trade and introduced a need-to-know which currently established library services were not equipped to satisfy. Further, industrial competition and secrecy were new factors which were formative causes of special library development.

Nor should the early establishment, in the Western world, of a number of national libraries, which had special subject interests, be forgotten. They, also, experienced and contributed towards solving the problems of handling this newer material. Similarly there were libraries attached to government offices and administrative departments which were special libraries in every meaning of the term and which played a decisive part in the development of special librarianship.

The important feature in the development of industrial libraries in Great Britain, a feature not parallelled in America, was that the early collections were generally formed on the personal initiative of a member of the research staff of the company, someone who had seen the growing importance of information to his own work. When the collections became too large for a part-time enthusiast to manage it was natural enough for an interested scientist or technologist to be detailed to organise them. An industrial organisation not infrequently has such people, who have not fulfilled their early promise of capability for original research yet whose services cannot in fairness be dispensed with, so two problems are solved at the same time. A number of these employees proved to have a real flair for information handling and became fascinated by its potential. With missionary zeal they launched themselves into their new career and did excellent work in it. They applied their inventive ability to the development of systems and communicated their enthusiasm, thus encouraging other firms to establish libraries.

This tendency to look internally for staff to continue libraries started by scientists naturally led to a preponderance of libraries in the charge of non-librarians. The few cases where outside help was sought and a qualified librarian appointed were, however, generally crowned with success chiefly because the type of person who would accept such unconventional library work had the right sort of personality and the necessary flexibility of outlook. The same outlook, as mentioned earlier, was found in those librarians who accepted posts in governmental special libraries.

The effect of this method of staffing special libraries at their genesis had a far-reaching effect on their development because there was little or no looking towards established librarianship for techniques. Systems to cope with the new needs tended thus to be worked out from first principles, and this was no bad thing as it is doubtful whether the methods of classical librarianship would have provided a satisfactory basis on which to build to encompass the complex bibliographical control of periodical and pamphlet literature (reports, standards and specifications) or non-book media. Nor were they designed to cope with a new emphasis on the information content of what was being handled, a matter of prime importance in special libraries. Thus there was concentration on detailed subject indexing for information retrieval rather than on classification. Further, methods had to be devised for the entirely new requirement of dissemination of information and for evaluation and presentation.

An accompanying disadvantage was that special librarianship often failed to benefit from well-tried and established techniques. Thus an unfortunate controversy, if not to say quarrel, arose between librarians and science-based information workers about the relative importance of knowledge of librarianship and subject knowledge for working success, and even about the fundamental nature of special librarianship itself. On the one hand some librarians held that the techniques of librarianship as applied to the classification and organisation of knowledge allowed more efficient finding of information in any subject field than was possible to subject-specialist non-librarians. On the other hand the latter claimed that, without knowledge of the area studied, searches for information would be without proper direction, user feedback would be impaired through lack of understanding, and, especially, evaluation of results would be impossible. Vested interests were involved because qualified librarians resented seeing a new area of what they felt to be their province being opened up by outsiders. The subject-based information workers saw ample justification in their success and further claimed that their new concern for information rather than for the format in which it was found, its evaluation for specific needs, and its dissemination even to those who had not requested it, together represented a difference in kind rather than in degree. Fortunately the polarisations caused by these arguments have now largely died away and a more commonsense attitude prevails in the acceptance of the fact that both librarianship and subject-knowledge are needed to work hand-in-hand for optimum effectiveness. It is this partnership which really constitutes work in a special library whether such a library be defined simply as one intended to serve a section of the community limited by interest in a particular subject or more narrowly to encompass only the information-seeking and disseminating features of such a library.

The term itself seems first to have been used in the United States when, in 1909, twenty-six librarians gathered together at a meeting of the American Library Association, then thirty-three years old, and decided that 'the demand of their jobs had actually created a new kind of library service – that of library service geared to meet the needs of specialised situations', and formed the Special Libraries Association. It was to be much later before any such moves were made in the UK although special libraries, in industry and in government departments, continued to be formed. The cooperative industrial research associations set up by the new Department of Scientific and Industrial Research shortly after the First World War also established libraries and three of these, the British Cotton Industry, the British Cast Iron and the British Non-Ferrous Metals Research Association were to make the first significant move. That the Library Association Annual Conference of 1922 included a section on industrial libraries is indication that its members were not entirely unaware of new developments as has since been frequently and unkindly suggested by special librarians. I am not one of those who believe that the Library Association in some way missed a wonderful opportunity and, in recounting events, I am concerned to fix responsibilities but not blame. After visiting the Special Libraries Association Conference in the US in 1923 Dr J. G. Pearce, who had just been appointed Director of the British Cast Iron Research Association, with Dr R. S. Hutton, Director of the British Non-Ferrous Metals Research Association, who had studied technical libraries on visits to the States, and his librarian A. F. Ridley, planned a conference of special librarians which was held in September 1924. (This was the same Dr Hutton who, in 1907, had started a movement in association with the *Manchester Guardian* to persuade Manchester Corporation officials to visit the USA to inspect some of the good libraries available to industry there. The visit was made and led to the establishment in 1922 of a Scientific and Technical branch of the Manchester Public Library.) Ridley acted as organising secretary of the Conference and there were eighty-four delegates amongst whom were some professional librarians. Although those who attended emphasised that they had no intention of forming a new Association, a Council or Standing Committee was set up and expressed its desire for cooperation with the Library Association. There must, however, have been a later change of heart as by May of the following year the Committee assumed the name Association of Special Libraries and Information Bureaux, and eventually became incorporated in 1927 as a company limited by guarantee. In discussion at the original conference E. Wyndham Hulme stated that the Library Association had contemplated the formation of a special library section some seven or eight years earlier but he was mis-remembering. The *Library Association Record* of the time shows that the proposal was for a club or society for non-municipal librarians, especially for the senior officers of state, university and professional association librarians, the only type of special librarians to whom the LA then made any appeal. To Wyndham Hulme's suggestion that it would have been better had the conference been linked with one of the Library Association's meetings, Dr Hutton replied that although he had a great respect for the professional librarian his view was that for the moment the need was 'to discuss these questions in an entirely independent meeting so as to mobilise the interest of a wide field of library users'. This seems to have become the official view of the Committee and, although some quite friendly joint meetings were held with the Library Association, special librarianship in Great Britain from this time onwards, as in the United States, developed separately from the librarians' professional association.

From this distance of time it can be seen that special librarianship had to grow in this way, and that it could not have evolved so effectively, if at all, directly from conventional librarianship as it then existed. As has been said, the concentration on information rather than on the particular format in which it was transmitted, and the recognition of the need for selection and evaluation followed by dissemination whether asked for or not, were new concepts calling for new techniques. With little to build upon, the approach of many special librarians was largely empirical, but they had the advantage of forming a small profession of enthusiasts who knew each other and shared experience freely. Lacking knowledge of, and therefore uncommitted to classification as a tool, they experimented from first principles with indexing methods and taught themselves, by so doing, how to marshall terms and achieve vocabulary control. The inverted index and its associated ingenious mechanical devices for obtaining combination of terms was invented in special libraries and so were numerous other devices, systems and ruses to enable minimal staffs to carry out circulation of periodicals, replication of records and the filing of information in the most readily-accessible way. One of the key features which differentiates a special library from all other kinds is that it is a closed system – a black box with input and output. Within the box are both the information provider and the user, working together in a cooperative enterprise, each equally part of their employing organisation. The rules of the operation are that the output to input ratio must be a maximum. There must be a profit of some kind or the system has failed. An optimum relationship exists between the information user and provider and together they must work out their roles in the process of locating and using information. It has thus always been a part of the work of a special library to optimise methods and to be cost-conscious, balancing the outlay in acquiring information against the value accruing from its being put to use. It is significant that many of the special libraries were associated with the handling of scientific and technical matters and with organisations having commercial interests. They were also largely concerned with providing information for innovation. Thus their staffs tended to be more numerate than those usually associated with public libraries and were able to give mathematical treatment to indexing and to the study of system effectiveness. They well understood the diminishing returns situation of information seeking and so the return actually needed could be used to determine the appropriate level of effort put in. This diminishing returns situation was also seen by special librarians to apply to library processes such as cataloguing and indexing. In such processes it becomes too costly to attempt to attain perfection, an acceptable approximation being much cheaper. There will be some loss of effectiveness in operation but such loss can be controlled to calculable level. Before special libraries came on the scene no real attempt to measure library processes had been made.

I have elsewhere considered the effect of the Royal Society's Scientific Information Conference of 1948. Many papers were presented and a plethora of recommendations emerged, few of which were ever implemented, but the actual holding of the conference at all was of the greatest importance because it gave special librarianship and information work top-level public recognition and respectability for the first time. It was always easier after this to obtain Government or other support for new developments.

Exchange of information and experience took place through Aslib for many years and its conferences and Proceedings were the major sources of spread of knowledge about special librarianship. The number of trained librarians employed in such libraries, however, rose steadily. Those who were chartered found no undue problems of divided loyalty as Aslib was primarily an association of libraries and the Library Association depended on individual membership. The control of the Library

Association was firmly in the hands of the far more numerous municipal librarians so librarians in academic and special libraries were ill-served by it but they were steadily and increasingly making their presence felt. Unfortunately the Library Association, staunch in its belief that librarians and information officers were all members of one profession and that there were no characteristics peculiar to scientific literature which called for a different kind of librarianship, was often militant in defence of its qualifications and there was no shortage of antagonists to express contrary views. The height of the controversy was in the early 1950s when the correspondence columns of the *Library Association Record* were full of it, the same statements and counter statements appearing *ad nauseam*. The heat of the fury concentrated on the question of what training special librarians should have. The paradox was that, even while maintaining that no special training was needed, librarians seemed as anxious as scientific information officers to create qualifications for special librarianship. Indeed part of the difficulty special librarians had experienced arose because employers were genuinely at a loss, in the absence of recognised qualifications for the job, to know how best to make appointments. Training courses and available examinations were for a number of years quite inadequate. The LA had a paper on commercial and technical libraries in its 1928 syllabus but it was clearly intended for departmental librarians in public libraries. Dr Baker of the University College School of Librarianship, a moving spirit in the formation of Aslib, offered in 1929 a modification of the Librarianship course which would allow science graduates to enter and study in their own subject area instead of English literature. Too few people applied for the course until the early 1930s when it was further amended and part-time lecturers were brought in from industry, the research associations and government libraries to give a more practical emphasis. Aslib ran short courses from 1943 onwards to supplement the educational nature of their earlier conferences. As early as 1931 the Library Association had offered a specialised alternative paper (part of the standard examination, not merely an additional specialist certificate) on University and Special libraries. By 1947 the Association added a certificate of proficiency in special librarianship to its syllabus,

and in 1949 a further paper on the subject approach to the
literature of the Arts and Sciences.

The next revision of syllabus took place in 1950 when papers on
the literature and librarianship of science and technology
covering a wide range of sub-topics were introduced in response
to pressure from the special librarian members of the
Association. None of these measures, however, went far enough
and when, in 1953, Aslib (the new name for the Association of
Special Libraries and Information Bureaux) gave its whole
Annual Conference to the subject of Education and Training,
the discussion on Elizabeth Maciewicz's paper 'Education for
special librarianship in Great Britain' crystallised into a
proposal by R. B. Stokes, enthusiastically supported by most of
those present, that Council give careful consideration to the
desirability of making a formal approach to the Library
Association with a view to ensuring an exhaustive joint
investigation of all aspects of the training requirements of
special librarians. A joint working party came into being but ran
into difficulties because some of its members wished Aslib to
become directly involved with examinations and the LA
representatives were opposed to this. Nevertheless, progress was
made towards agreeing on the core topics which would have to
be included. Meanwhile a number of members of Aslib pressed
strongly for their Association to enter the examination field,
a move which would have required an amendment to the
Articles of Association and which the Director, Leslie Wilson,
was extremely reluctant to accept. He did not wish to have an
open split with the Library Association, some of whose
members were also active in Aslib, nor was he at all anxious to
undertake the complex and onerous duties of running a whole
examination system. As an alternative he suggested the
possibility of Aslib's establishing a Register of information
workers, access to which would depend on the possession of
appropriate qualifications and approved experience. The
proposal was first mooted at an Annual General Meeting during
the Brighton Conference of 1956, when postponement was
urged pending the results of the joint discussions with the
Library Association. Nevertheless, under internal pressures two
matters continued to be examined within Aslib. The first was

the Register; the second the formation of a new Institute for Information Science which would be an examining body maintaining close relationship with Aslib but having a separate constitution. The supporters of the Register formally raised it again at the Scarborough Conference AGM in 1957, but after some discussion the vote was 200 to 26 against the proposal, a defeat so clear that it was never again considered. Similarly those who had desired a new examining institute, notably J. Farradane, C. Hanson and F. Liebesny, then realised that there was little hope of achieving it under an Aslib umbrella. They therefore held an independent meeting on 23 January 1958 which resulted in the formation of the Institute of Information Scientists 'To promote and maintain high standards in scientific and technical information work and to establish qualifications for those engaged in the profession'. The body became incorporated on 1 October 1959. Its definition of information scientist required that he should remain 'primarily a scientist capable of evaluating the information he gathered and of exercising an advisory function'. The examination syllabus of the Institute was produced by February 1961 and courses started at the Northampton College of Advanced Technology (now part of the City University, London) in October of the same year. Meanwhile, following the defeat of the Register, Aslib's interest in training was followed up less strongly and in 1964 the Library Association itself produced its new syllabus, leaning heavily on the agreements concerning core subjects and offering the first really constructive introduction to special librarianship with a well thought out syllabus including handling and dissemination of information. Aslib's contribution to training during this period, apart from assistance in the joint discussions, was of a totally different kind. Recognising that there was a real gap they commissioned, and in 1955 published under my editorship, a *Handbook of special librarianship and information work* written by a panel of practising experts recognised to be at the top of the profession. This became the definitive work and ran through a number of editions, providing vital information to those engaged in special libraries whether as librarians or information officers, and also serving as a students' text. Aslib had, during these years, stepped up their programme of short courses which had been found especially valuable to mature staff working in

special libraries. It also introduced the Subject Groups as a
forum for exchange of information and mutual assistance.

In parallel with these developments in the training for special
librarianship, many changes took place in the Library
Association's attitude to its members working in special libraries
and information bureaux whose needs had been somewhat
neglected. Several senior government librarians and a few
industrial librarians with librarianship qualifications played a key
role in fostering this change of heart. A University and
Research Section was set up to unite librarians with non-public
library interests and also to prevent the loss of these members
who might have formed a separate Association as had happened
in America. These librarians felt they had to fight to obtain
adequate representation of their interests and at one point in 1950
their committee openly quarrelled with Council on a matter
relating to qualifications and resigned *en bloc*. The replacement
committee managed to maintain tolerable, if uneasy relations,
but soon came to the conclusion that some of their problems
arose from divergence of needs and opinions betwen the purely
academic librarians and those with more specialist interests. A
new section for Reference and Research Libraries was proposed,
and inaugurated on 28 November 1950 and this, now the
Reference, Special and Information Section, has continued ever
since to represent special library interests within the Library
Association. A Medical Libraries Group was formed in 1947 and
an Industrial Librarians Group in December 1970. Special and
academic librarians were in the early 1950s still, however, a long
way from having any real power in the Association or say in its
policies, although their numbers steadily grew. They were to
make little progress until in 1959 the Association appointed a
new Secretary, Hugh Barry, who came with experience of
another professional society. One of his earliest tasks was to
review the organisation and structure of the Association which
he did with extreme boldness producing, in May 1960,
far-reaching proposals which for the first time gave groups
representing minority interests a chance to play their part. His
proposal was that a number of Council places be reserved for
National and University and Special Librarians who should be
voted there by their own colleagues working in those kinds of

library. The proposals were accepted in January 1961 and the
first Councillors under the scheme took their seats in January
1962. This was the greatest step forward towards integrating the
profession.

For a number of years a small group of special librarians had
steadfastly refused to become involved in the librarian
versus information officer controversy and, dividing their
interests between the two Associations, had acted as couriers
between them taking the heat out of arguments, reconciling
differing viewpoints and enabling clearer understanding. It was
now possible for these people to hold office in both
Associations and operate to good effect at higher levels. If the
Royal Society Scientific Information Conference had given
public respectability to special librarians this was the move
which gave an accolade much more difficult to achieve,
respectability amongst their colleagues in all types of library.
The integration was far less painful than either side had
expected. By 1969 it was completely acceptable when the
Association invited an industrial librarian, who was a past
Chairman of Aslib Council, to be its President, though special
librarians of earlier years would have thought it impossible.

It is not possible to present even a potted history of special
libraries without making reference to several notable boosts
which they received. Amongst these the effects of two World
Wars cannot be overlooked. The first found Britain so badly
placed in regard to research effort that in the immediate postwar
years attempts were made to redress the balance. An Advisory
Council for Scientific and Industrial Research was established in
1916 and a sum of £1,000,000 (then a very considerable amount)
was earmarked to set up a series of cooperative industrial
research associations, the ones which were to take so active a
part in encouraging the formation of industrial libraries and in
securing cooperation between them.

The Department of Scientific and Industrial Research followed
and most government departments established libraries which
became models of their type and centres from which
information of many kinds, technical and statistical particularly,

became available through cooperation with industrial libraries. The Science Museum played a significant part by instituting interloan arrangements and by its pioneering work in creating a massive card bibliography classified by the UDC and made freely available to bona fide enquirers who by this means had detailed subject bibliographies available on demand, on their specific interests. Although this massive activity was destined to follow the dinosaur into oblivion it undoubtedly had a catalytic effect on special libraries. Out of the loans scheme, which was backed by an official supplementary system and much private interlending between special libraries, eventually grew the British Lending Library. This is still used primarily by special libraries rather than public libraries, though their usage has vastly increased. The Second World War had a more traumatic effect on special libraries. Libraries had developed rapidly during the war because it was vitally important to have rapid access to information in an unprecedentedly technological conflict. This time, however, the following peace was less happy. The libraries were still vital to help the industries which supported them to look for new products and outlets, and as a consequence many at this time began to expand into provision of commercial information. But money was becoming increasingly tighter and cost-effectiveness more important. In this respect it has to be admitted that industrial special librarians have had one signal failure. They have not been able to drive home to management the truism that the tighter the economy the more vital it is to have effective information services. The support of industrial research is in a similar and related situation and requires an act of faith. By no means all searches for information or attempts at innovation are productive, hence it is all too easy for management to ignore the long-term gain in the desire for present economy. Thus special libraries have always tended to share, with the research effort they support, fluctuations of funding roughly in step with the general economic state of their companies. What has happened in recent years, however, has been cutting-back of a different and more serious nature. Ten or twenty years ago there was in industry a fundamental belief in the intrinsic value of research and it was the habit of technologically-based companies to give places on their Boards to Research Directors. The purpose of such firms was to make chemicals, textiles, electronic devices or whatever, thereby giving a service to their customers. Innovation was a matter of pride with them and that it paid off was, though pleasant, a matter of lesser importance. The new approach is different. Company Boards have been infiltrated by accountants and financiers and the primary aim is to make money, an aim which, in the short term at least, can more quickly be achieved by introduction of gimmicky design changes than by involvement in more expensive long-term research. If there should be any important new invention which might jeopardise business by making their product competitively less desirable, then the largest companies rely on their finance to buy out rivals or at least to enter into licensing agreements. Thus there has been a deliberate opting out of research and a tendency to leave it to the smaller firms which must innovate to expand and then find themselves taken over if success crowns their efforts. Such firms cannot so readily support libraries because special libraries have a minimum size below which they are not able to operate satisfactorily and justify the appointment of staff. This tendency to reduce the level of research and make interim savings has unfortunately been aggravated by a deep trough in the economy, and together these factors have led to gross cut-backs in industrial library services and considerable redundancy of special librarians. It is all the more serious because not only can special libraries not operate at all unless of a certain size, they do not mothball satisfactorily or idle inexpensively. A special library which is just kept ticking over is necessarily inefficient since it is in the active exploitation of stock that profit lies. Thus moderate reductions in funding may produce marked decline in effectiveness and lead to subsequent total closure. There have been previous fluctuations in fortunes but this is the first time that closures and redundancies have been experienced, with resultant disillusionment in an area formerly thought of as offering secure and desirable employment. It remains to be seen whether, when the economy recovers, any permanent damage will be found to have been done. While I believe that industry may yet come to see the error it has made, which can only have contributed to reduce the long-term success in world markets of British firms against more information-conscious competitors, one permanent effect is certain. Professional people in general have long memories and if highly qualified librarians are once again to be attracted to industrial special libraries they will expect to be paid on a higher rate than formerly to compensate for the risk-factor of possible future insecure tenure of employment. It is commendable that government departments, although their libraries have suffered from economy measures, have not opted out of involvement with information and that their libraries remain.

A further serious threat to special library services from the accountants' mentality, stupidly applied, is that in many companies (and also, under funding pressures, in the research associations) attempts have been made to cost out services to user departments or even at the point-of-sale. While it is essential continually to strive towards cost-effectiveness and wherever possible to seek for profitability some, if not most, of the benefits of a library service cannot readily be evaluated in financial terms. One can sometimes set a value on a particular item of information and estimate its cost, but for the most part the acceptance of the ultimate necessity of libraries is largely an act of faith, albeit one for which some large degree of justification can be found. Most of the ordinary articles and services we take for granted are more expensive than generally realised. Anyone faced with a daily invoice for the 'real' cost of his clothes calculated against the few hours each garment is worn might well prefer to join a nudist colony. Yet this is the kind of argument often used against paying for information services.

This present tendency to relegate research to the smaller firms raises an important question for the future of information in Britain because one problem which has never been more than partially solved is that which became widely known and discussed as 'the small firm problem'. Always, in Britain, a significant part of our industrial production has taken place in quite small firms, many too small to be likely to join research associations, although it would be to their great advantage to do so. They are thus very badly placed in regard to information for problem-solving. The Department of Scientific and Industrial Research made an especial study of the matter and various attempts have been made to resolve the dilemma. Different types of regional Offices and local Industrial Liaison Officers have been tried, drawing on government departments, research associations, and local technical or public libraries for their information. The major stumbling block has always been the difficulty of making contacts within the firms, gaining the necessary confidence and, even more, making such firms aware that they need information. In my opinion the lack of success stems from lack of vigour and courage in tackling the problem. Insufficient funds, mostly on a temporary basis, have been provided, resulting in failure to attract the right calibre of staff, and the supporting of a referral type of service only. I would like to have seen full scale industrial information units set up in association with trading estates or other concentrations of small industry. Once these had demonstrated their effectiveness they could have become supported cooperatively and new ones then opened elsewhere. Any purely referral service is bound to prove unsatisfactory over a period as there is always some loss in transmission of enquiries and the essence of effective information work is close contact between the librarian and user of information.

It is partly for this reason that computerisation of information retrieval has, on the whole, proved disappointing. On the surface it would appear to be an area of obvious potential because of the large amount of routine activity associated with the tagging of documents according to their subject content and the subsequent matching of these labels with enquiries. In reality, however, the process is not so simple. The information officer stands in unique creative relationship to his enquirer. This relationship cannot be imitated or replaced by any one-for-one matching process. There is rarely a single perfect answer to the real-life enquiry because the enquirer is usually looking for a lead, the better to develop his ideas or project, and for this there will often be a plurality of valid, acceptable answers from which a choice dependent on the circumstances and resources of the enquirer will have to be made. Whichever lead is chosen (either by the information worker at his stage of selection or by the enquirer from what is passed on to him) will turn the searcher in a different direction. To this extent the choice is critical but some other choice might also have led to a satisfactory, though

different, endpoint. Even those retrieval systems which permit
on-line scanning of the data base and some interaction by the
searcher are pathetically clumsy in their lack of flexibility in
comparison with a trained information worker whose experience
encompasses not only how to consult sources of information but
also the individual characteristics of his enquirer. It is not easy
for the classical librarian to understand that the answers given by
an experienced special librarian may legitimately differ
according to the person who makes the enquiry because the
lead he needs is dependent on his own powers to act on the
result. This recognition of the interdependence of the provider
and user of information, and of the information and its
application is one of the significant contributions which special
librarians have made to librarianship in general. They are only
too well aware that all information is valueless unless it is put to
use. Thus pertinence is of much more value than mere relevance.

In my own consideration of the practical application of
information I further pointed out that in the continuum of
knowledge there is at any given time an active and changing
band of knowledge which alone is conceptually and socially
acceptable for the development of new ideas and innovative
progress. Because of this, there is nothing to be feared from the
information explosion since the laws which prevent infinite
expansion inevitably limit the size of the active band according
to the resources available to work upon it. In this lies the fallacy
of classical librarianship which deemed it necessary and desirable
that all information, past and present, should be stored
permanently and organised to have equal accessibility, and
which had great faith in the comprehensive bibliography as a
tool to help research workers. In reality innovation can just as
easily be stifled by too much information as it can be inhibited by
too little. An enquirer only persists until he has found a
satisfactory answer to his question or a promising lead and
thereafter all further information on the matter ceases to be of
interest to him and is ignored and wasted.

The most successful developments of computerisation in special
libraries have tended to arise as a by-product of the use of the

computer as an aid to printing processes in the production of abstracting journals. Thus material is available on magnetic tape as an extensive data base and can, if suitably classified or tagged, be searched by computer to provide information to match enquiries or be matched against individual profiles to create a selective dissemination of information service. Unfortunately for special librarianship, however, such services have been offered directly to individual scientists backed by advertising material which implies that a new era in information dissemination has arrived. The fact that these tools, like the abstract services on which they are based, require interpretation and evaluation, and need to be supplemented by information from other sources has been overlooked by many industrial companies who have thought the new services a cheap alternative to their libraries – with disastrous results. Once again it is a situation in which the creativity of a special librarian is essential if the time of the ultimate user of information is not to be wasted, and for many years it has been accepted that 'save the time of the reader' should be the first, not the fourth, law of special librarianship.

Another important contribution of special librarians to library principles in general has been mentioned in passing earlier in this article, that is their contribution to indexing and retrieval methods. The inverted index represents an inversion of concept as well as a physical inversion of the file. The combination of ideas is fundamental in innovation and the inverted approach facilitates such combination. Classification puts knowledge into order in a manner which is thought likely to be useful, in anticipation of the kind of enquiries which will in future be made. Post-coordinate systems, on the other hand, use keywords which isolate significant features in documents so that they represent, not the subject of the document (what it is about) but rather the message (what is said about that subject). Subsequently interests of users are expressed in terms of combinations of keywords. If similar combinations are present in the documents indexed by a system then those documents must be pertinent. This is not necessarily the case when a document is found by a classified system because then it may be on the right subject (ie is relevant) but not say anything useful about it to the particular enquirer. This is the difference which has been stressed earlier, between relevance and pertinence.

Another feature which has assumed importance in special libraries is presentation of information because it has been realised that information may be both relevant and pertinent to an individual but still be unusable if presented in a form which he cannot understand or is unattractive to him. Thus the same material may have to be disseminated in more than one form according to the particular readers for whom it is intended. From the industrial library sphere can be taken the example of the differing needs of management, research workers and shop floor operatives for information about a new process or product likely to be of value to the company concerned.

Where information is culled from world-wide sources then translation can become necessary and it is common for translations to be prepared in and published by special libraries. This matter was deemed of such importance by the Institute of Information Scientists that a reading knowledge of at least two useful (in the context of the subject concerned) languages was required for Institute membership.

Throughout all special librarianship runs the constant need to consider information in a mathematical way, introducing concepts from statistics, probability theory and Boolean algebra to enable the processes of retrieval of information to be understood and maximised for greatest efficiency. The concept that librarianship is as much a science as an art has represented a broadening of its horizons and a gain in its applicability. The work of Dr Bradford on scatter and of the Science Library on the factors which caused scientists to request particular articles were the first attempts to apply scientific principles to the investigation of usage of library materials and subsequently to use in library planning the results of measurements made. Before this time librarians had taken it for granted that they 'knew' what users needed, but these beliefs were not subjected to critical fact-finding scrutiny until special librarians began to do so in order to demonstrate the cost-effectiveness of libraries to cost accountants and to their own scientific colleagues. Out of these early investigations grew more sophisticated research which revealed the mathematical relationships between recall and relevance, discovered parallels between the usage of scientific periodicals and laws of economics, and not only refined the laws of scatter but also found application for them in the diminishing-returns situation of making searches for information on specific topics. Obsolescence has been quantified and applied to stock-building and to planning, and been found to follow relatively simple mathematical laws. It is understandable that the greater portion of the research carried out into information science and special librarianship has taken place through Aslib rather than through the Library Association. The contribution of private industry, government departments, research associations and schools of librarianship has been significant. From 1965 onwards the largest single source of support for such research has been the Office for Scientific and Technical Information (now the Research Division of the British Library). Aslib began around this time to regard itself as the research association for the information industry and certainly managed to attract many earmarked grants to its research department. B. J. Perry of the British Library Research and Development Department sees three main strands in UK information science research: the first is the evolution of techniques for testing information retrieval systems, the second the application of computational linguistics to the information field, and the third the application of statistical association techniques for automatic classification. The latter two are certainly complex and long-term projects and the pay-off will be for the future. Of more immediate value is the work, which Perry did not highlight, in which attention has been usefully focussed on management problems of special libraries and information units. It is interesting to see that Perry, in his review of information science research, finds it possible to pass quickly over the major research projects on mechanised information systems and library automation which have been the main talking points in information work for the last ten years. 'However valuable has been the research and development that has been carried out to make these systems work', he says, 'and however valuable these systems are themselves, they have contributed little to our understanding of what information is

and how we use it and how we should organise it to use it even
more efficiently. Their real value is that they have helped us to
cope with the crisis caused by the accelerating production of
more and more recorded material, and this they have done well,
but not as well as they could have done had we known more
about the nature and processing of information'. These views
are in accord with mine that mechanisation is largely an
irrelevance to the nature and understanding of special
librarianship. It may change the speed with which certain
functions can be carried out but it does not change the functions.
An unexpected effect of the way in which research was financed
arose because both Aslib and the Library Association were in
competition for research grants from the one official source.
Discreet but firm pressure was exerted on both organisations to
enter into joint discussion towards eventual amalgamation. A
joint liaison committee was set up in 1967 bringing in also the
Institute of Information Scientists, the Society of Indexers and
the Society of Archivists. However, there proved to be too many
areas of disagreement. Disputes about education, qualifications,
and the division of research inhibited really close collaboration.
The situation which remains is one of mutual goodwill and
willingness to cooperate and the organisations continue to meet
at director/secretary level. But special librarians still have
divided allegiance to Aslib, the Library Association and the
Institute of Information Scientists.

The lack of ready access to research funds has to some extent
proved an unfortunate limitation to what the Library
Association has been able to do for special librarians. This has
from time to time caused the Association to seek for other ways
of serving them. Most notable of these was to commission in
1964 an independent Working Party under the Chairmanship of
Major-General C. Lloyd, to enquire into and report on the
Scientific Library Services of the United Kingdom. This report,
which was published in 1968, dealt with the existing pattern of
specialist library services for scientists and technologists, and
their training, and also made an investigation into the provision,
acquisition and organisation of scientific and technical
information. It cannot be said that its impact was as great as
intended, largely because its many recommendations, although

sound, were somewhat vaguely directed. To take one example, a recommendation that 'as a matter of urgency the number of specialist scientific and technical librarians and literature information workers should be increased at local level' is fine, but its implementation extremely complex and dependent on many other correct decisions having been taken by a number of different employing authorities.

In some respects British special librarians have been better provided with a forum for their publications than have public and academic librarians. It was perhaps more important for them because not only had they their way to make but also the exchange of information was both natural and vital to them. Aslib was active in the preparation of such important reference tools as the *Aslib Directory* and produced an information newsheet for its members, a monthly journal *Aslib Proceedings* and, later, a special journal *The Journal of Documentation* for more scholarly research papers. In addition articles on special librarianship were occasionally accepted for publication in the *Library Association Record*, the *Journal of Librarianship*, *Library World*, and *Librarian and Book World* (which for a time printed a special library column). Finally British special librarians seem to have contributed regularly to American and other foreign special library and information journals which have always circulated over here. The Library Association published some books relating to special libraries although not so much to special librarianship, which is rather surprising since their examinations deal with this subject. It is interesting to scan quickly through these journals for past years in search of special library trends but not so easy to be sure that one has found any! In the early years most papers, understandably, related to specific industrial or other special libraries and the systems developed within them to solve problems as they arose. Then followed a period of polemics in the information officer-versus librarian controversy and relating to their preferred education and training. After this there was a long period of consolidation in which attention was focussed on indexing methods, thesaurus construction, computerisation and other mechanisation. It was during this time that more philosophical articles on information theory became common and jargon proliferated. Attention was also drawn to the problems of special library management. I now see a return to the more severely practical paper, perhaps mirroring the present harsher conditions under which special librarians are having to operate, when day-to-day difficulties tend to concentrate the mind on practicality rather than on theory and attempts to foretell the future.

In this present article, however, I must make some attempt to predict the future. In making such predictions it is usual to analyse the past and to derive from it some pattern which might allow of forward extrapolation. Unfortunately special libraries over the last decade have not followed the normal rules of survival by which the fittest survive and the weak die out. Many of the most successful special library services have been the ones to go to the wall under the seemingly arbitrary decision of managements. The general shift of emphasis away from research and those services, such as special libraries, which supported it, has already been mentioned as part of the pattern leading to a downtrend. Another important feature which has contributed to special library decline has been the widespread occurrence of takeovers, mergers and nationalisation in industry. A reason frequently put forward in favour of the merging of firms is that it is possible to reap great benefits of economy when services are shared. Thus once the firms are merged, they are under pressure to show immediate cost-cutting. Library services are often the first to suffer cuts in staff and resources and this undermines their effectiveness and leaves them more vulnerable to the criticism that they are giving poor value for the money spent on them. Sometimes the library of one of the firms may be closed, leaving the other to cope with double the number of users, half of whom are geographically at a distance. This separation is especially damaging to efficiency because close contact between the library and its users is vital if the very best operating conditions are to be maintained in what is an essentially personal service. The final result is always that a loss of efficiency is followed by a fall in usage which is in turn taken as good reason for withdrawing support even further until the stage may be reached when management thinks it has good enough cause to close the library entirely. There is never any attempt at proper appraisal of the service before the cutting process begins. Where reason plays so small a part in decisions it is difficult to guess how far the decline may go or when it might be halted or reversed, especially as decision-making has been seen to have moved into the hands of those who are not research- or information-orientated in their thought, and do not understand the potentialities of either. Matters have gone so far that it is not easy to be optimistic of the outcome and it seems likely that Britain has opted out of special librarianship to such a degree as to have seriously undermined its powers to hold its own in the world as an innovative nation. If economic recovery takes place in spite of this fact (that is, for other reasons) then it is probable that both research and the special libraries supporting it will share in the general upsurge, as they always have done although, as I have shown earlier, the recovery will not be complete and there may in future be a greater reliance on external sources of information. Industry and government should now realise that a great mistake has been made and should pioneer a reversal of the present trend so that special libraries may play their part in Britain's return to a sound economy.

Bibliography

Ashworth, W. ed *Handbook of special librarianship and information work* 3rd ed, Aslib, 1967. 624p. *Also* Batten, W. E. ed 4th ed, Aslib, 1975. 430p.

Ashworth, W. Information in Britain. *Aslib Proc* 23 (12), December 1971, 635–644.

Ashworth, W. Special libraries in the UK in recent years. *in* Barr, K. *and* Line, M. *Essays on information and libraries* Clive Bingley, 1975, 19–27.

Ashworth, W. The Information Explosion. *Libr Ass Rec* 76 (4), April 1974, 63–68, 71.

Burkett, J. ed *Special library and information services in the United Kingdom* 2nd rev ed, Library Association, 1965. 366p.

Library Association. *Scientific library services* Library Association, 1968. 82p.

Mackiewicz, E. Education for special librarianship in Great Britain. *Aslib Proc* 5 (4), November 1953, 286–292.

Scarfe, D. Future patterns of information services for industry and commerce. *Aslib Proc* 27 (3), March 1975, 80–89.

Urquhart, D. J. Looking backwards and forwards. *Aslib Proc* 27 (6), June 1975, 230–238.

Chapter Fifteen

School libraries

Norman Beswick

The year 1970 was one of great hope for British school librarianship. New educational methods were revolutionising teachers' approaches to libraries, and requiring drastic changes in policy and provision. New, exciting schools and school buildings were being planned and created, with the library at the heart of things both conceptually and physically. The number of professional librarians employed in schools was slowly increasing. The Library Association published its first ever standards for school libraries, establishing a model of provision considerably in advance of current practice but in line with aspiration. Moreover, the premier national curriculum development agency, the Schools Council, not only conceived and financed a research project into the organisation of learning resources in schools, but had requested the major education library in the country to conduct it.

It was understandable, therefore, that many were prepared to prophesy that school librarianship would be the new major growth area for the library profession in Great Britain during the seventies and eighties. This was partly influenced by the singular lack of growth in this field during so many previous decades. Compared with USA and Canada, for instance, our provision had been primitive. There was no way to go but up – if we were going anywhere at all. Subsequent economic difficulties have aroused misgivings, and it is already clear that many hoped-for developments in school libraries will not now occur in this decade. We shall be fortunate to maintain the progress that has been achieved so far. Nonetheless the factors determining that progress, and occasioning the changes of attitude and demand underlying it, remain, giving some grounds for cautious hope.

There were always exceptions, but in general it can safely be said that school libraries in the period before the Second World War existed, primarily, in grammar and 'public' schools; they were rarely if ever found in elementary schools in the local authority sector. The basic purpose of the school library was to provide supplementary, cultural and recreational reading, typically for older pupils in the upper forms. Almost without exception, it was under the care of a teacher acting as librarian; usually he was a member of the English department, and had no formal qualifications in librarianship nor any means of acquiring them. Bookstocks were small, funds were low, and although much dedicated work was done, sometimes showing an unusual degree of imagination and commitment, it could not be said that the library played more than a peripheral role in most schools, or in the work of any other subject department.

The postwar reorganisation of secondary education consequent upon the 1944 Education Act brought into being secondary technical and secondary modern schools, alongside the grammar schools, and it became the policy of the Ministry of Education (later the Department of Education and Science) to insist that any new secondary school buildings should include a room specifically designated as the school library (whatever might in fact subsequently happen therein). However, there are still secondary schools in older buildings where the library room is heavily in use as a class room for most of the day, and where library activities of even the most cautiously traditional kind are virtually restricted to lunch breaks and after school, with all the limitations this implies.

Primary schools, meanwhile, rarely had library rooms at all, and there was much discussion as to whether they were even necessary. Most agreed that strong classroom collections were important for the younger children, and it is only in recent years that additional central collections, often in corridors or converted cloakrooms, have come into their own. In new

open-plan junior schools, the abolition of corridors has often
left room within the building regulations for the creation of
library areas, but this is still not mandatory.

It was natural that teacher-librarians should develop their own
characteristic view of their professional role, based upon their
own special interests and such demands as their other colleagues
had felt encouraged to make on their services; and this
self-image was necessarily seen in the context of their very
crowded day, with only the occasional period free of classroom
commitments and therefore in theory available to them for work
in or for the library. Many teacher-librarians went through
brief spells of trying out home-made systems, but lacked any
training or clerical assistance (at least, from adults). Library
housekeeping procedures therefore tended to be simplified with
little change from public library branch practice. A notable
exception was in classification; Fegan and Cant's *Cheltenham
classification*, first published in 1937, is an interesting example of a
carefully planned scheme based upon the then typical school
curriculum subject divisions, and demand has been sufficient to
warrant a recent new and revised edition. In addition, many
professional librarians, working through the School Library
Association, have produced modifications of standard
procedures which teacher-librarians have found helpful.

The major concentration of interest was, naturally and properly,
less on processes than on teaching. Inevitably in the
circumstances, but to the regret of some, this has tended to
mirror the interests of the parent English Department rather
than those of other teachers, although where such teachers did
become involved varied and innovative activities often resulted.
Teacher-librarians concentrated on the development of the
enjoyment of reading, and on the acquisition of simple 'library
skills', and in consequence many libraries have played an
important part in the personal and emotional development of
their patrons. When, in the 1950s, the then London County
Council set a precedent by allowing secondary schools of
suitable size to appoint full-time chartered librarians, the
appointees generally continued this policy, often drawing
enthusiastically upon their library-school studies of children's

literature; and their full-time professional presence in the library added considerably to the efficiency of the organisation as well as increasing the possibilities of its further use.

The later fifties and the whole of the sixties were years of ferment and change in British education (as they were also for schools elsewhere). Teachers increasingly recognised the challenges represented by the knowledge explosion (with the emergence of new subject disciplines and the partial merging of many others) and by technical, social and industrial changes in our society. It was becoming less possible to forecast the requirements of tomorrow's adult in terms of command of factual knowledge, and more important to think in terms of skills, understanding and the ability to continue learning. Studies of children in the process of learning, while not resulting in any unified learning theory, were nonetheless revealing the importance of individual motivation and commitment, as well as the great differences in the way individuals responded to particular teaching methods and strategies. Experience of the 'selective principle' upon which the secondary school system had been based had revealed unexpected problems and discrepancies, and this, allied to political and other pressures, led to a steady acceleration of 'comprehensivisation', the amalgamation of different secondary schools together into one non-selective institution. Similar trends led to a re-examination of 'streaming', the placing of pupils within a school into different 'streams' or classes according to ability, and much more teaching within schools tended to be of mixed-ability classes, requiring different methods of teaching from the old-fashioned expository lesson.

At the same time, increasing investigation of 'programmed learning' had led to greater recognition of the usefulness of systematic analysis in the preparation and planning of individualised work, including building elements of the learner's own responses into the design. Programmed learning begins with detailed specification of 'objectives', including the knowledge to be communicated and the skills to be learned, as well as how the successful achievement of these objectives will be recognised in practice; it is followed by the delineation of small, easily-grasped steps in a sequence and the careful planning of learner-responses at each stage. This methodology proved useful even for teachers who disliked the narrow 'tramlines' of many programmed units, and gave a design structure for more open-ended learning activities which could allow learners to proceed at the pace best suited to them as individuals. Improvement in reprographic techniques made it easier for teachers themselves to produce attractive 'starter packs', booklets or assemblages of material which could be used as bases for further pupil activity and research. Similarly, advances in technology made possible more flexible and imaginative use of the audio-visual formats previously regarded as 'teaching aids' (ie to accompany formal presentations). The recognition that 'teaching aids' could also be 'learning aids', and that slides, filmstrips and tapes, as well as maps, charts, models, cuttings, prints, specimens and realia, could be used by pupils as individual study items, greatly expanded the range of possibilities open in enquiry and research; it became less likely that pupils would copy uncomprehendingly from the nearest encyclopaedia, allowed for the development of visual and aural literacy, and greatly increased the variety of sensory stimuli which could be used to provoke learning. Like books, they were 'learning resources'.

The new curricula developed during the nineteen-sixties therefore made greater use of the pupil's own active participation in learning. Nuffield Science courses set out deliberately to get the pupil 'thinking like a scientist'; and the curricula developed by the Nuffield/Schools Council Humanities Curriculum Project set the teacher in an unaccustomed posture as 'neutral chairman' while the class grappled with controversial issues by means of discussion based on large and varied assemblages of information and opinion. 'Team teaching' initiated the exploration of inter-disciplinary themes, blending well-prepared lecture-presentations – often including film or other audio-visual items – to large assemblies, with research and investigation by pupils individually or in small groups; teachers with different subject specialisms cooperated in planning and exposition, and supervised activity work in their own areas.

It would be mistaken to assume that these developments were universal, or that where they occurred they necessarily resulted in the demise of the 'formal lesson'. A few schools dedicated to innovation (such as Countesthorpe in Leicestershire) made very extensive use of the new 'resource-based' teaching strategies; many others employed them for particular subject fields, or during particular periods of the year, or sometimes with particular types of pupil, such as those who found themselves unwillingly staying an extra year after the raising of the school leaving age to sixteen; some schools never altered their ways at all. Many primary schools had in their various ways pioneered such methods long before their discovery by teachers in the secondary sector, and they are implicit in the practice of the 'integrated day' adopted in a substantial minority of such schools. Success in such ventures is very much dependent on the quality of initial planning and preparation, and on the organised acquisition, production and utilisation of the requisite learning resources.

The implications for the school library will be apparent. As often happens, initial experiments with resource-based learning included the building up of separate collections of resources, often called 'resource banks' or 'resource centres', and based in departmental areas. Such resource collections consisted mainly of reprographic and (less frequently) audio-visual items, produced by the teachers in imitation of the many packs and kits being produced by Schools Council curriculum development projects. It became clear, however, that such collections were difficult to maintain, and that they neglected a valuable and substantial collection of learning resources already in existence: the school library. Increasingly, therefore, the library became intimately involved in the planning for resource-based learning, and part of this involvement consisted of collecting, storing and making available a wide range of learning materials in printed, duplicated and audio-visual formats: a simple extension of its normal supply function.

This was not, however, the only type of involvement. True, both teachers and pupils needed access to a wide range of learning resources, calling for a good index to facilitate the subject approach: but some of these items were departmental holdings which it made good sense to store in other parts of the school. Thus the library's catalogue became a comprehensive index of the school's learning materials, a much-needed key to what had previously been semi-secret hoards, and revealing unsuspected degrees of duplication and mutual interest. A coordinated index could be a first step towards more economic acquisition policies. Moreover, the materials often needed equipment for their use. Schools lacked the funds for extra purchases, but could make viewers, projectors and recorders available for individual or group use by pooling the general audiovisual equipment held (again) departmentally. This sometimes meant that the library was the coordinating agency for equipment borrowing, again enabling more economic use of existing items.

Much of the material to be presented to or studied by the pupil was available from commercial suppliers and publishers, but some of it was produced by teachers themselves, in an attempt to match individual needs and take advantage of local circumstances. Schools began to find advantages in some kind of centralised or coordinated production unit, bringing together the reprographic equipment held by the school (duplicators, copiers and transparency makers) and sometimes also the more sophisticated audio-visual production equipment such as photographic, audio and video machinery. The Inner London Education Authority trained and provided, to appropriate schools, a Media Resources Officer whose speciality was resources design consultancy and production, and MROs worked in close collaboration with librarians in the recognition that production was a valuable mode of acquisition. In other areas, resources production and resources librarianship tended to become coordinated into one organisation. This should not be understood as the library 'taking over' a production role, but participating in a wider agency whose objectives were total support to teachers and pupils in resource-based activities.

In such schools, instead of the library being a cultural and recreational arm of the English Department, it found itself involved in the very heart of the curriculum. Pupils came to it, in classes, groups or individually, in a wide range of subject contexts, concerned with the discovery of information from all available formats. Teachers came to it in the preparation of such activities, looking for existing materials and devising extra resources of their own. It was a mistake to say, as some people at first did, that the change was the addition to the library of non-book materials; what was different was the degree of use. Schools did not 'add a resource centre to their library'; on the contrary, they 'used their library as a resource centre'. Thus increasingly it became natural to embody this concept in the name of the organisation; there is some dispute as to where the usage began, but the Library Association standards in 1970 embodied the new name in its title: 'School library resource centres'.

In the Inner London Education Authority, secondary schools actively employing resource-based learning had two full-time members of staff concerned with its support: the Media Resources Officer and the (chartered) librarian. After some initial suspicion, relationships between the two professional groups have developed favourably and understanding has led to excellent examples of cooperation. No other education authority at present employs MROS, and very few as a matter of policy support the employment of chartered librarians, although this has not always precluded individual schools finding their way round the regulations. Somerset, Nottinghamshire and Cheshire, among others, have adopted a policy of providing chartered librarians, particularly in new schools, and there is no doubt that such provision has been considered much more favourably of late in other areas where till recently it would have met stiff teacher-resistance. In the meantime, schools continue to manage with teacher-librarians, and where resource-based learning has been a firm commitment to the school, headmasters have increasingly tended to timetable the teacher-librarian more helpfully so that time is available for his or her presence within the library resource centre. In Codsall Comprehensive School, for instance, the teacher-librarian was recently available for LRC work for three-quarters of the week, and the library was 'covered' for the other quarter by a fellow-teacher equally sympathetic to the work.

Overall coordination of the library, production and curriculum development elements of resource-based learning has typically been in the hands of a senior member of teaching staff, sometimes at deputy head level, often with the title Head of Resources; such people have often developed in-service training of teachers as part of their function, and brought in the librarian or teacher-librarian to cooperate in this important work. What is common to most schools of this type is the flexible and creative nature of their organisation; it is often very difficult to delineate where the library begins and ends as a unit; its staffing may well be shared with a production unit and its reader-guidance sometimes be undertaken by a librarian, or a teacher-librarian, or a teacher. All one can say is that here are a number of people and activities wherein most of the traditional elements of librarianship can, among other things, be distinguished.

Local education authorities have sought to provide a basis of support for school resources work in many ways, most of them involving new areas of cooperation not previously much explored. One development has been the community school, where the provision of a new educational institution has enabled an LEA to link services together. Nottinghamshire has an example of a school and public library using the same building, enabling library staff to serve both types of customer. In Manchester, the new Abraham Moss Centre includes a comprehensive school, further education college, community centre and branch library in the one building, working in concert and sharing resources; the library resource centre runs upwards through the middle of the building, serving a different type of clientele on each level. Such developments are controversial and it will be interesting to see how they fare over a period of years.

Support for schools over the recent decade has come from teachers centres, which not only provide a meeting place for in-service courses and curriculum planning discussions between schools, but also increasingly provide types of expensive reprographic and audio-visual production equipment which small schools cannot afford, enabling teachers to share the work of resources creation with their colleagues in other schools.

Teachers centres have often put on displays of books and other resource materials, and there have been suggestions that the collocation of a teachers centre with a public library branch would sometimes be of mutual advantage. Oxfordshire has pioneered the linking of teachers centres into a small network, coordinated from a curriculum centre in Kidlington, making available to schools the best and most successful sets of learning materials made by teachers within the county. Librarians have been closely concerned with the county's resources planning and a useful report was produced jointly in 1971.

An even more ambitious cooperative scheme has been experimentally developed in the south-west, based upon Exeter University Institute of Education. Financed first by Gulbenkian, and later by Philips Electrical, the Institute set up a Regional Resources Centre in collaboration with the Institute Library, which initially provided information and advice and produced certain types of learning resource on demand. This has now developed into a network of schools, other educational institutions, teachers centres and supportive agencies, demonstrating that in educational innovation it is as much the personal contacts and pooling of experiences as it is sharing of physical materials that gets an experiment off the ground. Meanwhile, Somerset, Leicestershire and (outstandingly) Wiltshire have established active multimedia lending and exhibition services to schools and colleges, and many public libraries have developed admirable processing, supply and project loans services together with informed guidance from their Schools Library Services.

Nationally, the pre-eminent body until very recently has been the School Library Association, founded in January 1937 after a preliminary meeting the previous summer. A School Libraries section of the Library Association, formed at around the same time (December 1936) eventually merged with the SLA in 1945. The School Library Association has pursued an active publication programme, including guides to periodicals and reference books, cataloguing rules for school libraries, a drastic simplification of the Dewey Decimal Classification intended mainly for primary schools, and numerous reports and policy statements. Its journal, *The School Librarian*, first published termly but now a well-established quarterly, contains very substantial and helpful sections of book reviewing in the educational and children's publishing fields; its feature articles discuss teaching matters involving the library, technical routines, and matters of policy concern (such as the employment of chartered librarians). The interests and character of the SLA are fairly shown by the decidedly 'literary' concern of the journal; thirty-four out of some ninety articles in twenty-two consecutive recent issues were about literary authors or themes, and no other school subject or its literature was explicitly considered, although there was one general article on non-fiction books for factual information. Equally noteworthy is the fact that, despite its formidable book reviewing team, no audio-visual materials are reviewed or discussed.

The rapid development of school libraries after the Second World War led to the urgent need for some form of professional accreditation and training for teacher-librarians. In 1956, discussions between the Library Association and the SLA resulted in an agreed syllabus and a jointly-validated Teacher-Librarian Certificate, examinations for which have been held annually ever since. No courses were provided by either Association for these examinations, and although some were provided in evening classes at further education colleges and elsewhere, the bulk of the examinees prepared for the Certificate by their own private study; the failure rate was frequently 50% and more. The Certificate was not accepted by any employing body for automatic increment or promotion, nor was appointment as teacher-librarian normally dependent upon possession of it, although in some cases it undoubtedly helped. Furthermore, the Certificate was not related to any other qualification in librarianship or teaching, and could not become a foundation for the achievement of chartered librarian status. A Working Party of the LA, the SLA and the Association of Teachers in Colleges and Departments of Education, has recently produced new syllabuses and procedures.

It has always been the view of the School Library Association that the person in charge of the school library should be a fully qualified teacher, able to play a full part in the educational exploitation of the collection. The Library Association, on the other hand, feels strongly that the organisation of a modern school library resource centre should be 'centred upon the skills of a chartered librarian'. In the further education field, it has for some years been possible for librarians to gain a teaching qualification at Garnett College. A number of recent developments have increased the prospects of those wishing to become dually qualified teacher-librarians in the schools field. Since 1969, a one-year full-time course for graduate experienced teachers has been offered at University College London, for a diploma which satisfies the course regulations of the Library Association towards accreditation as a chartered librarian. (This course is now taught at the London Institute of Education Library.) Since 1974, a one-year course for experienced chartered librarians has been offered at the Froebel Institute College of Education in London, for a certificate which gives a recognised teaching qualification. Students at the Schools of Librarianship at Newcastle and Liverpool Polytechnics can take a three-year degree course in librarianship, which can be translated into an honours degree plus a teaching qualification by the addition of a fourth year of planned study. Leeds Polytechnic School of Librarianship has plans along these lines, and also offers opportunities for qualified teachers to gain a degree in librarianship by part-time study. Finally, at Lough-borough University, a four-year joint degree in Education and Librarianship, leading to full dual qualification, has been offered since 1974.

Other courses in librarianship for teachers are offered by Birmingham University Institute of Education, by the University of Lancaster Institute of Education at Edge Hill College, and by College of Librarianship Wales, but these courses have not been discussed with the LA for chartering purposes. There are many unresolved difficulties about dual qualification, notably the different and sometimes incompatible salary scales and pensions schemes under which teachers and librarians are appointed, and also the two qualifying periods after the fulfilment of examination requirements, but some determined individuals have already achieved the dual status by their own initiative and this could well be the trend of the future.

The Bullock Report *A language for life* (1975) gave considerable support to the importance of the school library in the language and reading development of the child, as well as to the concept of the library as a resource centre. Much of its data revealed how far we still have to go to achieve even a successful library service of a traditional kind in schools, and by implication how unsuccessful the English Department-oriented teacher librarianship tradition has been by its own terms. The report endorsed the view that 'ideally, all school librarians should be doubly qualified in teaching and librarianship, and we hope this will be the pattern of future development'. When it is remembered that the Bullock Committee was concerned only with one aspect, albeit an important one, of the child's school experience, the case for more thorough-going staffing policies becomes almost overwhelming.

This feeling has been very much in the minds of the Library Association Sub-Committee on School Library Resource Centres, whose regular meetings over more than five years produced not only a series of policy statements but also the first authoritative standards for school library resource centres in this country. (The first American standards were approved in 1918, and published by ALA in 1920.) *School library resource centres: recommended standards for policy and provision* was published in 1970, and a *Supplement on nonbook materials* published in 1972. These standards were exacting by comparison with the reality in most schools, although there are schools in London and Nottinghamshire, for instance, which come very near to meeting them in many respects. A completely revised edition is under way at the time of writing and should appear during 1977. Such standards by their very nature set targets for attainment; comparison with the recommendations for expenditure established each year by the former Association of Education Committees, and with such published figures as are available of what schools actually spend (as, for instance, given in the Bullock Report, 307–8) shows how far we have yet to go if our performance is to equal our theoretical base.

Research into school libraries in Britain is at present very limited and one must hope for much more as teachers' interest gives us a livelier organisation to investigate. Keith Evans has summarised in *Research in librarianship* 3 (4), May 1970, 39–48, the results of his own very critical investigation into the provision, organisation and use of libraries in secondary schools, with special reference to Wales, for an MA (Education) thesis. Useful short dissertations are produced by students for the University of Birmingham Institute of Education diploma, and Dr P. Platt, the Institute librarian, can furnish a complete up-to-date list. The three-year Schools Council Resource Centre Project, based on the University of London Institute of Education Library, 1970–73, undertook a survey of existing practice in the resource centre field, and followed this with a detailed study of six pilot schools in the process of developing a school library resource centre within existing financial and other provision; as the research officer was the author of this chapter he refers the reader modestly to the bibliography.

We have not had the funds nor the close attention of the education profession that has marked developments in North America, where a long history of the development and use of libraries in both elementary and secondary schools has drawn envious British eyes. None the less there are signs that at least some of our teaching colleagues require school library service as never before, and that some schools are prepared to go to surprising lengths in re-planning their apportionment of staffing, equipment, accommodation, and finance to give the library resource centre greater opportunities than it has previously had. This will not mean the abandonment of the tradition previously represented by the English-oriented teacher-librarian, but its extension to include other areas of the curriculum and of the pupil's life. The steady growth in the number of chartered librarians in schools, and the slow accumulation of dually qualified enthusiasts, may yet have an influence out of proportion to mere numbers. It will be many years before we have more than a pittance to work with, but one possibly heartening sign in the meantime has been the number of teachers and administrators who have begun to see the value of the library resource centre as a means of making the fullest use of

what funds and resources we have, rather than a pipe-dream that
must wait until some never-never decade of affluence for its
achievement.

Further reading

Beswick, Norman W. *School resource
centres: Schools Council Working Paper 43*
Evans/Methuen Educational, 1972.
Beswick, Norman W. *Organizing
resources: six case studies* Heinemann
Educational, 1975.
Briault, Eric. *Allocation and management
of resources in schools* Council for
Educational Technology, 1974.
(Occasional Paper no 6.)
Department of Education and Science.
*A language for life: report of the
Committee of Inquiry . . . under the
chairmanship of Sir Alan Bullock*
London: HMSO, 1975.
Library Association. *School library
resource centres: recommended standards for
policy and provision 1970. A supplement on
nonbook materials 1972.*

Morris, C. W. *et al*, eds. *Libraries in
secondary schools* ed C. W. Morris,
A. B. Russell, C. A. Stott. School
Library Association, 1972.
Shifrin, Malcolm. *Information in the
school library: an introduction to the
organisation of non-book materials*
Bingley, 1973.
Waite, Clifford *and* Colebourne,
Ronald, eds. *Not by books alone: a
symposium on library resources in schools*
School Library Association, 1975.
Walton, Jack *and* Ruck, John, eds.
Resources and resources centres Ward Lock
Education, 1975.

The impact of the computer

Michael F. Lynch *and* George W. Adamson

It was perhaps inevitable that the advent of a novel and
imperfectly understood technology, in the descriptions of which
the term 'information-processing' occurred repeatedly, should
have given rise to claims and predictions which can be viewed
variously as those of cranks or visionaries, depending on the
time-scales on which they are assessed. Today, for instance,
mechanised translation from one natural language to another
tends to be viewed as a pipe-dream, attainable only in the long
term, as a result of our present ignorance of the manipulations of
language and of meaning necessary to produce adequate
translations. While many over-optimistic claims have been made
for the benefits to be gained from applying computer technology
to the problems of library and information work, tangible
attainments are already apparent, although their implications for
many libraries are still limited and often indirect.

The impact of computer technology on library and information
work and the benefit it brings can be assessed under two main
heads. The first is the rationalisation of the production
processes involved in the preparation of national bibliographies
and of the abstracting and indexing publications covering the
scientific and technical periodical literature. In both instances,
computer-based systems provide printed publications with no
reduction in the graphic qualities expected for such resources,
and with advantages in the time-scales in which increasing
volumes of new materials are dealt with. In addition to replacing
traditional labour-intensive typesetting procedures, the systems
provide facilities for simplification of work flows, reduction of

keyboarding and proof-reading effort, and greater degrees of control of complex data-management processes.

The second main thrust is in the direction of providing organised forms of access to these and similar, locally-compiled, data-bases, involving a variety of levels of technology. These involve varying degrees of integration of computer systems with two further technologies, based again on the very rapid developments in micro-electronics – telecommunications and micrography. The levels of technology are apparent in the particular combinations of these three components used. Thus access may be by means of wholly conventional catalogues, indexes and the like, the direct products of data-base compilation systems. Somewhat less conventionally, microform by-products of machine-readable data-bases make these resources more widely available, reducing updating, as well as production, material and transport costs, although with some reduction in their initial acceptability. Periodic selective searches of the data-bases are the basis for selective dissemination services, while on-line interactive searching, with facsimile transmission in the future, offers users remote from the system a novel and immediate channel to large collections of bibliographic records of a variety of types – monograph details, periodical, patent and report literature.[1]

These bibliographic information systems provide only the navigational information with which the user, whether librarian or library user, can identify and locate material of concern to him. Only the storage media and the mechanisms for manipulation are in principle novel, for the information content is substantially unchanged. However, the trend is clearly towards reducing the dependence of users on locally obtainable resources, and towards greater articulation of the library and information networks, and thus towards a greater degree of resource-sharing than was previously practicable. This last is increasingly dictated by the realities of the economic situation of the present decade.

For many libraries, the dominant factor has been the need to rationalise certain labour-intensive technical processes, so that much emphasis has been placed on the control of the library's internal stock records, in respects such as circulation control, ordering, accessioning and cataloguing, where the advantages sought include the ability to handle increased numbers of transactions without corresponding increases in staff effort or numbers, or in overall costs. For the most part, it has been left to the special libraries and the newer information services such as INSPEC and UKCIS to investigate and promote the information retrieval systems which have perhaps enjoyed a more eye-catching position, but which have yet to reach a truly significant proportion of those in a position to benefit from these services.

In all of this, the Office for Scientific and Technical Information (OSTI), now the British Library Research and Development Department, has played an active role in the support of research and development, with much of the funds going toward the more expensive systems development work required both in publication systems and in data-base management and access systems.[2] With particular emphasis on the evaluation of systems and services, the presence in the British scene of an agency charged with promoting improvements in techniques for information dissemination and use has provided a focus and a coordinating centre for many of the activities discussed in this Chapter. Aslib, too, has played an important role, firstly through the expertise in information systems analysis and design which its research department has built up, and secondly through its educational role, expressed in part through its special interest Groups.

Data-base compilation and distribution activities

During the mid- and late 60s the principal British secondary information services, including the British National Bibliography, the Institution of Electrical Engineers, and the Commonwealth Agricultural Bureaux, as well as many smaller organisations, initiated programmes aimed at converting their operations, and primarily their complex publication activities, to computer-based systems. The work of BNB was closely coordinated with that of the Library of Congress within the MARC project, for which internationally agreed standards for the specification and representation of catalogue records in machine-readable form were drawn up.[3] The work of IEE within the INSPEC system, as also that of CAB, followed closely on analogous developments in the US. In all of these cases, the approach is similar. The capture of diverse bibliographic records in machine-readable form leads to the production of archival data-bases from which a range of publications, complete with a variety of indexes, is prepared *via* computer typesetting. Simultaneously, production of microform versions of the publications, where appropriate, is also undertaken. At the same time the data-bases themselves are made available for distribution on a subscription basis to other centres for local utilisation.

Another form of international collaboration is instanced in the contribution of input from material published in Britain to two US systems. Thus the British Lending Library prepares input from the biomedical field for the US National Library of Medicine MEDLARS system, and the UK Chemical Information Service of the Chemical Society, treats chemical publications in a similar fashion for the Chemical Abstracts Service of the Americal Chemical Society, both in return for rights in the corresponding data-bases.[4]

There can be little doubt that these activities, although prosaic, are the more important aspect of computer applications in economic terms, but their impact on operations in the majority of libraries is slight, since the publications themselves show little change. Distribution of the data-bases in machine-readable form is becoming significant as a source of revenue for the secondary services in science and technology, with subscriptions taken up in many countries and by international organisations, but distribution of the MARC data-base to British libraries, as is noted later in the Chapter, is still limited, and for the most part awaits development of other forms of distributive systems.

Information retrieval systems

Special libraries have been particularly active in this respect, with developments taking a number of different patterns, depending often on the balance of emphasis between internally and externally generated information. The library and information services of many industrial organisations in the chemical, pharmaceutical and agricultural chemical spheres, as well as elsewhere, have invested heavily in computer-based retrieval systems, both for scientific and for techno-commercial information. Published information is acquired by the purchase of subscriptions to data-bases from organisations such as the Chemical Abstracts Service, Derwent Publications Ltd, or the Institute for Scientific Information, and converted for use internally, where they may be combined with internal report literature. Systems such as ASSASSIN, developed at ICI Agricultural Division, and used by many of that company's divisions, provide for a wide range of forms of display, including microfilm indexes, as well as for selective dissemination and retrospective searches. Shell Research Ltd, at Woodstock, has also been well to the fore in the development of a computer-based information system for coverage of the external literature, and demonstrates the cost-effectiveness of such an appraisal.[5]

In more specialised respects, such as the storage of chemical structure information, and of associated biological test data, the pharmaceutical industry has also invested strongly; here the CROSSBOW system, developed at ICI Pharmaceuticals Division, is particularly noteworthy.

In the main, the emphasis has been on the development of relatively low-technology systems, operated in batch-processing mode, which calls for periodic computer runs. If frequent, eg, on a 24-hour basis, these permit selective searches to be run, the output being produced as line-printer output. If much less frequent, eg monthly or quarterly, the output is more likely to be a paper- or microform-based output, such as KWIC and KWOC indexes, incremental or cumulated, which provide organised listings which can be consulted directly.

As always in this area, the main problem arises from the fact that, whether in absolute or relative terms, the data-bases are voluminous, and their activities, ie the number of times a search or a consultation is made, low in number. Compromises between numbers of listings to be consulted, the timeliness of these resources, and processing costs must always be sought. Only infrequently, and then primarily on a national or international basis, and for the large scientific and technical data-bases with wide interest, are on-line systems warranted, with their high investments in data-bases and in hardware and software systems. None the less, notable progress has been made in these directions, although the most notable systems have operated outside Britain, within the European Community as instanced by the European Space Agency's system at Frascati in Italy, now widely accessible by dial-up facilities from Britain as from the rest of Europe, and in the US. Here the main systems are the MEDLINE, Lockheed, and System Development Corporation services, all of which are now seeing rapidly increasing use within Britain.

The immediacy of access to large retrospective files of bibliographic information, coupled with the facilities for interaction during the development of a search profile, have proved to be a major advantage of on-line systems. The guidance provided to the user during the search process, by display of the numbers of references selected and the citations themselves, and in some instances, of the vocabulary structure, is more analogous to the normal literature search carried out with conventional resources, and overcomes much of the uncertainty encountered in preparing a search for batch-processing use, where the result may not be known for days or weeks, and where a similar time penalty attends attempts at improvement.

These advantages, however, are gained only by distributing the high costs over many users so that high activity results in acceptable costs to the individual. Remote access to such data-bases is made possible only through the development of telecommunications facilities, including dial-up services, leased lines, and networks. In practical terms, their use involves a teletype machine, a visual display unit with printer, or a fast typewriter terminal, together with a modem or acoustic coupler, and a telephone line, which the library must acquire or have available at appropriate times. The tariffs for heavy use of remote dial-up facilities at peak times are substantial, as are those of leased lines. Increasingly, however, the implementation of time-sharing networks, of which EURONET is one of the few intended chiefly for information use in the present context, reduces this component of the costs. Again, advanced techniques, such as packet-switching networks, in which tariffs are not based on the period for which the connection is sustained, may well prove attractive. EPSS, the GPO's Experimental Packet Switched System, is an instance of the latter development, already familiar through the US ARPANET, with connections using satellite transmission to a number of European centres.

The implications of these rapid technological changes are complex, both for libraries and for their users, not least in that libraries in many organisations do not administer the budgets for the use of information services such as these. Where they do, the countervailing claims of traditional and novel access methods need resolution, especially with current levels of inflation making heavy inroads into budgets and necessitating swingeing cuts. The subscriptions to the SDI services are not cheap. A personal profile may cost between £50 and £150 a year, with searches of more general interest, such as the INSPEC Topics and UKCIS Macroprofiles being rather less expensive. Again, the charges for use of the on-line systems can be reckoned to be at least £35 per hour.

Libraries serving research needs in the higher education sphere have moved in this direction through the appointment of Information Officers, part of whose role is to consider ways of utilising technologically advanced services. Many of these early appointments were made with the aid of an OSTI programme, and their work has been furthered through the programme to evaluate on-line techniques in this context.

The computer-based current awareness services have already made some impact, but rather an uneven one on the British library scene; on-line systems are still too novel in the British context for accurate prognostications to be made of the rate at which they will become widespread, or the balance between them and current awareness services. None the less, if the North American experience can be used cautiously as a predictor of future trends, it is certain that librarians, and particularly those in special libraries, will be giving serious consideration to the benefits they bring, in spite of the seemingly high costs.

Automation of library housekeeping

The application of computers to library housekeeping operations has attracted a lot of effort over the last decade and this effort has produced a large number of operational systems. A report[6] based on a survey[7] carried out with a cut-off date of March 1973 states that 'In March 1973, 135 UK libraries had a total of 425 operational computer applications run on a total of 146 computers'. Another report[8] shows that the number of operational computer-based loans systems increased by about 50% between mid-1973 and mid-1975. Thus, a large number of computer-based systems are now operational and, until very recently, at least, this number has been increasing very rapidly.

This area of activity is well served by a few sources which contain a large amount of information about the design and implementation of computer-based library housekeeping systems. A very useful periodical is *Program* which contains many substantial papers on library automation in the UK, and occasionally papers on activities abroad.[9] VINE, a Very Informal NEwsletter[10] which is produced from Southampton University Library by an Information Officer for Library Automation with financial support from the British Library, provides 'an up-to-date picture of work being done in UK library automation which has not been reported elsewhere' and is also a very useful publication. An excellent textbook in this area is R. T. Kimber's *Automation in libraries*,[3] and DES,[11] Aslib[12] and SCONUL[13] have produced useful guides. A large number of research projects have been described in OSTI and British Library Research and Development Department (BLR & DD) reports and in occasional publications by the organisations carrying out the research.

The coverage of the literature on systems description and

implementation is very good but on other aspects it is not yet adequate. It is difficult to find from the literature detailed information on why particular schemes were started, and why one alternative was chosen rather than another. This may be partly because such discussion would expose the political factors lying behind the decisions. Some of these are mentioned by Wainwright.[12] Information is also sadly lacking on the experience of running the systems and of the attitudes of users and all levels of staff. A good reason for this perhaps is that most systems have not been running for long and are still subject to major changes. When such information is made available it will be extremely valuable. In the meantime, gaps in the literature have to be covered by informal exchanges and it would be advisable for anyone moving into library automation to consult with experienced practitioners before making commitments.

From the number of computer-based systems now in operation it is obvious that a large number of librarians will, at some time in their career, work in a library which uses a computer for some part of its housekeeping activities. It is thus important that librarians should have some knowledge of the potentials and limitations of computers so that they do not become completely dependent upon outside experts. Organisations with educational responsibilities have recognised the need for courses in this area. For example, in the Postgraduate School of Librarianship and Information Science at Sheffield University, all students take courses on computer use in libraries and information units, most take at least one course in computer programming, and some students take other optional courses and carry out research studies in this area.

The introduction of computers on a large scale into library processing has produced a number of new tasks for librarians in the analysis, planning, implementation and maintenance of computer-based systems. It would probably be agreed by the people employed in these positions that they have interesting jobs. However, there have been unpublished comments from some people actually carrying out their day to day work using some automated systems that their work has become less interesting, or involves less contact with the public, since

computers were introduced. There have also been unpublished
reports that library users' attitudes change on the introduction
of computers, and some users may be more willing to accuse a
computerised system of making mistakes. A thorough
investigation of the attitudes of staff and users to
computerisation would undoubtedly produce results of
importance for library managers and this seems to be a
promising area for library surveyors to study.

One factor which favours the use of computers is that once a
record has been created in machine-readable form, all or parts of
it may be re-used in many different processes without the need to
recreate the record, an aspect of the data-base compilation
activities already mentioned. For example, a partial catalogue
record may be created for the acquisition process, this record
can be expanded on receipt of the item to give a full catalogue
entry, and this entry may be re-used many times in producing
catalogues or lists. Parts of the record may also be used on
automatically produced recall notices.

In the local use of MARC tapes the size of the back file makes
handling the whole file inconvenient. This difficulty has been
overcome by the selective dissemination of MARC records. In the
future this may be accomplished by having a file containing
MARC compatible records of as many items as possible on-line at
one location. Individual libraries could then send their
requirements for catalogue records by dialling-up the central
computer. Such a system has been operating successfully for
some time in the US[14] and the British Library are working on
one. It seems unlikely however, that the need to have some
cataloguing carried out locally will ever disappear completely.

There are several ways in which a library can gain access to a
computer but the majority of libraries use computers and
computer staff belonging to their parent organisations. Often
such facilities can be used at no extra cost to its own budget
although, obviously, at a cost to the parent body. The demands
which a library makes upon a computer service may be very
high. Its files are large and may have to be accessed frequently.
It also needs to have a guaranteed turnaround of computer jobs

if the standard of service to its users is to be maintained. The library may not have very high priority as a computer user and so the level of service it receives probably depends upon there being surplus computer capacity available. If this surplus disappears then there could be difficulties in obtaining the necessary facilities, and there are unpublished reports of libraries meeting this problem.

The other methods of gaining access to a computer do not suffer from this problem. A few libraries, eg the Birmingham Libraries Cooperative Mechanisation Project (BLCMP), have bought computer time at commercial rates from computer bureaux. A small but increasing number of libraries are purchasing their own mini-computers and the group of South Western Academic Libraries[15] (Bristol, Cardiff and Exeter Universities) with financial support from BLR & DD are sharing the cost of purchasing and running a computer to which each library will have on-line access.

An estimate of the progress made in this area may be made from the increasing availability of specialised equipment, computer programs and computer-readable data bases. In library automation, use has always been made of standard computers, data preparation equipment and programmes, but now a range of specialised items is available. Because of the cost of developing specialised equipment, programmes or data bases, it is advisable for a library wherever possible to use items already available rather than developing them from scratch itself.

A recent article on UK computer-based loans systems[8] lists eight types of data collection units which would be able to handle the large rate at which data are collected in a busy lending library. Some of this equipment was developed specially for library applications and other items were modified for library use. Computer programmes for aspects of library housekeeping are available from ICL, Dataskill and BL Bibliographic Services Division (BLBSD) amongst others; and some libraries, for example Southampton University Library, have made their programmes available to others. BLBSD can now supply catalogue records from a retrospective file of UK publications going back to

1950 and of US publications going back to 1968. Records for current UK and US publications are available on BL and LC MARC tapes. BLCMP have produced a file of about 20,000 serials records in a MARC based format, and the size of this data base is to be increased.

One of the choices confronting the librarian planning the introduction of a computer is that between off-line and on-line working. In off-line working files may only be updated and inquiries run at intervals, perhaps daily or less frequently. With on-line working updating is carried out immediately and a completely up to date file may be interrogated at any time. A comprehensive on-line system will usually give a higher level of service than is possible with an off-line system; however, the difference in levels of service may be quite small compared with the difference in the levels of cost. The majority of computer applications have been off-line, but there have been a small number of on-line systems implemented, for example the circulation systems at IBM, Hursley[16] and MOD Foulness,[17] and the acquisition and cataloguing system of Cheshire County Libraries.[18]

Some other techniques are available, or should become available in the near future, which will give some of the advantages of on-line working without incurring the cost of continuous access to a large, remote mainframe computer.

A compromise, both in level of service and cost between on-line and off-line systems, is offered by hybrid systems.[19] In a hybrid system the small, highly active files are kept in a mini-computer in the library, and up to date files may be interrogated at any time. Large files or files with low activity are kept at a large, remote computer, and may only be updated or interrogated at less frequent intervals.

The use of trapping stores in computer-based loans systems allows a file of numbers to be kept on-line at a data collection unit. The store is not programmable but is small and cheap and it allows data to be checked automatically with information in the store, at the time of generation. The store can thus give immediate warnings about books or borrowers who have to be intercepted. In the future, use may be made of data collection devices which have programmable stores.

Some of the library processes which have been automated demand large amounts of input or output. In the past this would have caused major problems, but developments have overcome these to a large extent. The catalogue of an academic or public library is a large document, and if it had to be produced on a line printer it would be expensive and frequent updates would be ruled out. The use of computer output microform methods which have very high data transfer rates avoids this difficulty. In loans systems large numbers of transactions are generated; for example, a large public lending library might generate 10,000 or more transactions in a day. Putting this data into a computer by manual methods would be slow and subject to error, but the use of automatic data collection equipment allows large amounts of data to be collected swiftly and with very low error rates, and most computer-based loans-systems use such equipment.

There has been a great deal of progress in computer applications in library housekeeping in the last ten years, both in terms of the number of systems implemented and in the variety of approaches available. It is reasonable to ask why this has happened. There are very few reports of costs or staff being reduced because of the implementation of computer-based systems. A more usual claim is that the level of service will be maintained or improved under the pressure of increasing demand at less cost by a computer-based system than by a manual system, ie expenditure will rise less rapidly with the computer-based system. In view of the potential gains and the momentum behind computerisation, and given reasonable economic conditions, progress in this area should continue.

References

1. Lynch, M. F. *Computer-based information services in science and technology – principles and techniques* Stevenage: Peter Peregrinus Ltd, 1974.

2. *OSTI – the first five years* London: HMSO, 1971.

3. Kimber, R. T. *Automation in libraries* 2nd ed Oxford: Pergamon, 1974.

4. Kent, A. K. An appraisal of the British scene. *In The future of cooperative information processing in Europe* Noordwijk: ESRO Scientific and Technical Information Branch, SP–102, 1974, 45–50.

5. Dammers, H. F. Information planning and economic realities. *Ibid*, 9–21.

6. Duchesne, R. M. The use of computers in British libraries and information services: an analysis. *Program* 8 (4), 1974, 183–190.

7. Wilson, C. W. J., ed. *Directory of operational computer applications in United Kingdom libraries and information units* Aslib, 1973. ISBN 0 85142 0540.

8. Young, R. C. United Kingdom computer-based loans systems: a review. *Program* 9 (3), 1975, 102–114.

9. *Program: news of computers in libraries* Aslib, London, 1966 – ISSN 0033 0337.

10. *VINE: A Very Informal Newsletter on Library Automation* ed P. J. D. Bramall, Southampton University Library, 1971 – ISSN 0305 5728.

11. Vickers, P. H. *Automation guidelines for public libraries.* DES Library Information Series no 6, HMSO, 1975. ISBN 0 11 270269 4.

12. Wainwright, Jane. *Computer provision in British libraries* Occasional Publication no 16, Aslib, 1975. ISBN 0 85142 069 9.

13. Higham, N. *Computer needs for university library operations* SCONUL, 1973, ISBN 0 900210 02 8.

14. Kilgour, G. F., Long, P. L., Landgraff, A. L., Wyckoff, J. A. The shared cataloguing system of the Ohio College Library Center. *J Libr Autom* 5 (3) 1972, 157–183.

15. Hudson, R. F. B. SWALCAP on-line circulation system: plans and progress. *Program* 9 (3), 1975, 133–142.

16. VINE no 9, 1974, 11–13.

17. Eunson, B. G. UPDATE – an on-line loans control system in use in a small research library. *Program* 8 (2) 1974, 88–101.

18. Berriman, S. G. *and* Pilliner, J. Cheshire County Library acquisitions and cataloguing system. *Program* 7 (1), 1973, 38–59.

19. Buckland, M. F. *and* Gallivan, B. Circulation control: off-line, on-line or hybrid. *J Lib Autom* 5 (1), 1972, 30–38.

International activities

K. C. Harrison

The Library Association has not found it easy in recent years to
organise its role in international librarianship. This is not to say
that British librarians are not interested in the international
aspects of their work. Actually, the reverse is true: there is
almost an embarrassment of activity. But the Council has had
some difficulty in deciding how best to harness this interest. A
suggestion first made in *Focus*[1] that the LA should set up an
International Relations Division on the lines of that belonging
to the American Library Association was taken up with alacrity
by many members of the Council and by many individual
members, but ideals were confronted with realities, and the
blunt truth is that the LA cannot afford an International Relations
Division at the moment, nor even in the foreseeable future.

It is worth mentioning that, two or three years ago, the
American Library Association was forced to disband its
International Relations Division because of financial stringency.
Furthermore, the ALA had been receiving sums of US
Government money to help in its international activities, and
there was very little hope of the LA getting parallel sums from
the British Government.

But if it is thought that the debates on whether or not the LA
should set up an International Relations Division were
fruitless, let this be straightaway denied. Instead, the debates
gave impulse to the LA Council to decide to set up an
International Relations Sub-Committee of the Executive and, at
the time of writing, this is still operating. The Sub-Committee

was formed in the middle of 1973, and its original purpose was
to supervise the disbursement of an annual grant which had been
made to the LA by the British Council. The Sub-Committee was
warmly welcomed by the International and Comparative
Librarianship Group, though it was thought by many that, with
four members only, it was not big enough.

It was not long, however, before the LA Council had to widen
the Sub-Committee's terms of reference. The Executive began to
direct more and more business to the Sub-Committee, so that
early in 1975 the Sub-Committee became entirely responsible for
advising the Executive and the Council on international
relations and activities. The International and Comparative
Librarianship Group, which had demonstrated its initiative by
inviting a member of the LA Sub-Committee to attend its Group
committee meetings, was given reciprocal facilities, so that a
representative of the Group is now coopted on to the LA
International Relations Sub-Committee.

This was a useful step forward which has been generally
welcomed, but although it has led to clear improvements in the
links between the Council and the ICLG, nobody could pretend
that these are not capable of further improvement. Although the
LA's Sub-Committee has demonstrated its hospitality by a
willingness to consider, often favourably, all suggestions and
propositions coming from the ICLG, the AAL and other
Branches, Groups and Sections, there still remains a need to
define in greater detail the roles and responsibilities of the many
sections of the LA which from time to time have international
implications in their work.

At the time of writing (January 1976) a new committee structure
of the LA Council has just come into operation. Apart from the
Executive Coordinating Committee, there are now only three
committees of the Council, one of which, the General Purposes
Committee, has international relations as one of its many and
varied responsibilities. At its first meeting, the General Purposes
Committee confirmed the appointment of an International
Relations Sub-Committee, and this provides the opportunity,
through cooptions, to increase the involvement of Branches

and Groups in the overall international policies of the
Association.

A wider involvement

I would also hope that such moves would result in involving
more young librarians in this international work. The AAL has, in
recent years, amassed considerable experience in arranging
international tours, both in Britain for overseas librarians, and
for British librarians visiting foreign countries. The ICLG has so
far been rather more theoretical in its approach, but it has done
positive work with the publication of its journal *Focus*, which
improves with every issue, and by arranging conferences and
meetings which have resulted in the exchange and the
publication of valuable current information on library
development in different parts of the world. The London and
Home Counties Branch of the LA has for many years shown
initiative by inviting European librarians to Britain for
conference and study tours, while its J. D. Stewart Travelling
Bursary has been instrumental in enlarging the international
experience of many a young librarian.

Outside the LA, some of the library schools have developed their
international work in positive ways. For example, since 1973 the
College of Librarianship Wales has run a successful International
Graduate Summer School in Librarianship and Information
Science, and from the same year the Liverpool School of
Librarianship has each September presented a Summer School
devoted to aspects of European librarianship.

It is the garnering together of these and other contributions to
international librarianship that I would like to see as the job of
the LA's International Relations Sub-Committee, and I am sure
we are moving steadily in this direction. Meanwhile, the LA does
much more international work than is generally realised by
members. Impressive numbers of visiting librarians from
overseas arrive at Headquarters, announced and unannounced,
but all are received cordially by the senior staff, with conducted
tours and exchanges of information being the order of the day.
The LA also arranges nationwide library tours both for

individual visitors from overseas and for groups. It has initiated invitations to overseas library associations to send guests to the LA Conference. It maintains close liaison with the British Council and its advice and help is always at the disposal of interested bodies and individuals, as well as to members of course.

Those who criticise the LA's shortcomings in international activities are really criticising its undue modesty. Obviously more should be done to acquaint members with their Association's work in this field: a start was made in March 1975 with an article in the *Record*.[2] Such publicity ought to be made continuous.

The British Council

Mentions have been made of the British Council, and no chapter on the international activities of British librarianship could possibly be complete without some further references, even though the work of the British Council is already well known. Like many other official bodies, the British Council has had to curtail its work in recent years owing to financial shortfalls, but it still maintains many libraries overseas, and its librarians frequently act as the agents for administering the ODA Book Presentation Programme to public, school and college libraries in many developing countries. The British Council also has a Libraries Panel on which the LA has representation. This Panel provides a useful forum for discussing British Council library problems, but it does not meet as often as it might.

From 1972 to 1975 the British Council made grants to the Library Association totalling £4000 in order to encourage relations with librarians in Western Europe. It was this act which led, as we have seen, to the establishment of an International Relations Sub-Committee by the LA. Good use was made of the British Council grants. Through them, the LA made specific grants helping individual librarians to visit European libraries for specific research projects. In addition, British librarianship was able to forge new and hopefully lasting contacts with libraries and librarians in Spain and in Italy. During 1974 some Italian librarians paid an official visit to

Britain, and a party of British librarians toured Italian libraries. In 1975 similar arrangements took place with Spain. As well as seeing library buildings and conversing with librarians, opportunities were provided in both Italy and Spain for the British visitors to have useful exchanges with those in authority who have responsibilities for library development.

The long-term benefits of these exchange visits may not be seen for some time to come, but any future improvements in Italian and Spanish librarianship may well owe a great deal to the impetus provided by the British Council grants. It should prove to be money well spent.

Links with Europe

The United Kingdom became part of the European Community on 1 January 1973, and some members of the Library Association began to think of the need for a library association covering the member-nations of the Community. The LA took up the idea and circularised other library associations in the EC. The replies were, to say the least, unenthusiastic. One or two were definitely against the idea, most kept their options open, and only a small minority were enthusiastically in favour. The door was, however, kept ajar by those library associations which asked for more information as to the aims and objectives of such a body. The ECLA, if one may coin yet another acronym, has not yet come into being, but the LA meanwhile takes every opportunity to discuss the project.

The opponents of ECLA indicated that there were already more than enough library associations in the international field. They pointed particularly to IFLA, while the Danes drew attention to the continuing existence of the triennial Anglo-Scandinavian Public Library Conferences. These arguments can, however, be countered by pointing out that IFLA is a world-wide body with programmes which are already over-full, while the Anglo-Scandinavian get-togethers concern public librarians only. In fact, the Anglo-Scandinavian Public Library Conferences could well offer a good model for ECLA. The meetings could be held about every three years, in one country after another. They would, of course, try to be of value to librarians of all types of libraries, and they could be followed by brief study tours.

To those who say there are already too many international associations and meetings, I would counter by saying that there are not enough. Interest in international and comparative librarianship is bound to grow. What is needed are more opportunities for a wider spectrum of librarians, and especially younger librarians, to take part in these activities.

The Anglo-Scandinavian Public Library Conferences have continued to thrive; in recent years they have been held at Cambridge, England, in 1967, at Koli, Finland, in 1970, and at Rättvik, Sweden, in 1973. By the time these words are in print, the Eighth Anglo-Scandinavian Conference will have taken place in 1976 at Brighton, England. While it is true to say that the conferences have more or less conformed to their original formulae, that at Brighton had to be confined to reduced numbers because of the increasing organisational costs. Before Brighton there were between sixty-five and seventy delegates, but in 1976 the numbers had to be confined to just over fifty. There were ten delegates each from Denmark, Finland, Norway, Sweden and the UK, plus one from Ireland and some additional speakers.

It will be a great pity if international library conferences have to be curtailed or abandoned on financial grounds, but there is no doubt that steeply rising accommodation costs and air fares pose great threats for the future.

IFLA

One of the bodies which has been hoist with the petard of its own success in recent years is IFLA. From the mid-1960s onwards, attendances at the IFLA General Council meetings were rising at the rate of an additional 100 or so every year. By the 1970s, when the IFLA meetings were successively held at Moscow, Liverpool, Budapest, Grenoble and Washington DC, attendances of 1000 or more were recorded. At Oslo in 1975 this was drastically reduced by limiting the number of delegates from each country, but adding to them those serving on the Board, the Programme Development Committee, and the Standing Committees. In the event, less than 400 were at the Oslo meetings, though 'accompanying persons' increased the total to over 500.

As it happened, Oslo provided the wrong kind of conference to assess the new policy because it was mainly concerned with revising the IFLA Statutes and there were few opportunities, either at plenary or sectional levels, for delegates to get down to professional matters. In 1976 IFLA will be going through yet another experimental year, since it is holding a professional meeting at Seoul, South Korea, followed by the General Council at Lausanne. The revised Statutes come up for final approval at Lausanne, and, at the time of writing, it must be everybody's hope that not too much valuable time will be spent on this item.

Not even 1977 will be a normal IFLA year, because the organisation celebrates its fiftieth anniversary that year. This is in some ways an unfortunate clash with the Library Association Centenary, but at least the two celebratory conferences, that of IFLA in Brussels and that of the LA in London, have been kept apart by one month. With Brussels 1977 being presumably devoted to IFLA anniversary matters, it seems as though we must wait until 1978 to see IFLA operating normally again, though under its new Statutes.

Members of the LA have supported IFLA since its foundations, and many are the contributions which have been made by British librarians. The names of Bishop, Cashmore, McColvin, Chaplin and Anthony Thompson are indelibly connected with IFLA, while in 1970 Sir Frank Francis completed a memorable six-year term of office as President. During his stewardship IFLA widened its horizons both geographically and professionally and British librarianship takes justifiable pride in Sir Frank's contributions to the international scene through IFLA.

The LA greatly increased its official representation to the annual

IFLA General Council meetings in 1964, sending ten or eleven delegates, comprising the Honorary Officers and the chairmen of standing committees. This state of affairs continued for some years, despite some attempts by the Executive to cut down the size of the delegation on economy grounds. These efforts were consistently rejected by the Council, which preferred the larger delegation. Towards the end of 1975, however, the combination of a new LA committee structure, added to the undeniable economic facts of life caused by escalating air fares, hotel accommodation and subsistence expenses, caused another new look at this question. It is to be hoped that the pendulum does not have to swing too far in the opposite direction. Ten or eleven LA representatives may be too many in the circumstances, but four or five would be too few.

The object of LA representation is to ensure that the Council and the membership as a whole are kept informed of the varied activities of IFLA. Since, however, LA representatives have by tradition contributed much to IFLA's own development, any panic reduction of British representation would be a bad thing for IFLA as well as for the LA. It is suggested that the British official delegation should never be less than seven, and it should preferably be eight.

UNESCO

Another area in which British contributions to international library development are maintained is through the agency of UNESCO. When the IFLA Standards for Public Libraries were being revised by a Working Party on which British representation was strong, UNESCO asked IFLA to look at its Public Library Manifesto. IFLA referred this task to its Working Party, with the result that in 1973 the updated *Standards for public libraries*[3] was published by IFLA, and the publication included the revised UNESCO Public Library Manifesto. The document as a whole is of prime importance to the development of public libraries in the world today and, if properly applied, is capable of making a signal and tangible contribution to librarianship.

Other British contributions made through UNESCO have been achieved mainly at individual rather than at Association level. If a list were to be compiled, it would include many writings by British librarians for the *Unesco Bulletin for Libraries,* as well as much practical work undertaken in various parts of the world on a consultancy basis. These assignments have been, and are being, undertaken in the fields of academic librarianship and library education, as well as in the public library area. UNESCO can always rely upon British support whenever it is sought, either from individual librarians or from the Library Association itself.

Commonwealth Library Assciation

The Library Association was intimately concerned in the formation in 1972 of the Commonwealth Library Association, or COMLA as it is now known. Indeed it is not overstating the case to say that without LA assistance it is unlikely that the Commonwealth body would ever have been started. What happened was that in 1970 the LA was approached by the Commonwealth Foundation which suggested the establishment of a Commonwealth association of librarians. The Commonwealth Foundation, since its formation in 1966, had already been instrumental in setting up Commonwealth-wide bodies for other professions, and now thought it high time for a similar organisation for librarianship. After discussions at officer level, the LA Executive and Council approved the concept in principle. It so happened that in 1971 with the IFLA General Council meeting in Liverpool there would be a large number of influential librarians from Commonwealth countries visiting Britain, so the LA asked the Commonwealth Foundation if it would support financially an exploratory meeting to be held at LA Headquarters in London.

This request was granted and the meeting duly took place in September 1971. Those present heard details of the idea and returned to their own countries on the understanding that they would consult their own library associations and let the LA know in due course whether or not they would support the formation of a Commonwealth Library Association. Nigeria offered Lagos as a meeting place for the inaugural conference and, with almost

unanimous support, this took place in November 1972. A total
of twenty countries with library associations was represented,
plus Canada which at that time was the only country which had
still not decided whether or not to support the venture. Soon
after the Lagos meeting the Canadian Library Association did
join COMLA.

Many historic decisions were made at Lagos. A constitution and
financial regulations were approved, officers and committee were
elected, subscriptions agreed, Jamaica was approved as the
location for the secretariat, conditions of appointment for a
Secretary were agreed, and a future programme of activities was
explored.

Two working parties were created, one led by Paul Xuereb
(Malta) with the object of facilitating exchanges and internships
for library personnel within the Commonwealth, and the other
convened by Harrison Bryan (Australia) and designed to work
towards the mutual recognition of librarians' qualifications.
Both these working parties began operations in 1973, mainly by
correspondence, and the rest of that year, as far as COMLA was
concerned, was occupied by advertising for, and appointing, a
secretary, and in establishing the secretariat at the Professional
Centre in Kingston, Jamaica.

It had been agreed at Lagos that the Executive of six members
should endeavour to meet at intervals of approximately
eighteen months, and this ideal was achieved when in March
1974 the committee met at the LA Headquarters in London. For
most members it was a first opportunity to meet the COMLA
Secretary, Mrs C. P. Fray. Interim reports from the working
parties were received by the Executive, which also took many
decisions and began to formulate plans for COMLA Council II to
be held in Kingston in November 1975.

Meanwhile COMLA, which does not see itself in competition with
other library associations, whether international, regional or
national, had joined IFLA, and the present writer, in his capacity
as COMLA President, was able to convene useful and
well-attended COMLA sessions during the IFLA meetings at

Washington DC in November 1974 and at Oslo, Norway, in August 1975.

In November 1975, despite financial difficulties, COMLA Council II took place at the Professional Centre, Kingston, Jamaica. A meeting of the Executive was held on Sunday 16 November, and the Council met during the ensuing three days. Compared with the twenty-one countries represented at Lagos, COMLA Council II was attended by representatives from thirty-three Commonwealth countries, plus three delegates from affiliated members. The total membership at the end of 1975 was in fact thirty-nine countries, while more than eighty individual libraries were supporting COMLA as affiliated members.

The Council meeting was extremely busy. The constitution and financial regulations were examined and amended, subscriptions were revised and a future programme was agreed, as was the submission of a budget for 1976–77. New officers and Executive were also elected. The Council learnt with pleasure that nine issues of the Newsletter had been published and circulated, but it wanted to see this publication come out as a regular quarterly, and to be in printed form. Members were also glad to hear from Bermuda, Botswana, Malawi and others that the formation of library associations in their countries was imminent. This was especially good news, since one of the COMLA objectives is to encourage the formation of library associations in those countries where they do not yet exist.

COMLA Council II did not devote any time to the reports of its two working parties, because these were topics for a COMLA Seminar held during the three days immediately following the Council meeting. This was codirected by Paul Xuereb and Harrison Bryan, and it was supported financially by the Commonwealth Fund for Technical Cooperation (CFTC). Indeed, the very existence of COMLA has led to considerable support for Commonwealth librarianship from CFTC. No fewer than ten recommendations emerged from the Seminar, and action on these is awaited with interest at the time of writing.

It would seem that COMLA has got off to a good start. The

Commonwealth Foundation has expressed its pleasure with the progress made, and it has so far been generous in funding COMLA activities. Whether the Foundation will be able to go on increasing its subventions in an era of economic stringency remains to be seen. For its part, the Library Association receives frequent reports from its COMLA representative, and it has given much tangible help to Commonwealth library associations and to many individual librarians from Commonwealth countries.

INTAMEL

The International Association of Metropolitan City Libraries (INTAMEL) is a subsection of the Public Libraries Committee of IFLA and has been so since its formation in 1967. Although the Library Association itself had nothing to do with the formation of INTAMEL, many leading members of the LA were concerned and have in fact played important parts in its development. George Chandler, when City Librarian of Liverpool, was INTAMEL's first President, while Godfrey Thompson and the present writer have carried out three-year stints as Secretary-Treasurer.

INTAMEL membership comprehends those metropolitan cities serving populations of 400,000 and over, and British librarianship may be proud of the fact that, soon after the new international body was formed, the public library authorities of all British cities in this population group had become members.

The attempt has been made for INTAMEL to organise a general meeting each year, also for its Executive to meet during the IFLA General Council. Although the need for an international body to study the specific problems of metropolitan city public libraries had been mooted at Prague in 1966 and agreed informally at Toronto in 1967, it was left to Britain to stage the official inaugural meeting at which the constitution was approved and a future programme arranged. This was done at Liverpool in 1968, and the city librarians from overseas were later able to embark on study tours taking in Birmingham, Manchester, Sheffield, Westminster and the City of London.

The Liverpool arrangements became the model for future
INTAMEL general meetings and study tours. In 1969
Gothenburg was the host, followed in subsequent years by
Tokyo, Baltimore, Milan, Delhi, and then Hamburg in 1974. The
study tours to such other cities as Stockholm, Copenhagen,
Osaka, Kyoto, Tokyo, Washington DC, Boston, Toronto,
Rome, Florence, Calcutta, Bremen and Berlin, helped those
members who attended to assemble some unique experiences of
comparative international librarianship, while the papers
presented at the meetings have been made available to wider
audiences through the pages of *International Library Review*.[4]

After its first triennium, INTAMEL widened its outlook in 1971 by
devoting increasing attention to the problems of metropolitan
library provision in developing countries. With funds
generously provided by the International Development
Research Center of Canada, INTAMEL was able to invite librarians
from Accra, Cairo, Colombo, Delhi, Lagos, Mexico City and
Tehran to its 1972 general meetings in Milan, Florence and
Rome. The following year, with UNESCO assistance, delegates
from Barbados, Ghana, Malaysia, Hong Kong, Nigeria and Sri
Lanka attended the INTAMEL meetings in Delhi and Calcutta.

During these contacts with colleagues from developing
countries a great deal of information was assembled relating to
the special problems facing such cities as Lagos, Colombo,
Delhi and others. It was decided to conduct a pilot investigation
in the hope that the conclusions reached might be transplanted
with a view to solving the library problems of large cities
wherever they may be located. Lagos was selected for this pilot
survey and, again with Canadian IDRC financial support,
Laverne Carroll of Oklahoma University visited Lagos to
consult with Nigerian librarians and authorities and to set up a
local research group. The investigation proceeded and the
intention was to produce a report for consideration by INTAMEL
members, who would then hold their annual meeting at Lagos in
1975, with a study tour to Accra.

A combination of circumstances, headed chiefly by the current
economic situation, led to very poor support for the Lagos

meeting, only four representatives from other countries being able to attend. There is no doubt that INTAMEL has lost some of its momentum for the time being, but, writing before the event, it can be said that plans are firmly fixed for the 1976 annual meeting to be held in Paris, with a study tour taking in Lyon, Toulouse and Bordeaux. It is expected that the Lagos final report will be considered during these meetings, that it will be published soon afterwards, and that it will fulfil the expectation of being useful to city library authorities in other developing countries.

Meanwhile, INTAMEL continues to expand its membership. There were over 100 cities at the last count, and British cities such as Liverpool, Glasgow, Edinburgh, Westminster and the City of London remain active members, being almost ever-present attenders at the general meetings.

Envoi

The international work and commitments of the LA have not always met with universal approval from members in the past, but happily the opposition has dwindled noticeably in recent years. If the International Relations Sub-Committee can fulfil its second term of reference which reads: 'to coordinate the proposed international relations activities of all Branches, Groups and Sections . . . to ensure a reasonable balance in international relations activity'; if more of the library schools can be persuaded to extend their interest in international librarianship; if grants from such bodies as the British Council and the Commonwealth Foundation can be continued and expanded; and if a larger number of young librarians can be given a taste of international librarianship through visits, study tours, meetings and conferences – if all these ideals can be achieved, it can only lead to a better calibre of librarians serving their users more efficiently in the world of tomorrow.

References

1. Harrison, K. C. An International Relations Office for the LA ? *Focus on International and Comparative Librarianship* 5/6, April, 1970.

2. Haslam, D. D. The Association's work: I International relations activities. *Libr Ass Rec* 77 (3) March 1975, 54.

3. IFLA. *Standards for public libraries*
Pullach/München: Verlag
Dokumentation, 1973.

4. *International Library Review* Reprints
from **4** (4) (1972), **5** (1) (1973) and
6 (5), (1974) 107.

Chapter Eighteen

Professional education, research and development

Wilfred L. Saunders

Education and training

On a centenary occasion one is inevitably moved to wonder
whatever our predecessors of a hundred years before would have
thought of what is happening today, to speculate about the
incredulity with which they would have viewed the practices and
procedures of 1976. In no aspect of our professional activity is
this more the case than with the arrangements for professional
education and training. Here the changes have indeed been
revolutionary: from the 1877 position of no formal education
and training at all we have progressed to our present situation of
sixteen full-time institutions – several of them headed by
Professors of librarianship – presenting a complex array of
full-time courses leading to Diplomas, Bachelor's and Master's
degrees, even the ultimate academic accolade of the Doctorate.
Perhaps even more astonishing is the fact that this has been no
even, century-long progression: most of the spectacular burst of
change and new development goes back no further than thirty
years. Much of it, indeed, has come about within an even shorter
period of time: since 1964.

The changes have been of two kinds: first of all a dramatic
increase in the scale of the professional education operation; and
secondly an enhancement of its quality, with accompanying
changes of attitude, objectives and general philosophy. In this
chapter I shall therefore deal not only with the more factual
aspects of the centenary year educational scene, but also with
some of the more intangible, qualitative considerations.

To appreciate the full significance of the changes it is worth
reminding ourselves of the situation up to 1964 – only twelve
years ago. Before that time professional education for
librarianship in Britain was a largely part-time operation in
which ten schools of librarianship prepared students for
examinations set by the Library Association. Some of the
students were graduates but the vast majority were
non-graduates who had come into library work at 16 or 17 years
of age and over the years were taking the series of Library
Association examinations which culminated in the Fellowship.
Graduates and non-graduates followed the same courses: I
myself recall as a part-time lecturer in the Birmingham Library
School having had in the same class for the Literature of social
and political ideas a raw 17-year-old, more or less straight from
school, and an Oxford graduate in Politics.

There was, in fact, one exception to all of this – the University
College London School of Librarianship and Archives, with a
one-year full-time postgraduate diploma which could lead to
exemption from the ALA and, *via* its later Part 2, from most of
the FLA examinations; but the number of students accounted for
by the London School was relatively very small indeed.

The other library schools were attached to colleges of commerce
or technology – institutions which in most cases were operating
at a low academic level. Their staffs were small – perhaps three or
four full-time lecturers supplemented by part-timers; and the
students' lecture programme was correspondingly heavy.
Teaching loads were extremely high – twenty, twenty-five or
even more hours a week – and the matter of advanced study or
research did not, of course, arise. Methods – and in most cases
the requirements of the LA syllabus – were geared up to pretty
solid absorption of a lot of factual information, and there was a
heavy bias towards the *techniques* of librarianship.

After 1964 all of this changed – more or less literally overnight.
The Library Association altered the structure of its examination
system to make the ALA the basic professional qualification; the
FLA was still available, but as an 'extra', so to speak, after

producing a thesis, and not many people were expected to attempt it. The prerequisite qualifications for studying to be a librarian were upgraded to the same as those for minimum university entrance, which meant that the new entrant to the profession would usually come in at 18 after taking GCE 'A' levels, not at 16 or 17. As the new syllabus called for two years of full-time study, the part-time approach became for practical purposes a thing of the past. One consequence of all of this was that most of these non-graduate students entered library school straight from school, with no practical experience, and placements for short spells of practical experience became a library school responsibility – in some cases requiring the designation of a member of library school staff as training or liaison officer.

For the schools this new situation had profound consequences. A two-year course in itself meant a doubling in size of the student body; an exclusively full-time basis presented new and very attractive educational opportunities; the higher entrance requirements lifted the academic level at which courses could be conducted, and likewise the level of operation that could be expected of the student in the educational situation; the revised syllabus was moving towards more emphasis on principles, less on techniques and the swallowing of large lumps of knowledge; and increasingly, the schools saw their proper concern as being with education, not training, the latter being most effectively and appropriately carried out 'in-service', in the actual working situation. Assessed course-work in practical subjects began to replace practical work carried out under examination conditions. Even more important, there began to take place a gradual devolution of examining responsibility from the LA to the schools themselves so that teaching and examining began to become – as they should be – part of the same process.

Side by side with these changes, in the second half of the sixties, we were experiencing a great shortage of librarians. Combined with the doubling of the duration of the course from one to two years, this led to almost irresistible pressure to expand the size of the library schools, a pressure to which they were more than willing to respond. In almost no time at all most of the non-university schools were up to 150–200 full-time students or more, the two largest being well over 300.

With greater student numbers came increases in staff: the LA laid down a one to ten staff/student ratio to qualify for internal examining and the CNAA, of which more later, adopted a similar yardstick. So library schools that for a dozen or fifteen years or more had got along with a very small number of full-time staff found themselves fifteen, twenty, even thirty or more strong, and occupying positions of considerable importance in their parent institutions. At national level a group of full-time teachers which had grown to 300 or more strong began to represent an increasingly influential voice in professional affairs. At this point it is relevant to mention, too, that there has also developed an active Library Education Group (LEG) of the Library Association, while the heads of library schools meet together periodically as ABLISS – the Association of British Library and Information Science Schools. The latter body still seems, in the view of some of its members, to be in search of a significant role, though it is undoubtedly of value as a forum, at head of school level.

If the non-university library schools were undergoing rapid change, so, too, were their parent institutions. The government's post-Robbins Report educational policy was not only to increase the number and size of the universities but to create some thirty powerful institutions called polytechnics, to be formed in most places by combining existing colleges of technology, of commerce, and of art, into a single unit; as polytechnics they would drop all their lower-level teaching and concentrate on work at or near degree level. This group of new institutions was intended to be rather more practically orientated than the universities, less academic, and, unlike the universities, with no commitment to pure research – though with applied research responsibilities in the service of their local communities. Nearly all the library schools were in institutions which were to be designated as polytechnics and they have benefited enormously from the improvement of the general educational environment which has come about with polytechnic status – including, of course, very substantially increased funds, for in recent years the Treasury has been looking far more benevolently on these new institutions than on the universities.

So we had a new LA syllabus, full-time education over a two-year period, a move towards internal examining, much larger schools, greatly expanded staffs, and a vastly improved educational environment. But there was still another – and extremely important – strand in the new fabric which was being created. From 1964 it ceased to be the case that only universities could award degrees. There was created a Council for National Academic Awards (CNAA), empowered to authorise higher educational institutions (which normally means polytechnics) to present three or four-year courses approved by the Council, successful completion of which would qualify for the Council's Bachelor's degrees. Courses with a vocational element were to be particularly encouraged.

This opportunity to participate in degree work, with all the enhanced status that would go with it, was naturally a very great attraction to the emergent polytechnics, and it could not have come at a better time for their schools of librarianship. As a subject, librarianship was a 'natural' for CNAA work. The academic prerequisites for the two-year students coming to the schools of librarianship were already at minimum university entrance level. The staffs had expanded – but even more importantly, they had expanded by attracting into teaching many of the brightest and most imaginative of the younger generation of librarians. They were just the people to respond to the challenge of devising new courses, pitched at a high enough level to persuade a very rigorous CNAA Librarianship Board that they were bachelor's-degree-worthy. There was a ferment of planning, of innovation, of rethinking the whole approach to library science; the outcome of all of this, by this centenary year, is that virtually all the non-university schools now offer at least one CNAA course, at Bachelor's level. Normally the syllabuses include supporting subjects from outside librarianship – eg Economics, or English – but orientated towards the needs of librarianship. This has, of course, involved joint planning with the other teaching departments concerned – itself a very beneficial exercise.

It should be made clear at this point that planning for bachelor's degree work of this sort has not been restricted to the CNAA courses – the University School of Librarianship at Strathclyde in fact pioneered the whole idea of first degrees in librarianship, and in addition to Strathclyde the Loughborough University of Technology and the University of Wales both offer bachelor's degrees in librarianship, the latter being taught by the College of Librarianship Wales, which has allied itself with the university for this purpose.

Side by side with – in fact slightly preceding – this move towards bachelor's degree work, the polytechnic schools have taken the opportunity arising from the 1964 syllabus changes to present a special one-year course for postgraduates, leading to the ALA *via* the LA's Postgraduate Professional route. The present situation, therefore, is that most of the non-university schools have a changing 'mix' of students: postgraduates working for an LA or CNAA qualification; undergraduates working for a three or four-year bachelor's degree; and two-year course students, working for the LA Associateship. To this may be added, in some cases, the possibility of reading for the CNAA's Master's degrees.

What we are now seeing is a fairly constant annual output of between 1400 and 1500 qualified people of all three principal varieties; but within that total the number of two-year non-graduates is declining as the output of bachelor's degree graduates increases, while the postgraduate total holds fairly steady – largely as a consequence of the limited number of postgraduate bursaries and studentships. It is the view of many that the two-year course will virtually have disappeared before many years have passed, and the day of the completely graduate profession will have arrived. This will not be without its problems. The two-year product has an important role to play in the British library scene, but individual schools are understandably prone to see more prestige and greater educational opportunities in building up their degree work. By

the time this volume appears, the future may be a little more
certain, as a reconvened Library Association committee is at
present examining the whole matter of professional education in
the future.

Attention has so far been concentrated on the non-university
schools, which are mostly in polytechnics, because that is where
growth and change have been seen at their most spectacular; but
equally significant developments have been taking place on the
university front. Up to 1964, as has been said, there was only one
university school, the University College London School of
Librarianship and Archives. But in 1964 there started up a
second – the Postgraduate School of Librarianship at Sheffield,
which later became the Postgraduate School of Librarianship
and Information Science; and this was rapidly followed by a
library school in a Scottish university – Strathclyde – and in a
Northern Irish university – Queen's University Belfast. Later,
but catching up very fast, was founded a further university
school – at the Loughborough University of Technology. The
College of Librarianship Wales, our largest school, and a
'monotechnic', has allied itself as we have seen with the
University of Wales and teaches courses for bachelor's-degree
and postgraduate qualifications, which are actually awarded by
that university. Most recently of all, it has now become possible
(with the recognition of its courses by the Library Association)
to include in a survey such as this the City University Centre for
Information Science.

The Belfast and Strathclyde Schools present courses for both
postgraduates and non-graduates: the City, University College
London and Sheffield Schools are exclusively postgraduate.
Though Belfast and Strathclyde do look outside their countries
for students, it is probably fair to say that they are thought of as
predominantly serving Ireland and Scotland, respectively. The
other schools draw from the entire range of UK universities and,
of course, to some extent from overseas. In Sheffield for
instance, though three universities – Oxford, Cambridge and
London – are more heavily represented than the rest, the sixty or
so postgraduates normally cover thirty or more universities
between them. In general terms the distinctive role of the

university schools is to attract and educate graduates of high academic calibre – often considerably higher than would be found on the polytechnic schools' postgraduate courses. This is particularly true of University College London and Sheffield, where an upper second-class or a first-class honours degree is a normal entrance requirement.

A full analysis of the students enrolled in the various schools and of the qualifications for which they are working is given in Table 18.1. It is perhaps worth while to examine this range of qualifications a little more closely.

Table 18.1

Total output of successful students, 1974/5

	2-year Course for Non-graduates	Bachelor's Degree	Post-graduate Diploma	MA **	MSC **	Total
Aberdeen	36		23			59
Aberystwyth, CLW	34	49	168			251
Belfast	2		37			39
Birmingham	62	24	29			115
Brighton	39					39
Leeds		42	34‡			76
Liverpool		25	38			63
London						
City University					24	24
Ealing	96		61			157
PNL	65	12	103			180
UCL			49			49
Loughborough*	61	27	39			127
Manchester	47	21	34			102
Newcastle	40	20	32			92
Sheffield				41	18	59
Strathclyde		19	37			56
Total	482	239	684	41	42	1,488

* This covers both the University and the College of Technology.
** Basic professional qualifications, not including post-qualification Master's degrees or Master's degrees by thesis.
‡ This figure is for January 1975 enrolments.

It must first of all be made clear that at Master's degree level there are at least three types of qualification. There is a Master's degree which is a first, basic professional qualification – notably the City University M SC in Information Science and the three Sheffield University Master's degrees (MA in Librarianship – for humanities graduates, M SC in Information Studies – for science and technology graduates, and MA in Information Studies – for social scientists). As befits their level, the courses for these degrees are of greater rigour than the various postgraduate diploma courses and of longer duration: a full calendar year instead of an academic year of eight or nine months. They also qualify for the highest level of student grant: the DES Studentships.

In addition, there are Master's degrees by research – offered by all the university schools, and, increasingly, by the non-university schools, under CNAA auspices. Then there are Master's degrees at post-qualification level for experienced and professionally qualified librarians, often made up of an advanced study element combined with a dissertation of some sort: for example, UCL's MA, Queen's University Belfast's MLS, and Sheffield's post-qualification MA and M SC., come into this category. Unique in its way is a degree course at the Loughborough University of Technology, which enables a limited number of ALA's to achieve a Master's degree after a combination of third-year Bachelor's degree courses, a dissertation, and examinations on professional practice. Many of these post-qualification Master's degrees accept the Fellowship of the Library Association as a prerequisite for entry and most of them may be pursued by working practitioners on a part-time basis. They have provided a valuable route to graduate status for many senior practising librarians and teachers in polytechnic schools of librarianship who, while of graduate calibre by any standards, came into the profession when it was not normal, as it is today, for the most gifted school leavers to proceed straight to university.

Having much in common with the Sheffield-and City-taught Master's courses is the postgraduate diploma. It seems likely that these two types of postgraduate qualification will continue to provide the preferred background for senior posts in universities, though large numbers of librarians who qualify by these routes do in fact take up posts in other types of library.

The Bachelor's degree in librarianship, as may be seen from Table 18.1 is becoming of considerable significance and it is interesting to speculate about the future professional role of those who qualify in this way. Undoubtedly some of them will emerge at the top of the profession in years to come, but it seems not unreasonable to picture the majority of them as the 'middle-management' cadre of the future: neither more intellectually gifted nor more professionally dedicated than their non-graduate ALA and FLA counterparts of today, but having had the benefit of a longer and more demanding general and professional education – a general social and educational phenomenon, not restricted to librarianship.

The group of which it is difficult to speak with any certainty is that which emerges with a two-year, non-graduate qualification. In a future in which the graduate librarian is the norm they will obviously be at a competitive disadvantage and this is one reason for many schools having discontinued their two-year non-graduate courses. The other side of this coin, however, is an 'all chiefs and no Indians' situation, and for this as well as other reasons increasing attention is being paid in libraries and information units of all types to improving the utilisation of qualified staff and to the rationalising of staffing structures in general. It is not surprising that the role and future of non-graduate professionally qualified librarians has been a major professional preoccupation in recent years, that many schools are devising courses to 'top-up' ALA's into Bachelor's degrees, that those who fear a depleted middle-rank when there are no more 2-year ALA's are discussing possibilities for new courses at some sort of intermediate level, and that in general a great deal of thought is being given to the need for producing and training supportive staff at all levels.

Finally, attention must be drawn to the dramatic fall in recent years in the number of librarians attaining the Fellowship (only eighteen in 1975). Obviously the enhanced status of the ALA has

made this inevitable, but it is somewhat surprising that the
thesis route to Fellowship, rigorous as it may be, has not drawn
more candidates. Possibly, for graduates at least, the alternative
of a Master's degree has proved more attractive. Discussion on a
future role for the Fellowship still continues and it will be
surprising – not to say sad – if it does not stage a revival in some
form or other.

Enough has been said to make clear the range and complexity of
the routes to professional qualification in the Britain of this
centenary year. (For full details see the Library Association's
Students' handbook.) For the bewildered foreigner or layman it may
be some shred of comfort to know that there is still one
yardstick against which any recognised British qualification must
measure; namely, its acceptance by the Library Association as
giving exemption from the examinations leading to the
Associateship. Custodianship of the Register of Chartered
Librarians, and thereby of professional standards, is now the
most significant educational contribution of the LA. Under the
leadership of its Education Officer, Bernard Palmer (who has
probably been the greatest single influence of all time on British
professional education for librarianship), the LA has wisely
brought about the virtually complete devolution of its
examining monopoly of not so many years ago; but so long as it
controls entry to the Register its educational role will continue
to be both unique and indispensable.

Reference has already been made to some of the qualitative
changes which have taken place in professional education during
recent years: for example, the improved academic environments
in which the library schools are operating, exemplified in better
staff-student ratios, lighter lecture loads for both staff and
students, more intellectually demanding courses of study, and
the like. It is worth looking a little more closely, however, at
some of the changing ideas about *what* should be taught and
studied; for in some cases they represent changes of view which
raise questions about the very nature of librarianship. It is not
easy to isolate and identify these changes, to itemise them in a
neat and tidy way. Certainly they include a trend towards seeing
librarianship as part of a larger communications process – that

part which is concerned with the transfer of information from one mind to another, whether it be factual information or 'information' embodied in the stimuli projected by imaginative literature. To see librarianship from such a perspective requires a break from that 'institutional' approach which has seen our professional activity as something that necessarily takes place in buildings called libraries; it calls for a much more flexible approach, one which is hospitable, for example, to the idea of 'librarians' as members of research teams, as information specialists in a whole variety of working situations very different from the traditional librarianship of the past. Such a view-point is not mere academic theorising: it reflects, for example, the needs and to some extent the actualities of much of the information work carried out in local government departments, in commercial intelligence units, in industrial R & D. In terms of courses it is the approach which underlies the MA in Information Studies at Sheffield – a course for social science graduates which emphasises the social, 'communications' nature of library and information work; the graduates from this course are in fact tending to take up posts very different indeed from the traditional idea of librarianship.

There are other implications, too, in considering our profession from the point of view of its 'communications' role. Looked at in this way our concern becomes extended, quite naturally, to the generation of information – to publishing and the book trade, to data base creation; it becomes likewise extended to the non-documentary media of communication. These and other such considerations bring up in acute form for those responsible for the planning of courses of professional education the problem of scope and of boundaries.

In this connection it is not without interest and significance that a full-scale Master's degree thesis – the University of Wales MLIB of Kevin J. McGarry, in 1975 – was devoted to the sociology of communication as a foundation course in the education of the librarian; or that The Polytechnic of North London placed so much emphasis on a communications context for its pioneer honours degree course at bachelor's level.

Inevitably a communications emphasis encourages – and benefits from – a treatment more theoretical than that which has prevailed in the past. Reinforcing this in recent years has been an even more powerful influence towards a more theoretical approach to our subject, namely the impact of a burgeoning information science. As a term, information science is open to a great variety of interpretations and there are unfortunately distinct differences of meaning between the term as used in the UK, the USA and continental Europe. In a paper elsewhere[1] on the nature of information science, I have attempted to establish some of its relationships with librarianship. Above all, perhaps, I tried to make a case for ceasing to use the term information *science* to describe the actual *practice* of information work, so that it could be reserved for the study and establishment of the underlying theory and principles. Without dwelling at inappropriate length on this matter it is worth making the point that the study of information science to date has drawn on a whole range of disciplines: linguistics, cybernetics, psychology, computer science, mathematics, sociology, and others. Input of this kind into courses of professional education for librarianship is very apparent in some of the programmes developed in recent years, and one particularly striking consequence is the virtually complete acceptance by our professional educational community that librarians of the future will need to be numerate as well as literate. This is reinforced by the increasing prominence now given by library schools to the study of management and the resultant emphasis on quantitative thinking.

Of direct relevance to any account of change of this sort is an important OECD report[2] by Herbert Schur. Entitled *Education and training of information specialists for the 1970s*, it embodies thinking of a type which applies to librarians as well as information specialists. Indeed, the report has already had considerable influence in Library Association circles and in schools of library and information studies in Britain and in many other parts of the world.

Communication studies, information science, scientific management principles: all of these are having a powerful effect in reorientating, reshaping the courses followed by those who are being prepared in 1977 for the librarianship of the 80s, the 90s, and beyond – into the twenty-first century. None of this is change for its own sake, and certainly the fundamental and traditional knowledge of bibliographical structure and control and the study of the organisation of knowledge, which leads into modern information retrieval theory, are in no sense under threat. The changes which are coming about represent an encouragingly healthy response to social change, to increasingly sophisticated demands from increasingly demanding users, and to the challenge and opportunities offered by a rapidly developing information technology. Librarianship – itself potentially a most powerful agent for change – will neglect to respond to social and technological change at its peril, and the library schools have a special duty to be sensitive to such change.

There is perhaps an even more important sense in which the schools are concerned with change. The students passing through them today are going into a world in which few jobs are immune from quite fundamental changes during a practitioner's working life. At the practical level this implies for library schools a heavy and continuing responsibility for post-qualification courses of all sorts – from refresher courses to intensive courses on new techniques, from high-level advanced qualifications to workshops and exchange-of-experience seminars for middle and senior-level practitioners. The presentation of short courses has, in fact, become something of an 'industry' in the library and information world. Scrutiny of the British Library R & D Department's periodical *Directory of short courses in librarianship and information work* will show that Aslib is by far the most prolific source of such courses, but the library schools will also be seen to be making a not inconsiderable contribution.

In more general terms, it is up to the schools to ensure that 'education for change' is not a mere cliché. This will not be easy, but the portents are encouraging: in this centenary year our schools are in better heart than ever before; and even more importantly, the calibre of new entrants to the profession is higher than at any time within the recollection of the writer of this chapter.

Research and development

From consideration of 'change' it is an easy and natural
progression to the concluding section of this chapter – Research
and Development. To a university teacher brought up in the
British tradition, research is seen as an essential concomitant of
teaching – at the university level, at least – and the logic of
including it in a chapter devoted to education and training
would therefore seem to require no justification. It is natural,
however, that in this particular volume substantial attention
should also be devoted to research and development in the
chapter on the BL R & D Department, in the account of Aslib's
activities, and in the chapter on the Libraries Division of DES.
Aspects of R & D already covered in this way will therefore be
touched on only lightly in this present section.

To this writer the most remarkable fact about British R & D in
library and information science is that, except for work of a
bibliographical nature or with a distinctly literary bias, virtually
no such activity was being carried out until the mid-1960s. The
dramatic change in the situation can be gathered from the
chapter on the BL R & D Department, with its account of the great
range of its projects and up to £1 million a year available for
research; or from scrutinising the hundreds of projects set out in
the RADIALS *Bulletin* (Research And Development – Information
And Library Science). Indeed, the fact that such a bulletin is now
an important and necessary bibliographical tool is testimony in
itself to the scale of the profession's R & D effort.

It is as recently as 1965, at the Library Association's Harrogate
conference, that K. A. Mallaber was quite rightly castigating the
profession for neglect of its R & D responsibilities; but in that
very year OSTI was created and, as will be seen, this was probably
the most important single factor in transforming the profession's
approach to R & D. It is not without interest that within two
further years thinking had reached the stage at which the present
writer and his colleague H. Schur could be setting out in a report
on *Education and training for scientific and technological library and
information work*[3] (itself an OSTI-sponsored report) a
categorisation of levels and types of library and information

activity which took full account of the profession's need for
R & D personnel. It read as follows:

i   Production
ii   Development (and design)
iii Applied research
iv   Background research

By this centenary year the profession has progressed well on the
way towards making this categorisation a reality and it is worth
while taking a somewhat closer look at the forces which have
brought research and development in library and information
science to its present, extremely healthy state.

For effective and large-scale research and development in any
field, in any country, there are at least three basic prerequisites:
an adequate source (or sources) of funds, a supply of research
workers with the appropriate skills and competencies, and an
environment congenial and receptive to the idea of such activity.

The first of these – a source of funds – became available with the
creation, in 1965, of OSTI, now absorbed into the British Library,
as its Research and Development Department. In addition – and
by no means insignificantly – substantial funds have been made
available by the DES Libraries Division, described by Jones and
Sewell in Chapter Nine. These Library Division research
projects, however, have always been initiated with the objective
of providing information needed to meet the specific
administrative responsibilities and tasks of the Division,
whereas the funding activities of OSTI and its successor, BLR & D
Department, have been much more akin to those of the various
Research Councils. Between them, with BLR & D very much the
senior partner, the two organisations have provided funds on a
scale sufficient to provide the essential and basic impetus for the
profession's R & D.

The availability of funds did not of course in itself produce
library and information staff trained and competent in research
and available to carry out the various projects which were being
funded. As a new and emergent discipline library and

information science had no tradition like that of the established scientific subjects, by which a number of the most gifted graduates went on each year to undergo research training leading to a Doctor's or Master's degree by research. In this centenary year the situation is different: most of the university-based library schools are now in fact training postgraduate students for research degrees (though the number undergoing such training is still much too small). But for the research projects of those earlier years the profession had to 'grow its own', or import experienced researchers from other disciplines – for example chemistry, physics, statistics, linguistics. The first generation of those who learned on the job, or who came in from elsewhere, are now in many cases household names and have made their own substantial contributions to training others, and lack of research competence and experience is no longer the problem for our profession that it was in the second half of the 1960s and the early 1970s. It must be remembered, too, that library and information science is unusually receptive to a multi-disciplinary approach and that for the foreseeable future our professional research will continue to benefit by drawing on contributions from specialists in statistics, cybernetics, operational research, computer science, linguistics, psychology, sociology, economics and many other disciplines.

The third prerequisite for an effective national research effort in our field was a climate congenial to such activity and receptive attitudes on the part of the profession itself. Again, one is struck by the favourable conjunction of circumstances. At a time when OSTI was beginning to make available the funds necessary for R & D, rapid growth and development were focusing the attention of chief librarians in many large academic and public libraries on their need for far more comprehensive and apposite management information than had been available or required hitherto. By this time, too, Dr Urquhart, by his example within NLL and his proselytising to the library world at large, had transmitted with great effect the message that surveys, monitoring and self-examination were activities that paid large dividends in terms of effective and efficient service. Though still regarded with scepticism by some of SCONUL's chief librarian members, this sort of thinking was very congenial to many of the younger generation of chief librarians – particularly to some of those who were charged with creating new university libraries or with up-grading former CAT libraries in response to the 1963 Robbins Report expansion recommendations. Furthermore, it was just at this time that new university library schools were being created and one of them, at least – that at Sheffield – decided from its very earliest days that as a matter of policy it would devote substantial effort and resources to research. For these and many other reasons mid-1960s professional attitudes were distinctly more favourable to the idea of R & D than had ever been the case before.

What is particularly interesting, looking back in this centenary year, is the variety of settings in which this generally favourable climate caused research to blossom. Particularly important has been the involvement in R & D of several major academic libraries – for example, the university library of Cambridge, with library management research, Lancaster with its pioneer work in the application of operational research techniques to library and information work, Newcastle, Southampton and Loughborough with library automation, Durham with the PEBUL project, Newcastle Polytechnic with mobile library instruction units. These and other projects have meant that our British academic libraries have played a major role in the research activity of the last decade. It is unfortunate – though perhaps understandable – that this has not been matched by similar large-scale research activity by the public libraries.

The multi-disciplinary nature of our field has naturally meant large-scale involvement in library and information research of learned societies – such as the Chemical Society and the IEE – and a variety of university departments: Chemistry, Linguistics, Fuel Technology, Physiology, to mention but a few. Aslib, as will be clear from Chapter Two, has played a major role in its own right, with a powerful and experienced multi-disciplinary team working at a whole range of library and information problems.

Finally – and fittingly, in the context of this chapter – somewhat fuller reference should be made to the contribution to R & D of the library schools themselves. The mutually beneficial interaction of teaching and research is an article of faith for most of those whose work is in the field of higher education, but until recent years excessively heavy teaching loads, lack of resources and a generally unfavourable environment for research and development meant that such activity was very limited indeed. The growth, both in quantitative and qualitative terms, which came about from the mid-1960s, and which has been referred to already, laid the foundations for R & D activity in the Polytechnic library schools, though until the last few years the development of new courses, with all the administrative and allied demands of rapid expansion, have kept most of the Polytechnic schools too fully committed to leave much time or energy for research. An important exception to this, however, has been The Polytechnic of North London, which while developing new courses and expanding like the rest, has also completed, under the research leadership of its Reader, Jack Mills, a succession of substantial R & D projects over a wide field of professional topics. More recently, rapid development in R & D has taken place at the Leeds Polytechnic Department of Librarianship, the College of Librarianship Wales has stepped up its research activity, and other Polytechnic library schools, too, are beginning to undertake R & D work as their courses stabilise and their staffs can begin to lift their eyes a little from the day-to-day activity associated with very rapid expansion.

The most substantial research programme of all has been carried out in one of the university schools – that of the University of Sheffield Postgraduate School of Librarianship and Information Science. Since its establishment in 1964, the school has received more than £½ million in research grants and contracts, mainly from OSTI and its successor, the BL R & D Department, but also from DES, UNESCO, ICSU, OECD and other organisations. The school's objective has always been to achieve a balance in research between information science and the more traditional aspects of librarianship and, at the time of writing, its four principal projects employing eighteen senior research workers are concerned with the fields of library and information staffing, the library and information needs of social welfare departments, applications of communication theory to data base design, and user studies.

The latter merits somewhat fuller mention, for it embodies a new and important approach to research funding by BLR & D Department. A contract has been placed with the University to create a Centre for Research on User Studies with the present writer and Dr P. H. Mann (Reader in Sociology and a specialist in reading and readership) as joint project heads. It brings together a multidisciplinary team to build up a national centre for research, education and advice on user studies and – most importantly – it is funded for an initial period of five years. This provides an element of continuity and permanence for the research team that has been lacking in the normal short-period funding of research grants, and it seems likely to herald, to some extent at least, a new approach to the support of library and information science research.

It is gratifying to be able to conclude this section and, indeed, this chapter, by commending to the reader a useful publication on research, produced by the library schools as the result of the initiative of Dr Graham Jones of the School of Librarianship of the University of Strathclyde. It is an *Introductory guide to research in library and information studies in the UK*, edited by Dr Patricia Layzell Ward in association with Jack Burkett and Philip Whiteman on behalf of the ABLISS (Association of British Library and Information Science Schools) Working Party on Research.

References

1 W. L. Saunders, The nature of information science. *Inf Scientist* 8 (2), 1974, 57-70.
2. Schur, H. *Education and training of information specialists for the 1970s* (OECD DAS/STINFOR/72.9). Paris: OECD, 1972.

3. Schur, H. *and* Saunders, W. L. *Education and training for scientific and technological library and information work* London: HMSO, 1968.

Further reading

Department of Education and Science. *OSTI – the first five years* London: HMSO, 1971.

O'Hanlon, M. J. British library research and development: current projects and future trends. *Inf Scientist* 9 (3), 1975, 99–106.

The reader is also referred to the chapters on Professional Education, Research in Librarianship and Research in Information Science, in *British librarianship and information science, 1966–1970*. The successor to this volume, covering 1971–1975, should be near to publication at the time this present volume appears.

Index